MAP OF
CUSTER'S BATTLEFIELD
on the Little Big Horn River

A Cycle of the West

John G. Neihardt

A CYCLE OF THE West

The Song
of
Three Friends

The Song
of
Hugh Glass

The Song
of
Jed Smith

The Song
of the
Indian Wars

The Song
of
the Messiah

University of Nebraska Press: Lincoln & London

Fiftieth Anniversary Edition

This edition is limited to 1000 copies.
It commemorates the 50th anniversaries
of the completion of *The Cycle of the
West* and the establishment of the Uni-
versity of Nebraska Press.

The paper in this book meets the mini-
mum requirements of American National
Standard for Information Sciences –
Permanence of Paper for Printed Library
Materials, ANSI Z39.48-1984.

Library of Congress Cataloging in Publi-
cation Data
Neihardt, John Gneisenau, 1881–1973.
A cycle of the west/John G. Neihardt. –
50th anniversary ed.
p.   cm.
ISBN 0-8032-3323-X (cloth: alk. paper)
1. Fur trade – West (U.S.) – History –
Poetry. 2. Indians of North America –
Wars – Poetry. 3. West (U.S.) – History –
Poetry.
PS3527.E35C8 1991 811'.52–dc20
91-38033 CIP

Contents

The Song of Jed Smith

The Song of the Indian Wars

Introduction

In 1912, at the age of 31, I began work on the following cycle of heroic *Songs,* designed to celebrate the great mood of courage that was developed west of the Missouri River in the nineteenth century. The series was dreamed out, much of it in detail, before I began; and for years it was my hope that it might be completed at the age of 60—as it was. During the interval, more than five thousand days were devoted to the work, along with the fundamentally important business of being first a man and a father. It was planned from the beginning that the five *Songs,* which appeared at long intervals during a period of twenty-nine years, should constitute a single work. They are now offered as such. ❖ The period with which the *Cycle* deals was one of discovery, exploration and settlement—a genuine epic period, differing in no essential from the other great epic periods that marked the advance of the Indo-European peoples out of Asia and across Europe. It was a time of intense individualism, a time when society was cut loose from its roots, a time when an old culture was being overcome by that of a powerful people driven by the ancient needs and greeds. For this reason only, the word "epic" has been used in connection with the *Cycle*; it is properly descriptive of the mood and meaning of the time and of the material with which I have worked. There has been no thought of synthetic *Iliads* and *Odysseys,* but only of the richly human saga-stuff of a country that I knew and loved, and of a time in the very fringe of which I was a boy. ❖ This period began in 1822 and ended in 1890.

The dates are not arbitrary. In 1822 General Ashley and Major Henry led a band of a hundred trappers from St. Louis, "the Mother of the West," to the beaver country of the upper Missouri River. During the following year a hundred more Ashley-Henry men ascended the Missouri. Out of these trapper bands came all the great continental explorers after Lewis and Clark. It was they who discovered and explored the great central route by way of South Pass, from the Missouri River to the Pacific Ocean, over which the tide of migration swept westward from the 40's onward. ❖ *The Song of Three Friends* and *The Song of Hugh Glass* deal with the ascent of the river and with characteristic adventures of Ashley-Henry men in the country of the upper Missouri and the Yellowstone. ❖ *The Song of Jed Smith* follows the first band of Americans through South Pass to the Great Salt Lake, the first band of Americans to reach Spanish California by an overland trail, the first white men to cross the great central desert from the Sierras to Salt Lake. ❖ *The Song of the Indian Wars* deals with the period of migration and the last great fight for the bison pastures between the invading white race and the Plains Indians—the Sioux, the Cheyenne and the Arapahoe. ❖ *The Song of the Messiah* is concerned wholly with the conquered people and the worldly end of their last great dream. The period closes with the Battle of Wounded Knee in 1890, which marked the end of Indian resistance on the Plains. ❖ It will have been noted from the foregoing that the five *Songs* are linked in chronological order; but in addition to their progress in time and across the vast land, those who may feel as I have felt while the tales were growing may note a spiritual progression also—from the level of indomitable physical prowess to that of spiritual triumph in apparent worldly defeat. If any vital question be suggested in *The Song of Jed Smith*, for instance, there may be those who will find its age-old answer once again in the final *Song* of an alien people who also were men, and troubled. ❖ But, after all, "the play's the thing"; and while it is true that a knowledge of Western history and the topography of the country would be very helpful to a reader of the *Cycle,* such knowledge is not indispensable. For here are tales of men in struggle, triumph and defeat. ❖ Those readers who have not followed the development of the *Cycle* may wish to know, and are entitled to know, something of my fitness for the task assumed a generation ago and now completed. To those I may say that I did not experience the necessity of seeking material about which to write. The feel and mood of it were in the blood of my family, and my early experiences aroused a passionate awareness of it. My family came to Pennsylvania more than a generation before the Revolutionary War, in which fourteen of us fought; and, crossing the Alleghenies after the war, we did not cease pioneering until some of us reached Oregon. Any one of my heroes, from point of time, could have been my paternal grandfather, who was born in 1801. ❖ My maternal grandparents were covered-wagon people, and at the age of five I was living with them in a sod house on the upper Solomon in western Kansas. The buffalo had vanished from that country only a few years before, and the signs of them were everywhere. I have helped, as a little boy could, in "picking cow-chips" for winter fuel. If I write of hot-winds and grasshoppers, of prairie fires and blizzards, of dawns and noons and sunsets and nights, of brooding heat and thunderstorms in vast lands, I knew them early. They were the vital facts of my world, along with the talk of the old-timers who knew such fascinating things to talk about. ❖ I was a very little boy when my father introduced me to the Missouri River at Kansas City. It was flood time. The impression was tremendous, and a steadily growing desire to know what had happened on such a river led me directly to my heroes. Twenty years later, when I had come to know them well, I built a boat at Fort Benton, Montana, descended the Missouri in low water and against head winds, dreamed back the stories men had lived along the river, bend by bend. This experi-

ence is set forth in *The River and I*. ❖ In northern Ne-
braska I grew up at the edge of the retreating frontier,
and became intimately associated with the Omaha In-
dians, a Siouan people, when many of the old "long-
hairs" among them still remembered vividly the time that
meant so much to me. We were good friends. Later, I be-
came equally well acquainted among the Oglala Sioux, as
my volume, *Black Elk Speaks*, reveals; and I have never
been happier than while living with my friends among
them, mostly unreconstructed "long-hairs," sharing, as
one of them, their thoughts, their feelings, their rich
memories that often reached far back into the world of
my *Cycle*. ❖ When I have described battles, I have de-
pended far less on written accounts than upon the remi-
niscences of men who fought in them—not only Indians,
but whites as well. For, through many years, I was privi-
leged to know many old white men, officers and privates,
who had fought in the Plains Wars. Much of the material
for the last two *Songs* of the series came directly from
those who were themselves a part of the stories. ❖ For
the first three *Songs*, I was compelled to depend chiefly
upon early journals of travel and upon an intimate
knowledge of Western history generally. But while I
could not have known my earlier heroes, I have known
old men who had missed them, but had known men who
knew some of them well; and such memories at second
hand can be most illuminating to one who knows the
facts already. For instance, I once almost touched even
Jedediah Smith himself, the greatest and most mysterious
of them all, through an old plainsman who was an inti-
mate friend of Bridger, who had been a comrade of Jed!
❖ Such intimate contacts with soldiers, plainsmen, In-
dians and river men were an integral part of my life for
many years, and I cannot catalog them here. As for
knowledge of the wide land with which the *Cycle* deals,
those who know any part of it well will know that I have
been there too. ❖ Those who are not acquainted with
early Western history will find a good introduction to the

Cycle in Harrison Dale's *The Ashley-Henry Men*—or perhaps my own book, *The Splendid Wayfaring*. ❖ I can see now that I grew up on the farther slope of a veritable "watershed of history," the summit of which is already crossed, and in a land where the old world lingered longest. It is gone, and, with it, all but two or three of the old-timers, white and brown, whom I have known. My mind and most of my heart are with the young, and with the strange new world that is being born in agony. But something of my heart stays yonder, for in the years of my singing about a time and a country that I loved, I note, without regret, that I have become an old-timer myself! ❖ The foregoing was set down in anticipation of some questions that readers of good will, potential friends, might ask.

JOHN NEIHARDT
Columbia, Mo., 1948.

The Song
of Three Friends

To *Hilda*

λοω ρω ψαωκωπακοω επεωοεραι ακπα εη ωαδν
ρο ψαωκωπακοω επεωοεραι ακπα εη ωαδν ρο ψαωκ
ωπακοω επεωοεραι ακπα εη ωαδν ρο ψαωκωπακο

ASHLEY'S HUNDRED

I

Who now reads clear the roster of that band?
Alas, Time scribbles with a careless hand
And often pinchbeck doings from that pen
Bite deep, where deeds and dooms of mighty men
Are blotted out beneath a sordid scrawl!

One hundred strong they flocked to Ashley's call
That spring of eighteen hundred twenty-two;
For tales of wealth, out-legending Peru,
Came wind-blown from Missouri's distant springs,
And that old sireny of unknown things
Bewitched them, and they could not linger more.
They heard the song the sea winds sang the shore
When earth was flat, and black ships dared the steep
Where bloomed the purple perils of the deep
In dragon-haunted gardens. They were young.
Albeit some might feel the winter flung
Upon their heads, 'twas less like autumn's drift
Than backward April's unregarded sift
On stout oaks thrilling with the sap again.
And some had scarce attained the height of men,
Their lips unroughed, and gleaming in their eyes
The light of immemorial surprise
That life still kept the spaciousness of old
And, like the hoarded tales their grandsires told,
Might still run bravely.

                     For a little span
Their life-fires flared like torches in the van
Of westward progress, ere the great wind 'woke

To snuff them. Many vanished like a smoke
The blue air drinks; and e'en of those who burned
Down to the socket, scarce a tithe returned
To share at last the ways of quiet men,
Or see the hearth-reek drifting once again
Across the roofs of old St. Louis town.

And now no more the mackinaws come down,
Their gunwales low with costly packs and bales,
A wind of wonder in their shabby sails,
Their homing oars flung rhythmic to the tide;
And nevermore the masted keelboats ride
Missouri's stubborn waters on the lone
Long zigzag journey to the Yellowstone.
Their hulks have found the harbor ways that know
The ships of all the Sagas, long ago—
A moony haven where no loud gale stirs.
The trappers and the singing *voyageurs*
Are comrades now of Jason and his crew,
Foregathered in that timeless rendezvous
Where come at last all seekers of the Fleece.

Not now of those who, dying, dropped in peace
A brimming cup of years the song shall be:
From Mississippi to the Western Sea,
From Britain's country to the Rio Grande
Their names are written deep across the land
In pass and trail and river, like a rune.

Pore long upon that roster by the moon
Of things remembered dimly. Tangled, blear
The writing runs; yet presently appear
Three names of men that, spoken, somehow seem
Incantatory trumpets of a dream
Obscurely blowing from the hinter-gloom.
Of these and that inexorable doom
That followed like a hound upon the scent,
Here runs the tale.

THE UP-STREAM MEN

II

When Major Henry went
Up river at the head of Ashley's band,
Already there were robins in the land.
Home-keeping men were following the plows
And through the smoke-thin greenery of boughs
The scattering wild-fire of the fruit bloom ran.

Behold them starting northward, if you can.
Dawn flares across the Mississippi's tide;
A tumult runs along the waterside
Where, scenting an event, St. Louis throngs.
Above the buzzling voices soar the songs
Of waiting boatmen—lilting *chansonettes*
Whereof the meaning laughs, the music frets,
Nigh weeping that such gladness can not stay.
In turn, the herded horses snort and neigh
Like panic bugles. Up the gangplanks poured,
Go streams of trappers, rushing goods aboard
The snub-built keelboats, squat with seeming sloth—
Baled three-point blankets, blue and scarlet cloth,
Rum, powder, flour, guns, gauderies and lead.
And all about, goodbyes are being said.
Gauche girls with rainy April in their gaze
Cling to their beardless heroes, count the days
Between this parting and the wedding morn,
Unwitting how unhuman Fate may scorn
The youngling dream. For O how many a lad
Would see the face of Danger, and go mad
With her weird vixen beauty; aye, forget

This girl's face, yearning upward now and wet,
Half woman's with the first vague guess at woe!

And now commands are bellowed, boat horns blow
Haughtily in the dawn; the tumult swells.
The tow-crews, shouldering the long cordelles
Slack from the mastheads, lean upon the sag.
The keelboats answer lazily and drag
Their blunt prows slowly in the gilded tide.
A steersman sings, and up the riverside
The gay contagious ditty spreads and runs
Above the shouts, the uproar of the guns,
The nickering of horses.

             So, they say,
Went forth a hundred singing men that day;
And girlish April went ahead of them.
The music of her trailing garment's hem
Seemed scarce a league ahead. A little speed
Might yet almost surprise her in the deed
Of sorcery; for, ever as they strove,
A gray-green smudge in every poplar grove
Proclaimed the recent kindling. Aye, it seemed
That bird and bush and tree had only dreamed
Of song and leaf and blossom, till they heard
The young men's feet; when tree and bush and bird
Unleashed the whole conspiracy of awe!
Pale green was every slough about the Kaw;
About the Platte, pale green was every slough;
And still the pale green lingered at the Sioux,
So close they trailed the marching of the South.
But when they reached the Niobrara's mouth
The witchery of spring had taken flight
And, like a girl grown woman over night,
Young summer glowed.

              And now the river rose,
Gigantic from a feast of northern snows,

And mightily the snub prows felt the tide;
But with the loud, sail-filling South allied,
The tow-crews battled gaily day by day;
And seldom lulled the struggle on the way
But some light jest availed to fling along
The panting lines the laughter of the strong,
For joy sleeps lightly in the hero's mood.
And when the sky-wide prairie solitude
Was darkened round them, and the camp was set
Secure for well-earned sleep that came not yet,
What stories shaped for marvel or for mirth!—
Tales fit to strain the supper-tightened girth,
Looped yarns, wherein the veteran spinners vied
To color with a lie more glorified
Some thread that had veracity enough,
Spun straightway out of life's own precious stuff
That each had scutched and heckled in the raw.
Then thinner grew each subsequent guffaw
While drowsily the story went the rounds
And o'er the velvet dark the summer sounds
Prevailed in weird crescendo more and more,
Until the story-teller with a snore
Gave over to a dream a tale half told.

And now the horse-guards, while the night
    grows old,
With intermittent singing buffet sleep
That surges subtly down the starry deep
On waves of odor from the manless miles
Of summer-haunted prairie. Now, at whiles,
The kiote's mordant clamor cleaves the drowse.
The horses stamp and blow; about the prows
Dark waters chug and gurgle; as with looms
Bugs weave a drone; a beaver's diving booms,
Whereat bluffs grumble in their sable cowls.
The devil laughter of the prairie owls
Mocks mirth anon, like unrepentant sin.
Perceptibly at last slow hours wear thin

The east, until the prairie stares with morn,
And horses nicker to the boatman's horn
That blares the music of a day begun.

So through the days of thunder and of sun
They pressed to northward. Now the river shrank,
The grass turned yellow and the men were lank
And gnarled with labor. Smooth-lipped lads matured
'Twixt moon and moon with all that they
      endured,
Their faces leathered by the wind and glare,
Their eyes grown ageless with the calm far stare
Of men who know the prairies or the seas.
And when they reached the village of the Rees,
One scarce might say, This man is young, this old,
Save for the beard.

           Here loitered days of gold
And days of leisure, welcome to the crews;
For recently had come the wondrous news
Of beaver-haunts beyond the Great Divide—
So rich a tale 'twould seem the tellers lied,
Had they not much fine peltry to attest.
So now the far off River of the West
Became the goal of venture for the band;
And since the farther trail lay overland
From where the Great Falls thundered to no ear,
They paused awhile to buy more ponies here
With powder, liquor, gauds and wily words.
A horse-fond people, opulent in herds,
The Rees were; and the trade was very good.

Now camped along the river-fringing wood,
Three sullen, thunder-brewing, rainless days,
Those weathered men made merry in their ways
With tipple, euchre, story, jest and song.
The marksmen matched their cleverness; the strong
Wrestled the strong; and brawling pugilists

Displayed the boasted power of their fists
In stubborn yet half amicable fights.
And whisky went hell-roaring through the nights
Among the lodges of the fuddled Rees.
Thus merrily the trappers took their ease,
Rejoicing in the thread that Clotho spun;
For it was good to feel the bright thread run,
However eager for the snipping shears.

O joy long stifled in the ruck of years!
How many came to strange and bitter ends!
And who was merrier than those three friends
Whom here a song remembers for their woe?

Will Carpenter, Mike Fink and Frank Talbeau
Were they—each gotten of a doughty breed;
For in the blood of them the ancient seed
Of Saxon, Celt and Norman grew again.
The Mississippi reared no finer men,
And rarely the Ohio knew their peers
For pluck and prowess—even in those years
When stern life yielded suck but to the strong.
Nor in the hundred Henry took along
Was found their match—and each man knew it well.
For instance, when it suited Mike to tell
A tale that called for laughter, as he thought,
The hearer laughed right heartily, or fought
And took a drubbing. Then, if more complained,
Those three lacked not for logic that explained
The situation in no doubtful way.
"Me jokes are always funny" Mike would say;
And most men freely granted that they were.

A lanky, rangy man was Carpenter,
Quite six feet two from naked heel to crown;
And, though crow-lean, he brought the steelyard down
With twice a hundred notched upon the bar.
Nor was he stooped, as tall men often are;

A cedar of a man, he towered straight.
One might have judged him lumbering of gait,
When he was still; but when he walked or ran,
He stepped it lightly like a little man—
And such a one is very good to see.
Not his the tongue for quip or repartee;
His wit seemed slow; and something of the child
Came o'er his rough-hewn features, when he smiled,
To mock the porching brow and eagle nose.
'Twas when he fought the true import of those
Grew clear, though even then his mien deceived;
For less in wrath, he seemed, than mildly grieved—
Which made his blows no whit less true or hard.
His hair was flax fresh gleaming from the card;
His eyes, the flax in bloom.

     A match in might,
Fink lacked five inches of his comrade's height,
And of his weight scarce twenty pounds, they say.
His hair was black, his small eyes greenish gray
And restless as though feeling out of place
In such a jocund plenilunar face
That seemed made just for laughter. Then one saw
The pert pugnacious nose, the forward jaw,
The breadth of stubborn cheekbones, and one knew
That jest and fight to him were scarcely two,
But rather shifting phases of the joy
He felt in living. Careless as a boy,
Free handed with a gift or with a blow,
And giving either unto friend or foe
With frank good will, no man disliked him long.
They say his voice could glorify a song,
However loutish might the burden be;
And all the way from Pittsburg to the sea
The Rabelaisian stories of the rogue
Ran wedded to the richness of his brogue.
And wheresoever boatmen came to drink,
There someone broached some escapade of Fink

That well might fill the goat-hoofed with delight;
For Mike, the pantagruelizing wight,
Was happy in the health of bone and brawn
And had the code and conscience of the faun
To guide him blithely down the easy way.
A questionable hero, one might say:
And so indeed, by any civil law.
Moreover, at first glimpse of him one saw
A bull-necked fellow, seeming over stout;
Tremendous at a heavy lift, no doubt,
But wanting action. By the very span
Of chest and shoulders, one misjudged the man
When he was clothed. But when he stripped to swim,
Men flocked about to have a look at him,
Moved vaguely by that body's wonder-scheme
Wherein the shape of God's Adamic dream
Was victor over stubborn dust again!

O very lovely is a maiden, when
The old creative thrill is set astir
Along her blood, and all the flesh of her
Is shapen as to music! Fair indeed
A tall horse, lean of flank, clean-limbed for speed,
Deep-chested for endurance! Very fair
A soaring tree, aloof in violet air
Upon a hill! And 'tis a glorious thing
To see a bankfull river in the spring
Fight homeward! Children wonderful to see—
The Girl, the Horse, the River and the Tree—
As any suckled at the breast of sod;
Dissolving symbols leading back to God
Through vista after vista of the Plan!
But surely none is fairer than a man
In whom the lines of might and grace are one.

Bronzed with exposure to the wind and sun,
Behold the splendid creature that was Fink!
You see him strolling to the river's brink,

All ease, and yet tremendously alive.
He pauses, poised on tiptoe for the dive,
And momently it seems the mother mud,
Quick with a mystic seed whose sap is blood,
Mysteriously rears a human flower.
Clean as a windless flame the lines of power
Run rhythmic up the stout limbs, muscle-laced,
Athwart the ropy gauntness of the waist,
The huge round girth of chest, whereover spread
Enormous shoulders. Now above his head
He lifts his arms where big thews merge and flow
As in some dream of Michelangelo;
And up along the dimpling back there run,
Like lazy serpents stirring in the sun,
Slow waves that break and pile upon the slope
Of that great neck in swelling rolls, a-grope
Beneath the velvet softness of the skin.
Now suddenly the lean waist grows more thin,
The deep chest on a sudden grows more deep
And with the swiftness of a tiger's leap,
The easy grace of hawks in swooping flight,
That terrible economy of might
And beauty plunges outward from the brink.

Thus God had made experiment with Fink,
As proving how 'twere best that men might grow.

One turned from Mike to look upon Talbeau–
A little man, scarce five feet six and slim—
And wondered what his comrades saw in him
To justify their being thus allied.
Was it a sort of planetary pride
In lunar adoration? Hark to Mike:
"Shure I declare I niver saw his like—
A skinny whiffet of a man! And yit—
Well, do ye moind the plisint way we mit
And how he interjooced hisself that day?
'Twas up at Pittsburg, liquor flowin' fray

And ivrybody happy as a fool.
I cracked me joke and thin, as is me rule,
Looked round to view the havoc of me wit;
And ivrywan was doubled up wid it,
Save only wan, and him a scrubby mite.
Says I, and shure me language was polite,
'And did ye hear me little joke?' says I.
'I did' says he. 'And can't ye laugh, me b'y?'
'I can't' says he, the sassy little chap.
Nor did I git me hand back from the slap
I give him till he landed on me glim,
And I was countin' siventeen of him
And ivry dancin' wan of him was air!
Faith, whin I hit him he was niver there;
And shure it seemed that ivry wind that blew
Was peltin' knuckles in me face. Hurroo!
That toime, fer wance, I got me fill of fun!
God bless the little whiffet! It begun
Along about the shank of afthernoon;
And whin I washed me face, I saw the moon
A-shakin' wid its laughther in the shtrame.
And whin, betoimes, he wakened from his drame,
I says to him, 'Ye needn't laugh, me b'y:
A cliver little man ye are,' says I.
And Och, the face of me! I'm tellin' fac's—
Ye'd wonder did he do it wid an ax!
'Twas foine! 'Twas art!"

                         Thus, eloquent with pride,
Mike Fink, an expert witness, testified
To Talbeau's fistic prowess.

                            Now they say
There lived no better boatmen in their day
Than those three comrades; and the larger twain
In that wide land three mighty rivers drain
Found not their peers for skill in marksmanship.
Writes one, who made the long Ohio trip

With those boon cronies in their palmy days,
How once Mike Fink beheld a sow at graze
Upon the bank amid her squealing brood;
And how Mike, being in a merry mood,
Shot off each wiggling piglet's corkscrew tail
At twenty yards, while under easy sail
The boat moved on. And Carpenter could bore
A squirrel's eye clean at thirty steps and more—
So many say. But 'twas their dual test
Of mutual love and skill they liked the best
Of all their shooting tricks—when one stood up
At sixty paces with a whisky cup
Set brimming for a target on his head,
And felt the gusty passing of the lead,
Hot from the other's rifle, lift his hair.
And ever was the tin cup smitten fair
By each, to prove the faith of each anew:
For 'twas a rite of love between the two,
And not a mere capricious feat of skill.
"Och, shure, and can ye shoot the whisky, Bill?"
So Mike would end a wrangle. "Damn it, Fink!
Let's bore a pair of cups and have a drink!"
So Carpenter would stop a row grown stale.
And neither feared that either love might fail
Or either skill might falter.

                        Thus appear
The doughty three who held each other dear
For qualities they best could comprehend.

Now came the days of leisure to an end—
The days so gaily squandered, that would seem
To men at length made laughterless, a dream
Unthinkably remote; for Ilion held
Beneath her sixfold winding sheet of Eld
Seems not so hoar as bygone joy we prize
In evil days. Now vaguely pale the skies,
The glimmer neither starlight's nor the morn's.

A rude ironic merriment of horns
Startles the men yet heavy with carouse,
And sets a Ree dog mourning in the drowse,
Snout skyward from a lodge top. Sleepy birds
Chirp in the brush. A drone of sullen words
Awakes and runs increasing through the camp.
Thin smoke plumes, rising in the valley damp,
Flatten among the leathern tents and make
The whole encampment like a ghostly lake
Where bobbing heads of swimmers come and go,
As with the whimsy of an undertow
That sucks and spews them. Raising dust and din,
The horse-guards drive their shaggy rabble in
From nightlong grazing. *Voyageurs,* with packs
Of folded tents and camp gear on their backs,
Slouch boatward through the reek. But when prevails
The smell of frying pans and coffee pails,
They cease to sulk and, greatly heartened, sing
Till ponies swell the chorus, nickering,
And race-old comrades jubilate as one.

Out of a roseless dawn the heat-pale sun
Beheld them toiling northward once again—
A hundred horses and a hundred men
Hushed in a windless swelter. Day on day
The same white dawn o'ertook them on their way;
And daylong in the white glare sang no bird,
But only shrill grasshoppers clicked and whirred,
As though the heat were vocal. All the while
The dwindling current lengthened, mile on mile,
Meandrous in a labyrinth of sand.

Now e'er they left the Ree town by the Grand
The revellers had seen the spent moon roam
The morning, like a tipsy hag bound home.
A bubble-laden boat, they saw it sail
The sunset river of a fairy tale
When they were camped beside the Cannonball.

A spectral sun, it held the dusk in thrall
Nightlong about the Heart. The stars alone
Upon the cluttered Mandan lodges shone
The night they slept below the Knife. And when
Their course, long westward, shifted once again
To lead them north, the August moon was new.

The rainless Southwest wakened now and blew
A wilting, worrying, breath-sucking gale
That roared one moment in the bellied sail,
Next moment slackened to a lazy croon.
Now came the first misfortune. All forenoon
With line and pole the sweating boatmen strove
Along the east bank, while the horseguards drove
The drooping herd a little to the fore.
And then the current took the other shore.
Straight on, a maze of bar and shallow lay,
The main stream running half a mile away
To westward of a long low willow isle.
An hour they fought that stubborn half a mile
Of tumbled water. Down the running planks
The polesmen toiled in endless slanting ranks.
Now swimming, now a-flounder in the ooze
Of some blind bar, the naked cordelle crews
Sought any kind of footing for a pull;
While gust-bedevilled sails, now booming full,
Now flapping slack, gave questionable aid.

The west bank gained, along a ragged shade
Of straggling cottonwoods the boatmen sprawled
And panted. Out across the heat-enthralled,
Wind-fretted waste of shoal and bar they saw
The string of ponies ravelled up a draw
That mounted steeply eastward from the vale
Where, like a rampart flung across the trail,
A bluff rose sheer. Heads low, yet loath to graze,
They waxed and withered in the oily haze,
Now ponies, now a crawling flock of sheep.

Behind them three slack horseguards, half asleep,
Swayed limply, leaning on their saddle-bows.

The boat crews, lolling in a semi-doze,
Still watch the herd; nor do the gazers dream
What drama nears a climax over stream,
What others yonder may be watching too.
Now looming large upon the lucent blue,
The foremost ponies top the rim, and stare
High-headed down the vacancies of air
Beneath them; while the herders dawdle still
And gather wool scarce halfway up the hill—
A slumbrous sight beheld by heavy eyes.

But hark! What murmuring of far-flung cries
From yonder pocket in the folded rise
That flanks the draw? The herders also hear
And with a start glance upward to the rear.
Their spurred mounts plunge! What do they
        see but dust
Whipped skyward yonder in a freakish gust?
What panic overtakes them? Look again!
The rolling dust cloud vomits mounted men,
A ruck of tossing heads and gaudy gears
Beneath a bristling thicket of lean spears
Slant in a gust of onset!

                    Over stream
The boatmen stare dumfounded. Like a dream
In some vague region out of space and time
Evolves the swiftly moving pantomime
Before those loungers with ungirded loins;
Till one among them shouts *"Assiniboines!"*
And swelling to a roar, the wild word runs
Above a pellmell scramble for the guns,
Perceived as futile soon. Yet here and there
A few young hotheads fusillade the air,
And rage the more to know the deed absurd.

Some only grind their teeth without a word;
Some stand aghast, some grinningly inane,
While some, like watch-dogs rabid at the chain,
Growl curses, pacing at the river's rim.

So might unhappy spirits haunt the dim
Far shore of Styx, beholding outrage done
To loved ones in the region of the sun—
Rage goaded by its own futility!

For one vast moment strayed from time, they see
The war band flung obliquely down the slope,
The flying herdsmen, seemingly a-grope
In sudden darkness for their saddle guns.
A murmuring shock! And now the whole scene runs
Into a dusty blur of horse and man;
And now the herd's rear surges on the van
That takes the cue of panic fear and flies
Stampeding to the margin of the skies,
Till all have vanished in the deeps of air.
Now outlined sharply on the sky-rim there
The victors pause and taunt their helpless foes
With buttocks patted and with thumbs at nose
And jeers scarce hearkened for the wind's guffaw.
They also vanish. In the sunwashed draw
Remains no sign of what has come to pass,
Save three dark splotches on the yellow grass,
Where now the drowsy horseguards have their will.

At sundown on the summit of the hill
The huddled boatmen saw the burial squad
Tuck close their comrades' coverlet of sod—
Weird silhouettes on melancholy gray.
And very few found anything to say
That night; though some spoke gently of the dead,
Remembering what that one did or said
At such and such a time. And some, more stirred
With lust of vengeance for the stolen herd,

Swore vaguely now and then beneath their breath.
Some, brooding on the imminence of death,
Grew wistful of their unreturning years;
And some who found their praying in arrears
Made shift to liquidate the debt that night.

But when once more the cheerful morning light
Came on them toiling, also came the mood
Of young adventure, and the solitude
Sang with them. For 'tis glorious to spend
One's golden days large-handed to the end—
The good broadpieces that can buy so much!
And what may hoarders purchase but a crutch
Wherewith to hobble graveward?

                              On they pressed
To where once more the river led them west;
And every day the hot wind, puff on puff,
Assailed them; every night they heard it sough
In thickets prematurely turning sere.

Then came the sudden breaking of the year.

Abruptly in a waning afternoon
The hot wind ceased, as fallen in a swoon
With its own heat. For hours the swinking crews
Had bandied scarcely credible good news
Of clouds across the dim northwestward plain;
And they who offered wagers on the rain
Found ready takers, though the gloomy rack,
With intermittent rumbling at its back,
Had mounted slowly. Now it towered high,
A blue-black wall of night across the sky
Shot through with glacial green.

                              A mystic change!
The sun was hooded and the world went strange—
A picture world! The hollow hush that fell

Made loud the creaking of the taut cordelle,
The bent spar's groan, the plunk of steering poles.
A bodeful calm lay glassy on the shoals;
The current had the look of flowing oil.
They saw the cloud's lip billow now and boil—
Black breakers gnawing at a coast of light;
They saw the stealthy wraith-arms of the night
Grope for the day to strangle it; they saw
The up-stream reaches vanish in a flaw
Of driving sand: and scarcely were the craft
Made fast to clumps of willow fore and aft,
When with a roar the blinding fury rolled
Upon them; and the breath of it was cold.
There fell no rain.

        That night was calm and clear:
Just such a night as when the waning year
Has set aflare the old Missouri wood;
When Greenings are beginning to be good;
And when, so hollow is the frosty hush,
One hears the ripe persimmons falling—*plush!*—
Upon the littered leaves. The kindly time!
With cider in the vigor of its prime,
Just strong enough to edge the dullest wit
Should neighbor folk drop in awhile to sit
And gossip. O the dear flame-painted gloam,
The backlog's sputter on the hearth at home—
How far away that night! Thus many a lad,
Grown strangely old, remembered and was sad.
Wolves mourned among the bluffs. Like hanks of wool
Fog flecked the river. And the moon was full.

A week sufficed to end the trail. They came
To where the lesser river gives its name
And meed of waters to the greater stream.
Here, lacking horses, they must nurse the dream
Of beaver haunts beyond the Great Divide,
Build quarters for the winter trade, and bide

The coming up of Ashley and his band.
So up and down the wooded tongue of land
That thins to where the rivers wed, awoke
The sound of many axes, stroke on stroke;
And lustily the hewers sang at whiles—
The better to forget the homeward miles
In this, the homing time. And when the geese
With cacophonic councils broke the peace
Of frosty nights before they took to wing;
When cranes went over daily, southering,
And blackbirds chattered in the painted wood,
A mile above the river junction stood
The fort, adjoining the Missouri's tide.
Foursquare and thirty paces on a side,
A wall of sharpened pickets bristled round
A group of sod-roofed cabins. Bastions frowned
From two opposing corners, set to brave
A foe on either flank; and stout gates gave
Upon the stream, where now already came
The Indian craft, lured thither by the fame
Of traders building by the mating floods.

TO THE MUSSELSHELL

III

Now came at dawn a party of the Bloods,
Who told of having paddled seven nights
To parley for their people with the Whites,
The long way lying 'twixt a foe and foe;
For ever on their right hand lurked the Crow,
And on their left hand, the Assiniboine.
The crane-winged news, that where the waters join
The Long Knives built a village, made them sad;
Because the pastures thereabouts were bad,
Sustaining few and very scrawny herds.
So they had hastened hither, bringing words
Of kindness from their mighty men, to tell
What welcome waited on the Musselshell
Where stood the winter lodges of their band.

They rhapsodized the fatness of that land:
Lush valleys where all summer bison ran
To grass grown higher than a mounted man!
Aye, winter long on many a favored slope
The bison grazed with goat and antelope,
Nor were they ever leaner in the spring!
One heard the diving beaver's thundering
In all the streams at night; and one might hear
Uncounted bull elks whistle, when the year
Was painted for its death. Their squaws were good,
Strong bearers of the water and the wood,
With quiet tongues and never weary hands;
Tall as the fighting men of other lands,
And good to look upon. These things were so!

Why else then should Assiniboine and Crow
Assail the Bloods?

　　　　　　　　Now flaring up, they spoke
Of battles and their haters blown as smoke
Before the blizzard of their people's ire,
Devoured as grass before a prairie fire
That licks the heavens when the Northwind runs!
But, none the less, their warriors needed guns
And powder. Wherefor, let the Great White Chief
Return with them, ere yet the painted leaf
Had fallen. If so be he might not leave
This land of peoples skillful to deceive,
Who, needing much, had scarce a hide to sell—
Then send a party to the Musselshell
To trade and trap until the grass was young
And calves were yellow. With no forkéd tongue
The Bloods had spoken. Had the White Chief ears?

So Major Henry called for volunteers;
And Fink was ready on the word to go
"And chance the bloody naygurs"; then Talbeau,
Then Carpenter; and after these were nine,
In whom young blood was like a beading wine,
Who lusted for the venture.

　　　　　　　　　Late that night
The Bloods set out for home. With day's first light
The dozen trappers followed, paddling west
In six canoes. And whatso suited best
The whimsies of the savage or his needs,
The slim craft carried—scarlet cloth and beads,
Some antiquated muskets, powder, ball,
Traps, knives, and little casks of alcohol
To lubricate the rusty wheels of trade!

So, singing as they went, the blithe brigade
Departed, with their galloping canoes

Heeding the tune. They had no time to lose;
For long and stubborn was the upstream way,
And when they launched their boats at break of day
They heard a thin ice tinkle at the prows.

A bodeful silence and a golden drowse
Possessed the land. The Four Winds held their breath
Before a vast serenity of death,
Wherein it seemed the reminiscent Year—
A yearning ghost now—wrought about its bier
Some pale hallucination of its May.
Bleak stretched the prairie to the walls of day,
So dry, that where a loping kiote broke
Its loneliness, it smouldered into smoke:
And when a herd of bison rumbled past,
'Twas like a great fire booming in a blast,
The rolling smudge whereof concealed the flame.

Proceeding in the truce of winds, they came
In five days to the vale the Poplar drains.
A trailing flight of southbound whooping cranes,
Across the fading West, was like a scrawl
Of cabalistic warning on a wall,
And counselled haste. In seven days they reached
The point where Wolf Creek empties in, and beached
Their keels along its dusty bed. In nine,
Elk Prairie and the Little Porcupine,
Now waterless, had fallen to the rear.
The tenth sun failed them on the lone frontier
Where flows the turbid Milk by countless bends
And where Assiniboian country ends
And Blackfoot Land begins. The hollow gloom
All night resounded with the beaver's boom;
A wolf pack yammered from a distant hill;
Anon a rutting elk cried, like a shrill
Arpeggio blown upon a flageolet.
A half day more their lifting prows were set
To westward; then the flowing trail led south

Two days by many a bend to Hell Creek's mouth
Amid the Badlands. Gazing from a height,
The lookout saw the marching of the Night
Across a vast black waste of peaks and deeps
That could have been infernal cinder-heaps,
The relics of an ancient hell gone cold.

That night they saw a wild aurora rolled
Above the lifeless wilderness. It formed
Northeastwardly in upright waves that stormed
To westward, sequent combers of the bow
That gulfed Polaris in their undertow
And hurtled high upon the Ursine Isles
A surf of ghostly fire. Again, at whiles,
A shimmering silken veil, it puffed and swirled
As 'twere the painted curtain of the world
That fluttered in a rising gale of doom.
And when it vanished in the starry gloom
One said " 'Twill blow to-morrow."

                                        So it did.
Ere noon they raised the Half Way Pyramid
Southwestward; saw its wraith-like summit lift
And seem to float northwest against a drift
Of wind-whipped dust. The lunar hills about—
Where late a bird's note startled like a shout
The hush that seemed the body of old Time—
Now bellowed where the hoofs of Yotunheim
Foreran the grizzled legions of the Snow.
'Twas peep of day when it began to blow,
A zephyr growing stronger with the light,
And now by fits it churned the river white
And whipped the *voyageurs* with freezing spray.
The windward reaches took their breath away.
Ghost-white and numb with cold, from bend to bend,
Where transiently the wind became a friend
To drive them south, they battled; till at last
Around a jutting bluff they met a blast

That choked as with a hand upon their throats
The song they sang for courage; hurled their
     boats
Against the farther shore and held them pinned.

A sting of spitting snow was in the wind.
Southwest by west across the waste, where fell
A murky twilight, lay the Musselshell—
Two days of travel with the crow for guide.
Here must they find them shelter, and abide
The passing of the blizzard as they could.
The banks bore neither plum nor cottonwood
And all the hills were naked as a hand.
But where, debouching from the broken land,
A river in the spring was wont to flow,
A northward moving herd of buffalo
Had crossed the river, evidently bound
From failing pastures to the grazing ground
Along the Milk: and where the herd had passed
Was scattered *bois de vache* enough to last
Until the storm abated. So they packed
Great blanketfuls of sun-dried chips, and stacked
The precious fuel where the wind was stilled—
A pocket hemmed by lofty bluffs and filled
With mingled dusk and thunder; bore therein
Canoes and cargo, pitched their tents of skin
About a central heap of glowing chips,
And dined on brittle bull-meat dried in strips,
With rum to wash it down.

              It snowed all night.
The earth and heavens, in the morning light,
Were one white fury; and the stream ran slush.
Two days and nights the gale boomed; then a
     hush
Fell with the sun; and when the next dawn came—
A pale flare flanked by mockeries of flame—
The river lay as solid as the land.

Now caching half their goods, the little band
Resumed the journey, toiling under packs;
And twice they felt the morning at their backs,
A laggard traveller; and twice they saw
The sunset dwindle to a starry awe
Beyond the frozen vast, while still they pressed
The journey—bearded faces yearning west,
White as the waste they trod. Then one day more,
Southwestward, brought them to the jutting shore
That faced the goal.

        A strip of poplars stretched
Along a winding stream, their bare boughs etched
Black line by line upon a flat of snow
Blue tinted in the failing afterglow.
Humped ponies 'mid the drifts and clumps of sage
Went nosing after grudging pasturage
Where'er it chanced the blizzard's whimsic flaws
Had swept the slough grass bare. A flock of squaws
Chopped wood and chattered in the underbrush,
Their ax strokes thudding dully in the hush,
Their nasal voices rising shrill and clear:
And, circled 'neath a bluff that towered sheer
Beside the stream, snug lodges wrought of hide,
Smoke-plumed and glowing with the fires inside,
Made glad the gazers. Even as they stood,
Content to stare a moment, from the wood
The clamor deepened, and a running shout
Among the lodges brought the dwellers out,
Braves, squaws, papooses; and the wolf dogs bayed;
And up the flat the startled ponies neighed,
Pricking their ears to question what befell.

So came Fink's party to the Musselshell,
Gaunt, bearded, yet—how gloriously young
And then, what feasts of bison fleece and tongue
Of browned *boudin* and steaming humprib stew!
What roaring nights of wassailing they knew—

Gargantuan regales—when through the town
The fiery liquor ravined, melting down
The tribal hoard of beaver! How they made
Their merest gewgaws mighty in the trade!
Aye, merry men they were! Nor could they know
How even then there came that wraith of woe
Amongst them; some swift-fingered Fate that span
The stuff of sorrow, wove 'twixt man and man
The tangling mesh, that friend might ruin friend
And each go stumbling to a bitter end—
A threefold doom that now the Song recalls.

THE NET IS CAST

There was a woman.

IV

What enchantment falls
Upon that far off revel! How the din
Of jangling voices, chaffering to win
The lesser values, hushes at the words,
As dies the dissonance of brawling birds
Upon a calm before the storm is hurled!
Lo, down the age-long reaches of the world
What rose-breatht wind of ghostly music creeps!

And was she fair—this woman? Legend keeps
No answer; yet we know that she was young,
If truly comes the tale by many a tongue
That one of Red Hair's party fathered her.
What need to know her features as they were?
Was she not lovely as her lover's thought,
And beautiful as that wild love she wrought
Was fatal? Vessel of the world's desire,
Did she not glow with that mysterious fire
That lights the hearth or burns the rooftree down?
What face was hers who made the timeless town
A baleful torch forever? Hers who wailed
Upon the altar when the four winds failed
At Aulis? What the image that looked up
On Iseult from the contemplated cup
Of everlasting thirst? What wondrous face
Above the countless cradles of the race
Makes sudden heaven for the blinking eyes?

One face in truth! And once in Paradise
Each man shall stray unwittingly, and see—
In some unearthly valley where the Tree
With golden fruitage perilously fraught
Still stands—that image of God's afterthought.
Then shall the world turn wonderful and strange!

Who knows how came that miracle of change
To Fink at last? For he was not of such
As tend to prize one woman overmuch;
And legend has it that, from Pittsburg down
To Baton Rouge, in many a river town
Some blowsy Ariadne pined for Mike.
"It is me rule to love 'em all alike."
He often said, with slow, omniscient wink,
When just the proper quantity of drink
Had made him philosophic; "Glass or gourd,
Shure, now, they're all wan liquor whin they're
        poured!
Aye, rum is rum, me b'y!"

                            Alas, the tongue!
How glibly are its easy guesses flung
Against the knowing reticence of years,
To echo laughter in the time of tears,
Raw gusts of mocking merriment that stings!
Some logic in the seeming ruck of things
Inscrutably confutes us!

                            Now had come
The time when rum no longer should be rum,
But witchwine sweet with peril. It befell
In this wise, insofar as tongue may tell
And tongues repeat the little eyes may guess
Of what may happen in that wilderness,
The human heart. There dwelt a mighty man
Among the Bloods, a leader of his clan,
Around whose life were centered many lives,

For many sons had he of many wives;
And also he was rich in pony herds.
Wherefore, they say, men searched his lightest words
For hidden things, since anyone might see
That none had stronger medicine than he
To shape aright the stubborn stuff of life.
Among the women that he had to wife
Was she who knew the white man when the band
Of Red Hair made such marvel in the land,
She being younger then and little wise.
But in that she was pleasing to the eyes
And kept her fingers busy for her child
And bore a silent tongue, the great man smiled
Upon the woman, called her to his fire
And gave the Long Knife's girl a foster sire,
So that her maidenhood was never lean,
But like a pasture that is ever green
Because it feels a mountain's sunny flank.

Now in the season when the pale sun shrank
Far southward, like another kind of moon,
And dawns were laggard and the dark came soon,
It pleased the great man's whim to give a feast.
'Twas five days after Carpenter went east
With eight stout ponies and a band of three
To lift the cache; a fact that well might be
Sly father to the great man's festive mood—
A wistfully prospective gratitude,
Anticipating charity!

                    It chanced
That while the women sang and young men danced
About the drummers, and the pipe went round,
And ever 'twixt the songs arose the sound
Of fat dog stewing, Fink, with mournful eyes
And pious mien, lamented the demise
Of "pore owld Fido," till his comrades choked
With stifled laughter; soberly invoked

The plopping stew ("Down, Rover! Down, me lad!");
Discussed the many wives the old man had
In language more expressive than polite.
So, last of all his merry nights, that night
Fink clowned it, little dreaming he was doomed
To wear that mask of sorrow he assumed
In comic mood, thenceforward to the last.
For even as he joked, the net was cast
About him, and the mystic change had come,
And he had looked on rum that was not rum—
The Long Knife's daughter!

                Stooped beneath a pack
Of bundled twigs, she pushed the lodge-flap back
And entered lightly; placed her load of wood
Beside the fire; then straightened up and stood
One moment there, a shapely girl and tall.
There wasn't any drama: that was all.
But when she left, the wit had died in Fink.
He seemed a man who takes the one more drink
That spoils the fun, relaxes jaw and jowl
And makes the jester, like a sunstruck owl,
Stare solemnly at nothing.

            All next day
He moped about with scarce a word to say,
And no one dared investigate his whim.
But when the twilight came, there fell on him
A sentimental, reminiscent mood,
As though upon some frozen solitude
Within him, breathed a softening chinook,
Far strayed across the alplike years that look
On what one used to be and what one is.
And when he raised that mellow voice of his
In songs of lovers wedded to regret,
'Tis said that, unashamed, men's eyes grew wet,
So poignantly old memories were stirred.
And much his comrades marvelled as they heard

That ribald jester singing thus of love.
Nor could they solve the mystery thereof,
Until at dawn they saw him rise and take
A rifle of the latest Hawkin make,
Ball, powder, and a bolt of scarlet goods,
And hasten to the fringe of cottonwoods
Where rose the great man's lodge smoke. Then
    they knew;
For thus with gifts the Bloods were wont to woo
The daughter through the sire.

                The white sun burned
Midmost the morning steep when he returned
Without his load and humming as he went.
And hour by hour he squatted in his tent
And stared upon the fire; save now and then
He stirred himself to lift the flap again
And cast an anxious gaze across the snows
Where stood the chieftain's lodge. And well did those
Who saw him know what sight he hoped to see;
For 'twas the custom that the bride-to-be
Should carry food to him she chose to wed.
Meanwhile, with seemly caution, be it said,
Fink's men enjoyed a comedy, and laid
Sly wagers on the coming of the maid—
She would! She wouldn't! So the brief day waned.

Now when the sun, a frosty specter maned
With corruscating vapors, lingered low
And shadows lay like steel upon the snow,
An old squaw, picking faggots in the brush,
Saw that which set her shrieking in the hush.
"They come! They come!" Then someone shouted
    "Crows!"
The town spewed tumult, men with guns and bows,
Half clad and roaring; shrill hysteric wives
With sticks of smoking firewood, axes, knives;
Dogs, bristle-necked and snarling. So they pressed

To meet a foe, as from a stricken nest
The hornet swarm boils over.

                     Blinking, dazed
With sudden light and panic fear, they gazed
About the frozen waste; and then they saw
Eight laden ponies filing up the draw,
Their nostrils steaming, slack of neck and slow.
Behind them, stumbling in the broken snow,
Three weary trappers trudged, while in the lead
Strode Carpenter. A goodly sight, indeed!
Upstanding, eagle-faced and eagle-eyed,
The ease of latent power in his stride,
He dwarfed the panting pony that he led;
And when the level sunlight 'round his head
Made glories in the frosted beard and hair,
Some Gothic fighting god seemed walking there,
Strayed from the dim Hercynian woods of old.

How little of a story can be told!
Let him who knows what happens in the seed
Before the sprout breaks sunward, make the deed
A plummet for the dreaming deeps that surged
Beneath the surface ere the deed emerged
For neat appraisal by the rule of thumb!
The best of Clio is forever dumb,
To human ears at least. Nor shall the Song
Presume to guess and tell how all night long,
While roared the drunken orgy and the trade,
Doom quickened in the fancy of a maid,
The daughter of the Long Knife; how she saw,
Serenely moving through a spacious awe
Behind shut lids where never came the brawl,
That shining one, magnificently tall,
A day-crowned mortal brother of the sun.
Suffice it here that, when the night was done
And morning, like an uproar in the east,
Aroused the town still heavy with the feast,

All men might see what whimsic, fatal bloom
A soil, dream-plowed and seeded in the gloom,
Had nourished unto blowing in the day.

'Twas then the girl appeared and took her way
Across the snow with hesitating feet.
She bore a little pot of steaming meat;
And when midmost the open space, she turned
And held it up to where the morning burned,
As one who begs a blessing of the skies.
Unconscious of the many peeping eyes,
Erect, with wrapt uplifted face she stood—
A miracle of shapely maidenhood—
Before the flaming god. And many heard,
Or seemed to hear by piecing word to word,
The prayer she muttered to the wintry sky:
"O Sun, behold a maiden! Pure am I!
Look kindly on the little gift I give;
For, save you smile upon it, what can live?
Bright Father, hear a maiden!" Then, as one
Who finds new courage for a task begun,
She turned and hastened to the deed.

                                    They say
There was no dearth of gossiping that day
Among the lodges. Shrewish tongues there were
That clacked no happy prophecies of her.
And many wondered at the chieftain's whim.
The Long Knife's girl had wrought a spell on him;
Why else then was he silent? See her shrink
A moment there before the tent of Fink,
As one who feels a sudden sleety blast!
But look again! She starts, and hurries past!
All round the circled village, lodges yawn
To see how brazen in the stare of dawn
A petted girl may be. For now, behold!
Was ever maiden of the Bloods so bold?
She stops before another tent and stoops,

Her fingers feeling for the buckskin loops
That bind the rawhide flap. 'Tis opened wide.
The slant white light of morning falls inside,
And half the town may witness at whose feet
She sets the little pot of steaming meat—
'Tis Carpenter!

THE QUARREL

V

Perceptibly, at length,
The days grew longer, and the winter's strength
Increased to fury. Down across the flat
The blizzards bellowed; and the people sat
Fur-robed about the smoky fires that stung
Their eyes to streaming, when a freak gust flung
The sharp reek back with flaws of powdered snow.
And much the old men talked of long ago,
Invoking ghostly Winters from the Past,
Till cold snap after cold snap followed fast,
And none might pile his verbal snow so deep
But some athletic memory could heap
The drifts a trifle higher; give the cold
A greater rigor in the story told;
Put bellows to a wind already high.
And ever greater reverence thereby
The old men won from gaping youths, who heard,
Like marginalia to the living word,
The howling of the poplars tempest-bent,
The smoke-flap cracking sharply at the vent,
The lodge poles creaking eerily. And O!
The happy chance of living long ago,
Of having wrinkles now and being sires
With many tales to tell around the fires
Of days when things were bigger! All night long
White hands came plucking at the buckskin
    thong
That bound the door-flap, and the writhing dark
Was shrill with spirits. By the snuffling bark

Of dogs men knew that homesick ghosts were there.
And often in a whirl of chilling air
The weird ones entered, though the flap still held,
Built up in smoke the shapes they knew of eld,
Grew thin and long to vanish as they came.

Now had the scandal, like a sudden flame
Fed fat with grasses, perished in the storm.
The fundamental need of keeping warm
Sufficed the keenest gossip for a theme;
And whimsies faded like a warrior's dream
When early in the dawn the foemen cry.

The time when calves are black had blustered by—
A weary season—since the village saw
The chief's wife pitching for her son-in-law
The nuptial lodge she fashioned. Like a bow
That feels the arrow's head, the moon hung low
That evening when they gave the wedding gifts;
And men had seen it glaring through the rifts
Of wintry war as up the east it reeled,
A giant warrior's battle-bitten shield—
But now it braved no more the charging air.
Meanwhile the lodge of Carpenter stood there
Beside the chieftain's, huddled in the snows,
And, like a story everybody knows,
Was little heeded now.

         But there was one
Who seldom noted what was said or done
Among his comrades; he would sit and look
Upon the fire, as one who reads a book
Of woeful doings, ever on the brink
Of ultimate disaster. It was Fink:
And seeing this, Talbeau was sick at heart
With dreading that his friends might drift apart
And he be lost, because he loved them both.
But, knowing well Mike's temper, he was loath

To broach the matter. Also, knowing well
That silence broods upon the hottest hell,
He prayed that Fink might curse.

                              So worried past
The days of that estrangement. Then at last
One night when round their tent the blizzard roared
And, nestled in their robes, the others snored,
Talbeau could bear the strain no more and spoke.
He opened with a random little joke,
Like some starved hunter trying out the range
Of precious game where all the land is strange;
And, as the hunter, missing, hears the grim
And spiteful echo-rifles mocking him,
His own unmirthful laughter mocked Talbeau.
He could have touched across the ember-glow
Mike's brooding face—yet Mike was far away.
And O that nothing more than distance lay
Between them—any distance with an end!
How tireless then in running to his friend
A man might be! For suddenly he knew
That Mike would have him choose between the two.
How could he choose 'twixt Carpenter and Fink?
How idle were a choice 'twixt food and drink
When, choosing neither, one were sooner dead!

Thus torn within, and hoarse with tears unshed,
He strove again to find his comrade's heart:
"O damn it, Mike, don't make us drift apart!
Don't do it, Mike! This ain't a killin' fuss,
And hadn't ought to faze the three of us
That's weathered many a rough-and-tumble fight!
W'y don't you mind that hell-a-poppin' night
At Baton Rouge three years ago last fall—
The time we fit the whole damned dancin' hall
And waded out nigh belly-deep in men?
O who'd have said a girl could part us, then?
And, Mike, that fracas in the Vide Poche dive!

Can you forget it long as you're alive?—
A merry time! Us strollin' arm-in-arm
From drink to drink, not calculatin' harm,
But curious, because St. Louis town
Fair boiled with greasy mountain men, come down
All brag and beaver, howlin' for a spree!
And then—you mind?—a feller jostled me—
'Twas at the bar—a chap all bones and big.
Says he in French: 'You eater of a pig,
Make room for mountain men!' And then says you
In Irish, aimin' where the whiskers grew,
And landin' fair: 'You eater of a dog,
Make room for boatmen!' Like a punky log
That's water-soaked, he dropped. What happened then?
A cyclone in a woods of mountain men—
That's what! O Mike, you can't forget it now!
And what in hell's a woman, anyhow,
To memories like that?"

        So spoke Talbeau,
And, pausing, heard the hissing of the snow,
The snoring of the sleepers, and the cries
Of blizzard-beaten poplars. Still Fink's eyes
Upon the crumbling embers pored intent.
Then momently, or so it seemed, there went
Across that alien gaze a softer light,
As when bleak windows in a moony night
Flush briefly with a candle borne along.
And suddenly the weary hope grew strong
In him who saw the glimmer, and he said:
"O Mike, I see the good old times ain't dead!
Why don't you fellers shoot the whisky cup
The way you used to do?"

        Then Fink looked up.
'Twas bad the way the muscles twitched and worked
About his mouth, and in his eyes there lurked
Some crouchant thing. "To hell wid you!" he cried.

So love and hate that night slept side by side;
And hate slept well, but love lay broad awake
And, like a woman, for the other's sake
Eked out the lonely hours with worrying.

Now came a heartsick yearning for the spring
Upon Talbeau; for surely this bad dream
Would vanish with the ice upon the stream,
Old times be resurrected with the grass!
But would the winter ever, ever pass,
The howling of the blizzard ever cease?
So often now he dreamed of hearing geese
Remotely honking in the rain-washed blue;
And ever when the blur of dawn broke through
The scudding rack, he raised the flap to see,
By sighting through a certain forkéd tree,
How much the sun made northward.

                                    Then, one day,
The curtain of the storm began to fray;
The poplars' howling softened to a croon;
The sun set clear, and dusk revealed the moon—
A thin-blown bubble in a crystal bowl.
All night, as 'twere the frozen prairie's soul
That voiced a hopeless longing for the spring,
The wolves assailed with mournful questioning
The starry deeps of that tremendous hush.
Dawn wore the mask of May—a rosy flush.
It seemed the magic of a single bird
Might prove the seeing of the eye absurd
And make the heaped-up winter billow green.
On second thought, one knew the air was keen—
A whetted edge in gauze. The village fires
Serenely builded tenuous gray spires
That vanished in the still blue deeps of awe.
All prophets were agreed upon a thaw.
And when the morning stood a spearlength high,
There grew along the western rim of sky

A bank of cloud that had a rainy look.
It mounted slowly. Then the warm chinook
Began to breathe a melancholy drowse
And sob among the naked poplar boughs,
As though the prairie dreamed a dream of June
And knew it for a dream. All afternoon
The gale increased. The sun went down
    blood-red;
The young moon, perilously fragile, fled
To early setting. And the long night roared.

Tempestuously broke the day and poured
An intermittent glory through the rifts
Amid the driven fog. The sodden drifts
Already grooved and withered in the blast:
And when the flying noon stared down aghast,
The bluffs behind the village boomed with flood.
What magic in that sound to stir the blood
Of winter-weary men! For now the spring
No longer seemed a visionary thing,
But that which any morning might bestow.
And most of all that magic moved Talbeau;
For, scrutinizing Fink, he thought he saw
Some reflex of that February thaw—
A whit less curling of the upper lip.
O could it be returning comradeship,
That April not beholden to the moon
Nor chatteled to the sun?

               That afternoon
They played at euchre. Even Fink sat in;
And though he showed no eagerness to win,
Forgot the trumps and played his bowers wild,
There were not lacking moments when he
    smiled,
A hesitating smile 'twixt wan and grim.
It seemed his stubborn mood embarrassed him
Because regret now troubled it with shame.

The great wind died at midnight. Morning came,
Serene and almost indolently warm—
As when an early April thunder storm
Has cleansed the night and vanished with the gloom;
When one can feel the imminence of bloom
As 'twere a spirit in the orchard trees;
When, credulous of blossom, come the bees
To grumble 'round the seepages of sap.
So mused Talbeau while, pushing back the flap,
Instinctively he listened for a bird
To fill the hush. Then presently he heard—
And 'twas the only sound in all the world—
The trickle of the melting snow that purled
And tinkled in the bluffs above the town.
The sight of ragged Winter patched with brown,
The golden peace and, palpitant therein,
That water note, spun silverly and thin,
Begot a wild conviction in the man:
The wounded Winter weakened; now began
The reconciliation! Hate would go
And, even as the water from the snow,
Old comradeship come laughing back again!

All morning long he pondered, while the men
Played seven-up. And scarce a trick was played
But someone sang a snatch of song or made
A merry jest. And when the game was balked
By one who quite forgot his hand, and talked
Of things in old St. Louis, none demurred.
And thus, by noon, it seemed the lightest word
Of careless salutation would avail
To give a happy ending to the tale
Of clouded friendship. So he 'rose and went,
By studied indirection, to the tent
Of Carpenter, as one who takes the air.
And, as he raised the flap and entered there,
A sudden gale of laughter from the men
Blew after him. What music in it then!

What mockery, when memory should raise
So often in the coming nights and days
The ruthless echo of it!

                Click on click
Amid the whirlwind finish of a trick
The cards fell fast, while King and Queen and Ace,
With meaner trumps for hounds, pursued the chase
Of wily Knave and lurking Deuce and Ten;
When suddenly the game-enchanted men
Were conscious of a shadow in the place,
And glancing up they saw the smiling face
Of Carpenter, thrust in above Talbeau's.
"How goes it, Boys?" said he; and gaily those
Returned the greeting. "Howdy, Mike!" he said;
And with a sullen hanging of the head
Fink mumbled "Howdy!" Gruff—but what of
      that?
One can not doff displeasure like a hat—
'Twould dwindle snow-like.

              Nothing else would do
But Carpenter should play. Now Fink played too;
And, having brought his cherished ones together,
Talbeau surrendered to the languid weather
And, dreamily contented, watched the sport.
All afternoon the pictured royal court
Pursued its quarry in the mimic hunt;
And Carpenter, now gayer than his wont,
Lost much; while Fink, with scarce a word to say,
His whole attention fixed upon the play,
Won often. So it happened, when the sun
Was near to setting, that the day seemed won
For friendliness, however stood the game.
But even then that Unseen Player came
Who stacks the shuffled deck of circumstance
And, playing wild the Joker men call Chance,
Defeats the Aces of our certainty.

The cards were dealt and Carpenter bid three.
The next man passed the bid, and so the next.
Then Fink, a trifle hesitant and vexed,
Bid four on spades. And there was one who said
In laughing banter: "Mike, I'll bet my head
As how them spades of your'n 'll dig a hole!"
And in some subtle meaning of the soul
The wag was more a prophet than he knew.

Fink held the Ace and Deuce, and that made two:
His black King scored another point with Knave.
But Carpenter, to whom that Weird One gave
A band of lesser trumps to guard his Ten,
Lay low until the Queen had passed, and then
Swept in a last fat trick for Game, and scored.
And now the players slapped their knees and roared:
"You're set! You're in the hole! He set you, Mike!"

Then suddenly they saw Fink crouch to strike;
And ere they comprehended what they saw,
There came a thud of knuckles on a jaw
And Carpenter rolled over on the ground.
One moment in a breathless lapse of sound
The stricken man strove groggily to 'rise,
The emptiness of wonder in his eyes
Turned dreamily with seeming unconcern
Upon Mike's face, where now began to burn
The livid murder-lust. 'Twixt breath and breath
The hush and immobility of death
Made there a timeless picture. Then a yell,
As of a wild beast charging, broke the spell.
Fink sprang to crush, but midway met Talbeau
Who threw him as a collie dog may throw
A raging bull. But Mike was up again,
And wielding thrice the might of common men,
He gripped the little man by nape and thigh
And lightly lifted him and swung him high
And flung him; and the smitten tent went down.

Then 'rose a roar that roused the teeming town,
And presently a shouting rabble surged
About the wreck, whence tumblingly emerged
A knot of men who grappled Fink and clung.
Prodigiously he rose beneath them, flung
His smashing arms, man-laden, forth and back;
But stubbornly they gripped him, like a pack
That takes uncowed the maulings of a bear.
"Let Carpenter get up!" they cried. "Fight fair!
Fight fair! Fight fair!"

                    Quite leisurely the while
The stricken man arose, a sleepy smile
About his quiet eyes. Indeed, he seemed
As one but lately wakened, who has dreamed
A pleasing dream. But when he stroked his beard
And gazed upon his fingers, warmly smeared
With crimson from the trickle at his jaw,
His eyes went eagle-keen with what they saw.
The stupor passed. He hastily untied
His buckskin shirt and, casting it aside,
Stood naked to the hips. The tumult ceased
As, panting hard, the *voyageurs* released
Their struggling charge and, ducking to a swing
Of those freed arms, sought safety, scampering.

Fink also stripped his shirt; and as the man
Stood thus revealed, a buzz of wonder ran
Amid the jostling rabble. Few there were
Who in that moment envied Carpenter,
Serenely poised and waiting placid browed:
For shall a lonely cedar brave a cloud
Bulged big and shapen to the cyclone's whirl?
Lo, even as the body of a girl,
The body of the blond was smooth and white;
But vaguely, as one guesses at the might
Of silent waters running swift and deep,
One guessed what stores of power lay asleep

Beneath the long fleet lines of trunk and limb.
Thus God had made experiment with him;
And, groping for the old Adamic dream,
Had found his patterns in the tree and stream,
As Fink's in whirling air and hungry flame.

Now momently the picture there became
A blur of speed. Mike rushed. The tiptoe town
Craned eagerly to see a man go down
Before that human thunder gust. But lo!
As bends a sapling when the great winds blow,
The other squatted, deftly swayed aside,
And over him the slashing blows went wide.
Fink sprawled. But hardly had a spreading roar
O'errun the town, when silence as before
Possessed the scene; for Mike flashed back again
With flame-like speed, and suddenly the men
Clenched, leaning neck to neck.

                              Without a word,
Like horn-locked bulls that strive before the herd,
They balanced might with might; till Mike's hands
        whipped
Beneath the other's arm-pits, met and gripped
Across the broad white shoulders. Then began
The whole prodigious engine of the man
To bulge and roll and darken with the strain.
Like rivulets fed suddenly with rain,
The tall one's thews rose ropily and flowed
Converging might against the growing load
Of those tremendous arms that strove to crush.

Their labored breathing whistled in the hush.
One saw the blond man's face go bluish red,
As deeper, deeper sank Fink's shaggy head
Amid his heaped-up shoulder brawn. One knew
That very soon the taller of the two
Must yield and take that terrible embrace.

A tense hypnotic quiet filled the place.
The men were like two wrestlers in a dream
That holds an endless moment; till a scream
Fell stab-like on the hush. One saw Talbeau,
Jaws set, hands clenched, eyes wild, and bending low,
As though he too were struggling, slowly bowed
Beneath Fink's might. And then—

                    What ailed the crowd?
Swept over by a flurry of surprise,
They swayed and jostled, shouting battle-cries
And quips and jeers of savage merriment.
One moment they had seen the tall man bent,
About to break: then, falling back a-haunch,
His feet had plunged against the other's paunch
And sent Fink somersaulting.

                    Once again
A silence fell as, leaping up, the men
Were mingled briefly in a storm of blows.
Now, tripping like a dancer on his toes,
The blond man sparred; while, like a baited bear,
Half blinded with the lust to crush and tear,
Fink strove to clutch that something lithe and sleek
That stung and fled and stung. Upon his cheek
A flying shadow laid a vivid bruise;
Another—and his brow began to ooze
Slow drops that spattered on his bearded jaw.
Again that shadow passed—his mouth went raw,
And like a gunshot wound it gaped and bled.

Fink roared with rage and plunged with lowered head
Upon this thing that tortured, hurled it back
Amid the crowd. One heard a thud and smack
Of rapid blows on bone and flesh—and then
One saw the tall man stagger clear again
With gushing nostrils and a bloody grin,
And down his front the whiteness of the skin

Was striped with flowing crimson to the waist.
Unsteadily he wheeled about and faced
The headlong hate of his antagonist.
Now toe to toe and fist to flying fist,
They played at give and take; and all the while
The blond man smiled that riddle of a smile,
As one who meditates upon a jest.

Yet surely he was losing! Backward pressed,
He strove in vain to check his raging foe.
Fink lunged and straightened to a shoulder blow
With force enough to knock a bison down.
The other dodged it, squatting. Then the town
Discovered what a smile might signify.
For, even as the futile blow went by,
One saw the lithe white form shoot up close in,
A hooked white arm jab upward to the chin—
Once—twice—and yet again. With eyes a-stare,
His hands aloft and clutching at the air,
Fink tottered backward, limply lurched and fell.

Then came to pass what stilled the rabble's yell,
So strange it was. And 'round the fires that night
The wisest warriors, talking of the fight,
Could not explain what happened at the end.
No friend, they said, makes war upon a friend;
Nor does a foe have pity on a foe:
And yet the tall white chief had bathed with snow
The bloody mouth and battered cheek and brow
Of him who fell!

       Queer people, anyhow,
The Long Knives were—and hard to understand!

THE SHOOTING OF THE CUP

VI

Bull-roaring March had swept across the land,
And now the evangelic goose and crane,
Forerunners of the messianic Rain,
Went crying through the wilderness aloft.
Fog hid the sun, and yet the snow grew soft.
The monochrome of sky and poplar bough,
Drab tracery on drab, was stippled now
With swelling buds; and slushy water ran
Upon the ice-bound river that began
To stir and groan as one about to wake.

Now, while they waited for the ice to break,
The trappers fashioned bull-boats—willow wrought
To bowl-like frames, and over these drawn taut
Green bison hides with bison sinew sewn.
And much they talked about the Yellowstone:
How fared their comrades yonder since the fall?
And would they marvel at the goodly haul
Of beaver pelts these crazy craft should bring?
And what of Ashley starting north that spring
With yet another hundred? Did his prows
Already nose the flood?—Ah, cherry boughs
About St. Louis now were loud with bees
And white with bloom; and wading to the knees,
The cattle browsed along the fresh green sloughs!
Yes, even now the leaning cordelle crews
With word from home (so far away, alas!)
Led north the marching armies of the grass,
As 'twere the heart of Summertime they towed!

So while they shaped the willow frames and sewed
The bison hides, the trappers' hearts were light.
They talked no longer now about the fight.
That story, shaped and fitted part by part,
Unwittingly was rounded into art,
And, being art, already it was old.
When this bleak time should seem the age of gold,
These men, grown gray and garrulous, might tell
Of wondrous doings on the Musselshell—
How Carpenter, the mighty, fought, and how
Great Fink went down. But spring was coming now,
And who's for backward looking in the spring?

Yet one might see that Mike still felt the sting
Of that defeat; for often he would brood,
Himself the center of a solitude
Wherein the friendly chatter of the band
Was like a wind that makes a lonely land
Seem lonelier. And much it grieved Talbeau
To see a haughty comrade humbled so;
And, even more, he feared what wounded pride
Might bring to pass, before their boats could ride
The dawnward reaches of the April floods
And leave behind the village of the Bloods;
For now it seemed a curse was on the place.
Talbeau was like a man who views a race
With all to lose: so slowly crept the spring,
So surely crawled some formless fatal thing,
He knew not what it was. But should it win,
Life could not be again as it had been
And spring would scarcely matter any more.
The daybreak often found him at the shore,
A ghostly figure in the muggy light,
Intent to see what progress over night
The shackled river made against the chain.

And then at last, one night, a dream of rain
Came vividly upon him. How it poured!

A witch's garden was the murk that roared
With bursting purple bloom. 'Twas April weather,
And he and Mike and Bill were boys together
Beneath the sounding shingle roof at home.
He smelled the odor of the drinking loam
Still rolling mellow from the recent share;
And he could feel the meadow greening there
Beyond the apple orchard. Then he 'woke
And raised the flap. A wraith of thunder-smoke
Was trailing off along the prairie's rim.
Half dreaming yet, the landscape puzzled him.
What made the orchard seem so tall and lean?
And surely yonder meadow had been green
A moment since! What made it tawny now?
And yonder where the billows of the plow
Should glisten fat and sleek—?

                  The drowsy spell
Dropped off and left him on the Musselshell
Beneath the old familiar load of care.
He looked aloft. The stars had faded there.
The sky was cloudless. No, one lonely fleece
Serenely floated in the spacious peace
And from the distance caught prophetic light.
In truth he had heard thunder in the night
And dashing rain; for all the land was soaked,
And where the withered drifts had lingered, smoked
The naked soil. But since the storm was gone,
How strange that still low thunder mumbled on—
An unresolving cadence marred at whiles
By dull explosions! Now for miles and miles
Along the vale he saw a trail of steam
That marked the many windings of the stream,
As though the river simmered. Then he knew.
It was the sound of April breaking through!
The resurrection thunder had begun!
The ice was going out, and spring had won
The creeping race with dread!

His ringing cheers
Brought out the blinking village by the ears
To share the news; and though they could not know
What ecstasy of triumph moved Talbeau,
Yet lodge on lodge took up the joyous cry
That set the dogs intoning to the sky,
The drenched cayuses shrilly nickering.
So man and beast proclaimed the risen Spring
Upon the Musselshell.

And all day long
The warring River sang its ocean song.
And all that night the spirits of the rain
Made battle music with a shattered chain
And raged upon the foe. And did one gaze
Upon that struggle through the starry haze,
One saw enormous bodies heaved and tossed,
Where stubbornly the Yotuns of the Frost
With shoulder set to shoulder strove to stem
The wild invasion rolling over them.
Nor in the morning was the struggle done.
Serenely all that day the doughty Sun,
A banished king returning to his right,
Beheld his legions pouring to the fight,
Exhaustless; and his cavalries that rode—
With hoofs that rumbled and with manes that flowed
White in the war gust—crashing on the foe.
And all that night the din of overthrow
Arose to heaven from the stricken field;
A sound as of the shock of spear and shield,
Of wheels that trundled and the feet of hordes,
Of shrieking horses mad among the swords,
Hurrahing of attackers and attacked,
And sounds as of a city that is sacked
When lust for loot runs roaring through the night.
Dawn looked upon no battle, but a flight.
And when the next day broke, the spring flood flowed
Like some great host that takes the homeward road

With many spoils—a glad triumphal march,
Of which the turquoise heaven was the arch.
Now comes a morning when the tents are down
And packed for travel; and the whole Blood town
Is out along the waterfront to see
The trappers going. Dancing as with glee,
Six laden bull-boats feel the April tide
And sweep away. Along the riverside
The straggling, shouting rabble keeps abreast
A little while; but, longer than the rest,
A weeping runner races with the swirl
And loses slowly. 'Tis the Long Knife's girl,
Whom love perhaps already makes aware
How flows unseen a greater river there—
The never-to-be-overtaken days.
And now she pauses at the bend to gaze
Upon the black boats dwindling down the long
Dawn-gilded reach. A merry trapper's song
Comes liltingly to mock her, and a hand
Waves back farewell. Now 'round a point of land
The bull-boats disappear; and that is all—
Save only that long waiting for the fall
When he would come again.

                All day they swirled
Northeastwardly. The undulating world
Flowed by them—wooded headland, greening vale
And naked hill—as in a fairy tale
Remembered in a dream. And when the flare
Of sunset died behind them, and the air
Went weird and deepened to a purple gloom,
They saw the white Enchanted Castles loom
Above them, slowly pass and drift a-rear,
Dissolving in the starry crystal sphere
'Mid which they seemed suspended.
                      Late to camp,
They launched while yet the crawling valley damp
Made islands of the distant hills and hid

The moaning flood. The Half Way Pyramid
That noon stared in upon them from the south.
'Twas starlight when they camped at Hell Creek's mouth,
Among those hills where evermore in vain
The Spring comes wooing, and the April rain
Is tears upon a tomb. And once again
The dead land echoed to the songs of men
Bound dayward when the dawn was but a streak.
Halfway to noon they sighted Big Dry Creek,
Not choked with grave dust now, but carolling
The universal music of the spring.
Then when the day was midway down the sky,
They reached the Milk. And howsoe'er the eye
Might sweep that valley with a far-flung gaze,
It found no spot uncovered with a maze
Of bison moving lazily at browse—
Scarce wilder than a herd of dairy cows
That know their herdsman.

                Now the whole band willed
To tarry. So they beached their boats and killed
Three fatling heifers; sliced the juicy rumps
For broiling over embers; set the humps
And loins to roast on willow spits, and threw
The hearts and livers in a pot to stew
Against the time of dulling appetites.
And when the stream ran opalescent lights
And in a scarlet glow the new moon set,
The feast began. And some were eating yet,
And some again in intervals of sleep,
When upside down above the polar steep
The Dipper hung. And many tales were told
And there was hearty laughter as of old,
With Fink's guffaw to swell it now and then.
It seemed old times were coming back again;
That truly they had launched upon a trip
Whereof the shining goal was comradeship:
And tears were in the laughter of Talbeau,

So glad was he. For how may mortals know
Their gladness, save they sense it by the fear
That whispers how the very thing held dear
May pass away?

        The smoky dawn was lit,
And, suddenly become aware of it,
A flock of blue cranes, dozing on the sand,
With startled cries awoke the sprawling band
And took the misty air with moaning wings.
Disgruntled with the chill drab scheme of things,
Still half asleep and heavy with the feast,
The trappers launched their boats. But when the east
Burned rosily, therefrom a raw wind blew,
And ever with the growing day it grew
Until the stream rose choppily and drove
The fleet ashore. Camped snugly in a grove
Of cottonwoods, they slept. And when the gale,
Together with the light, began to fail,
They 'rose and ate and set a-drift again.

It seemed the solid world that mothers men
With twilight and the falling moon had passed,
And there was nothing but a hollow vast,
By time-outlasting stars remotely lit,
And they who at the central point of it
Hung motionless; while, rather sensed than seen,
The phantoms of a world that had been green
Stole by in silence—shapes that once were trees,
Black wraiths of bushes, airy traceries
Remembering the hills. Then sleep made swift
The swinging of the Dipper and the lift
Of stars that dwell upon the day's frontier;
Until at length the wheeling hollow sphere
Began to fill. And just at morningshine
They landed at the Little Porcupine.

Again they slept and, putting off at night,
They passed the Elk Horn Prairie on the right

Halfway to dawn and Wolf Creek. One night more
Had vanished when they slept upon the shore
Beside the Poplar's mouth. And three had fled
When, black against the early morning red,
The Fort that Henry builded heard their calls,
And sentries' rifles spurting from the walls
Spilled drawling echoes. Then the gates swung wide
And shouting trappers thronged the riverside
To welcome back the homing *voyageurs*.

That day was spent in sorting out the furs,
With eager talk of how the winter went;
And with the growing night grew merriment.
The hump and haunches of a bison cow
Hung roasting at the heaped-up embers now
On Henry's hearth. The backlog whined and popped
And, sitting squat or lounging elbow-propped,
Shrewd traders in the merchandise of tales
Held traffic, grandly careless how the scales
Tiptilted with a slight excessive weight.
And when the roast was finished, how they ate!
And there was that which set them singing too
Against the deep bass music of the flue,
While catgut screamed ecstatic in the lead,
Encouraging the voices used and keyed
To vast and windy spaces.

                    Later came
A gentler mood when, staring at the flame,
Men ventured reminiscences and spoke
About Kentucky people or the folk
Back yonder in Virginia or the ways
They knew in old St. Louis; till the blaze
Fell blue upon the hearth, and in the gloom
And melancholy stillness of the room
They heard the wind of midnight wail outside.
Then there was one who poked the logs and cried:
"Is this a weeping drunk? I swear I'm like
To tear my hair! Sing something lively, Mike!"

And Fink said nought; but after poring long
Upon the logs, began an Irish song—
A gently grieving thing like April rain,
That while it wakes old memories of pain,
Wakes also odors of the violet.
A broken heart, it seemed, could ne'er forget
The eyes of Nora, dead upon the hill.
And when he ceased the men sat very still,
As hearing yet the low caressing note
Of some lost angel mourning in his throat.
And afterwhile Mike spoke: "Shure, now," said he,
" 'Tis in a woman's eyes shtrong liquors be;
And if ye drink av thim—and if ye drink—"
For just a moment in the face of Fink
Talbeau beheld that angel yearning through;
And wondering if Carpenter saw too,
He looked, and lo! the guileless fellow—grinned!

As dreaming water, stricken by a wind,
Gives up the imaged heaven that it knows,
So Fink's face lost the angel. He arose
And left the place without a word to say.

The morrow was a perfect April day;
Nor might one guess—so friendly was the sun,
So kind the air—what thread at length was spun,
What shears were opened now to sever it.
No sullen mood was Mike's. His biting wit
Made gay the trappers busy with the fur;
Though more and ever more on Carpenter
His sallies fell, with ever keener whet.
And Carpenter, unskilled in banter, met
The sharper sally with the broader grin.
But, by and by, Mike made a jest, wherein
Some wanton innuendo lurked and leered,
About the Long Knife's girl. The place went weird
With sudden silence as the tall man strode
Across the room, nor lacked an open road

Among the men. A glitter in his stare
Belied the smile he bore; and, pausing there
With stiffened index finger raised and held
Before the jester's eyes, as though he spelled
The slow words out, he said: "We'll have no jokes
In just that way about our women folks!"
And Fink guffawed.

        They would have fought again,
Had not the Major stepped between the men
And talked the crisis by. And when 'twas past,
Talbeau, intent to end the strife at last,
Somehow persuaded Fink to make amends,
And, as a proof that henceforth they were friends,
Proposed the shooting of the whisky cup.
"Shure, b'y," said Mike, "we'll toss a copper up
And if 'tis heads I'll thry me cunning first.
As fer me joke, the tongue of me is cursed
Wid double j'ints—so let it be forgot!"
And so it was agreed.

        They cleared a spot
And flipped a coin that tinkled as it fell.
A tiny sound—yet, like a midnight bell
That sets wild faces pressing at the pane,
Talbeau would often hear that coin again,
In vivid dreams, to waken terrified.
'Twas heads.

        And now the tall man stepped aside
And, beckoning Talbeau, he whispered: "Son,
If anything should happen, keep my gun
For old time's sake. And when the Major pays
In old St. Louis, drink to better days
When friends were friends, with what he's owing me."
Whereat the little man laughed merrily
And said: "Old Horse, you're off your feed to-day;
But if you've sworn an oath to blow your pay,

I guess the three of us can make it good!
Mike couldn't miss a target if he would."
"Well, maybe so," said Carpenter, and smiled.

A windless noon was brooding on the wild
And in the clearing, eager for the show,
The waiting trappers chatted. Now Talbeau
Stepped off the range. The tall man took his place,
The grin of some droll humor on his face;
And when his friend was reaching for his head
To set the brimming cup thereon, he said:
"You won't forget I gave my gun to you
And all my blankets and my fixin's too?"
The small man laughed and, turning round,
        he cried:
"We're ready, Mike!"

                A murmur ran and died
Along the double line of eager men.
Fink raised his gun, but set it down again
And blew a breath and said: "I'm gittin' dhry!
So howld yer noddle shtiddy, Bill, me b'y,
And don't ye shpill me whisky!" Cedar-straight
The tall man stood, the calm of brooding Fate
About him. Aye, and often to the end
Talbeau would see that vision of his friend—
A man-flower springing from the fresh green sod,
While, round about, the bushes burned with God
And mating peewees fluted in the brush.

They heard a gun lock clicking in the hush.
They saw Fink sighting—heard the rifle crack,
And saw beneath the spreading powder rack
The tall man pitching forward.

                        Echoes fled
Like voices in a panic. Then Mike said:
"Bejasus, and ye've shpilled me whisky, Bill!"

A catbird screamed. The crowd stood very still
As though bewitched.

                                "And can't ye hear?" bawled Fink;
"I say, I'm dhry—and now ye've shpilled me drink!"
He stooped to blow the gasses from his gun.

And now men saw Talbeau. They saw him run
And stoop to peer upon the prostrate man
Where now the mingling blood and whisky ran
From oozing forehead and the tilted cup.
And in the hush a sobbing cry grew up:
"My God! You've killed him, Mike!"

                                Then growing loud,
A wind of horror blew among the crowd
And set it swirling round about the dead.
And over all there roared a voice that said:
"I niver mint to do it, b'ys, I swear!
The divil's in me gun!" Men turned to stare
Wild-eyed upon the center of that sound,
And saw Fink dash his rifle to the ground,
As 'twere the hated body of his wrong.

Once more arose that wailing, like a song,
Of one who called and called upon his friend.

THE THIRD RIDER

VII

It seemed the end, and yet 'twas not the end.
A day that wind of horror and surprise
Blew high; and then, as when the tempest dies
And only aspens prattle, as they will,
Though pines win silence and the oaks are still,
By furtive twos and threes the talk survived.
To some it seemed that men were longer lived
Who quarreled not over women. Others guessed
That love was bad for marksmanship at best—
The nerves, you know! Still others pointed out
Why Mike should have the benefit of doubt;
For every man, who knew a rifle, knew
That there were days you'd split a reed in two,
Off-hand at fifty paces; then, one day,
Why, somehow, damn your eyes, you'd blaze away
And miss a bull! No doubt regarding that!
"But," one replied, " 'tis what you're aiming at.
Not what you hit, determines skill, you know!"—
An abstract observation, apropos
Of nothing in particular, but made
As just a contribution to the trade
Of gunnery! And others would recall
The center of that silence in the hall
The night one lay there waiting, splendid, still,
And nothing left to wait for. Poor old Bill!
There went a man, by God! Who knew his like—
So meek in might? And some remembered Mike—
The hearth-lit room—the way he came to look
Upon that face—and how his shoulders shook
With sobbing as he moaned: "My friend! My friend!"

It seemed the end, and yet 'twas not the end,
Though men cared less to know what cunning gnome
Or eyeless thing of doom had ridden home
The deadly slug. And then there came a day
When Major Henry had a word to say
That seemed, at last, to lay the ghost to rest.
He meant to seek the River of the West
Beyond the range, immensely rich in furs,
And for the wiving prows of *voyageurs*
A virgin yearning. Yonder one might glide
A thousand miles to sunset, where the tide
Is tempered with an endless dream of May!
So much and more the Major had to say—
Words big with magic for the young men's ears.
And finally he called for volunteers—
Two men to hasten to the Moreau's mouth,
Meet Ashley's party coming from the south
And bid them buy more horses at the Grand
Among the Rees. Then, pushing through the band,
Mike Fink stood forth, and after him, Talbeau.

Now Henry thought 'twere wiser they should go
By land, although the river trail, he knew,
Were better. But a wind of rumor blew
Up stream. About the region of the Knife,
It seemed, the Grovans tarried, nursing strife
Because the Whites were favoring their foes
With trade for guns; and, looking on their bows,
The Grovans hated. So the rumor said.
And thus it came to pass the new trail led
About six days by pony to the south;
Thence eastward, five should find the Moreau's mouth
And Ashley toiling up among the bars.

The still white wind was blowing out the stars
When yawning trappers saw the two men row
Across the river with their mounts in tow—
A red roan stallion and a buckskin mare.
And now the ponies gain the far bank there

And flounder up and shake themselves like dogs.
And now the riders mount and breast the fogs
Flung down as wool upon the flat. They dip
And rise and float, submerging to the hip,
Turn slowly into shadow men, and fade.
And some have said that when the ponies neighed,
'Twas like a strangled shriek; and far ahead
Some ghostly pony, ridden by the dead,
Called onward like a bugle singing doom.
And when the valley floor, as with a broom,
Was swept by dawn, men saw the empty land.

Not now the Song shall tell of Henry's band
Ascending to the Falls, nor how they crossed
The Blackfoot trail, nor how they fought and lost,
Thrown back upon the Yellowstone to wait
In vain for Ashley's hundred. Yonder, Fate
Led southward through the fog, and thither goes
The prescient Song.

        The April sun arose
And fell; and all day long the riders faced
A rolling, treeless, melancholy waste
Of yellow grass; for 'twas a rainless time,
Nor had the baby green begun to climb
The steep-kneed hills, but kept the nursing draws.
And knee to knee they rode with scarce a pause,
Save when the ponies drank; and scarce a word,
As though the haunting silence of a third,
Who rode between them, shackled either tongue.
And when along the sloughs the twilight flung
Blue haze, and made the hills seem doubly bleak,
They camped beside a songless little creek
That crawled among the clumps of stunted plum
Just coming into bud. And both sat dumb
Beside a mewing fire, until the west
Was darkened and the shadows leaped and pressed
About their little ring of feeble light.

Then, moved by some vague menace in the night,
Fink forced a laugh that wasn't glad at all,
And joked about a certain saddle gall
That troubled him—a Rabelaisian quip
That in the good old days had served to strip
The drooping humor from the dourest jowl.
He heard the laughter of the prairie owl,
A goblin jeering. Gazing at the flame,
Talbeau seemed not to hear. But when there came
A cry of kiotes, peering all about
He said: "You don't suppose they'll dig him out?
I carried heavy stones till break of day.
You don't suppose they'll come and paw away
The heavy stones I packed, and pester Bill?"
"Huh uh," Fink grunted; but the evening chill
Seemed doubled on a sudden; so he sought
His blanket, wrapped it closely, thought and thought
Till drowsy nonsense tumbled through his skull.

Now at that time of night when comes a lull
On stormy life; when even sorrow sleeps,
And sentinels upon the stellar steeps
Sight morning, though the world is blind and dumb,
Fink wakened at a whisper: "Mike! He's come!
Look! Look!" And Mike sat up and blinked and saw.
It didn't walk—it burned along the draw—
Tall, radiantly white! It wasn't dead—
It smiled—it had a tin cup on its head—
Eh?—Gone!

            Fink stirred the embers to a flare.
What dream was this? The world seemed unaware
That anything at all had come to pass.
Contentedly the ponies nipped the grass
There in the darkness; and the night was still.
They slept no more, but nursed the fire until
The morning broke; then ate and rode away.

They weren't any merrier that day.
And each spoke little, save when Fink would swear
And smirch the virtue of the buckskin mare
For picking quarrels with the roan he rode.
(Did not the Northwind nag her like a goad,
And was there any other horse to blame?)

The worried day dragged on and twilight came—
A dusty gray. They climbed a hill to seek
Some purple fringe of brush that marked a creek.
The prairie seemed an endless yellow blur:
Nor might they choose but tarry where they were
And pass the cheerless night as best they could,
For they had seen no water-hole or wood
Since when the sun was halfway down the sky;
And there would be no stars to travel by,
So thick a veil of dust the great wind wove.
They staked their ponies in a leeward cove,
And, rolling in their blankets, swooned away.

Talbeau awoke and stared. 'Twas breaking day!
So soon? It seemed he scarce had slept a wink!
He'd have another snooze, for surely Fink
Seemed far from waking, sprawled upon the ground,
His loose mouth gaping skyward with a sound
As of a bucksaw grumbling through a knot.
Talbeau dropped back and dreamed the sun was hot
Upon his face. He tried but failed to stir;
Whereat he knew that he was Carpenter
And hot-breatht wolves were sniffing round his head!
He wasn't dead! He really wasn't dead!
Would no one come, would no one drive them off?
His cry for help was nothing but a cough,
For something choked him. Then a shrill long scream
Cut knife-like through the shackles of his dream,
And once again he saw the lurid flare
Of morning on the hills.

What ailed the mare?
She strained her tether, neighing. And the roan?
He squatted, trembling, with his head upthrown,
And lashed his tail and snorted at the blast.
Perhaps some prowling grizzly wandered past.
Talbeau sat up. What stifling air! How warm!
What sound was that? Perhaps a thunder storm
Was working up. He coughed; and then it broke
Upon him how the air was sharp with smoke;
And, leaping up, he turned and looked and knew
What birdless dawn, unhallowed by the dew,
Came raging from the northwest! Half the earth
And half the heavens were a burning hearth
Fed fat with grass inflammable as tow!
He shook Fink, yelling: "Mike, we've got to go!
All hell's broke loose!"

             They cinched the saddles on
With hands that fumbled; mounted and were gone,
Like rabbits fleeing from a kiote pack.
They crossed the valley, topped a rise, looked back,
Nor dared to gaze. The firm, familiar world,
It seemed, was melting down, and Chaos swirled
Once more across the transient realms of form
To scatter in the primal atom-storm
The earth's rich dust and potency of dreams.
Infernal geysers gushed, and sudden streams
Of rainbow flux went roaring up the skies
Through ghastly travesties of Paradise,
Where, drowsy in a tropic summertide,
Strange gaudy flowers bloomed and aged and
     died—
Whole seasons in a moment. Bloody rain,
Blown slant like April silver, spewed the plain
To mock the fallow sod; and where it fell
Anemones and violets of hell
Foreran the fatal summer.

Spurs bit deep.
Now down the hill where shadow-haunted sleep
Fell from the broken wind's narcotic breath,
The ponies plunged. A sheltered draw, where death
Seemed brooding in the silence, heard them pass.
A hollow, deep with tangled jointed grass,
Snatched at the frantic hoofs. Now up a slope
They clambered, blowing, at a stumbling lope
And, reined upon the summit, wheeled to stare.
The stallion snorted, and the rearing mare
Screamed at the sight and bolted down the wind.
The writhing Terror, scarce a mile behind,
Appeared to gain; while far to left and right
Its flanks seemed bending in upon the night—
A ten-league python closing on its prey.

No guiding hand was needed for the way;
Blind speed was all. So little Nature heeds
The fate of men, these blew as tumbleweeds
Before that dwarfing, elemental rage.
A gray wolf bounded from a clump of sage;
A rabbit left its bunchgrass nest and ran
Beside its foe; and neither dreaded Man,
The deadliest of all earth's preying things.
A passing knoll exploded into wings,
And prairie owls, befuddled by the light,
Went tumbling up like patches of the night
The burning tempest tattered.

Leaning low,
The gasping riders let the ponies go,
The little buckskin leading, while the roan
Strove hard a-flank, afraid to be alone
And nickering at whiles. And he who led,
By brief hypnotic lapses comforted,
Recalled the broad Ohio, heard the horns
The way they used to sing those summer morns
When he and Mike and—. There the dream went wrong

And through his head went running, like a song
That sings itself: 'He tried so hard to come
And warn us; but the grave had made him dumb,
And 'twas to show he loved us that he smiled.'
And of the other terror made a child
Whom often, for a panic moment's span,
Projections from the conscience of the man
Pursued with glaring eyes and claws of flame.
For this the dead arose, for this he came—
That grin upon his face!

         A blinding gloom
Crushed down; then, followed by a rolling boom,
There broke a scarlet hurricane of light
That swept the farthest reaches of the night
Where unsuspected hills leaped up aghast.
Already through the hollow they had passed
So recently, the hounding Terror sped!
And now the wind grew hotter. Overhead
Inverted seas of color rolled and broke,
And from the combers of the litten smoke
A stinging spindrift showered.

           On they went,
Unconscious of duration or extent,
Of everything but that from which they fled.
Now, sloping to an ancient river bed,
The prairie flattened. Plunging downward there,
The riders suddenly became aware
How surged, beneath, a mighty shadow-stream—
As though the dying Prairie dreamed a dream
Of yesterage when all her valleys flowed
With Amazons, and monster life abode
Upon her breast and quickened in her womb.
And from that rushing in the flame-smeared gloom
Unnumbered outcries blended in a roar.
The headlong ponies struck the sounding shore
And reared upon their haunches. Far and near,

The valley was a-flood with elk and deer
And buffalo and wolves and antelope
And whatsoever creature slough and slope
Along the path of terror had to give.
Torrential with the common will to live,
The river of unnumbered egos swept
The ponies with it. But the buckskin kept
The margin where the rabble frayed and thinned
And, breathing with the wheeze of broken wind,
The stallion clung to her.

      It came to pass
The valley yawned upon a sea of grass
That seemed to heave, as waves of gloom and glare
Ran over it; and, rising here and there,
Tall buttes made islands in the living tide
That roared about them. Still with swinging stride
And rhythmic breath the little buckskin ran
Among the herd, that opened like a fan
And scattered. But the roan was losing ground.
His breathing gave a gurgling, hollow sound,
As though his life were gushing from his throat.
His whole frame quivered like a scuttled boat
That slowly sinks; nor did he seem to feel
Upon his flank the biting of the steel
That made him bleed. Fink cut the rifle-boot
And saddle-bags away, to give the brute
Less burden.

    Now it happened, as they neared
A lofty butte whose summit glimmered weird
Beneath the lurid boiling of the sky,
Talbeau was startled by a frantic cry
Behind him; noted that he rode alone,
And, turning in the saddle, saw the roan
Go stumbling down and wither to a heap.
And momently, between a leap and leap,
The love of self was mighty in the man;

For now the Terror left the hills and ran
With giant strides along the grassy plains.
Dear Yesterdays fought wildly for the reins,
To-morrows for the spur. And then the mare
Heeled to the sawing bit and pawed the air
And halted, prancing.
                  Once again Talbeau
Looked back to where the sparks were blown as snow
Before that blizzard blast of scorching light,
And saw Fink running down the painted night
Like some lost spirit fleeing from the Wrath.

One horse—and who should ride it? All he hath
A man will give for life! But shall he give
For living that which makes it good to live—
The consciousness of fellowship and trust?
Let fools so prize a pinch of throbbing dust!
Now Fink should ride, and let the rest be hid.
He bounded from the mare; but, as he did,
The panic-stricken pony wheeled about,
Won freedom with a lunge, and joined the rout
Of fleeing shadows.

                Well, 'twas over now—
Perhaps it didn't matter anyhow—
They'd go together now and hunt for Bill!
And momently the world seemed very still
About Talbeau. Then Fink was at his side,
Blank horror in his face. "Come on!" he cried;
"The butte! We'll climb the butte!" And once again
Talbeau knew fear.

              Now, gripping hands, the men
Scuttled and dodged athwart the scattered flight
Of shapes that drifted in the flood of light,
A living flotsam; reached the bare butte's base,
Went scrambling up its leaning leeward face
To where the slope grew sheer, and huddled there.

And hotter, hotter, hotter grew the air,
Until their temples sang a fever tune.
The April night became an August noon.
Then, near to swooning in a blast of heat,
They heard the burning breakers boom and beat
About their lofty island, as they lay,
Their gaping mouths pressed hard against the clay,
And fought for every breath. Nor could they tell
How long upon a blistered scarp in hell
They gasped and clung. But suddenly at last—
An age in passing, and a moment, passed—
The torture ended, and the cool air came;
And, looking out, they saw the long slant flame
Devour the night to leeward.

        By and by
Drab light came seeping through the sullen sky.
They waited there until the morning broke,
And, like a misty moon amid the smoke,
The sun came stealing up.

        They found a place
Where rain had scarred the butte wall's western face
With many runnels; clambered upward there—
And viewed a panorama of despair.
The wind had died, and not a sound arose
Above those blackened leagues; for even crows
(The solitude embodied in a bird)
Had fled that desolation. Nothing stirred,
Save here and there a thin gray column grew
From where some draw still smouldered. And they
    knew
How universal quiet may appal
As violence, and, even as a wall,
Sheer vacancy confine.

        No horse, no gun!
Nay, worse; no hint of water hole or run

In all the flat or back among the hills!
Mere hunger is a goad that, ere it kills,
May drive the lean far down the hardest road:
But thirst is both a snaffle and a load;
It gripped them now. When Mike made bold to speak,
His tongue was like a stranger to his cheek.
"Shure, b'y," he croaked; " 'tis Sunday morn in hell!"
The sound seemed profanation; on it fell
The vast, rebuking silence.

                     Long they gazed
About them, standing silent and amazed
Upon the summit. West and north and east
They saw too far. But mystery, at least,
Was in the south, where still the smoke concealed
The landscape. Vistas of the unrevealed
Invited Hope to stray there as it please.
And presently there came a little breeze
Out of the dawn. As of a crowd that waits
Some imminent revealment of the Fates
That toil behind the scenes, a murmur 'woke
Amid the hollow hush. And now the smoke
Mysteriously stirs, begins to flow,
And giant shadow bulks that loom below
Seem crowding dawnward. One by one they lift
Above the reek, and trail the ragged drift
About their flanks. A melancholy scene!
Gray buttes and giddy gulfs that yawn between—
A Titan's labyrinth! But see afar
Where yonder canyon like a purple scar
Cuts zigzag through the waste! Is that a gleam
Of water in its deeps?

                  A stream! A stream!

Now scrambling down the runnels of the rain,
They struck across the devastated plain

Where losers of the night's mad race were strewn
To wait the wolves and crows.

           Mid-afternoon
Beheld them stripping at the river's bank.
They wallowed in the turbid stream and drank
Delicious beakers in the liquid mud;
Nor drank alone, for here the burning flood
Had flung its panting driftage in the dark.
The valley teemed with life, as though some Ark
That rode the deluge, spewed its cargo here:
Elk, antelope, wolves, bison, rabbits, deer,
Owls, crows—the greatest mingled with the least.
And when the men had drunk, they had a feast
Of liver, bolted dripping from a cow
Dead at the water's lip.

           Blue shadow now
Was mounting slowly up the canyon steep;
So, seeking for a better place to sleep,
They wandered down the margin of the stream.
'Twas scarce more real than walking in a dream
Of lonely craters in a lunar land
That never thrilled with roots. On either hand
The dwarfing summits soared, grotesque, austere,
And jaggéd fissures, sentinelled with fear,
Led back to mysteries of purple gloom.

They came to where a coulee, like a flume,
Rose steeply to the prairie. Thither hurled,
A roaring freshet of the herd had swirled,
Cascading to the river bed; and there,
Among the trampelled carcasses, the mare
Lay bloated near the water. She had run
With saddle, panniers, powder-horn and gun
Against the wind-thewed fillies of the fire,
And won the heat, to perish at the wire—
A plucky little brute!

VENGEANCE

VIII

They made a camp
Well up above the crawling valley damp,
And where no prowling beast might chance to come.
There was no fuel; but a flask of rum,
Thanks to the buckskin, dulled the evening chill.
And both grew mellow. Memories of Bill
And other nights possessed the little man;
And on and on his reminiscence ran,
As 'twere the babble of a brook of tears
Gone groping for the ocean of dead years
Too far away to reach. And by and by
The low voice sharpened to an anguished cry:
"O Mike! I said you couldn't miss the cup!"

Then something snapped in Fink and, leaping up,
He seized Talbeau and shook him as a rat
Is shaken by a dog. "Enough of that!"
He yelled; "And, 'faith, I'll sind ye afther Bill
Fer wan more wurrd! Ye fool! I mint to kill!
And, moind me now, ye'd better howld yer lip!"
Talbeau felt murder shudder in the grip
That choked and shook and flung him. Faint and dazed,
He sprawled upon the ground. And anger blazed
Within him, like the leaping Northern Light
That gives no heat. He wished to rise and fight,
But could not for the horror of it all.
Wild voices thronged the further canyon wall
As Fink raved on; and every word he said
Was like a mutilation of the dead
By some demonic mob.

And when at length
He heard Mike snoring yonder, still the strength
To rise and kill came not upon Talbeau.
So many moments of the Long Ago
Came pleading; and the gentle might thereof
United with the habit of old love
To weave a spell about the sleeping man.
Then drowsily the pondered facts began
To merge and group, as running colors will,
In new and vaguer patterns. Mike and Bill
Were bickering again. And someone said:
"Let's flip a copper; if it's tails, he's dead;
If heads, he's living. That's the way to tell!"
A spinning copper jangled like a bell.
But even as he stooped to pick it up,
Behold! the coin became a whisky cup
Bored smoothly through the center! "Look at this!"
He seemed to shout: "I knew Mike couldn't miss!
Bill only played at dying for a joke!"

Then laughter filled his dream, and he awoke.
The dawn was like a stranger's cold regard
Across the lifeless land, grotesquely scarred
As by old sorrow; and the man's dull sense
Of woe, become objective and immense,
Seemed waiting there to crush him.

                              Fink still slept;
And even now, it seemed, his loose mouth kept
A shape for shameless words, as though a breath,
Deep drawn, might set it gloating o'er the death
Of one who loved its jesting and its song.
And while Talbeau sat pondering the wrong
So foully done, and all that had been killed,
And how the laughter of the world was stilled
And all its wine poured out, he seemed to hear
As though a spirit whispered in his ear:
You won't forget I gave my gun to you!

And instantly the deep conviction grew
That 'twas a plea for justice from the slain.
Ah, not without a hand upon the rein,
Nor with an empty saddle, had the mare
Outrun the flame that she might carry there
The means of vengeance!

                        Yet—if Mike were dead!
He shuddered, gazing where the gray sky bled
With morning, like a wound. He couldn't kill;
Nor did it seem to be the way of Bill
To bid him do it. Yet the gun was sent.
For what?—To make Mike suffer and repent?
But how?

           Awhile his apathetic gaze
Explored yon thirst- and hunger-haunted maze,
As though he might surprise the answer there.
The answer came. That region of despair
Should be Mike's Purgatory! More than Chance
Had fitted circumstance to circumstance
That this should be! He knew it! And the plan,
Thus suddenly conceived, possessed the man.
It seemed the might of Bill had been reborn
In him.

         He took the gun and powder horn,
The water flasks and sun-dried bison meat
The panniers gave; then climbing to a seat
Above the sleeper, shouted down to him:
"Get up!" Along the further canyon rim
A multitude of voices swelled the shout.
Fink started up and yawned and looked about,
Bewildered. Once again the clamor ran
Along the canyon wall. The little man,
Now squinting down the pointed rifle, saw
The lifted face go pale, the stubborn jaw
Droop nervelessly. A twinge of pity stirred

Within him, and he marvelled as he heard
His own voice saying what he wished unsaid:
"It's Bill's own rifle pointing at your head;
Go east, and think of all the wrong you've done!"

Fink glanced across his shoulder where the sun
Shone level on the melancholy land;
And, feigning that he didn't understand,
Essayed a careless grin that went awry.
"Bejasus, and we'll not go there, me b'y,"
He said; "for shure 'tis hell widout the lights!"
That one-eyed stare along the rifle sights
Was narrowed to a slit. A sickening shock
Ran through him at the clucking of the lock.
He clutched his forehead, stammering: "Talbeau,
I've been yer frind—."

              "I'll give you three to go,"
The other said, "or else you'll follow Bill!
One—two—."

               Fink turned and scuttled down the hill;
And at the sight the watcher's eyes grew dim,
For something old and dear had gone from him—
His pride in one who made a clown of Death.
Alas, how much the man would give for breath!
How easily Death made of him the clown!

Now scrambling for a grip, now rolling down,
Mike landed at the bottom of the steep,
And, plunging in the river belly deep,
Struck out in terror for the other shore.
At any moment might the rifle's roar
Crash through that rearward silence, and the lead
Come snarling like a hornet at his head—
He felt the spot! Then presently the flood
Began to cool the fever in his blood,
And furtive self-derision stung his pride.

He clambered dripping up the further side
And felt himself a fool! He wouldn't go!
That little whiffet yonder was Talbeau!
And who was this that he, Mike Fink, had feared?
He'd go and see.

    A spurt of smoke appeared
Across the river, and a bullet struck—
Spat ping—beside him, spewing yellow muck
Upon his face. Then every cliff and draw
Rehearsed the sullen thunders of the law
He dared to question. Stricken strangely weak,
He clutched the clay and watched the powder reek
Trail off with glories of the level sun.
He saw Talbeau pour powder in his gun
And ram the wad. A second shot might kill!
That brooding like a woman over Bill
Had set the fellow daft. *A crazy man!*
The notion spurred him. Springing up, he ran
To where a gully cleft the canyon rim
And, with that one-eyed fury after him,
Fled east.

    The very buttes, grotesque and weird,
Seemed startled at the sight of what he feared
And powerless to shield him in his need.
'Twas more than man he fled from; 'twas a deed,
Become alive and subtle as the air,
That turned upon the doer. Everywhere
It gibbered in the echoes as he fled.
A stream of pictures flitted through his head:
The quiet body in the hearth-lit hall,
The grinning ghost, the flight, the stallion's fall,
The flame girt isle, the spectral morning sun,
And then the finding of the dead man's gun
Beside the glooming river. Flowing by,
These fused and focused in the deadly eye
He felt behind him.

                              Suddenly the ground
Heaved up and smote him with a crashing sound;
And in the vivid moment of his fall
He thought he heard the snarling rifle ball
And felt the one-eyed fury crunch its mark.
Expectant of the swooping of the dark,
He raised his eyes.—The sun was shining still;
It peeped about the shoulder of a hill
And viewed him with a quizzifying stare.
He looked behind him. Nothing followed there;
But Silence, big with dread-begotten sound,
Dismayed him; and the steeps that hemmed him round
Seemed plotting with a more than human guile.
He rose and fled; but every little while
A sense of eyes behind him made him pause;
And always down the maze of empty draws
It seemed a sound of feet abruptly ceased.
Now trotting, walking now, he labored east;
And when at length the burning zenith beat
Upon him, and the summits swam with heat,
And on the winding gullies fell no shade,
He came to where converging gulches made
A steep-walled basin for the blinding glare.
Here, fanged and famished, crawled the prickly pear;
Malevolent with thirst, the soap weed thrust
Its barbed stilettos from the arid dust,
Defiant of the rain-withholding blue:
And in the midst a lonely scrub oak grew,
A crooked dwarf that, in the pictured bog
Of its own shadow, squatted like a frog.
Fink, panting, flung himself beneath its boughs.
A mighty magic in the noonday drowse
Allayed the driving fear. A waking dream
Fulfilled a growing wish. He saw the stream
Far off as from a space-commanding height.
And now a phantasy of rapid flight
Transported him above the sagging land,
And with a sudden swoop he seemed to stand

Once more upon the shimmering river's brink.
His eyes drank deep; but when his mouth would drink,
A giant hornet from the other shore—
The generating center of a roar
That shook the world—snarled by.

                            He started up,
And saw the basin filling as a cup
With purple twilight! Gazing all around
Where still the flitting ghost of some great sound
Troubled the crags a moment, then was mute,
He saw along the shoulder of a butte,
A good three hundred paces from the oak,
A slowly spreading streak of rifle smoke
And knew the deadly eye was lurking there.
He fled again.

                About him everywhere
Amid the tangled draws now growing dim,
Weird witnesses took cognizance of him
And told abroad the winding way he ran.
He halted only when his breath began
To stab his throat. And lo, the staring eye
Was quenched with night! No further need he fly
Till dawn. And yet—. He held his breath to hear
If footsteps followed. Silence smote his ear,
The gruesome silence of the hearth-lit hall,
More dread than sound. Against the gully wall
He shrank and huddled with his eyes shut tight,
For fear a presence, latent in the night,
Should walk before him.

                      Then it seemed he ran
Through regions alien to the feet of Man,
A weary way despite the speed of sleep,
And came upon a river flowing deep
Between black crags that made the sky a well.
And eerily the feeble starlight fell

Upon the flood with water lilies strown.
But when he stooped, the stream began to moan,
And suddenly from every lily pad
A white face bloomed, unutterably sad
And bloody browed.

     A swift, erasing flame
Across the dusky picture, morning came.
Mike lay a moment, blinking at the blue;
And then the fear of yesterday broke through
The clinging drowse. For lo, on every side
The paling summits watched him, Argus-eyed,
In hushed anticipation of a roar.
He fled.

    All day, intent to see once more
The open plain before the night should fall,
He labored on. But many a soaring wall
Annulled some costly distance he had won;
And misdirected gullies, white with sun,
Seemed spitefully to baffle his desire.
The deeps went blue; on mimic dome and spire
The daylight faded to a starry awe.
Mike slept; and lo, they marched along the draw—
Or rather burned—tall, radiantly white!
A hushed procession, tunnelling the night,
They came, with lips that smiled and brows that bled,
And each one bore a tin cup on its head,
A brimming cup. But ever as they came
Before him, like a draught-struck candle flame
They shuddered and were snuffed.

       'Twas deep night yet
When Mike awoke and felt the terror sweat
Upon his face, the prickling of his hair.
Afraid to sleep, he paced the gully there
Until the taller buttes were growing gray.
He brooded much on flowing streams that day.

As with a weight, he stooped; his feet were slow;
He shuffled. Less and less he feared Talbeau
Behind him. More and more he feared the night
Before him. Any hazard in the light,
Or aught that might befall 'twixt living men,
Were better than to be alone again
And meet that dream!

          The deeps began to fill
With purple haze. Bewildered, boding ill,
A moaning wind awoke. 'Twould soon be dark.
Mike pondered. Twice Talbeau had missed the mark.
Perhaps he hadn't really meant to hit.
And surely now that flaring anger fit
Had burned away. It wasn't like the man
To hold a grudge. Mike halted, and began
To grope for words regretful of the dead,
Persuasive words about a heart that bled
For Bill. 'Twas all a terrible mistake.
"Plase now, a little dhrop fer owld toime's sake!"
With troublesome insistence, that refrain
Kept running through the muddle of his brain
And disarranged the words he meant to speak.
The trickle of a tear along his cheek
Consoled him. Soon his suffering would end.
Talbeau would see him weeping for his friend—
Talbeau had water!

          Now the heights burned red
To westward. With a choking clutch of dread
He noted how the dusk was gathering
Along the draws—a trap about to spring.
He cupped his hands about his mouth and cried:
"Talbeau! Talbeau!" Despairing voices died
Among the summits, and the lost wind pined.
It made Talbeau seem infinitely kind—
The one thing human in a ghostly land.
Where was he? Just a touch of that warm hand

Would thwart the dark! Mike sat against a wall
And brooded.

        By and by a skittering fall
Of pebbles at his back aroused the man.
He scrambled to his feet and turned to scan
The butte that sloped above him. Where the glow
Still washed the middle height, he saw Talbeau
Serenely perched upon a ledge of clay!
And Mike forgot the words he meant to say,
The fitted words, regretful of his deed.
A forthright, stark sincerity of need
Rough hewed the husky, incoherent prayer
He shouted to that Lord of water there
Above the gloom. A little drop to drink
For old time's sake!

        Talbeau regarded Fink
Awhile in silence; then his thin lips curled.
"You spilled the only drink in all the world!
Go on," he said, "and think of what you've done!"
Beyond the pointed muzzle of his gun
He saw the big man wither to a squat
And tremble, like a bison when the shot
Just nips the vital circle. Then he saw
A stooping figure hurry down the draw,
Grow dim, and vanish in the failing light.

'Twas long before Talbeau could sleep that night.
Some questioner, insistently perverse,
Assailed him and compelled him to rehearse
The justifying story of the friend
Betrayed and slain. But when he reached the end,
Still unconvinced the questioner was there
To taunt him with that pleading of despair—
For old time's sake! Sleep brought him little rest;
For what the will denied, the heart confessed
In mournful dreams. And when the first faint gray

Aroused him, and he started on his way,
He knew the stubborn questioner had won.
No brooding on the wrong that Mike had done
Could still that cry: "Plase now, fer owld toime's sake,
A little dhrop!" It made his eyeballs ache
With tears of pity that he couldn't shed.
No other dawn, save that when Bill lay dead
And things began to stare about the hall,
Had found the world so empty. After all,
What man could know the way another trod?
And who was he, Talbeau, to play at God?
Let one who curbs the wind and brews the rain
Essay the subtler portioning of pain
To souls that err! Talbeau would make amends!
Once more they'd drink together and be friends.
How often they had shared!

                He struck a trot,
Eyes fixed upon the trail. The sun rose hot;
Noon poured a blinding glare along the draws;
And still the trail led on, without a pause
To show where Mike had rested. Thirst began
To be a burden on the little man;
His progress dwindled to a dragging pace.
But when he tipped the flask, that pleading face
Arose before him, and a prayer denied
Came mourning back to thrust his need aside—
A little drop! How Mike must suffer now!
"I'm not so very thirsty, anyhow,"
He told himself. And almost any bend
Might bring him on a sudden to his friend.
He'd wait and share the water.

                Every turn
Betrayed a hope. The west began to burn;
Flared red; went ashen; and the stars came out
Dreams, colored by an unacknowledged doubt,
Perplexed the trail he followed in his sleep;

And dreary hours before the tallest steep
Saw dawn, Talbeau was waiting for the day.

Till noon he read a writing in the clay
That bade him haste; for now from wall to wall
The footmarks wandered, like the crabbéd scrawl
An old man writes. They told a gloomy tale.
And then the last dim inkling of a trail
Was lost upon a patch of hardened ground!

The red west saw him, like a nervous hound
That noses vainly for the vanished track,
Still plunging into gullies, doubling back,
And pausing now and then to hurl a yell
Among the ululating steeps. Night fell.
The starlit buttes still heard him panting by,
And summits weird with midnight caught his cry
To answer, mocking.

                    Morning brought despair;
Nor did he get much comfort of his prayer:
"God, let me find him! Show me where to go!"
Some greater, unregenerate Talbeau
Was God that morning; for the lesser heard
His own bleak answer echoed word for word:
Go on, and think of all the wrong you've done!

His futile wish to hasten sped the sun.
That day, as he recalled it in the dark,
Was like the spinning of a burning arc.
He nodded, and the night was but a swoon;
And morning neighbored strangely with the noon;
And evening was the noon's penumbral haze.

No further ran the reckoning of days.
'Twas evening when at last he stooped to stare
Upon a puzzling trail. A wounded bear,
It seemed, had dragged its rump across the sands

That floored the gullies now. But sprawling hands
Had marked the margin! Why was that? No doubt
Mike too had tarried here to puzzle out
What sort of beast had passed. And yet—how queer—
'Twas plain no human feet had trodden here!
A trail of hands! That throbbing in his brain
Confused his feeble efforts to explain;
And hazily he wondered if he slept
And dreamed again. Tenaciously he kept
His eyes upon the trail and labored on,
Lest, swooping like a hawk, another dawn
Should snatch that hope away.

                A sentry crow,
Upon a sunlit summit, saw Talbeau
And croaked alarm. The noise of many wings,
In startled flight, and raucous chatterings
Arose. What feast was interrupted there
A little way ahead? 'Twould be the bear!
He plodded on. The intervening space
Sagged under him; and, halting at the place
Where late the flock had been, he strove to break
A grip of horror. Surely now he'd wake
And see the morning quicken in the skies!

The thing remained!—It hadn't any eyes—
The pilfered sockets bore a pleading stare!

A long, hoarse wail of anguish and despair
Aroused the echoes. Answering, arose
Once more the jeering chorus of the crows.

The Song
of Hugh Glass

To *Sigurd*, scarcely three

When you are old enough to know
The joys of kite and boat and bow
And other suchlike splendid things
That boyhood's rounded decade brings,
I shall not give you tropes and rhymes;
But, rising to those rousing times,
I shall ply well the craft I know
Of shaping kite and boat and bow,
For you shall teach me once again
The goodly art of being ten.

Meanwhile, as on a rainy day
When 'tis not possible to play,
The while you do your best to grow
I ply the other craft I know
And strive to build for you the mood
Of daring and of fortitude
With fitted word and shapen phrase,
Against those later wonder-days
When first you glimpse the world of men
Beyond the bleaker side of ten.

GRAYBEARD AND GOLDHAIR

The year was eighteen hundred twenty three.

'Twas when the guns that blustered at the Ree
Had ceased to brag, and ten score martial clowns
Retreated from the unwhipped river towns,
Amid the scornful laughter of the Sioux.
A withering blast the arid South still blew,
And creeks ran thin beneath the glaring sky;
For 'twas a month ere honking geese would fly
Southward before the Great White Hunter's face:
And many generations of their race,
As bow-flung arrows, now have fallen spent.

It happened then that Major Henry went
With eighty trappers up the dwindling Grand,
Bound through the weird, unfriending barren-land
For where the Big Horn meets the Yellowstone;
And old Hugh Glass went with them.
                                   Large of bone,
Deep-chested, that his great heart might have play,
Gray-bearded, gray of eye and crowned with gray
Was Glass. It seemed he never had been young;
And, for the grudging habit of his tongue,
None knew the place or season of his birth.
Slowly he 'woke to anger or to mirth;
Yet none laughed louder when the rare mood fell,
And hate in him was like a still, white hell,
A thing of doom not lightly reconciled.
What memory he kept of wife or child

I

Was never told; for when his comrades sat
About the evening fire with pipe and chat,
Exchanging talk of home and gentler days,
Old Hugh stared long upon the pictured blaze,
And what he saw went upward in the smoke.

But once, as with an inner lightning stroke,
The veil was rent, and briefly men discerned
What pent-up fires of selfless passion burned
Beneath the still gray smoldering of him.
There was a rakehell lad, called Little Jim,
Jamie or Petit Jacques; for scarce began
The downy beard to mark him for a man.
Blue-eyed was he and femininely fair.
A maiden might have coveted his hair
That trapped the sunlight in its tangled skein:
So, tardily, outflowered the wild blond strain
That gutted Rome grown overfat in sloth.
A Ganymedes haunted by a Goth
Was Jamie. When the restive ghost was laid,
He seemed some fancy-ridden child who played
At manliness 'mid all those bearded men.
The sternest heart was drawn to Jamie then.
But his one mood ne'er linked two hours
          together.
To schedule Jamie's way, as prairie weather,
Was to get fact by wedding doubt and whim;
For very lightly slept that ghost in him.
No cloudy brooding went before his wrath
That, like a thunder-squall, recked not its path,
But raged upon what happened in its way.
Some called him brave who saw him on that day
When Ashley stormed a bluff town of the Ree,
And all save beardless Jamie turned to flee
For shelter from that steep, lead-harrowed
          slope.
Yet, hardly courage, but blind rage agrope
Inspired the foolish deed.

'Twas then old Hugh
Tore off the gray mask, and the heart shone through.
For, halting in a dry, flood-guttered draw,
The trappers rallied, looked aloft and saw
That travesty of war against the sky.
Out of a breathless hush, the old man's cry
Leaped shivering, an anguished cry and wild
As of some mother fearing for her child,
And up the steep he went with mighty bounds.
Long afterward the story went the rounds,
How old Glass fought that day. With gun for club,
Grim as a grizzly fighting for a cub,
He laid about him, cleared the way, and so,
Supported by the firing from below,
Brought Jamie back. And when the deed was done,
Taking the lad upon his knee: "My Son,
Brave men are not ashamed to fear," said Hugh,
"And I've a mind to make a man of you;
So here's your first acquaintance with the law!"
Whereat he spanked the lad with vigorous paw
And, having done so, limped away to bed;
For, wounded in the hip, the old man bled.

It was a month before he hobbled out,
And Jamie, like a fond son, hung about
The old man's tent and waited upon him.
And often would the deep gray eyes grow dim
With gazing on the boy; and there would go—
As though Spring-fire should waken out of snow—
A wistful light across that mask of gray.
And once Hugh smiled his enigmatic way,
While poring long on Jamie's face, and said:
"So with their sons are women brought to bed,
Sore wounded!"
                    Thus united were the two:
And some would dub the old man 'Mother Hugh';
While those in whom all living waters sank
To some dull inner pool that teemed and stank

With formless evil, into that morass
Gazed, and saw darkly there, as in a glass,
The foul shape of some weakly envied sin.
For each man builds a world and dwells therein.
Nor could these know what mocking ghost of Spring
Stirred Hugh's gray world with dreams of blossoming
That wooed no seed to swell or bird to sing.
So might a dawn-struck digit of the moon
Dream back the rain of some old lunar June
And ache through all its craters to be green.
Little they know what life's one love can mean,
Who shrine it in a bower of peace and bliss:
Pang dwelling in a puckered cicatrice
More truly figures this belated love.
Yet very precious was the hurt thereof,
Grievous to bear, too dear to cast away.
Now Jamie went with Hugh; but who shall say
If 'twas a warm heart or a wind of whim,
Love, or the rover's teasing itch in him,
Moved Jamie? Howsoe'er, 'twas good to see
Graybeard and Goldhair riding knee to knee,
One age in young adventure. One who saw
Has likened to a February thaw
Hugh's mellow mood those days; and truly so,
For when the tempering Southwest wakes to blow
A phantom April over melting snow,
Deep in the North some new white wrath is brewed.
Out of a dim-trailed inner solitude
The old man summoned many a stirring story,
Lived grimly once, but now shot through with glory
Caught from the wondering eyes of him who heard—
Tales jaggéd with the bleak unstudied word,
Stark saga-stuff. "A fellow that I knew,"
So nameless went the hero that was Hugh—
A mere pelt merchant, as it seemed to him;
Yet trailing epic thunders through the dim,
Whist world of Jamie's awe.
                              And so they went,
One heart, it seemed, and that heart well content

With tale and snatch of song and careless laughter.
Never before, and surely never after,
The gray old man seemed nearer to his youth—
That myth that somehow had to be the truth,
Yet could not be convincing any more.

Now when the days of travel numbered four
And nearer drew the barrens with their need,
On Glass, the hunter, fell the task to feed
Those four score hungers when the game should fail.
For no young eye could trace so dim a trail,
Or line the rifle sights with speed so true.
Nor might the wistful Jamie go with Hugh;
"For," so Hugh chaffed, "my trick of getting game
Might teach young eyes to put old eyes to shame.
An old dog never risks his only bone."
'Wolves prey in packs, the lion hunts alone'
Is somewhat nearer what he should have meant.

And so with merry jest the old man went;
And so they parted at an unseen gate
That even then some gust of moody fate
Clanged to betwixt them; each a tale to spell—
One in the nightmare scrawl of dreams from hell,
One in the blistering trail of days a-crawl,
Venomous footed. Nor might it ere befall
These two should meet in after days and be
Graybeard and Goldhair riding knee to knee,
Recounting with a bluff, heroic scorn
The haps of either tale.
                              'Twas early morn
When Hugh went forth, and all day Jamie rode
With Henry's men, while more and more the goad
Of eager youth sore fretted him, and made
The dusty progress of the cavalcade
The journey of a snail flock to the moon;
Until the shadow-weaving afternoon
Turned many fingers nightward—then he fled,
Pricking his horse, nor deigned to turn his head

At any dwindling voice of reprimand;
For somewhere in the breaks along the Grand
Surely Hugh waited with a goodly kill.
Hoofbeats of ghostly steeds on every hill,
Mysterious, muffled hoofs on every bluff!
Spurred echo horses clattering up the rough
Confluent draws! These flying Jamie heard.
The lagging air droned like the drowsy word
Of one who tells weird stories late at night.
Half headlong joy and half delicious fright,
His day-dream's pace outstripped the plunging steed's.
Lean galloper in a wind of splendid deeds,
Like Hugh's, he seemed unto himself, until,
Snorting, a-haunch above a breakneck hill,
The horse stopped short—then Jamie was aware
Of lonesome flatlands fading skyward there
Beneath him, and, zigzag on either hand,
A purple haze denoted how the Grand
Forked wide 'twixt sunset and the polar star.

A-tiptoe in the stirrups, gazing far,
He saw no Hugh nor any moving thing,
Save for a welter of cawing crows, a-wing
About some banquet in the further hush.
One faint star, set above the fading blush
Of sunset, saw the coming night, and grew.
With hand for trumpet, Jamie gave halloo;
And once again. For answer, the horse neighed.
Some vague mistrust now made him half afraid—
Some formless dread that stirred beneath the will
As far as sleep from waking.
                              Down the hill,
Close-footed in the skitter of the shale,
The spurred horse floundered to the solid vale
And galloped to the northwest, whinnying.
The outstripped air moaned like a wounded thing,
But Jamie gave the lie unto his dread.
"The old man's camping out to-night," he said,

"Somewhere about the forks, as like as not;
  And there'll be hunks of fresh meat steaming hot,
  And fighting stories by a dying fire!"

The sunset reared a luminous phantom spire
That, crumbling, sifted ashes down the sky.

Now, pausing, Jamie sent a searching cry
Into the twilit river-skirting brush,
And in the vast denial of the hush
The champing of the snaffled horse seemed loud.

Then, startling as a voice beneath a shroud,
A muffled boom woke somewhere up the stream
And, like vague thunder hearkened in a dream,
Drawled back to silence. Now, with heart abound,
Keen for the quarter of the perished sound,
The lad spurred gaily; for he doubted not
His cry had brought Hugh's answering rifle shot.
The laggard air was like a voice that sang,
And Jamie half believed he sniffed the tang
Of woodsmoke and the smell of flesh a-roast;
When presently before him, like a ghost,
Upstanding, huge in twilight, arms flung wide,
A gray form loomed. The wise horse reared and shied,
Snorting his inborn terror of the bear!
And in the whirlwind of a moment there,
Betwixt the brute's hoarse challenge and the charge,
The lad beheld, upon the grassy marge
Of a small spring that bullberries stooped to scan,
A ragged heap that should have been a man,
A huddled, broken thing—and it was Hugh!

There was no need for any closer view.
As, on the instant of a lightning flash
Ere yet the split gloom closes with a crash,
A landscape stares with every circumstance
Of rock and shrub—just so the fatal chance

Of Hugh's one shot, made futile with surprise,
Was clear to Jamie. Then before his eyes
The light whirled in a giddy dance of red;
And, doubting not the crumpled thing was dead
That was a friend, with but a skinning knife
He would have striven for the hated life
That triumphed there: but with a shriek of fright
The mad horse bolted through the falling night,
And Jamie, fumbling at his rifle boot,
Heard the brush crash behind him where the brute
Came headlong, close upon the straining flanks.
But when at length low-lying river banks—
White rubble in the gloaming—glimmered near,
A swift thought swept the mind of Jamie clear
Of anger and of anguish for the dead.
Scarce seemed the raging beast a thing to dread,
But some foul-playing braggart to outwit.
Now hurling all his strength upon the bit,
He sank the spurs, and with a groan of pain
The plunging horse, obedient to the rein,
Swerved sharply streamward. Sliddering in the sand,
The bear shot past. And suddenly the Grand
Loomed up beneath and rose to meet the pair
That rode a moment upon empty air,
Then smote the water in a shower of spray.
And when again the slowly ebbing day
Came back to them, a-drip from nose to flank,
The steed was scrambling up the further bank,
And Jamie saw across the narrow stream,
Like some vague shape of fury in a dream,
The checked beast ramping at the water's rim.
Doubt struggled with a victor's thrill in him,
As, hand to buckle of the rifle-sheath,
He thought of dampened powder; but beneath
The rawhide flap the gun lay snug and dry.
Then as the horse wheeled and the mark went by—
A patch of shadow dancing upon gray—
He fired. A sluggish thunder trailed away;

The spreading smoke-rack lifted slow, and there,
Floundering in a seethe of foam, the bear
Hugged yielding water for the foe that slew!

Triumphant, Jamie wondered what old Hugh
Would think of such a "trick of getting game"!
"Young eyes" indeed!—And then that memory came,
Like a dull blade thrust back into a wound.
One moment 'twas as though the lad had swooned
Into a dream-adventure, waking there
To sicken at the ghastly land, a-stare
Like some familiar face gone strange at last.
But as the hot tears came, the moment passed.
Song snatches, broken tales—a troop forlorn,
Like merry friends of eld come back to mourn—
O'erwhelmed him there. And when the black bulk
        churned
The star-flecked stream no longer, Jamie turned,
Recrossed the river and rode back to Hugh.

A burning twist of valley grasses threw
Blear light about the region of the spring.
Then Jamie, torch aloft and shuddering,
Knelt there beside his friend, and moaned: "O Hugh,
If I had been with you—just been with you!
We might be laughing now—and you are dead."
With gentle hand he turned the hoary head
That he might see the good gray face again.
The torch burned out, the dark swooped back, and then
His grief was frozen with an icy plunge
In horror. 'Twas as though a bloody sponge
Had wiped the pictured features from a slate!
So, pillaged by an army drunk with hate,
Home stares upon the homing refugee.
A red gout clung where either brow should be;
The haughty nose lay crushed amid the beard,
Thick with slow ooze, whence like a devil leered
The battered mouth convulsed into a grin.

Nor did the darkness cover, for therein
Some torch, unsnuffed, with blear funereal flare,
Still painted upon black that alien stare
To make the lad more terribly alone.

Then in the gloom there rose a broken moan,
Quick stifled; and it seemed that something stirred
About the body. Doubting that he heard,
The lad felt, with a panic catch of breath,
Pale vagrants from the legendry of death
Potential in the shadows there. But when
The motion and the moaning came again,
Hope, like a shower at daybreak, cleansed the dark,
And in the lad's heart something like a lark
Sang morning. Bending low, he crooned: "Hugh,
        Hugh,
It's Jamie—don't you know?—I'm here with you."

As one who in a nightmare strives to tell—
Shouting across the gap of some dim hell—
What things assail him; so it seemed Hugh heard,
And flung some unintelligible word
Athwart the muffling distance of his swoon.

Now kindled by the yet unrisen moon,
The East went pale; and like a naked thing
A little wind ran vexed and shivering
Along the dusk, till Jamie shivered too
And worried lest 'twere bitter cold where Hugh
Hung clutching at the bleak, raw edge of life.
So Jamie rose, and with his hunting-knife
Split wood and built a fire. Nor did he fear
The staring face now, for he found it dear
With the warm presence of a friend returned.
The fire made cozy chatter as it burned,
And reared a tent of light in that lone place.
Then Jamie set about to bathe the face
With water from the spring, oft crooning low,

"It's Jamie here beside you—don't you know?"
Yet came no answer save the labored breath
Of one who wrestled mightily with Death
Where watched no referee to call the foul.

The moon now cleared the world's end, and the
     owl
Gave voice unto the wizardry of light;
While in some dim-lit chancel of the night,
Snouts to the goddess, wolfish corybants
Intoned their wild antiphonary chants—
The oldest, saddest worship in the world.

And Jamie watched until the firelight swirled
Softly about him. Sound and glimmer merged
To make an eerie void, through which he urged
With frantic spur some whirlwind of a steed
That made the way as glass beneath his speed,
Yet scarce kept pace with something dear that fled
On, ever on—just half a dream ahead:
Until it seemed, by some vague shape dismayed,
He cried aloud for Hugh, and the steed neighed—
A neigh that was a burst of light, not sound.
And Jamie, sprawling on the dewy ground,
Knew that his horse was sniffing at his hair,
While, mumbling through the early morning air,
There came a roll of many hoofs—and then
He saw the swinging troop of Henry's men
A-canter up the valley with the sun.

Of all Hugh's comrades crowding round, not one
But would have given heavy odds on Death;
For, though the graybeard fought with sobbing
     breath,
No man, it seemed, might break upon the hip
So stern a wrestler with the strangling grip
That made the neck veins like a purple thong
Tangled with knots. Nor might Hugh tarry long

There where the trail forked outward far and dim;
Or so it seemed. And when they lifted him,
His moan went treble like a song of pain,
He was so tortured. Surely it were vain
To hope he might endure the toilsome ride
Across the barrens. Better let him bide
There on the grassy couch beside the spring.
And, furthermore, it seemed a foolish thing
That eighty men should wait the issue there;
For dying is a game of solitaire
And all men play the losing hand alone.

But when at noon he had not ceased to moan,
And fought still like the strong man he had been,
There grew a vague mistrust that he might win,
And all this be a tale for wondering ears.
So Major Henry called for volunteers,
Two men among the eighty who would stay
To wait on Glass and keep the wolves away
Until he did whatever he should do.
All quite agreed 'twas bitter bread for Hugh,
Yet none, save Jamie, felt in duty bound
To run the risk—until the hat went round,
And pity wakened, at the silver's clink,
In Jules Le Bon.

     'He would not have them think
That mercenary motives prompted him.
But somehow just the grief of Little Jim
Was quite sufficient—not to mention Hugh.
He weighed the risk. As everybody knew,
The Rickarees were scattered to the West:
The late campaign had stirred a hornet's nest
To fill the land with stingers (which was so),
And yet—'
    Three days a southwest wind may blow
False April with no drop of dew at heart.
So Jules ran on, while, ready for the start,

The pawing horses nickered and the men,
Impatient in their saddles, yawned. And then,
With brief advice, a round of bluff good-byes
And some few reassuring backward cries,
The troop rode up the valley with the day.

Intent upon his friend, with naught to say,
Sat Jamie; while Le Bon discussed at length
The reasonable limits of man's strength—
A self-conducted dialectic strife
That made absurd all argument for life
And granted but a fresh-dug hole for Hugh.
'Twas half like murder. Yet it seemed Jules knew
Unnumbered tales accordant with the case,
Each circumstantial as to time and place
And furnished with a death's head colophon.

Vivaciously despondent, Jules ran on.
'Did he not share his judgment with the rest?
You see, 'twas some contusion of the chest
That did the trick—heart, lungs and all that, mixed
In such a way they never could be fixed.
A bear's hug—ugh!'
                           And often Jamie winced
At some knife-thrust of reason that convinced
Yet left him sick with unrelinquished hope.
As one who in a darkened room might grope
For some belovéd face, with shuddering
Anticipation of a clammy thing;
So in the lad's heart sorrow fumbled round
For some old joy to lean upon, and found
The stark, cold something Jamie knew was there.
Yet, womanlike, he stroked the hoary hair
Or bathed the face; while Jules found tales to tell—
Lugubriously garrulous.
                              Night fell.
At sundown, day-long winds are like to veer;
So, summoning a mood of relished fear,

Le Bon remembered dire alarms by night—
The swoop of savage hordes, the desperate fight
Of men outnumbered: and, like him of old,
In all that made Jules shudder as he told,
His the great part—a man by field and flood
Fate-tossed. Upon the gloom he limned in blood
Their situation's possibilities:
Two men against the fury of the Rees—
A game in which two hundred men had failed!
He pointed out how little it availed
To run the risk for one as good as dead;
Yet, Jules Le Bon meant every word he said,
And had a scalp to lose, if need should be.

That night through Jamie's dreaming swarmed the
    Ree.
Gray-souled, he wakened to a dawn of gray,
And felt that something strong had gone away,
Nor knew what thing. Some whisper of the will
Bade him rejoice that Hugh was living still;
But Hugh, the real, seemed somehow otherwhere.
Jules, snug and snoring in his blanket there,
Was half a life the nearer. Just so, pain
Is nearer than the peace we seek in vain,
And by its very sting compells belief.
Jules woke, and with a fine restraint of grief
Saw early dissolution. 'One more night,
And then the poor old man would lose the fight—
Ah, such a man!'
           A day and night crept by,
And yet the stubborn fighter would not die,
But grappled with the angel. All the while,
With some conviction, but with more of guile,
Jules colonized the vacancy with Rees;
Till Jamie felt that looseness of the knees
That comes of oozing courage. Many men
May tower for a white-hot moment, when
The wild blood surges at a sudden shock;

But when, insistent as a ticking clock,
Blind peril haunts and whispers, fewer dare.
Dread hovered in the hushed and moony air
The long night through; nor might a fire be lit,
Lest some far-seeing foe take note of it.
And day-long Jamie scanned the blank sky rim
For hoof-flung dust clouds; till there woke in him
A childish anger—dumb for ruth and shame—
That Hugh so dallied.
                            But the fourth dawn came
And with it lulled the fight, as on a field
Where broken armies sleep but will not yield.
Or had one conquered ? Was it Hugh or Death?
The old man breathed with faintly fluttering breath,
Nor did his body shudder as before.
Jules triumphed sadly. 'It would soon be o'er;
So men grew quiet when they lost their grip
And did not care. At sundown he would slip
Into the deeper silence.'
                            Jamie wept,
Unwitting how a furtive gladness crept
Into his heart that gained a stronger beat.
So cities, long beleaguered, take defeat—
Unto themselves half traitors.
                            Jules began
To dig a hole that might conceal a man;
And, as his sheath knife broke the stubborn sod,
He spoke in kindly vein of Life and God
And Mutability and Rectitude.
The immemorial funerary mood
Brought tears, mute tribute to the mother-dust;
And Jamie, seeing, felt each cutting thrust
Less like a stab into the flesh of Hugh.
The sun crept up and down the arc of blue
And through the air a chill of evening ran;
But, though the grave yawned, waiting for the man,
The man seemed scarce yet ready for the grave.

Now prompted by a coward or a knave
That lurked in him, Le Bon began to hear
Faint sounds that to the lad's less cunning ear
Were silence; more like tremors of the ground
They were, Jules said, than any proper sound—
Thus one detected horsemen miles away.
For many moments big with fate, he lay,
Ear pressed to earth; then rose and shook his head
As one perplexed. "There's something wrong," he said.
And—as at daybreak whiten winter skies,
Agape and staring with a wild surmise—
The lad's face whitened at the other's word.
Jules could not quite interpret what he heard;
A hundred horse might noise their whereabouts
In just that fashion; yet he had his doubts.
It could be bison moving, quite as well.
But if 'twere Rees—there'd be a tale to tell
That two men he might name should never hear.
He reckoned scalps that Fall were selling dear,
In keeping with the limited supply.
Men, fit to live, were not afraid to die!

Then, in that caution suits not courage ill,
Jules saddled up and cantered to the hill,
A white dam set against the twilight stream;
And as a horseman riding in a dream
The lad beheld him; watched him clamber up
To where the dusk, as from a brimming cup,
Ran over; saw him pause against the gloom,
Portentous, huge—a brooder upon doom.
What did he look upon?
                                Some moments passed;
Then suddenly it seemed as though a blast
Of wind, keen-cutting with the whips of sleet,
Smote horse and rider. Haunched on huddled feet,
The steed shrank from the ridge, then, rearing,
        wheeled
And took the rubbly incline fury-heeled.

Those days and nights, like seasons creeping slow,
Had told on Jamie. Better blow on blow
Of evil hap, with doom seen clear ahead,
Than that monotonous, abrasive dread,
Blind gnawer at the soul-thews of the blind.
Thin-worn, the last heart-string that held him kind;
Strung taut, the final tie that kept him true
Now snapped in Jamie, as he saw the two
So goaded by some terrifying sight.
Death riding with the vanguard of the Night,
Life dwindling yonder with the rear of Day!
What choice for one whom panic swept away
From moorings in the sanity of will?

Jules came and summed the vision of the hill
In one hoarse cry that left no word to say:
"Rees! Saddle up! We've got to get away!"

Small wit had Jamie left to ferret guile,
But fumblingly obeyed Le Bon; the while
Jules knelt beside the man who could not flee:
For big hearts lack not time for charity
However thick the blows of fate may fall.
Yet, in that Jules Le Bon was practical,
He could not quite ignore a hunting knife,
A flint, a gun, a blanket—gear of life
Scarce suited to the customs of the dead!

And Hugh slept soundly in his ample bed,
Star-canopied and blanketed with night,
Unwitting how Venality and Fright
Made hot the westward trail of Henry's men.

THE AWAKENING

II

No one may say what time elapsed, or when
The slumberous shadow lifted over Hugh:
But some globose immensity of blue
Enfolded him at last, within whose light
He seemed to float, as some faint swimmer might,
A deep beneath and overhead a deep.
So one late plunged into the lethal sleep,
A spirit diver fighting for his breath,
Swoops through the many-fathomed glooms of death,
Emerging in a daylight strange and new.

Rousing a languid wonder, came on Hugh
The quiet, steep-arched splendor of the day.
Agrope for some dim memory, he lay
Upon his back, and watched a lucent fleece
Fade in the blue profundity of peace
As did the memory he sought in vain.
Then with a stirring of mysterious pain,
Old habit of the body bade him rise;
But when he would obey, the hollow skies
Broke as a bubble punctured, and went out.

Again he woke, and with a drowsy doubt,
Remote unto his horizontal gaze
He saw the world's end kindle to a blaze
And up the smoky steep pale heralds run.
And when at length he knew it for the sun,
Dawn found the darkling reaches of his mind,
Where in the twilight he began to find

Strewn shards and torsos of familiar things.
As from the rubble in a place of kings
Men school the dream to build the past anew,
So out of dream and fragment builded Hugh,
And came upon the reason of his plight:
The bear's attack—the shot—and then the night
Wherein men talked as ghosts above a grave.

Some consciousness of will the memory gave:
He would get up. The painful effort spent
Made the wide heavens billow as a tent
Wind-struck, the shaken prairie sag and roll.
Some moments with an effort at control
He swayed, half raised upon his arms, until
The dizzy cosmos righted, and was still.
Then would he stand erect and be again
The man he was: an overwhelming pain
Smote him to earth, and one unruly limb
Refused the weight and crumpled under him.

Sickened with torture he lay huddled there,
Gazing about him with a great despair
Proportioned to the might that felt the chain.
Far-flung as dawn, collusive sky and plain
Stared bleak denial back.

                 Why strive at all?—
That vacancy about him like a wall,
Yielding as light, a granite scarp to climb!
Some little waiting on the creep of time,
Abandonment to circumstance; and then—

Here flashed a sudden thought of Henry's men
Into his mind and drove the gloom away.
They would be riding westward with the day!
How strange he had forgot! That battered leg
Or some scalp wound, had set his wits a-beg!
Was this Hugh Glass to whimper like a squaw?
Grimly amused, he raised his head and saw—

The empty distance: listened long and heard—
Naught but the twitter of a lonely bird
That emphasized the hush.

                              Was something wrong?
'Twas not the Major's way to dally long,
And surely they had camped not far behind.
Now woke a query in his troubled mind—
Where was his horse? Again came creeping back
The circumstances of the bear's attack.
He had dismounted, thinking at the spring
To spend the night—and then the grisly thing—
Of course the horse had bolted; plain enough!
But why was all the soil about so rough
As though a herd of horses had been there?
The riddle vexed him till his vacant stare
Fell on a heap of earth beside a pit.
What did that mean? He wormed his way to it,
The newly wakened wonder dulling pain.
No paw of beast had scooped it—that was plain.
'Twas squared; indeed, 'twas like a grave, he thought.
A grave—a grave—the mental echo wrought
Sick fancies! Who had risen from the dead?
Who, lying there, had heard above his head
The ghostly talkers deaf unto his shout?

Now searching all the region round about,
As though the answer were a lurking thing,
He saw along the margin of the spring
An ash-heap and the litter of a camp.
Suspicion, like a little smoky lamp
That daubs the murk but cannot fathom it,
Flung blear grotesques before his groping wit.
Had Rees been there? And he alive? Who then?
And were he dead, it might be Henry's men!
How many suns had risen while he slept?
The smoky glow flared wildly, and he crept,
The dragged limb throbbing, till at length he found
The trail of many horses westward bound;

And in one breath the groping light became
A gloom-devouring ecstasy of flame,
A dazing conflagration of belief!

Plunged deeper than the seats of hate and grief,
He gazed about for aught that might deny
Such baseness: saw the non-committal sky,
The prairie apathetic in a shroud,
The bland complacence of a vagrant cloud—
World-wide connivance! Smilingly the sun
Approved a land wherein such deeds were done;
And careless breezes, like a troop of youth,
Unawed before the presence of such truth,
Went scampering amid the tousled brush.
Then bye and bye came on him with a rush
His weakness and the consciousness of pain,
While, with the chill insistence of a rain
That pelts the sodden wreck of Summer's end,
His manifest betrayal by a friend
Beat in upon him. Jamie had been there;
And Jamie—Jamie—Jamie did not care!

What no man yet had witnessed, the wide sky
Looked down and saw; a light wind idling by
Heard what no ear of mortal yet had heard:
For he—whose name was like a magic word
To conjure the remote heroic mood
Of valiant deed and splendid fortitude,
Wherever two that shared a fire might be,—
Gave way to grief and wept unmanfully.
Yet not as they for whom tears fall like dew
To green a frosted heart again, wept Hugh.
So thewed to strive, so engined to prevail
And make harsh fate the zany of a tale,
His own might shook and tore him.
                                           For a span
He lay, a gray old ruin of a man
With all his years upon him like a snow.

And then at length, as from the long ago,
Remote beyond the other side of wrong,
The old love came like some remembered song
Whereof the strain is sweet, the burden sad.
A retrospective vision of the lad
Grew up in him, as in a foggy night
The witchery of semilunar light
Mysteriously quickens all the air.
Some memory of wind-blown golden hair,
The boyish laugh, the merry eyes of blue,
Wrought marvelously in the heart of Hugh,
As under snow the dæmon of the Spring.
And momently it seemed a little thing
To suffer; nor might treachery recall
The miracle of being loved at all,
The privilege of loving to the end.
And thereupon a longing for his friend
Made life once more a struggle for a prize—
To look again upon the merry eyes,
To see again the wind-blown golden hair.
Aye, one should lavish very tender care
Upon the vessel of a hope so great,
Lest it be shattered, and the precious freight,
As water on the arid waste, poured out.
Yet, though he longed to live, a subtle doubt
Still turned on him the weapon of his pain:
Now, as before, collusive sky and plain
Outstared his purpose for a puny thing.

Praying to live, he crawled back to the spring,
With something in his heart like gratitude
That by good luck his gun might furnish food,
His blanket, shelter, and his flint, a fire.
For, after all, what thing do men desire
To be or have, but these condition it?
These with a purpose and a little wit,
And howsoever smitten, one might rise,
Push back the curtain of the curving skies,
And come upon the living dream at last.

Exhausted, by the spring he lay and cast
Dull eyes about him. What did it portend?
Naught but the footprints of a fickle friend,
A yawning grave and ashes met his eyes!
Scarce feeling yet the shock of a surprise,
He searched about him for his flint and knife;
Knew vaguely that his seeking was for life,
And that the place was empty where he
      sought.
No food, no fire, no shelter! Dully wrought
The bleak negation in him, slowly crept
To where, despite the pain, his love had kept
A shrine for Jamie undefiled of doubt.
Then suddenly conviction, like a shout,
Aroused him. Jamie—Jamie was a thief!
The very difficulty of belief
Was fuel for the simmering of rage,
That grew and grew, the more he strove to gage
The underlying motive of the deed.
Untempered youth might fail a friend in need;
But here had wrought some devil of the will,
Some heartless thing, too cowardly to kill,
That left to Nature what it dared not do!

So bellowsed, all the kindled soul of Hugh
Became a still white hell of brooding ire,
And through his veins regenerating fire
Ran, driving out the lethargy of pain.
Now once again he scanned the yellow plain,
Conspirant with the overbending skies;
And lo, the one was blue as Jamie's eyes,
The other of the color of his hair—
Twin hues of falseness merging to a stare,
As though such guilt, thus visibly immense,
Regarded its effect with insolence!

Alas for those who fondly place above
The act of loving, what they chance to love;
Who prize the goal more dearly than the way!

For time shall plunder them, and change betray,
And life shall find them vulnerable still.

A bitter-sweet narcotic to the will,
Hugh's love increased the peril of his plight;
But anger broke the slumber of his might,
Quickened the heart and warmed the blood that ran
Defiance for the treachery of Man,
Defiance for the meaning of his pain,
Defiance for the distance of the plain
That seemed to gloat, 'You can not master me.'
And for one burning moment he felt free
To rise and conquer in a wind of rage.
But as a tiger, conscious of the cage,
A-smoulder with a purpose, broods and waits,
So with the sullen patience that is hate's
Hugh taught his wrath to bide expedience.

Now cognizant of every quickened sense,
Thirst came upon him. Leaning to the spring,
He stared with fascination on a thing
That rose from giddy deeps to share the draught—
A face, it was, so tortured that it laughed,
A ghastly mask that Murder well might wear;
And while as one they drank together there,
It was as though the deed he meant to do
Took shape and came to kiss the lips of Hugh,
Lest that revenge might falter. Hunger woke;
And from the bush with leafage gray as smoke,
Wherein like flame the bullberries glinted red
(Scarce sweeter than the heart of him they fed),
Hugh feasted.
   And the hours of waiting crept,
A-gloom, a-glow; and though he waked or slept,
The pondered purpose or a dream that wrought,
By night, the murder of his waking thought,
Sustained him till he felt his strength returned.
And then at length the longed-for morning burned

And beckoned down the vast way he should crawl—
That waste to be surmounted as a wall,
Sky-rims and yet more sky-rims steep to climb—
That simulacrum of enduring Time—
The hundred empty miles 'twixt him and where
The stark Missouri ran!

                    Yet why not dare?
Despite the useless leg, he could not die
One hairsbreadth farther from the earth and sky,
Or more remote from kindness.

THE CRAWL

Straight away

III

Beneath the flare of dawn, the Ree land lay,
And through it ran the short trail to the goal.
Thereon a grim turnpikeman waited toll:
But 'twas so doomed that southering geese should flee
Nine times, ere yet the vengeance of the Ree
Should make their foe the haunter of a tale.

Midway to safety on the northern trail
The scoriac region of a hell burned black
Forbade the crawler. And for all his lack,
Hugh had no heart to journey with the suns:
No suppliant unto those faithless ones
Should bid for pity at the Big Horn's mouth.

The greater odds for safety in the South
Allured him; so he felt the midday sun
Blaze down the coulee of a little run
That dwindled upward to the watershed
Whereon the feeders of the Moreau head—
Scarce more than deep-carved runes of vernal rain.
The trailing leg was like a galling chain,
And bound him to a doubt that would not pass.
Defiant clumps of thirst-embittered grass
That bit parched earth with bared and fang-like roots;
Dwarf thickets, jealous for their stunted fruits,
Harsh-tempered by their disinheritance—
These symbolized the enmity of Chance
For him who, with his fate unreconciled,

Equipped for travel as a weanling child,
Essayed the journey of a mighty man.

Like agitated oil the heat-waves ran
And made the scabrous gulch appear to shake
As some reflected landscape in a lake
Where laggard breezes move. A taunting reek
Rose from the grudging seepage of the creek,
Whereof Hugh drank and drank, and still would drink.
And where the mottled shadow dripped as ink
From scanty thickets on the yellow glare,
The crawler faltered with no heart to dare
Again the torture of that toil, until
The master-thought of vengeance 'woke the will
To goad him forth. And when the sun quiesced
Amid ironic heavens in the West—
The region of false friends—Hugh gained a rise
Whence to the fading cincture of the skies
A purpling panorama swept away.
Scarce farther than a shout might carry, lay
The place of his betrayal. He could see
The yellow blotch of earth where treachery
Had digged his grave. O futile wrath and toil!
Tucked in beneath yon coverlet of soil,
Turned back for him, how soundly had he slept!
Fool, fool! to struggle when he might have crept
So short a space, yet farther than the flight
Of swiftest dreaming through the longest night,
Into the quiet house of no false friend.

Alas for those who seek a journey's end—
They have it ever with them like a ghost:
Nor shall they find, who deem they seek it most,
But crave the end of human ends—as Hugh.

Now swoopingly the world of dream broke through
The figured wall of sense. It seemed he ran
As wind above the creeping ways of man,

And came upon the place of his desire,
Where burned, far-luring as a beacon-fire,
The face of Jamie. But the vengeful stroke
Bit air. The darkness lifted like a smoke—
And it was early morning.
                  Gazing far,
From where the West yet kept a pallid star
To thinner sky where dawn was wearing through,
Hugh shrank with dread, reluctant to renew
The war with that serene antagonist.
More fearsome than a smashing iron fist
Seemed that vast negativity of might;
Until the frustrate vision of the night
Came moonwise on the gloom of his despair.
And lo, the foe was naught but yielding air,
A vacancy to fill with his intent!
So from his spacious bed he 'rose and went
Three-footed; and the vision goaded him.

All morning southward to the bare sky rim
The rugged coulee zigzagged, mounting slow;
And ever as it 'rose, the lean creek's flow
Dwindled and dwindled steadily, until
At last a scooped-out basin would not fill;
And thenceforth 'twas a way of mocking dust.
But, in that Hugh still kept the driving lust
For vengeance, this new circumstance of fate
Served but to brew more venom for his hate,
And nerved him to avail the most with least.
Ere noon the crawler chanced upon a feast
Of bread-root sunning in a favored draw.
A sentry gopher from his stronghold saw
Some three-legged beast, bear-like, yet not a bear,
With quite misguided fury digging where
No hapless brother gopher might be found.
And while, with striped nose above his mound,
The sentinel chirped shrilly to his clan
Scare-tales of that anomaly, the man

Devoured the chance-flung manna of the plains
That some vague reminiscence of old rains
Kept succulent, despite the burning drouth.

So with new vigor Hugh assailed the South,
His pockets laden with the precious roots
Against that coming traverse, where no fruits
Of herb or vine or shrub might brave the land
Spread rooflike 'twixt the Moreau and the Grand.

The coulee deepened; yellow walls flung high,
Sheer to the ragged strip of blinding sky,
Dazzled and sweltered in the glare of day.
Capricious draughts that woke and died away
Into the heavy drowse, were breatht as flame.
And midway down the afternoon, Hugh came
Upon a little patch of spongy ground.
His thirst became a rage. He gazed around,
Seeking a spring; but all about was dry
As strewn bones bleaching to a desert sky;
Nor did a clawed hole, bought with needed strength,
Return a grateful ooze. And when at length
Hugh sucked the mud, he spat it in disgust.
It had the acrid tang of broken trust,
The sweetish, tepid taste of feigning love!

Still hopeful of a spring somewhere above,
He crawled the faster for his taunted thirst.
More damp spots, no less grudging than the first,
Occurred with growing frequence on the way,
Until amid the purple wane of day
The crawler came upon a little pool!
Clear as a friend's heart, 'twas, and seeming cool—
A crystal bowl whence skyey deeps looked up.
So might a god set down his drinking cup
Charged with a distillation of haut skies.
As famished horses, thrusting to the eyes
Parched muzzles, take a long-sought water-hole,

Hugh plunged his head into the brimming bowl
As though to share the joy with every sense.
And lo, the tang of that wide insolence
Of sky and plain was acrid in the draught!
How ripplingly the lying water laughed!
How like fine sentiment the mirrored sky
Won credence for a sink of alkali!
So with false friends. And yet, as may accrue
From specious love some profit of the true,
One gift of kindness had the tainted sink.
Stripped of his clothes, Hugh let his body drink
At every thirsting pore. Through trunk and limb
The elemental blessing solaced him;
Nor did he rise till, vague with stellar light,
The lone gulch, buttressing an arch of night,
Was like a temple to the Holy Ghost.
As priests in slow procession with the Host,
A gusty breeze intoned—now low, now loud,
And now, as to the murmur of a crowd,
Yielding the dim-torched wonder of the nave.
Aloft along the dusky architrave
The wander-tale of drifting stars evolved;
And Hugh lay gazing till the whole resolved
Into a haze.
                    It seemed that Little Jim
Had come to share a merry fire with him,
And there had been no trouble 'twixt the two.
And Jamie listened eagerly while Hugh
Essayed a tangled tale of bears and men,
Bread-root and stars. But ever now and then
The shifting smoke-cloud dimmed the golden hair,
The leal blue eyes; until with sudden flare
The flame effaced them utterly—and lo,
The gulch bank-full with morning!
                                        Loath to go,
Hugh lay beside the pool and pondered fate.
He saw his age-long pilgrimage of hate
Stretch out—a fool's trail; and it made him cringe;

For still amid the nightly vision's fringe
His dull wit strayed, companioned with regret.
But when the sun, a tilted cauldron set
Upon the gulch rim, poured a blaze of day,
He rose and bathed again, and went his way,
Sustaining wrath returning with the toil.

At noon the gulch walls, hewn in lighter soil,
Fell back; and coulees dense with shrub and vine
Climbed zigzag to the sharp horizon line,
Whence one might choose the pilotage of crows.
He labored upward through the noonday doze.
Of breathless shade, where plums were turning red
In tangled bowers, and grapevines overhead
Purpled with fruit to taunt the crawler's thirst.
With little effort Hugh attained the first;
The latter bargained sharply ere they sold
Their luscious clusters for the hoarded gold
Of strength that had so very much to buy.
Now, having feasted, it was sweet to lie
Beneath a sun-proof canopy; and sleep
Came swiftly.

       Hugh awakened to some deep
Star-snuffing well of night. Awhile he lay
And wondered what had happened to the day
And where he was and what were best to do.
But when, fog-like, the drowse dispersed, he knew
How from the rim above the plain stretched far
To where the evening and the morning are,
And that 'twere better he should crawl by night,
Sleep out the glare. With groping hands for sight,
Skyward along the broken steep he crawled,
And saw at length, immense and purple-walled—
Or sensed—the dusky mystery of plain.
Gazing aloft, he found the capsized Wain
In mid-plunge down the polar steep. Thereto
He set his back; and far ahead there grew,
As some pale blossom from a darkling root,

The star-blanched summit of a lonely butte,
And thitherward he dragged his heavy limb.

It seemed naught moved. Time hovered over him,
An instant of incipient endeavor.
'Twas ever thus, and should be thus forever—
This groping for the same armful of space,
An insubstantial essence of one place,
Extentless on a weird frontier of sleep.
Sheer deep upon unfathomable deep
The flood of dusk bore down without a sound,
As ocean on the spirits of the drowned
Awakened headlong leagues beneath the light.

So lapsed the drowsy æon of the night—
A strangely tensile moment in a trance.
And then, as quickened to somnambulance,
The heavens, imperceptibly in motion,
Were altered as the upward deeps of ocean
Diluted with a seepage of the moon.
The butte-top, late a gossamer balloon
In mid-air tethered hovering, grew down
And rooted in a blear expanse of brown,
That, lifting slowly with the ebb of night,
Took on the harsh solidity of light—
And day was on the prairie like a flame.

Scarce had he munched the hoarded roots, when came
A vertigo of slumber. Snatchy dreams
Of sick pools, inaccessible cool streams,
Lured on through giddy vacancies of heat
In swooping flights; now hills of roasting meat
Made savory the oven of the world,
Yet kept remote peripheries and whirled
About a burning center that was Hugh.
Then all were gone, save one, and it turned blue
And was a heap of cool and luscious fruit,
Until at length he knew it for the butte

Now mantled with a weaving of the gloam.
   It was the hour when cattle straggle home.
Across the clearing in a hush of sleep
They saunter, lowing; loiter belly-deep
Amid the lush grass by the meadow stream.
How like the sound of water in a dream
The intermittent tinkle of yon bell.
A windlass creaks contentment from a well,
And cool deeps gurgle as the bucket sinks.
Now blowing at the trough the plow-team drinks;
The shaken harness rattles. Sleepy quails
Call far. The warm milk hisses in the pails
There in the dusky barn-lot. Crickets cry.
The meadow twinkles with the glowing fly.
One hears the horses munching at their oats.
The green grows black. A veil of slumber floats
Across the haunts of home-enamored men.

Some freak of memory brought back again
The boyhood world of sight and scent and sound:
It perished, and the prairie ringed him round,
Blank as the face of fate. In listless mood
Hugh set his face against the solitude
And met the night. The new moon, low and far,
A frail cup tilted, nor the high-swung star,
It seemed, might glint on any stream or spring
Or touch with silver any toothsome thing.
The kiote voiced the universal lack.
As from a nether fire, the plain gave back
The swelter of the noon-glare to the gloom.
In the hot hush Hugh heard his temples boom.
Thirst tortured. Motion was a languid pain.
Why seek some further nowhere on the plain?
Here might the kiotes feast as well as there.
So spoke some loose-lipped spirit of despair;
And still Hugh moved, volitionless—a weight
Submissive to that now unconscious hate,
As darkling water to the hidden moon.

Now when the night wore on in middle swoon,
The crawler, roused from stupor, was aware
Of some strange alteration in the air.
To breathe became an act of conscious will.
The starry waste was ominously still.
The far-off kiote's yelp came sharp and clear
As through a tunnel in the atmosphere—
A ponderable, resonating mass.
The limp leg dragging on the sun-dried grass
Produced a sound unnaturally loud.

Crouched, panting, Hugh looked up but saw no cloud.
An oily film seemed spread upon the sky
Now dully staring as the open eye
Of one in fever. Gasping, choked with thirst,
A childish rage assailed Hugh, and he cursed:
'Twas like a broken spirit's outcry, tossed
Upon hell's burlesque sabbath for the lost,
And briefly space seemed crowded with the voice.

To wait and die, to move and die—what choice?
Hugh chose not, yet he crawled; though more and more
He felt the futile strife was nearly o'er.
And as he went, a muffled rumbling grew,
More felt than heard; for long it puzzled Hugh.
Somehow 'twas coextensive with his thirst,
Yet boundless; swollen blood-veins ere they burst
Might give such warning, so he thought. And still
The drone seemed heaping up a phonic hill
That towered in a listening profound.
Then suddenly a mountain peak of sound
Came toppling to a heaven-jolting fall!
The prairie shuddered, and a raucous drawl
Ran far and perished in the outer deep.

As one too roughly shaken out of sleep,
Hugh stared bewildered. Still the face of night
Remained the same, save where upon his right

The moon had vanished 'neath the prairie rim.
Then suddenly the meaning came to him.
He turned and saw athwart the northwest sky,
Like some black eyelid shutting on an eye,
A coming night to which the night was day!
Star-hungry, ranged in regular array,
The lifting mass assailed the Dragon's lair,
Submerged the region of the hounded Bear,
Out-topped the tall Ox-Driver and the Pole.
And all the while there came a low-toned roll,
Less sound in air than tremor in the earth,
From where, like flame upon a windy hearth,
Deep in the further murk sheet-lightning flared.
And still the southern arc of heaven stared,
A half-shut eye, near blind with fever rheum;
And still the plain lay tranquil as a tomb
Wherein the dead reck not a menaced world.

What turmoil now? Lo, ragged columns hurled
Pell-mell up stellar slopes! Swift blue fires leap
Above the wild assailants of the steep!
Along the solid rear a dull boom runs!
So light horse squadrons charge beneath the guns.
Now once again the night is deathly still.
What ghastly peace upon the zenith hill,
No longer starry? Not a sound is heard.
So poised the hush, it seems a whispered word
Might loose all noises in an avalanche.
Only the black mass moves, and far glooms blanch
With fitful flashes. The capricious flare
Reveals the butte-top tall and lonely there
Like some gray prophet contemplating doom.

But hark! What spirits whisper in the gloom?
What sibilation of conspiracies
Ruffles the hush—or murmuring of trees,
Ghosts of the ancient forest—or old rain,
In some hallucination of the plain,

A frustrate phantom mourning? All around,
That e'er evolving, ne'er resolving sound
Gropes in the stifling hollow of the night.

Then—once—twice—thrice—a blade of blinding light
Ripped up the heavens, and the deluge came—
A burst of wind and water, noise and flame
That hurled the watcher flat upon the ground.
A moment past Hugh famished; now, half drowned,
He gasped for breath amid the hurtling drench.

So might a testy god, long sought to quench
A puny thirst, pour wassail, hurling after
The crashing bowl with wild sardonic laughter
To see man wrestle with his answered prayer!

Prone to the roaring flaw and ceaseless flare,
The man drank deeply with the drinking grass;
Until it seemed the storm would never pass
But ravin down the painted murk for aye.
When had what dreamer seen a glaring day
And leagues of prairie pantingly aquiver?
Flame, flood, wind, noise and darkness were a river
Tearing a cosmic channel to no sea.

The tortured night wore on; then suddenly
Peace fell. Remotely the retreating Wrath
Trailed dull, reluctant thunders in its path,
And up along a broken stair of cloud
The Dawn came creeping whitely. Like a shroud
Gray vapors clung along the sodden plain.
Up rose the sun to wipe the final stain
Of fury from the sky and drink the mist.
Against a flawless arch of amethyst
The butte soared, like a soul serene and white
Because of the katharsis of the night.

All day Hugh fought with sleep and struggled on
Southeastward; for the heavy heat was gone

Despite the naked sun. The blank Northwest
Breathed coolly; and the crawler thought it best
To move while yet each little break and hollow
And shallow basin of the bison-wallow
Begrudged the earth and air its dwindling store.
But now that thirst was conquered, more and more
He felt the gnaw of hunger like a rage.
And once, from dozing in a clump of sage,
A lone jackrabbit bounded. As a flame
Hope flared in Hugh, until the memory came
Of him who robbed a sleeping friend and fled.
Then hate and hunger merged; the man saw red,
And momently the hare and Little Jim
Were one blurred mark for murder unto him—
Elusive, taunting, sweet to clutch and tear.
The rabbit paused to scan the crippled bear
That ground its teeth as though it chewed a root.
But when, in witless rage, Hugh drew his boot
And hurled it with a curse, the hare loped off,
Its critic ears turned back, as though to scoff
At silly brutes that threw their legs away.

Night like a shadow on enduring day
Swooped by. The dream of crawling and the act
Were phases of one everlasting fact:
Hugh woke, and he was doing what he dreamed.
The butte, outstripped at eventide, now seemed
Intent to follow. Ever now and then
The crawler paused to calculate again
What dear-bought yawn of distance dwarfed the hill.
Close in the rear it soared, a Titan still,
Whose hand-in-pocket saunter kept the pace.

Distinct along the southern rim of space
A low ridge lay, the crest of the divide.
What rest and plenty on the other side!
Through what lush valleys ran what crystal brooks!
And there in virgin meadows wayside nooks
With leaf and purple cluster dulled the light!

All day it seemed that distant Pisgah Height
Retreated, and the tall butte dogged the rear.
At eve a stripéd gopher chirping near
Gave Hugh an inspiration. Now, at least,
No thieving friend should rob him of a feast.
His great idea stirred him as a shout.
Off came a boot, a sock was ravelled out.
The coarse yarn, fashioned to a running snare,
He placed about the gopher's hole with care,
And then withdrew to hold the yarn and wait.
The nightbound moments, ponderous with fate,
Crept slowly by. The battered gray face leered
In expectation. Down the grizzled beard
Ran slaver from anticipating jaws.
Evolving twilight hovered to a pause.
The light wind fell. Again and yet again
The man devoured his fancied prey: and then
Within the noose a timid snout was thrust.
His hand unsteadied with the hunger lust,
Hugh jerked the yarn. It broke.

              Down swooped the night,
A shadow of despair. Bleak height on height,
It seemed, a sheer abyss enclosed him round.
Clutching a strand of yarn, he heard the sound
Of some infernal turmoil under him.
Grimly he strove to reach the ragged rim
That snared a star, until the skyey space
Was darkened with a roof of Jamie's face.
And then the yarn was broken, and he fell.
A-tumble like a stricken bat, his yell
Woke hordes of laughers down the giddy yawn
Of that black pit—and suddenly 'twas dawn.

Dream-dawn, dream-noon, dream-twilight! Yet, possest
    By one stern dream more clamorous than the rest,
Hugh headed for a gap that notched the hills,
Where through a luring murmur of cool rills,

A haunting smell of verdure seemed to creep.
By fits the wild adventure of his sleep
Became the cause of all his waking care,
And he complained unto the empty air
How Jamie broke the yarn.

                The sun and breeze
Had drunk all shallow basins to the lees,
But now and then some gully, choked with mud,
Retained a turbid relict of the flood.
Dream-dawn, dream-noon, dream-night! And still
    obsessed
By that one dream more clamorous than the rest,
Hugh struggled for the crest of the divide.
And when at length he saw the other side,
'Twas but a rumpled waste of yellow hills!
The deep-sunk, wiser self had known the rills
And nooks to be the facture of a whim;
Yet had the pleasant lie befriended him,
And now the brutal fact had come to stare.

Succumbing to a langorous despair,
He mourned his fate with childish uncontrol
And nursed that deadly adder of the soul,
Self-pity. Let the crows swoop down and feed,
Aye, batten on a thing that died of need,
A poor old wretch betrayed of God and Man!
So peevishly his broken musing ran,
Till, glutted with the luxury of woe,
He turned to see the butte, that he might know
How little all his striving could avail
Against ill-luck. And lo, a finger-nail,
At arm-length held, could blot it out of space!
A goading purpose and a creeping pace
Had dwarfed the Titan in a haze of blue!
And suddenly new power came to Hugh
With gazing on his masterpiece of will.
So fare the wise on Pisgah.

Down the hill,
Unto the higher vision consecrate,
Now sallied forth the new triumvirate—
A Weariness, a Hunger and a Glory—
Against tyrannic Chance. As in a story
Some higher Hugh observed the baser part.
So sits the artist throned above his art,
Nor recks the travail so the end be fair.
It seemed the wrinkled hills pressed in to stare,
The arch of heaven was an eye a-gaze.
And as Hugh went, he fashioned many a phrase
For use when, by some friendly ember-light,
His tale of things endured should speed the night
And all this gloom grow golden in the sharing.
So wrought the old evangel of high daring,
The duty and the beauty of endeavor,
The privilege of going on forever,
A victor in the moment.
                        Ah, but when
The night slipped by and morning came again,
The sky and hill were only sky and hill
And crawling but an agony of will.
So once again the old triumvirate,
A buzzard Hunger and a viper Hate
Together with the baser part of Hugh,
Went visionless.
                        That day the wild geese flew,
Vague in a gray profundity of sky;
And on into the night their muffled cry
Haunted the moonlight like a far farewell.
It made Hugh homesick, though he could not tell
For what he yearned; and in his fitful sleeping
The cry became the sound of Jamie weeping,
Immeasurably distant.
                        Morning broke,
Blear, chilly, through a fog that drove as smoke
Before the booming Northwest. Sweet and sad
Came creeping back old visions of the lad—

Some trick of speech, some merry little lilt,
The brooding blue of eyes too clear for guilt,
The wind-blown golden hair. Hate slept that day,
And half of Hugh was half a life away,
A wandering spirit wistful of the past;
And half went drifting with the autumn blast
That mourned among the melancholy hills;
For something of the lethargy that kills
Came creeping close upon the ebb of hate.
Only the raw wind, like the lash of Fate,
Could have availed to move him any more.
At last the buzzard beak no longer tore
His vitals, and he ceased to think of food.
The fighter slumbered, and a maudlin mood
Foretold the dissolution of the man.
He sobbed, and down his beard the big tears ran.
And now the scene is changed; the bleak wind's cry
Becomes a flight of bullets snarling by
From where on yonder summit skulk the Rees.
Against the sky, in silhouette, he sees
The headstrong Jamie in the leaden rain.
And now serenely beautiful and slain
The dear lad lies within a gusty tent.

Thus vexed with doleful whims the crawler went
Adrift before the wind, nor saw the trail;
Till close on night he knew a rugged vale
Had closed about him; and a hush was there,
Though still a moaning in the upper air
Told how the gray-winged gale blew out the day.
Beneath a clump of brush he swooned away
Into an icy void; and waking numb,
It seemed the still white dawn of death had come
On this, some cradle-valley of the soul.
He saw a dim, enchanted hollow roll
Beneath him, and the brush thereof was fleece;
And, like the body of the perfect peace
That thralled the whole, abode the break of day.

It seemed no wind had ever come that way,
Nor sound dwelt there, nor echo found the place
And Hugh lay lapped in wonderment a space,
Vexed with a snarl whereof the ends were lost,
Till, shivering, he wondered if a frost
Had fallen with the dying of the blast.
So, vaguely troubled, listlessly he cast
A gaze about him: lo, above his head
The gray-green curtain of his chilly bed
Was broidered thick with plums! Or so it seemed,
For he was half persuaded that he dreamed;
And with a steady stare he strove to keep
That treasure for the other side of sleep.

Returning hunger bade him rise; in vain
He struggled with a fine-spun mesh of pain
That trammelled him, until a yellow stream
Of day flowed down the white vale of a dream
And left it disenchanted in the glare.
Then, warmed and soothed, Hugh rose and feasted there,
And thought once more of reaching the Moreau.

To southward with a painful pace and slow
He went stiff-jointed; and a gnawing ache
In that hip-wound he had for Jamie's sake
Oft made him groan—nor wrought a tender mood:
The rankling weapon of ingratitude
Was turned again with every puckering twinge.

Far down the vale a narrow winding fringe
Of wilted green betokened how a spring
There sent a little rill meandering;
And Hugh was greatly heartened, for he knew
What fruits and herbs might flourish in the slough,
And thirst, henceforth, should torture not again.

So day on day, despite the crawler's pain,
All in the windless, golden autumn weather,

These two, as comrades, struggled south together—
The homeless graybeard and the homing rill:
And one was sullen with the lust to kill,
And one went crooning of the moon-wooed vast;
For each the many-fathomed peace at last,
But oh the boon of singing on the way!
So came these in the golden fall of day
Unto a sudden turn in the ravine,
Wherefrom Hugh saw a flat of cluttered green
Beneath the further bluffs of the Moreau.

With sinking heart he paused and gazed below
Upon the goal of so much toil and pain.
Yon green had seemed a paradise to gain
The while he thirsted where the lonely butte
Looked far and saw no toothsome herb or fruit
In all that yellow barren dim with heat.
But now the wasting body cried for meat,
And sickness was upon him. Game should pass,
Nor deign to fear the mighty hunter Glass,
But curiously sniffing, pause to stare.

Now while thus musing, Hugh became aware
Of some low murmur, phasic and profound,
Scarce risen o'er the border line of sound.
It might have been the coursing of his blood,
Or thunder heard remotely, or a flood
Flung down a wooded valley far away.
Yet that had been no weather-breeding day;
'Twould frost that night; amid the thirsty land
All streams ran thin; and when he pressed a hand
On either ear, the world seemed very still.

The deep-worn channel of the little rill
Here fell away to eastward, rising, rough
With old rain-furrows, to a lofty bluff
That faced the river with a yellow wall.
Thereto, perplexed, Hugh set about to crawl,

Nor reached the summit till the sun was low.
Far-spread, shade-dimpled in the level glow,
The still land told not whence the murmur grew;
But where the green strip melted into blue
Far down the winding valley of the stream,
Hugh saw what seemed the tempest of a dream
At mimic havoc in the timber-glooms.
As from the sweeping of gigantic brooms,
A dust cloud deepened down the dwindling river;
Upon the distant tree-tops ran a shiver
And huddled thickets writhed as in a gale.

On creeps the windless tempest up the vale,
The while the murmur deepens to a roar,
As with the wider yawning of a door.
And now the agitated green gloom gapes
To belch a flood of countless dusky shapes
That mill and wrangle in a turbid flow—
Migrating myriads of the buffalo
Bound for the winter pastures of the Platte!

Exhausted, faint with need of meat, Hugh sat
And watched the mounting of the living flood.
Down came the night, and like a blot of blood
The lopped moon weltered in the dust-bleared East.
Sleep came and gave a Barmecidal feast.
About a merry flame were simmering
Sweet haunches of the calving of the Spring,
And tender tongues that never tasted snow,
And marrow bones that yielded to a blow
Such treasure! Hugh awoke with gnashing teeth,
And heard the mooing drone of cows beneath,
The roll of hoofs, the challenge of the bull.
So sounds a freshet when the banks are full
And bursting brush-jams bellow to the croon
Of water through green leaves. The ragged moon
Now drenched the valley in an eerie rain:
Below, the semblance of a hurricane;

Above, the perfect calm of brooding frost,
Through which the wolves in doleful tenson tossed
From hill to hill the ancient hunger-song.
In broken sleep Hugh rolled the chill night long,
Half conscious of the flowing flesh below.
And now he trailed a bison in the snow
That deepened till he could not lift his feet.
Again, he battled for a chunk of meat
With some gray beast that fought with icy fang.
And when he woke, the wolves no longer sang;
White dawn athwart a white world smote the hill,
And thunder rolled along the valley still.

Morn, wiping up the frost as with a sponge,
Day on the steep and down the nightward plunge,
And Twilight saw the myriads moving on.
Dust to the westward where the van had gone,
And dust and muffled thunder in the east!
Hugh starved while gazing on a Titan feast.
The tons of beef, that eddied there and swirled,
Had stilled the crying hungers of the world,
Yet not one little morsel was for him.

The red sun, pausing on the dusty rim,
Induced a panic aspect of his plight:
The herd would pass and vanish in the night
And be another dream to cling and flout.
Now scanning all the summit round about,
Amid the rubble of the ancient drift
He saw a bowlder. 'Twas too big to lift,
Yet he might roll it. Painfully and slow
He worked it to the edge, then let it go
And breathlessly expectant watched it fall.
It hurtled down the leaning yellow wall,
And bounding from a brushy ledge's brow,
It barely grazed the buttocks of a cow
And made a moment's eddy where it struck.

In peevish wrath Hugh cursed his evil luck,
And seizing rubble, gave his fury vent
By pelting bison till his strength was spent:
So might a child assail the crowding sea!
Then, sick at heart and musing bitterly,
He shambled down the steep way to the creek,
And having stayed the tearing buzzard beak
With breadroot and the waters of the rill,
Slept till the white of morning o'er the hill
Was like a whisper groping in a hush.
The stream's low trill seemed loud. The tumbled
    brush
And rumpled tree-tops in the flat below,
Upon a fog that clung like spectral snow,
Lay motionless; nor any sound was there.
No frost had fallen, but the crystal air
Smacked of the autumn, and a heavy dew
Lay hoar upon the grass. There came on Hugh
A picture, vivid in the moment's thrill,
Of martialed corn-shocks marching up a hill
And spiked fields dotted with the pumpkin's gold.
It vanished; and, a-shiver with the cold,
He brooded on the mockeries of Chance,
The shrewd malignity of Circumstance
That either gave too little or too much.

Yet, with the fragment of a hope for crutch,
His spirit rallied, and he rose to go,
Though each stiff joint resisted as a foe
And that old hip-wound battled with his will.
So down along the channel of the rill
Unto the vale below he fought his way.
The frore fog, rifting in the risen day,
Revealed the havoc of the living flood—
The river shallows beaten into mud,
The slender saplings shattered in the crush,
All lower leafage stripped, the tousled brush
Despoiled of fruitage, winter-thin, aghast.

And where the avalanche of hoofs had passed
It seemed nor herb nor grass had ever been.
And this the hard-won paradise, wherein
A food-devouring plethora of food
Had come to make a starving solitude!

Yet hope and courage mounted with the sun.
Surely, Hugh thought, some ill-begotten one
Of all that striving mass had lost the strife
And perished in the headlong stream of life—
A feast to fill the bellies of the strong,
That still the weak might perish. All day long
He struggled down the stricken vale, nor saw
What thing he sought. But when the twilight awe
Was creeping in, beyond a bend arose
A din as though the kiotes and the crows
Fought there with shrill and raucous battle cries.

Small need had Hugh to ponder and surmise
What guerdon beak and fang contended for.
Within himself the oldest cause of war
Brought forth upon the instant fang and beak.
He too would fight! Nor had he far to seek
Amid the driftwood strewn about the sand
For weapons suited to a brawny hand
With such a purpose. Armed with club and stone
He forged ahead into the battle zone,
And from a screening thicket spied his foes.

He saw a bison carcass black with crows,
And over it a welter of black wings,
And round about, a press of tawny rings
That, like a muddy current churned to foam
Upon a snag, flashed whitely in the gloom
With naked teeth; while close about the prize
Red beaks and muzzles bloody to the eyes
Betrayed how worth a struggle was the feast.

Then came on Hugh the fury of the beast—
To eat or to be eaten! Better so
To die contending with a living foe,
Than fight the yielding distance and the lack.
Masked by the brush he opened the attack,
And ever where a stone or club fell true,
About the stricken one an uproar grew
And brute tore brute, forgetful of the prey,
Until the whole pack tumbled in the fray
With bleeding flanks and lacerated throats.
Then, as the leader of a host who notes
The cannon-wrought confusion of the foe,
Hugh seized the moment for a daring blow.

The wolf's a coward, who, in goodly packs,
May counterfeit the courage that he lacks
And with a craven's fury crush the bold.
But when the disunited mass that rolled
In suicidal strife, became aware
How some great beast that shambled like a bear
Bore down with roaring challenge, fell a hush
Upon the pack, some slinking to the brush
With tails a-droop; while some that whined in pain
Writhed off on reddened trails. With bristled mane
Before the flying stones a bolder few
Snarled menace at the foe as they withdrew
To fill the outer dusk with clamorings.
Aloft upon a moaning wind of wings
The crows with harsh, vituperative cries
Now saw a gray wolf of prodigious size
Devouring with the frenzy of the starved.
Thus fell to Hugh a bison killed and carved;
And so Fate's whims mysteriously trend—
Woe in the silken meshes of the friend,
Weal in the might and menace of the foe.
But with the fading of the afterglow
The routed wolves found courage to return:
Amid the brush Hugh saw their eye-balls burn;

And well he knew how futile stick and stone
Should prove by night to keep them from their own.
Better is less with safety, than enough
With ruin. He retreated to a bluff,
And scarce had reached it when the pack swooped in
Upon the carcass.

                All night long, the din
Of wrangling wolves assailed the starry air,
While high above them in a brushy lair
Hugh dreamed of gnawing at the bloody feast.

Along about the blanching of the east,
When sleep is weirdest and a moment's flight,
Remembered coextensive with the night,
May teem with hapful years; as light in smoke
Upon the jumble of Hugh's dreaming broke
A buzz of human voices. Once again
He rode the westward trail with Henry's men—
Hoof-smitten leagues consuming in a dust.
And now the nightmare of that broken trust
Was on him, and he lay beside the spring,
A corpse, yet heard the muffled parleying
Above him of the looters of the dead:
But when he might have riddled what they said,
The babble flattened to a blur of gray—
And lo, upon a bleak frontier of day,
The spent moon staring down! A little space
Hugh scrutinized the featureless white face,
As though 'twould speak. But when again the sound
Grew up, and seemed to come from under ground,
He cast the drowse, and peering down the slope,
Beheld what set at grapple fear and hope—
Three Indian horsemen riding at a jog!
Their ponies, wading belly-deep in fog,
That clung along the valley, seemed to swim,
And through a thinner vapor moving dim,
The men were ghost-like.

                Could they be the Sioux?

Almost the wish became belief in Hugh.
Or were they Rees? As readily the doubt
Withheld him from the hazard of a shout.
And while he followed them with baffled gaze,
Grown large and vague, dissolving in the haze,
They vanished westward.

                Knowing well the wont
Of Indians moving on the bison-hunt,
Forthwith Hugh guessed the early riders were
The outflung feelers of a tribe a-stir
Like some huge cat gone mousing. So he lay
Concealed, impatient with the sleepy day
That dawdled in the dawning. Would it bring
Good luck or ill? His eager questioning,
As crawling fog, took on a golden hue
From sunrise. He was waiting for the Sioux,
Their parfleche panniers fat with sun-dried maize
And wasna! From the mint of evil days
He would coin tales and be no begging guest
About the tribal feast-fires burning west,
But kinsman of the blood of daring men.
And when the crawler stood erect again—
O Friend-Betrayer at the Big Horn's mouth,
Beware of someone riding from the South
To do the deed that he had lived to do!

Now when the sun stood hour-high in the blue,
From where a cloud of startled blackbirds rose
Down stream, a panic tumult broke the doze
Of windless morning. What unwelcome news
Embroiled the parliament of feathered shrews?
A boiling cloud against the sun they lower,
Flackering strepent; now a sooty shower,
Big-flaked, squall-driven westward, down they
    flutter
To set a clump of cottonwoods a-sputter
With cold black fire! And once again, some shock

Of sight or sound flings panic in the flock—
Gray boughs exploding in a ruck of birds!

What augury in orniscopic words
Did yon swart sibyls on the morning scrawl?

Now broke abruptly through the clacking brawl
A camp-dog's barking and a pony's neigh;
Whereat a running nicker fled away,
Attenuating to a rearward hush;
And lo! in hailing distance 'round the brush
That fringed a jutting bluff 's base like a beard
Upon a stubborn chin out-thrust, appeared
A band of mounted warriors! In their van
Aloof and lonely rode a gnarled old man
Upon a piebald stallion. Stooped was he
Beneath his heavy years, yet haughtily
He wore them like the purple of a king.
Keen for a goal, as from the driving string
A barbed and feathered arrow truly sped,
His face was like a flinty arrow-head,
And brooded westward in a steady stare.
There was a sift of winter in his hair,
The bleakness of brown winter in his look.
Hugh saw, and huddled closer in his nook.
Fled the bright dreams of safety, feast and rest
Before that keen, cold brooder on the West,
As gaudy leaves before the blizzard flee.
'Twas Elk Tongue, fighting chieftain of the Ree,
With all his people at his pony's tail—
Full two-score lodges emptied on the trail
Of hunger!
                    On they came in ravelled rank,
And many a haggard eye and hollow flank
Made plain how close and pitilessly pressed
The enemy that drove them to the West—
Such foeman as no warrior ever slew.
A tale of cornfields plundered by the Sioux

Their sagging panniers told. Yet rich enough
They seemed to him who watched them from the
    bluff;
Yea, pampered nigh the limit of desire!
No friend had filched from them the boon of fire
And hurled them shivering back upon the beast.
Erect they went, full-armed to strive, at least;
And nightly in a cozy ember-glow
Hope fed them with a dream of buffalo
Soon to be overtaken. After that,
Home with their Pawnee cousins on the Platte,
Much meat and merry-making till the Spring.
On dragged the rabble like a fraying string
Too tautly drawn. The rich-in-ponies rode,
For much is light and little is a load
Among all heathen with no Christ to save!
Gray seekers for the yet begrudging grave,
Bent with the hoeing of forgotten maize,
Wood-hewers, water-bearers all their days,
Toiled 'neath the life-long hoarding of their packs.
And nursing squaws, their babies at their backs
Whining because the milk they got was thinned
In dugs of famine, strove as with a wind.
Invincibly equipped with their first bows
The striplings strutted, knowing, as youth knows,
How fair life is beyond the beckoning blue.
Cold-eyed the grandsires plodded, for they knew,
As frosted heads may know, how all trails merge
In what lone land. Raw maidens on the verge
Of some half-guessed-at mystery of life,
In wistful emulation of the wife
Stooped to the fancied burden of the race;
Nor read upon the withered granddam's face
The scrawled tale of that burden and its woe.
Slant to the sagging poles of the travaux,
Numb to the squaw's harsh railing and the goad,
The lean cayuses toiled. And children rode
A-top the household plunder, wonder-eyed

To see a world flow by on either side,
From blue air sprung to vanish in blue air,
A river of enchantments.

                  Here and there
The camp-curs loped upon a vexing quest
Where countless hoofs had left a palimpsest,
A taunting snarl of broken scents. And now
They sniff the clean bones of the bison cow,
Howl to the skies; and now with manes a-rough
They nose the man-smell leading to the bluff;
Pause puzzled at the base and sweep the height
With questioning yelps. Aloft, crouched low in
      fright,
Already Hugh can hear the braves' guffaws
At their scorned foeman yielded to the squaws'
Inverted mercy and a slow-won grave.
Since Earth's first mother scolded from a cave
And that dear riddle of her love began,
No man has wrought a weapon against man
To match the deadly venom brewed above
The lean, blue, blinding heart-fires of her love.
Well might the hunted hunter shrink aghast!
But thrice three seasons yet should swell the past,
So was it writ, ere Fate's keen harriers
Should run Hugh Glass to earth.

                The hungry curs
Took up again the tangled scent of food.
Still flowed the rabble through the solitude—
A thinning stream now of the halt, the weak
And all who had not very far to seek
For that weird pass whereto the fleet are slow,
And out of it keen winds and numbing blow,
Shrill with the fleeing voices of the dead.
Slowly the scattered stragglers, making head
Against their weariness as up a steep,
Fled westward; and the morning lay asleep
Upon the valley fallen wondrous still.

Hugh kept his nook, nor ventured forth, until
The high day toppled to the blue descent,
When thirst became a master, and he went
With painful scrambling down the broken scarp,
Lured by the stream, that like a smitten harp
Rippled a muted music to the sun.

Scarce had he crossed the open flat, and won
The half-way fringe of willows, when he saw,
Slow plodding up the trail, a tottering squaw
Whose years made big the little pack she bore.
Crouched in the brush Hugh watched her. More
    and more
The little burden tempted him. Why not?
A thin cry throttled in that lonely spot
Could bring no succor. None should ever know,
Save him, the feasted kiote and the crow,
Why one poor crone found not the midnight fire.
Nor would the vanguard, quick with young desire,
Devouring distance westward like a flame,
Regret this ash dropped rearward.
                  On she came,
Slow-footed, staring blankly on the sand—
So close now that it needed but a hand
Out-thrust to overthrow her; aye, to win
That priceless spoil, a little tent of skin,
A flint and steel, a kettle and a knife!
What did the dying with the means of life,
That thus the fit-to-live should suffer lack?

Poised for the lunge, what whimsy held him back?
Why did he gaze upon the passing prize,
Nor seize it? Did some gust of ghostly cries
Awaken round her—whisperings of Eld,
Wraith-voices of the babies she had held,
Guarding the milkless paps, the withered womb?
Far down a moment's cleavage in the gloom
Of backward years Hugh saw her now—nor saw

The little burden and the feeble squaw,
But someone sitting haloed like a saint
Beside a hearth long cold. The dream grew faint;
And when he looked again, the crone was gone
Beyond a clump of willow.

                         Crawling on,
He reached the river. Leaning to a pool
Calm in its cup of sand, he saw—a fool!
A wild, wry mask of mirth, a-grin, yet grim,
Rose there to claim identity with him
And ridicule his folly. Pity? Faugh!
Who pitied this, that it should spare a squaw
Spent in the spawning of a scorpion brood?

He drank and hastened down the solitude,
Fleeing that thing which fleered him, and was Hugh.
And as he went his self-accusing grew
And with it, anger; till it came to seem
That somehow some sly Jamie of a dream
Had plundered him again; and he was strong
With lust of vengeance and the sting of wrong,
So that he travelled faster than for days.

Now when the eve in many-shaded grays
Wove the day's shroud, and through the lower lands
Lean fog-arms groped with chilling spirit hands,
Hugh paused perplexed. Elusive, haunting, dim,
As though some memory that stirred in him,
Invasive of the real, outgrew the dream,
There came upon the breeze that stole up stream
A whiff of woodsmoke.

                    'Twixt a beat and beat
Of Hugh's deluded heart, it seemed the sweet
Allure of home.—A brief way, and one came
Upon the clearing where the sumach flame
Ran round the forest-fringe; and just beyond
One saw the slough grass nodding in the pond
Unto the sleepy troll the bullfrogs sung.

And then one saw the place where one was young—
The log-house sitting on a stumpy rise.
Hearth-lit within, its windows were as eyes
That love much and are faded with old tears.
It seemed regretful of a life's arrears,
Yet patient, with a self-denying poise,
Like some old mother for her bearded boys
Waiting sweet-hearted and a little sad.—
So briefly dreamed a recrudescent lad
Beneath gray hairs, and fled.

                Through chill and damp
Still groped the odor, hinting at a camp,
A two-tongued herald wooing hope and fear.
Was hospitality or danger near?
A Sioux war-party hot upon the trail,
Or laggard Rees? Hugh crawled across the vale,
Toiled up along a zigzag gully's bed
And reached a bluff's top. In a smudge of red
The West burned low. Hill summits, yet alight,
And pools of gloom anticipating night
Mottled the landscape to the dull blue rim.
What freak of fancy had imposed on him?
Could one smell home-smoke fifty years away?
He saw no fire; no pluming spire of gray
Rose in the dimming air to woo or warn.

He lay upon the bare height, fagged, forlorn,
And old times came upon him with the creep
Of subtle drugs that put the will to sleep
And wreak doom to the soothing of a dream.
So listlessly he scanned the sombrous stream,
Scarce seeing what he scanned. The dark increased;
A chill wind wakened from the frowning east
And soughed along the vale.

                    Then with a start
He saw what broke the torpor of his heart
And set the wild blood free. From where he lay
An easy point-blank rifle-shot away,

Appeared a mystic germinating spark
That in some secret garden of the dark
Upreared a frail, blue, nodding stem, whereon
A ruddy lily flourished—and was gone!
What miracle was this? Again it grew,
The scarlet blossom on the stem of blue,
And withered back again into the night.

With pounding heart Hugh crawled along the height
And reached a point of vantage whence, below,
He saw capricious witch-lights dim and glow
Like far-spent embers quickened in a breeze.
'Twas surely not a camp of laggard Rees,
Nor yet of Siouan warriors hot in chase.
Dusk and a quiet bivouacked in that place.
A doddering vagrant with numb hands, the Wind
Fumbled the dying ashes there, and whined.
It was the day-old camp-ground of the foe!

Glad-hearted now, Hugh gained the vale below,
Keen to possess once more the ancient gift.
Nearing the glow, he saw vague shadows lift
Out of the painted gloom of smouldering logs—
Distorted bulks that bristled, and were dogs
Snarling at this invasion of their lair.
Hugh charged upon them, growling like a bear,
And sent them whining.
                              Now again to view
The burgeoning of scarlet, gold and blue,
The immemorial miracle of fire!
From heaped-up twigs a tenuous smoky spire
Arose, and made an altar of the place.
The spark-glow, faint upon the grizzled face,
Transformed the kneeling outcast to a priest;
And, native of the light-begetting East,
The Wind became a chanting acolyte.
These two, entempled in the vaulted night,
Breathed conjuries of interwoven breath.

Then, hark!—the snapping of the chains of Death!
From dead wood, lo!—the epiphanic god!

Once more the freightage of the fennel rod
Dissolved the chilling pall of Jovian scorn.
The wonder of the resurrection morn,
The face apocalyptic and the sword,
The glory of the many-symboled Lord,
Hugh, lifting up his eyes about him, saw!
And something in him like a vernal thaw,
Voiced with the sound of many waters, ran
And quickened to the laughter of a man.

Light-heartedly he fed the singing flame
And took its blessing: till a soft sleep came
With dreaming that was like a pleasant tale.

The far white dawn was peering up the vale
When he awoke to indolent content.
A few shorn stars in pale astonishment
Were huddled westward; and the fire was low.
Three scrawny camp-curs, mustered in a row
Beyond the heap of embers, heads askew,
Ears pricked to question what the man might do,
Sat wistfully regardant. He arose;
And they, grown canny in a school of blows,
Skulked to a safer distance, there to raise
A dolorous chanting of the evil days,
Their gray breath like the body of a prayer.
Hugh nursed the sullen embers to a flare,
Then set about to view an empty camp
As once before; but now no smoky lamp
Of blear suspicion searched a gloom of fraud
Wherein a smirking Friendship, like a bawd,
Embraced a coward Safety; now no grief,
'Twixt hideous revelation and belief,
Made womanish the man; but glad to strive,
With hope to nerve him and a will to drive,

He knew that he could finish in the race.
The staring impassivity of space
No longer mocked; the dreadful skyward climb,
Where distance seemed identical with time,
Was past now; and that mystic something, luck,
Without which worth may flounder in the ruck,
Had turned to him again.

          So flamelike soared
Rekindled hope in him as he explored
Among the ash-heaps; and the lean dogs ran
And barked about him, for the love of man
Wistful, yet fearing. Surely he could find
Some trifle in the hurry left behind—
Or haply hidden in the trampled sand—
That to the cunning of a needy hand
Should prove the master-key of circumstance:
For 'tis the little gifts of grudging Chance,
Well husbanded, make victors.

          Long he sought
Without avail; and, crawling back, he thought
Of how the dogs were growing less afraid,
And how one might be skinned without a blade.
A flake of flint might do it: he would try.
And then he saw—or did the servile eye
Trick out a mental image like the real?
He saw a glimmering of whetted steel
Beside a heap now washed with morning light!

Scarce more of marvel and the sense of might
Moved Arthur when he reached a hand to take
The fay-wrought brand emerging from the lake,
Whereby a kingdom should be lopped of strife,
Than Hugh now, pouncing on a trader's knife
Worn hollow in the use of bounteous days!

And now behold a rich man by the blaze
Of his own hearth—a lord of steel and fire!
Not having, but the measure of desire

Determines wealth. Who gaining more, seek most,
Are ever the pursuers of a ghost
And lend their fleetness to the fugitive.
For Hugh, long goaded by the wish to live,
What gage of mastery in fire and tool!—
That twain wherewith Time put the brute to school,
Evolving Man, the maker and the seer.

'Twixt urging hunger and restraining fear
The gaunt dogs hovered round the man; while he
Cajoled them in the language of the Ree
And simulated feeding them with sand,
Until the boldest dared to sniff his hand,
Bare-fanged and with conciliative whine.
Through bristled mane the quick blade bit the spine
Below the skull; and as a flame-struck thing
The body humped and shuddered, withering;
The lank limbs huddled, wilted.

                            Now to skin
The carcass, dig a hole, arrange therein
And fix the pelt with stakes, the flesh-side up.
This done, he shaped the bladder to a cup
On willow withes, and filled the rawhide pot
With water from the river—made it hot
With roasted stones, and set the meat a-boil.
Those days of famine and prodigious toil
Had wrought bulimic cravings in the man,
And scarce the cooking of the flesh outran
The eating of it. As a fed flame towers
According to the fuel it devours,
His hunger with indulgence grew, nor ceased
Until the kettle, empty of the feast,
Went dim, the sky and valley, merging, swirled
In subtle smoke that smothered out the world.
Hugh slept.

                And then—as divers, mounting, sunder
A murmuring murk to blink in sudden wonder
Upon a dazzling upper deep of blue—

He rose again to consciousness, and knew
The low sun beating slantly on his face.

Now indolently gazing round the place,
He noted how the curs had revelled there—
The bones and entrails gone; some scattered hair
Alone remaining of the pot of hide.
How strange he had not heard them at his side!
And granting but one afternoon had passed,
What could have made the fire burn out so fast?
Had daylight waned, night fallen, morning crept,
Noon blazed, a new day dwindled while he slept?
And was the friendlike fire a Jamie too?
Across the twilit consciousness of Hugh
The old obsession like a wounded bird
Fluttered.
          He got upon his knees and stirred
The feathery ash; but not a spark was there.
Already with the failing sun the air
Went keen, betokening a frosty night.
Hugh winced with something like the clutch of fright.
How could he bear the torture, how sustain
The sting of that antiquity of pain
Rolled back upon him—face again the foe,
That yielding victor, fleet in being slow,
That huge, impersonal malevolence?

So readily the tentacles of sense
Root in the larger standard of desire,
That Hugh fell farther in the loss of fire
Than in the finding of it he arose.
And suddenly the place grew strange, as grows
A friend's house, when the friend is on his bier,
And all that was familiar there and dear
Puts on a blank, inhospitable look.
Hugh set his face against the east, and took
That dreariest of ways, the trail of flight.
He would outcrawl the shadow of the night

And have the day to blanket him in sleep.
But as he went to meet the gloom a-creep,
Bemused with life's irrational rebuffs,
A yelping of the dogs among the bluffs
Rose, hunger-whetted, stabbing; rent the pall
Of evening silence; blunted to a drawl
Amid the arid waterways, and died.
And as the echo to the sound replied,
So in the troubled mind of Hugh was wrought
A reminiscent cry of thought to thought
That, groping, found an unlocked door to life:
The dogs—keen flint to skin one—then the knife
Discovered. Why, that made a flint and steel!
No further with the subtle foe at heel
He fled; for all about him in the rock,
To waken when the needy hand might knock,
A savior slept! He found a flake of flint,
Scraped from his shirt a little wad of lint,
Spilled on it from the smitten stone a shower
Of ruddy seed; and saw the mystic flower
That genders its own summer, bloom anew!

And so capricious luck came back to Hugh;
And he was happier than he had been
Since Jamie to that unforgiven sin
Had yielded, ages back upon the Grand.
Now he would turn the cunning of his hand
To carving crutches, that he might arise,
Be manlike, lift more rapidly the skies
That crouched between his purpose and the mark.
The warm glow housed him from the frosty dark,
And there he wrought in very joyous mood
And sang by fits—whereat the solitude
Set laggard singers snatching at the tune.
The gaunter for their hunt, the dogs came soon
To haunt the shaken fringes of the glow,
And, pitching voices to the timeless woe,
Outwailed the lilting. So the Chorus sings

Of terror, pity and the tears of things
When most the doomed protagonist is gay.
The stars swarmed over, and the front of day
Whitened above a white world, and the sun
Rose on a sleeper with a task well done,
Nor roused him till its burning topped the blue.

When Hugh awoke, there woke a younger Hugh,
Now half a stranger; and 'twas good to feel
With ebbing sleep the old green vigor steal,
Thrilling, along his muscles and his veins,
As in a lull of winter-cleansing rains
The gray bough quickens to the sap a-creep.
It chanced the dogs lay near him, sound asleep,
Curled nose to buttock in the noonday glow.
He killed the larger with a well-aimed blow,
Skinned, dressed and set it roasting on a spit;
And when 'twas cooked, ate sparingly of it,
For need might yet make little seem a feast.

Fording the river shallows, south by east
He hobbled now along a withered rill
That issued where old floods had gashed the hill—
A cyclopean portal yawning sheer.
No storm of countless hoofs had entered here:
It seemed a place where nothing ever comes
But change of season. He could hear the plums
Plash in the frosted thicket, over-lush;
While, like a spirit lisping in the hush,
The crisp leaves whispered round him as they fell.
And ever now and then the autumn spell
Was broken by an ululating cry
From where far back with muzzle to the sky
The lone dog followed, mourning. Darkness came;
And huddled up beside a cozy flame,
Hugh's sleep was but a momentary flight
Across a little shadow into light.

So day on day he toiled: and when, afloat
Above the sunset like a stygian boat,
The new moon bore the spectre of the old,
He saw—a dwindling strip of blue outrolled—
The valley of the tortuous Cheyenne.
And ere the half moon sailed the night again,
Those far lone leagues had sloughed their garb
    of blue,
And dwindled, dwindled, dwindled after Hugh,
Until he saw that Titan of the plains,
The sinewy Missouri. Dearth of rains
Had made the Giant gaunt as he who saw.
This loud Chain-Smasher of a late March thaw
Seemed never to have bellowed at his banks;
And yet, with staring ribs and hollow flanks,
The urge of an indomitable will
Proclaimed him of the breed of giants still;
And where the current ran a boiling track,
'Twas like the muscles of a mighty back
Grown Atlantean in the wrestler's craft.

Hugh set to work and built a little raft
Of driftwood bound with grapevines. So it fell
That one with an amazing tale to tell
Came drifting to the gates of Kiowa.

THE RETURN OF THE GHOST

IV

Not long Hugh let the lust of vengeance gnaw
Upon him idling; though the tale he told
And what report proclaimed him, were as gold
To buy a winter's comfort at the Post.
"I can not rest; for I am but the ghost
  Of someone murdered by a friend," he said,
"So long as yonder traitor thinks me dead,
  Aye, buried in the bellies of the crows
  And kiotes!"
                Whereupon said one of those
Who heard him, noting how the old man shook
As with a chill: "God fend that one should look
With such a blizzard of a face for me!"
For he went grayer like a poplar tree
That shivers, ruffling to the first faint breath
Of storm, while yet the world is still as death
Save where, far off, the kenneled thunders bay.

So brooding, he grew stronger day by day,
Until at last he laid the crutches by.
And then one evening came a rousing cry
From where the year's last keelboat hove in view
Around the bend, its swarthy, sweating crew
Slant to the shouldered line.
                          Men sang that night
In Kiowa, and by the ruddy light
Of leaping fires amid the wooden walls
The cups went round; and there were merry brawls
Of bearded lads no older for the beard;

And laughing stories vied with tales of weird
By stream and prairie trail and mountain pass,
Until the tipsy Bourgeois bawled for Glass
To 'shame these with a man's tale fit to hear.'

The graybeard, sitting where the light was blear,
With little heart for revelry, began
His story, told as of another man
Who, loving late, loved much and was betrayed.
He spoke unwitting how his passion played
Upon them, how their eyes grew soft or hard
With what he told; yet something of the bard
He seemed, and his the purpose that is art's,
Whereby men make a vintage of their hearts
And with the wine of beauty deaden pain.
Low-toned, insistent as October rain,
His voice beat on; and now and then would flit
Across the melancholy gray of it
A glimmer of cold fire that, like the flare
Of soundless lightning, showed a world made bare,
Green Summer slain and all its leafage stripped.

And bronze jaws tightened, brawny hands were
        gripped,
As though each hearer had a fickle friend.
But when the old man might have made an end,
Rounding the story to a peaceful close
At Kiowa, songlike his voice arose,
The grinning gray mask lifted and the eyes
Burned as a bard's who sees and prophesies,
Conning the future as a time long gone.
Swaying to rhythm the dizzy tale plunged on
Even to the cutting of the traitor's throat,
And ceased—as though a bloody strangling smote
The voice of that gray chanter, drunk with doom.
And there was shuddering in the blue-smeared gloom
Of fallen fires. It seemed the deed was done
Before their eyes who heard.

The morrow's sun,
Low over leagues of frost-enchanted plain,
Saw Glass upon his pilgrimage again,
Northbound as hunter for the keelboat's crew.
And many times the wide autumnal blue
Burned out and darkened to a deep of stars;
And still they toiled among the snags and bars—
Those lean up-stream men, straining at the rope,
Lashed by the doubt and strengthened by the hope
Of backward winter—engines wrought of bone
And muscle, panting for the Yellowstone,
Bend after bend and yet more bends away.
Now was the river like a sandy bay
At ebb-tide, and the far-off cutbank's boom
Mocked them in shallows; now 'twas like a flume
With which the toilers, barely creeping, strove.
And bend by bend the selfsame poplar grove,
Set on the selfsame headland, so it seemed,
Confronted them, as though they merely dreamed
Of passing one drear point.
So on and up
Past where the tawny Titan gulps the cup
Of Cheyenne waters, past the Moreau's mouth;
And still wry league and stubborn league fell south,
Becoming haze and weary memory.
Then past the empty lodges of the Ree
That gaped at cornfields plundered by the Sioux;
And there old times came mightily on Hugh,
For much of him was born and buried there.
Some troubled glory of that wind-tossed hair
Was on the trampled corn; the lonely skies,
So haunted with the blue of Jamie's eyes,
Seemed taunting him; and through the frosted wood
Along the flat, where once their tent had stood,
A chill wind sorrowed, and the blackbirds' brawl
Amid the funeral torches of the Fall
Ran raucously, a desecrating din.

Past where the Cannon Ball and Heart come in
They labored. Now the Northwest 'woke at last.
The gaunt bluffs bellowed back the trumpet blast
Of charging winds that made the sandbars smoke.
To breathe now was to gulp fine sand, and choke:
The stinging air was sibilant with whips.
Leaning the more and with the firmer grips,
Still northward the embattled toilers pressed
To where the river yaws into the west.
There stood the Mandan village.

Now began
The chaining of the Titan. Drift-ice ran.
The wingéd hounds of Winter ceased to bay.
The stupor of a doom completed lay
Upon the world. The biting darkness fell.
Out in the night, resounding as a well,
They heard the deckplanks popping in a vise
Of frost; all night the smithies of the ice
Reëchoed with the griding jar and clink
Of ghostly hammers welding link to link:
And morning found the world without a sound.
There lay the stubborn Prairie Titan bound,
To wait the far-off Heraclean thaw,
Though still in silent rage he strove to gnaw
The ragged shackles knitting at his breast.

And so the boatman won a winter's rest
Among the Mandan traders: but for Hugh
There yet remained a weary work to do.
Across the naked country west by south
His purpose called him at the Big Horn's mouth—
Three hundred miles of winging for the crow;
But by the river trail that he must go
'Twas seven hundred winding miles at least.

So now he turned his back upon the feast,
Snug ease, the pleasant tale, the merry mood,

And took the bare, foot-sounding solitude
Northwestward. Long they watched him from
    the Post,
Skied on a bluff-rim, fading like a ghost
At gray cock-crow; and hooded in his breath,
He seemed indeed a fugitive from Death
On whom some tatter of the shroud still clung.
Blank space engulfed him.

                Now the moon was young
When he set forth; and day by day he strode,
His scarce healed wounds upon him like a load;
And dusk by dusk his fire outflared the moon
That waxed until it wrought a spectral noon
At nightfall. Then he came to where, awhirl
With Spring's wild rage, the snow-born Titan girl,
A skyey wonder on her virgin face,
Receives the virile Yellowstone's embrace
And bears the lusty Seeker for the Sea.
A bleak, horizon-wide serenity
Clung round the valley where the twain lay dead.
A winding sheet was on the marriage bed.

'Twas warmer now; the sky grew overcast;
And as Hugh strode southwestward, all the vast
Gray void seemed suddenly astir with wings
And multitudinary whisperings—
The muffled sibilance of tumbling snow.
It seemed no more might living waters flow,
Moon gleam, star glint, dawn smoulder through,
    bird sing,
Or ever any fair familiar thing
Be so again. The outworn winds were furled.
Weird weavers of the twilight of a world
Wrought, thread on kissing thread, the web of doom.
Grown insubstantial in the knitted gloom,
The bluffs loomed eerie, and the scanty trees
Were dwindled to remote dream-traceries
That never might be green or shield a nest.

All day with swinging stride Hugh forged southwest
Along the Yellowstone's smooth-paven stream,
A dream-shape moving in a troubled dream;
And all day long the whispering weavers wove.
And close on dark he came to where a grove
Of cottonwoods rose tall and shadow-thin
Against the northern bluffs. He camped therein
And with cut boughs made shelter as he might.

Close pressed the blackness of the snow-choked night
About him, and his fire of plum wood purred.
Athwart a soft penumbral drowse he heard
The tumbling snowflakes sighing all around,
Till sleep transformed it to a Summer sound
Of boyish memory—susurrant bees,
The Southwind in the tousled apple trees
And slumber flowing from their leafy gloom.

He wakened to the cottonwoods' deep boom.
Black fury was the world. The northwest's roar,
As of a surf upon a shipwreck shore,
Plunged high above him from the sheer bluff's verge;
And, like the backward sucking of the surge,
Far fled the sobbing of the wild snow-spray.

Black blindness grew white blindness—and 'twas day.
All being now seemed narrowed to a span
That held a sputtering wood fire and a man;
Beyond was tumult and a whirling maze.
The trees were but a roaring in a haze;
The sheer bluff-wall that took the blizzard's charge
Was thunder flung along the hidden marge
Of chaos, stridden by the ghost of light.
White blindness grew black blindness—and 'twas night
Wherethrough nor moon nor any star might grope.

Two days since, Hugh had killed an antelope
And what remained sufficed the time of storm.

The snow, banked round his shelter, kept him warm
And there was wood to burn for many a day.

The third dawn, oozing through a smudge of gray,
Awoke him. It was growing colder fast.
Still from the bluff high over boomed the blast,
But now it took the void with numbing wings.
By noon the woven mystery of things
Frayed raggedly, and through a sudden rift
At length Hugh saw the beetling bluff-wall lift
A sturdy shoulder to the flying rack.
Slowly the sense of distances came back
As with the waning day the great wind fell.
The pale sun set upon a frozen hell.
The wolves howled.

                  Hugh had left the Mandan town
When, heifer-horned, the maiden moon lies down
Beside the sea of evening. Now she rose
Scar-faced and staring blankly on the snows
While yet the twilight tarried in the west;
And more and more she came a tardy guest
As Hugh pushed onward through the frozen waste
Until she stole on midnight shadow-faced,
A haggard spectre; then no more appeared.

'Twas on that time the man of hoary beard
Paused in the early twilight, looming lone
Upon a bluff-rim of the Yellowstone,
And peered across the white stream to the south
Where in the flatland at the Big Horn's mouth
The new fort stood that Henry's men had built.
What perfect peace for such a nest of guilt!
What satisfied immunity from woe!
Yon sprawling shadow, pied with candle-glow
And plumed with sparkling wood-smoke, might
        have been
A homestead with the children gathered in

To share its bounty through the holidays.
Hugh saw their faces round the gay hearth-blaze:
The hale old father in a mood for yarns
Or boastful of the plenty of his barns,
Fruitage of honest toil and grateful lands;
And, half a stranger to her folded hands,
The mother with October in her hair
And August in her face. One moment there
Hugh saw it. Then the monstrous brutal fact
Wiped out the dream and goaded him to act,
Though now to act seemed strangely like a dream.

Descending from the bluff, he crossed the stream,
The dry snow fifing to his eager stride.
Reaching the fort stockade, he paused to bide
The passing of a whimsy. Was it true?
Or was this but the fretted wraith of Hugh
Whose flesh had fed the kiotes long ago?

Still through a chink he saw the candle-glow,
So like an eye that brazened out a wrong.
And now there came a flight of muffled song,
The rhythmic thudding of a booted heel
That timed a squeaking fiddle to a reel!
How swiftly men forget! The spawning Earth
Is fat with graves; and what is one man worth
That fiddles should be muted at his fall?
He should have died and did not—that was all.
Well, let the living jig it! He would turn
Back to the night, the spacious unconcern
Of wilderness that never played the friend.

Now came the song and fiddling to an end,
And someone laughed within. The old man winced,
Listened with bated breath, and was convinced
'Twas Jamie laughing! Once again he heard.
Joy filled a hush 'twixt heart-beats like a bird;
Then like a famished cat his lurking hate

Pounced crushingly.
                          He found the outer gate,
Beat on it with his shoulder, raised a cry.
No doubt 'twas deemed a fitful wind went by;
None stirred. But when he did not cease to shout,
A door creaked open and a man came out
Amid the spilling candle-glimmer, raised
The wicket in the outer gate and gazed
One moment on a face as white as death,
Because the beard was thick with frosted breath
Made mystic by the stars. Then came a gasp,
The clatter of the falling wicket's hasp,
The crunch of panic feet along the snow;
And someone stammered huskily and low:
"My God! I saw the Old Man's ghost out there!"
'Twas spoken as one speaks who feels his hair
Prickle the scalp. And then another said—
It seemed like Henry's voice—"The dead are dead:
What talk is this, Le Bon? You saw him die!
Who's there?"
                          Hugh strove to shout, to give the lie
To those within; but could not fetch a sound.
Just so he dreamed of lying under ground
Beside the Grand and hearing overhead
The talk of men. Or was he really dead,
And all this but a maggot in the brain?

Then suddenly the clatter of a chain
Aroused him, and he saw the portal yawn
And saw a bright rectangled patch of dawn
As through a grave's mouth—no, 'twas candlelight
Poured through the open doorway on the night;
And those were men before him, bulking black
Against the glow.
                          Reality flashed back;
He strode ahead and entered at the door.
A falling fiddle jangled on the floor
And left a deathly silence. On his bench

The fiddler shrank. A row of eyes, a-blench
With terror, ran about the naked hall.
And there was one who huddled by the wall
And hid his face and shivered.

                      For a spell
That silence clung; and then the old man: "Well,
Is this the sort of welcome that I get?
'Twas not my time to feed the kiotes yet!
Put on the pot and stew a chunk of meat
And you shall see how much a ghost can eat!
I've journeyed far if what I hear be true!"

Now in that none might doubt the voice of Hugh,
Nor yet the face, however it might seem
A blurred reflection in a flowing stream,
A buzz of wonder broke the trance of dread.
"Good God!" the Major gasped; "We thought you dead!
Two men have testified they saw you die!"
"If they speak truth," Hugh answered, "then I lie
Both here and by the Grand. If I be right,
Then two lie here and shall lie from this night.
Which are they?"

               Henry answered: "Yon is one."

The old man set the trigger of his gun
And gazed on Jules who cowered by the wall.
Eyes blinked, expectant of the hammer's fall;
Ears strained, anticipative of the roar.
But Hugh walked leisurely across the floor
And kicked the croucher, saying: "Come, get up
And wag your tail! I couldn't kill a pup!"
Then turning round: "I had a faithful friend;
No doubt he too was with me to the end!
Where's Jamie?"

            "Started out before the snows
For Atkinson."

JAMIE

V

        The Country of the Crows,
Through which the Big Horn and the Rosebud run,
Sees over mountain peaks the setting sun;
And southward from the Yellowstone flung wide,
It broadens ever to the morning side
And has the Powder on its vague frontier.
About the subtle changing of the year,
Ere even favored valleys felt the stir
Of Spring, and yet expectancy of her
Was like a pleasant rumor all repeat
Yet none may prove, the sound of horses' feet
Went eastward through the silence of that land.
For then it was there rode a little band
Of trappers out of Henry's Post, to bear
Dispatches down to Atkinson, and there
To furnish out a keelboat for the Horn.
And four went lightly, but the fifth seemed worn
As with a heavy heart; for that was he
Who should have died but did not.

                        Silently
He heard the careless parley of his men,
And thought of how the Spring should come again,
That garish strumpet with her world-old lure,
To waken hope where nothing may endure,
To quicken love where loving is betrayed.
Yet now and then some dream of Jamie made
Slow music in him for a little while;
And they who rode beside him saw a smile

Glimmer upon that ruined face of gray,
As on a winter fog the groping day
Pours glory through a momentary rift.
Yet never did the gloom that bound him, lift;
He seemed as one who feeds upon his heart
And finds, despite the bitter and the smart,
A little sweetness and is glad for that.

Now up the Powder, striking for the Platte
Across the bleak divide the horsemen went;
Attained that river where its course is bent
From north to east: and spurring on apace
Along the wintry valley, reached the place
Where from the west flows in the Laramie.
Thence, fearing to encounter with the Ree,
They headed eastward through the barren land
To where, fleet-footed down a track of sand,
The Niobrara races for the morn—
A gaunt-loined runner.

          Here at length was born
Upon the southern slopes the baby Spring,
A timid, fretful, ill-begotten thing,
A-suckle at the Winter's withered paps:
Not such as when announced by thunder-claps
And ringed with swords of lightning, she would ride,
The haughty victrix and the mystic bride,
Clad splendidly as never Sheba's Queen,
Before her marching multitudes of green
In many-bannered triumph! Grudging, slow,
Amid the fraying fringes of the snow
The bunch-grass sprouted; and the air was chill.
Along the northern slopes 'twas winter still,
And no root dreamed what Triumph-over-Death
Was nurtured now in some bleak Nazareth
Beyond the crest to sunward.
          On they spurred
Through vacancies that waited for the bird,

And everywhere the Odic Presence dwelt.
The Southwest blew, the snow began to melt;
And when they reached the valley of the Snake,
The Niobrara's ice began to break,
And all night long and all day long it made
A sound as of a random cannonade
With rifles snarling down a skirmish line.

The geese went over. Every tree and vine
Was dotted thick with leaf-buds when they saw
The little river of Keyapaha
Grown mighty for the moment. Then they came,
One evening when all thickets were aflame
With pale green witch-fires and the windflowers blew,
To where the headlong Niobrara threw
His speed against the swoln Missouri's flank
And hurled him roaring to the further bank—
A giant staggered by a pigmy's sling.
Thence, plunging ever deeper into Spring,
Across the greening prairie east by south
They rode, and, just above the Platte's wide mouth,
Came, weary with the trail, to Atkinson.

There all the vernal wonder-work was done:
No care-free heart might find aught lacking there.
The dove's call wandered in the drowsy air;
A love-dream brooded in the lucent haze.
Priapic revellers, the shrieking jays
Held mystic worship in the secret shade.
Woodpeckers briskly plied their noisy trade
Along the tree-boles, and their scarlet hoods
Flashed flame-like in the smoky cottonwoods.
What lacked? Not sweetness in the sun-lulled breeze;
The plum bloom murmurous with bumblebees
Was drifted deep in every draw and slough.
Not color; witcheries of gold and blue
The dandelion and the violet
Wove in the green. Might not the sad forget,

The happy here have nothing more to seek?
Lo, yonder by that pleasant little creek,
How one might loll upon the grass and fish
And build the temple of one's wildest wish
'Twixt nibbles! Surely there was quite enough
Of wizard-timber and of wonder-stuff
To rear it nobly to the blue-domed roof!

Yet there was one whose spirit stood aloof
From all this joyousness—a gray old man,
No nearer now than when the quest began
To what he sought on that long winter trail.

Aye, Jamie had been there; but when the tale
That roving trappers brought from Kiowa
Was told to him, he seemed as one who saw
A ghost, and could but stare on it, they said:
Until one day he mounted horse and fled
Into the North, a devil-ridden man.
"I've got to go and find him if I can,"
Was all he said for days before he left.

And what of Hugh? So long of love bereft,
So long sustained and driven by his hate,
A touch of ruth now made him desolate.
No longer eager to avenge the wrong,
With not enough of pity to be strong
And just enough of love to choke and sting,
A gray old hulk amid the surge of Spring
He floundered on a lee-shore of the heart.

But when the boat was ready for the start
Up the long watery stairway to the Horn,
Hugh joined the party. And the year was shorn
Of blooming girlhood as they forged amain
Into the North; the late green-mantled plain
Grew sallow; and the ruthless golden shower
Of Summer wrought in lust upon the flower

That withered in the endless martyrdom
To seed. The scarlet quickened on the plum
About the Heart's mouth when they came
   thereto;
Among the Mandans grapes were turning blue,
And they were purple at the Yellowstone.
A frosted scrub-oak, standing out alone
Upon a barren bluff top, gazing far
Above the crossing at the Powder's bar,
Was spattered with the blood of Summer slain.
So it was Autumn in the world again,
And all those months of toil had yielded nought
To Hugh. (How often is the seeker sought
By what he seeks—a blind, heart-breaking game!)
For always had the answer been the same
From roving trapper and at trading post:
Aye, one who seemed to stare upon a ghost
And followed willy-nilly where it led,
Had gone that way in search of Hugh, they said—
A haggard, blue-eyed, yellow-headed chap.

And often had the old man thought, 'Mayhap
He'll be at Henry's Post and we shall meet;
And to forgive and to forget were sweet:
'Tis for its nurse that Vengeance whets the tooth!
And oh the golden time of Jamie's youth,
That it should darken for a graybeard's whim!'
So Hugh had brooded, till there came on him
The pity of a slow rain after drouth.

But at the crossing of the Rosebud's mouth
A shadow fell upon his growing dream.
A band of Henry's traders, bound down stream,
Who paused to traffic in the latest word—
Down-river news for matters seen and heard
In higher waters—had not met the lad,
Not yet encountered anyone who had.

Alas, the journey back to yesterwhiles!
How tangled are the trails! The stubborn miles,
How wearily they stretch! And if one win
The long way back in search of what has been,
Shall he find aught that is not strange and new?

Thus wrought the melancholy news in Hugh,
As he turned back with those who brought the news;
For more and more he dreaded now to lose
What doubtful seeking rendered doubly dear.
And in the time when keen winds stripped the year
He came with those to where the Poplar joins
The greater river. There Assinoboines,
Rich from the Summer's hunting, had come down
And flung along the flat their ragged town,
That traders might bring goods and winter there.

So leave the heartsick graybeard. Otherwhere
The final curtain rises on the play.
'Tis dead of Winter now. For day on day
The blizzard wind has thundered, sweeping wide
From Mississippi to the Great Divide
Out of the North beyond Saskatchewan.
Brief evening glimmers like an inverse dawn
After a long white night. The tempest dies;
The snow-haze lifts. Now let the curtain rise
Upon Milk River valley, and reveal
The stars like broken glass on frosted steel
Above the Piegan lodges, huddled deep
In snowdrifts, like a freezing flock of sheep.
A crystal weight the dread cold crushes down
And no one moves about the little town
That seems to grovel as a thing that fears.

But see! a lodge-flap swings; a squaw appears,
Hunched with the sudden cold. Her footsteps creak
Shrill in the hush. She stares upon the bleak,
White skyline for a moment, then goes in.

We follow her, push back the flap of skin,
Enter the lodge, inhale the smoke-tanged air
And blink upon the little faggot-flare
That blossoms in the center of the room.
Unsteady shadows haunt the outer gloom
Wherein the walls are guessed at. Upward, far,
The smoke-vent now and then reveals a star
As in a well. The ancient squaw, a-stoop,
Her face light-stricken, stirs a pot of soup
That simmers with a pleasant smell and sound.
A gnarled old man, cross-legged upon the ground,
Sits brooding near. He feeds the flame with sticks;
It brightens. Lo, a leaden crucifix
Upon the wall! These heathen eyes, though dim,
Have seen the white man's God and cling to Him,
Lest on the sunset trail slow feet should err.

But look again. From yonder bed of fur
Beside the wall a white man strives to rise.
He lifts his head, with yearning sightless eyes
Gropes for the light. A mass of golden hair
Falls round the face that sickness and despair
Somehow make old, albeit he is young.
His weak voice, stumbling to the mongrel tongue
Of traders, flings a question to the squaw:
"You saw no Black Robe? Tell me what you saw!"
And she, brief-spoken as her race, replies:
"Heaped snow—sharp stars—a kiote on the rise."

The blind youth huddles moaning in the furs.
The firewood spits and pops, the boiled pot purrs
And sputters. On this little isle of sound
The sea of winter silence presses round—
One feels it like a menace.

                      Now the crone
Dips out a cup of soup, and having blown
Upon it, takes it to the sick man there

And bids him eat. With wild, unseeing stare
He turns upon her: "Why are they so long?
I can not eat! I've done a mighty wrong;
It chokes me! Oh no, no, I must not die
Until the Black Robe comes!" His feeble cry
Sinks to a whisper. "Tell me, did they go—
Your kinsmen?"

    "They went south before the snow."
"And will they tell the Black Robe?"

       "They will tell."

The crackling of the faggots for a spell
Seems very loud. Again the sick man moans
And, struggling with the weakness in his bones,
Would gain his feet, but can not. "Go again,
And tell me that you see the bulks of men
Dim in the distance there."

      The squaw obeys;
Returns anon to crouch beside the blaze,
Numb-fingered and a-shudder from the night.
The vacant eyes that hunger for the light
Are turned upon her: "Tell me what you saw!
Or maybe snowshoes sounded up the draw.
Quick, tell me what you saw and heard out there!"
"Heaped snow—sharp stars—big stillness
  everywhere."

One clutching at thin ice with numbing grip
Cries while he hopes; but when his fingers slip,
He takes the final plunge without a sound.
So sinks the youth now, hopeless. All around
The winter silence presses in; the walls
Grow vague and vanish in the gloom that crawls
Close to the failing fire.

     The Piegans sleep.
Night hovers midway down the morning steep.
The sick man drowses. Nervously he starts
And listens; hears no sound except his heart's
And that weird murmur brooding stillness makes.

But stealthily upon the quiet breaks—
Vague as the coursing of the hearer's blood—
A muffled, rhythmic beating, thud on thud,
That, growing nearer, deepens to a crunch.
So, hungry for the distance, snowshoes munch
The crusted leagues of Winter, stride by stride.
A camp-dog barks; the hollow world outside
Brims with the running howl of many curs.

Now wide-awake, half risen in the furs,
The youth can hear low voices and the creak
Of snowshoes near the lodge. His thin, wild shriek
Startles the old folk from their slumberings:
"He comes! The Black Robe!"
                              Now the door-flap swings,
And briefly one who splutters Piegan, bars
The way, then enters. Now the patch of stars
Is darkened with a greater bulk that bends
Beneath the lintel. "Peace be with you, friends!
And peace with him herein who suffers pain!"
So speaks the second comer of the twain—
A white man by his voice. And he who lies
Beside the wall, with empty, groping eyes
Turned to the speaker: "There can be no peace
For me, good Father, till this gnawing cease—
The gnawing of a great wrong I have done."

The big man leans above the youth: "My son—"
(Grown husky with the word, the deep voice breaks,
And for a little spell the whole man shakes
As with the clinging cold) "—have faith and hope!
'Tis often nearest dawn when most we grope.
Does not the Good Book say, Who seek shall find?"

"But, Father, I am broken now and blind,
And I have sought, and I have lost the way."
To which the stranger: "What would Jesus say?
Hark! In the silence of the heart 'tis said—
By their own weakness are the feeble sped;

The humblest feet are surest for the goal;
The blind shall see the City of the Soul.
Lay down your burden at His feet to-night."

Now while the fire, replenished, bathes in light
The young face scrawled with suffering and care,
Flinging ironic glories on the hair
And glinting on dull eyes that once flashed blue,
The sick one tells the story of old Hugh
To him whose face, averted from the glow,
Still lurks in gloom. The winds of battle blow
Once more along the steep. Again one sees
The rescue from the fury of the Rees,
The graybeard's fondness for the gay lad; then
The westward march with Major Henry's men
With all that happened there upon the Grand.

"And so we hit the trail of Henry's band,"
The youth continues; "for we feared to die:
And dread of shame was ready with the lie
We carried to our comrades. Hugh was dead
And buried there beside the Grand, we said.
Could any doubt that what we said was true?
They even praised our courage! But I knew!
The nights were hell because I heard his cries
And saw the crows a-pecking at his eyes,
The kiotes tearing at him. O my God!
I tried and tried to think him under sod;
But every time I slept it was the same.
And then one night—I lay awake—he came!
I say he came—I know I hadn't slept!
Amid a light like rainy dawn, he crept
Out of the dark upon his hands and knees.
The wound he got that day among the Rees
Was like red fire. A snarl of bloody hair
Hung round the eyes that had a pleading stare,
And down the ruined face and gory beard
Big tear-drops rolled. He went as he appeared,
Trailing a fog of light that died away.

And I grew old before I saw the day.
O Father, I had paid too much for breath!
The Devil traffics in the fear of death,
And may God pity anyone who buys
What I have bought with treachery and lies—
This rat-like gnawing in my breast!

                                        "I knew
I couldn't rest until I buried Hugh;
And so I told the Major I would go
To Atkinson with letters, ere the snow
Had choked the trails. Jules wouldn't come along;
He didn't seem to realize the wrong;
He called me foolish, couldn't understand.
I rode alone—not south, but to the Grand.
Daylong my horse beat thunder from the sod,
Accusing me; and all my prayers to God
Seemed flung in vain at bolted gates of brass.
And in the night the wind among the grass
Hissed endlessly the story of my shame.

"I do not know how long I rode: I came
Upon the Grand at last, and found the place,
And it was empty. Not a sign or trace
Was left to show what end had come to Hugh.
And oh that grave! It gaped upon the blue,
A death-wound pleading dumbly for the slain.
I filled it up and fled across the plain,
And somehow came to Atkinson at last.
And there I heard the living Hugh had passed
Along the river northward in the Fall!
O Father, he had found the strength to crawl
That long, heart-breaking distance back to life,
Though Jules had taken blanket, steel and knife,
And I, his trusted comrade, had his gun!

"They said I'd better stay at Atkinson,
Because old Hugh was surely hunting me,
White-hot to kill. I did not want to flee

Or hide from him. I even wished to die,
If so this aching cancer of a lie
Might be torn out forever. So I went,
As eager as the homesick homeward bent,
In search of him and peace.
                                        But I was cursed.
For even when his stolen rifle burst
And spewed upon me this eternal night,
I might not die as any other might;
But God so willed that friendly Piegans came
To spare me yet a little unto shame.
O Father, is there any hope for me?"

"Great hope indeed, my son!" so huskily
The other answers. "I recall a case
Like yours—no matter what the time and place—
'Twas somewhat like the story that you tell;
Each seeking and each sought, and both in hell;
But in the tale I mind, they met at last."

The youth sits up, white-faced and breathing fast:
"They met, you say? What happened? Quick!
      Oh quick!"

"The old man found the dear lad blind and sick
And both forgave—'twas easy to forgive—
For oh we have so short a time to live—'
Whereat the youth: "Who's here? The Black Robe's gone!
Whose voice is this?"

                                The gray of winter dawn
Now creeping round the door-flap, lights the place
And shows thin fingers groping for a face
Deep-scarred and hoary with the frost of years
Whereover runs a new springtide of tears.

"O Jamie, Jamie, Jamie—I am Hugh!
There was no Black Robe yonder—Will I do?"

The Song

of Jed Smith

For Sigurd's Wife *Maxine*

The valley was beginning to forget
The dead June day, but southward clearly yet
The peaks remembered.

I

                      Trappers by their gear,
With four trail-weary horses grazing near,
Two men were sitting, leaning on their packs.
Still as the shadows purpling at their backs,
They gazed upon the smoke that rose between,
Thin-fingered. From the canyon of the Green,
Low-toned but mighty in the solitude,
A never-never moaning voiced the mood
Some reminiscent waking dream had cast
Upon them. Henry's Fork that hurried past
Ran full of distant voices, muffled mirths.
A meadowlark, in gratitude for Earth's
Lush shielding, with a mounting bar that broke,
Enriched the quiet.

              And the elder spoke,
Stirring the embers into sudden fire:
"Well, that's a queer one! Was I nodding, Squire?
I swear I saw it!"

             Lifted in surprise,
With thick, black beard belying boyish eyes,
A flame-bright face regarded him. "What's queer?
I wasn't looking, Art; just sitting here
And seeing things myself."

               The failing flare,
Across the elder's grizzling beard and hair,

Revealed the mien of one whom many snows
Would leave green-hearted. "No, I didn't doze,"
He said; "and I was thinking nothing more
Than what to do about that saddle sore
The old mare's got; and it was only now,
All still and empty. Suddenly, somehow,
I tell you, it was eighteen twenty-five!
This valley came alive with fires, alive
With men and horses! Rings on glowing rings
Of old-time faces sang as liquor sings
After a drouth; and laughter shook the night
Where someone, full of meat and getting tight,
Spun lies the way Black Harris used to do.
Then it was now again, and only you
Were sitting yonder."

      "Art, you make me dry,"
The other said, "you make me want to cry
Into my whiskers. Thirteen years away!
That's better than a million miles, I'd say,
Without a horse, and all the country strange!"
Now while they mused there came an eerie
    change
Upon the world. From where the day lay dead
The ghost thereof in streamered glory fled
Across the sky, transfiguring the scene.
Amazed amidst the other-worldly green
That glowed along the flat, as though a shout
Had startled them, they stood and stared about,
Searching the muted landscape of a dream.

There *was* a cry. The bluffs along the stream
Awoke to mock it. On a low rise there
To westward, vivid in the radiant air,
They saw a horseman coming at a jog,
A pack-mule plodding after, and a dog
That rushed ahead now, halted, muzzle high,
And howled.

The light-blown bubble of the sky,
As with a final strain of splendor, broke.
The peaks forgot; and like a purple smoke
Night settled in the valley.

                Looming dim,
The rider neared the shadows greeting him
Beside the embers, while the outer gloam
Neighed welcome. "Hitch and make yourself at
      home,"
One bantered: "Hang your hat upon a star,
The house is yours. Whatever else you are,
It's not a horsethief by the nag you've got!"

The stranger laughed. "If supper's in the pot,
The nag has served me well enough," he said,
Dismounting. To the growling dog, "Down, Jed,
Old-timer! They've invited us to eat."

Now hand found hand. "Except for beaver meat,
And jerked at that, you'll find the cupboard bare,"
One said; "and, short of Taos, we'll have to share
Our drinking yonder with the bird and beast."

"I never make this valley but to feast,
And water won't keep ghosts away," replied
The stranger, fumbling at the horse's side
And stripping off the saddle. "Anyhow,
The hump and haunches of a yearling cow
Have fagged the old mule here. If that won't do
To make a good old-fashioned rendezvous,
I've come from Taos—the jug's full!"

                   Bluffs to heights
Hurrahed with glee, and in the outer night's
Star-bearing silence troubled for a space
The somber summits.

              "Come and show your face!"

The elder cried. "I'll swear, if I don't know
That voice—though he went wolfing years ago—
My name's not Black!" He seized the other's hand
And drew him to the embers. Stirred and fanned,
They reddened till the fed twigs took the spark,
And, cut upon the onyx of the dark,
A shaven face shone—sensitive and lean,
With eyes that narrowed less upon the seen
Than with some inward gazing. Leather-skinned,
It was, hard-bitten by the worldly wind;
But more the weather of a mind that seeks
In solitude had etched upon the cheeks
A cryptic story.

       "Holy smoke!" cried Black;
"Look, Squire! Unless it be a spook come back
To haunt us, old Bob Evans hasn't fed
The kiotes yet!"

       A joyful warwhoop fled
Along the valley. Eager voices, blent
In greeting, quickened into merriment.
The dog barked gaily and the horses neighed.
Impatiently the laden pack-mule brayed
Sardonic comment.

II

             Now the jug went round
The glowing circle, while the fat hump browned
And sputtered, dripping. Night, immense and still,
With stars keen-whetted by the mountain chill,
Dreamed deep around the trio, snugly housed
In living light. From where the horses browsed,
The blowing loudened in a lapse of speech.
A wolf howled, and the farthest empty reach
Of vastness mourned, as though God dreamed in vain
And 'wakened, filling with a wail of pain
The nightmare void of uncreated good.

The dog whined, bristling.

               Cozy in the wood,
The tongued flame purred content. Again the bright,
Brief moment vanquished the appalling night
Of timelessness.

            The youngest laughed, and said:
"Is this a wake? If one of us is dead,
Just count me in among the other two
And cut a chunk of meat!"

             "A rendezvous,"
Mused Evans, with a far, unfocussed gaze
Upon the other. "Ghosts of better days,
With laughters never to be laughed again,
And singing from the lips of lusty men
Gone dust forever! Listen! Can you hear?
I ought to know. I've heard them year by year
With every June!"

"Well, let them drink with us!"
The youngest chuckled. "Bob, you loony cuss,
I like you; but you always lived too far
Above the belly where the doin's are
That make men happy. This child ought to know!"
With jug presented, "Spooks of long ago,"
He mocked, "here's looking at you! Bye and bye
We'll be as dead as you! But now, we're dry,
And men at that! Tough luck to be a ghost!
Old-timers, skoal! Here's how!"

                              He drank the toast
And snorted.

               "Squire," laughed Black, "as Milton wrote,
The place for education—mind, I quote!—
The place for education in your head
Ain't there at all! According to old Jed,
Bob's half a poet! Why, that look of his
Can see what never was and really is
Because it isn't—if you get the way
My stick floats! It was on the Snake one day.
Alone and far from home, we sat there glum,
Remembering how many friends had come
To crow meat since we crossed the Great Divide;
And, after long, he looked at me and sighed
And said: 'I wish I knew where Evans went.
The man's a scholar. Only accident
Has made him less than poet.' Who but he
Was like to know?"

                     The Squire laughed merrily.
"Be easy with me, Art, until I'm tight.
You'll be surprised, come later in the night,
And nothing in the jug, how clear and quick
I get the drift of any crazy stick
A man can float! Why, Boys, I used to grieve

And weep for men too sober to believe
Black Harris when he squared away to lie,
And me well educated! Hope to die,
I could believe him better when he lied!
You mind his forest that was putrified?
Him peeking through that underbrush of hair
And whiskers at the whole gang howling there,
Short-breatht with meat and three sheets in the wind,
Save only Jed, the man that never sinned,
Stone-sober, looking down his long, thin nose!
You mind? Old Harris and the 'Rapahoes
Hell-bent for hair—and plenty!—had a race.
The old man won, and came upon a place
Where trees soared taller than a tree can soar,
And then some taller! And the queerest roar
Ran high among them—pines in stormy weather—
And like a million castanets together,
The green leaves clicked, though not a zephyr stirred.
And in the branches, on his holy word,
Queer birds, like none this side of Jordan, sang.
'And would ye think,' says he, 'the whole shebang
Was putrified!' 'It must've made a smell
To kill a polecat!' someone says. 'Aw, hell!'
Says he, disgusted; 'How could such rock be?
The place was putrified, and every tree
Was agate and the birds was agate too!
That roar up yonder was a wind that blew
Before God's whiskers sprouted—yes, and man
Was only mud yet. When the place began
To putrify, the thing came on so strong
And fast, it caught that wind and every song
Them birds was singing at the time, you see!'"
The far-flung, many-echoed gaiety
Became a chuckle. "Harris never wed—
For long. 'The truth and me is hitched,' he said;
'I'll lick the man that tries to put asunder!'
Bob, who poured lightning in that jug, I wonder?

I half believe him! Pretty soon I will!
Let's have the meat now, Shakespeare!"

                                    Silent still,
The other brooded with an empty stare.

"I mind," Black said. "We sat right over there
Beyond the horses. . . . What a bunch of men!
This valley will not see their like again
Until the evening and the dawn swap places
And days run backwards! I can see their faces
While Harris took his time to be exact
And dealt with each new whopper like a fact
That 'twould have been dishonest to forget!
Fitzpatrick, Ashley, Jackson, and Sublette!
Jim Bridger, newly bearded, half a boy
For all his doings! Hanna and McCoy,
La Plant, Reubasco, Harry Rogers, Ranne,
Luzano, Gobel, Gaither—man by man,
I see them laughing yonder, soon to die,
The men who followed Smith—and you and I
Return alone, Bob, out of thirty-two!
Jim Beckwourth, filled with tales of derring-do,
And hero of them all, to let him say,
Guffawing at the very sober way
That Harris had of flirting with his wife!
And old Jed Smith—!"

                                    He drew his hunting knife,
And absently awhile he whetted it
Upon his boot. Then, having carved a spit
For each, he sliced the succulently rare
Fat meat and passed it.

                                    "I can see him there—
The way his wide-set eyes turned slits of blue
When he was thinking; how his brown hair grew
In waves that broke like surf about his ears.

I knew him longest in his hardest years,
And seldom did he fail to keep it trim
And shave—as though he felt God's eye on him,
No matter what the hardship or the weather.
I see the way his straight brows grew together,
And knitted at a run of scurvy talk;
The nose that made you think about a hawk;
The lean six feet of man-stuff, shouldered wide,
Too busy with a dream that grew inside
For laughter. He was seeing all the white
Map westward as a page on which to write,
For men to read, the story of a land
Still lying empty as the Maker's hand
Before creation. From the Great Salt Lake,
Between the Colorado and the Snake,
From burning sand to high Sierra snow,
He wrote it. Some day men will read and
     know
The man he was. It does me good to boast
I knew him longest."

              "But I loved him most,"
Said Evans, rousing with a weary air
Of slow return, his heart still otherwhere,
Remote and lonely; and the low voice took,
As from the gentle burning of his look,
A hint of smoke. "I loved him most; and yet
I failed him."

            "Aw, drink hearty and forget!
You're far too sober, Bob!" the younger said,
Passing the jug. "Too bad about old Jed!
'Twas seven years ago we heard somewhere
A parcel of Comanches got his hair
Away down yonder on the Cimarrone."

"He died alone," the other said; "alone;
And where his bones are lying no one knows.

The fed wolves sang his dirge, and feasting crows
Were his ironic mourners."

     "Let him rest
In peace," the younger bantered. "At the best,
Dying's a one-man job! Hurrah for now!
He must have gone to heaven anyhow;
I never saw him having any fun!
That's right, old-timer! Have another one,
And send the O-be-joyful 'round the ring!
We'll drink to good old Jed gone angeling—
But he won't like it if he's looking down!
He'll cock that one scarred brow of his, and frown
Without a word; the scar he got that day
He argued with the bear up Big Horn way
And came off best—a bit the worse for wear—
Some ribs caved in. But when you saw the bear,
Heart-stabbed and belly-slashed—well, you began
To know that Jedediah was a man
For all his Bible-reading, parson ways!
And so here's to you, 'Diah! Happy days!
Meat in the pot and sign in every stream!"

He drank, and passed the jug.

     "And some great dream
To lead, and may the strange trail never end!"
The elder added.

    "And no faithless friend,"
The other murmured, drinking.

III

Now the deep,
Tremendous silence of the night asleep
Possessed the little tent of light again.
A-haunch, head cocked, the dog surveyed the men.
One drooping ear for doubt and one pricked ear
For hope, he watched the red meat disappear
In alien mouths, commenting with a hurt,
Ingratiating whimper, and alert
To catch the morsels casually thrown.
The muted thunder of the canyon's moan,
The Fork's low murmur, the contented sound
Of grazing in the dark, made more profound
The sense of silence heavy on the world.

The feasting done, the dog lay down and curled
A tawny back against the ember light,
The slender, wolfish muzzle snuggled tight
Against a shaggy buttock. One eye slept,
And one, upon the verge of slumber, kept
Uneasy vigil lest the feast resume.

Now slowly shrank the circle of the gloom,
Chill-edged. Aroused from indolent content,
The Squire arose, yawned lazily, and went
Into the dark. An ax's *clink* and *chock*
Broke brittle on the everlasting rock
Of stillness, bluff and peak with flying shard
Resounding. Stooping low and breathing hard,
He reappeared at length; and having shed
His burden on the fire, sat down and said:
"That turn deserves another! Pass the juice!"

He took a swig, then made his girdle loose,
Sighed with eupeptic pleasure, being sated,
And chuckled: "Boys, I'm going educated,
The way you don't get cross-eyed with a book!
Just now out yonder when I stopped to look
Around and listen, all at once there came
A funny sort of feeling. 'Twas the same
Old 'Diah used to give me years ago:
A feel of something you could never know,
Except that it was big and still and dim
And had a secret. If you stuck with him,
Most any minute everything would change.
The mountains and the valleys would be strange,
And there'd be rivers like no common river—
A sort of evening-before-Christmas shiver
All up the backbone, like a youngster knows.

It was the time we wintered with the Crows
In 'twenty three and 'four, when I first felt
That way about him. Snow began to melt
Along Wind River. Winter wasn't done,
But in the soft late February sun
You heard the gulches roar. A big chinook
Was booming when we saddled up and took
The trail that led across the Great Divide.
And who had ever seen the other side
The Shining Mountains? Indians, and such
Assorted varmints, didn't matter much,
We being humans! It was waiting yet,
Since God A'mighty finished it, to get
The first real, honest seeing from our eyes!

We followed up Sweetwater. No surprise!
A frozen crick, and everything was old
About it. But we felt it getting cold
And colder as we rode along the flat,
Smooth valley westward, and we knew from that
How we were climbing. Mountains fell away—

Just sort of melted. Then the second day,
The word came down the line: 'We're in the Pass!'

But there was only common yellow grass
And sagebrush on a prairie, rolling wide
From common hills along the nearer side
To far peaks looking like a broken saw
Ahead and to the right across the draw
Along Sweetwater. Antelope were there
Beside the crick—like critters anywhere
In anybody's meadow. Empty skies
Were straight ahead above a little rise
Notched crooked like a hind-sight out of true.
There wasn't any shoutingful to-do
About it! But I galloped to the head
To have a look, and rode beside old Jed.
He didn't see me, didn't say a word
To anybody. Pretty soon he spurred
A ways ahead, reined suddenly, and stopped.
From where we sat and looked, the prairie dropped
Along the easy shoulder of a hill
Into a left-hand valley. Things got still
And kind of strange. The others, gathered round,
Quit talking, and there wasn't any sound
Except a bridle made it. Then it came—
That funny sort of feeling, just the same
I had out there a little while ago—
A feel of something you could never know,
But it was something big and still and dim
That wouldn't tell. It seemed to come from him
Just looking down the Sandy towards the Green
That had been waiting yonder to be seen
A million winters and a million springs
And summers! 'Twas the other side of things—
Another world!

        You gather I was wet
Behind the ears; a pea-green youngster yet,

Just turning seventeen, and wild as hell.
That river had been doing pretty well
Without us; and, as any beaver knows,
A river is a ditch where water flows,
And any side's the other where you ain't!
I mind I wondered was he going to faint,
Or was he praying, maybe, when he bent
His head. I caught him at it in his tent
That winter once! But even if he was,
It seemed the sort of thing a fellow does
With just that sort of feeling . . . Well, they say
We live to learn."

       "It's just the other way,"
Said Evans dryly. "Mostly we forget;
But 'Diah never did."

       "A few nips yet,
And you'll be even wiser than your 'teens,"
The elder chaffed. "I know what Evans means.
There's something sort of thrilling that you know
Until you learn so much that isn't so,
There's no room left inside for what you knew!
I felt a bit like that about him, too,
And me an oldster. He was hard and grim
And man a-plenty; but he had in him
What made you feel the world had just begun!
Queer how we call him old! Just thirty one—
Or maybe two—the year that he went under!"
"He had the humble wisdom that is wonder,"
Mused Evans.

       "Well, let's have another smile,"
The younger countered, laughing. "Afterwhile,
The way I'm getting wise and wiser still,
I'll bawl for milk! Where was I? Oh—the hill
Above the Promised Land—and 'Diah praying!
Leastwise, he didn't faint. Then he was saying
How that was where the water ran both ways,

And over there beyond the valley haze
The great Pacific rolled! I heard it roar—
Almost!

It was a couple years before
That funny feeling left me. All the way
Down Little Sandy and the Big next day,
It grew and grew till it was everywhere,
And not a 'tarnal thing but sagebrush there,
And sage hens! Every time a covey broke
From cover—like a gun-shot lacking smoke—
It hit me like a signal something queer
Around us had been waiting for, to hear
And happen—if you gather what I mean!
And when we struck the valley of the Green,
'Twas beaver heaven!

Listen to it moan
Out yonder, like a dog without a bone!
Lend me your bosom, Arthur, if I weep!
I'd give a leg to see the slow Spring creep
Among the willows by the stream once more
The way it did that year of 'twenty four
And everything brand new! Them days are dead,
And gone forever—followed after Jed
To heaven! Mind to quit and settle down,
And keep a cow and wife somewheres near
        town
And be a Christian!"

"Well, why don't you quit?"
The elder chuckled.

"Had a spell of it,"
The other answered. "Wasn't nothing there!
And even if it just ain't anywhere,
Out this way it's got room enough to be!
Get humpbacked looking for a living! Me?
What for? To have a funeral, and all

The neighbors happy for a chance to bawl
About how much they always thought of you—
And mostly didn't! Such a nice grave too,
With posies on it! When I rise to shine,
I'll take the belly of a wolf for mine,
The same as Jed!"

                 Rejecting with disgust
This wrinkled desert of our mortal dust,
He tapped the fount of phantom youth again,
And raised a war-whoop. Blackfeet fighting men
Flung far defiance, then no longer prowled
The silence. And the dog leaped up and growled
Through bared teeth ready for the throat of harm;
Then, looking sheepish at the false alarm,
Lay down and grumbled. Hard to understand—
These men were!

                  "Better raise this child by hand
On water, Bob?" Black anxiously inquired.
And, with the high disdain of the inspired,
Expansively the younger gestured. "Art,"
He said, "you old pig-eater[1] in your heart,
And hardly yet half wintered at the best,
You've got no tender feelings in your breast,
No tender feelings! Telling me to quit!
Been drinking, eh? And just can't carry it
The way a mountain man like me can do!

Well, to resume, as I was telling you
Before you up and started telling me,
If things could be the way they used to be
Them days with Jed, I'd give a leg or so
And run barefooted! Art, I'd even throw

1. *Mangeur de lard,* signifying a greenhorn in the mountains—one
who had not yet wintered in the country and lived on wild game.

Your mare in, and the sore upon her back,
If boot was needed!"

                     "Why the boot?" said Black;
"You've traded all your legs off."

                         Mournfully
The other shook his head. "And you and me
Old pardners, Arthur! Now, as like as not,
We'll never see them days. And all for what?
A bag of bones!"

                 He wiped away a tear
That wasn't there—but might have been, to hear
The timbre of a changing mood that came
Into his voice. "'Twill never be the same
Till Jed comes riding that cayuse of his.
I wonder where in hell this Heaven is!
A long ways off, and nary blade of grass
Nor water hole beyond the narrow pass
Across the Shining Mountains; and the snow
Horse-deep and getting deeper, maybe! . . . No,
Not even Jed could make it back alive!

'Twas just the same the year of 'twenty five.
A summer and a winter and a spring—
And still the other side of everything
Was Christmas for the shaver that was me.
Who knew what might be hanging on the tree?
If God and 'Diah did, they wouldn't tell!
We had been trapping westward quite a spell,
With sign a-plenty. Beaver packs had put
The whole caboodle, mostly, flat a-foot,
And made the Crow cayuses cuss our luck,
If horses can. And then one day we struck
A river in the mountains flowing west
Among thick brush—so thick, we climbed a crest
To have a look at where the canyon led.

And, holy smoke! The way I thought of Jed
Had turned into a picture! Still and dim
And big with secrets! No horizon rim,
So far it was! You looked and looked, and then
From where you ended you began again
And looked a little farther. Bye and bye,
The country—just—got—thinner—and was sky,
Blue hazy, and the secrets hiding yet.
You fumbled round inside of you to get
A word, and drew a lungful fit to shout it;
But there was nothing you could do about it,
Except to look. Nohow, it couldn't be—
And there it was! You rubbed your eyes to see
Queer ranges to the southward, built of smoke,
As if you'd just been dreaming them, and 'woke
And couldn't quite remember. Pretty soon
You'd wake all over, and 'twould be the moon
That you were in, or anywhere not made
To pasture human critters. Half afraid,
You looked a little nearer there below;
And there was snow that couldn't have been snow
Around a sea of ice that wasn't ice,
Or was it? When you blinked and saw it twice,
'Twas more like water foaming at the lip,
And yet it didn't move. A crazy ship
That was an island had been sailing there
Forever—hadn't gotten anywhere,
And wouldn't. Wasn't any use in motion—
No place to go to!

                        Could it be the ocean—
The Great Pacific? All at once, it could!
You held your breath—it *was*! From where we stood
And saw the sky and water mix, almost
You got a glimmer of the China coast,
Low-lying! Just look hard enough, you might!

Well, there was plenty arguing that night!
It was, it wasn't, and it was again

All over. But the was-ers won it when
We made the lake shore, even though it wasn't!
If lakes taste salty and the ocean doesn't,
Why 'twasn't ocean! Try it on your tongue!
The very sand was salt! The water stung,
Lead-heavy with it!

                  Nothing seemed to care,
Excepting us and sea-gulls screaming there
Above us that it *was* the ocean too!
The rest just went on knowing what it knew
And being what it was, and didn't take
No interest in whether 'twas a lake
Or ocean, neither one! It sort of slept,
The way it had a million years, and kept
A secret you were half-way scared to know!
Seems funny! Only thirteen years ago,
And nary secret hiding anywhere!
You're only here again when you get there,
And then it's there again when you get here!
A bag of tricks!

                  He went away the year
Of 'twenty six. We rendezvoused in June,
And then he left. Some river of the moon
That he went chasing after, seemed to me—
The wonderfulest river that could be,
Because there wasn't any where it flowed
Off westward there and made an easy road
To the Pacific—which we knew by then
The salt lake wasn't. Saw him once again,
On Bear Lake, when you three came back half dead
From California, Bob. And what a Jed!
A buzzard wouldn't eat him! Made me glad
He didn't take me!

                  Now I wish he had—
I wish he had."

IV

"You're getting sober, Squire,"
Black said, and, sighing, stirred the dreamy fire
Until the dozing logs awoke in flame;
"Or else—which seems to figure out the same—
It's only getting human makes you sad.
You wish he'd taken you, and if he had
You'd know, with inside knowledge of the thing,
How buzzards soar, what makes the kiotes sing
Such mournful ditties, what the crows regret
With all their cawing. Maybe so—and yet,
Who ever saw a wolf with bowels of brass
Or bird with iron gizzard? Let it pass,—
Or, rather, let the jug!"

He rose and scanned
The stars awhile, eyes shaded with a hand
Against the groundling dazzle. "Night is new,"
He yawned; "and there's another nip or two
Left in the Dipper yonder, tipped to pour
Whatever angels drink. There's even more
Left in the jug. So here's regards to those
Bone-scattered where the Colorado flows
Among the damned Mojaves, and beside
The Umpqua where it bitters with the tide
Among the marshes—Jedediah's men!
And may they rise and follow him again
The other side of Jordan! Drink the toast,
Bob Evans!"

"—Even to the cosmic coast,"
The other said, and drank, "where all stars cease,

And seas of silence answer with their peace
The petulant impertinence of life!"

"And here's to when I keep that cow and wife,"
The youngest bantered, "—just as like to be!"

"But when," said Black, "we started for the sea
That summer, Bob, not one of seventeen,
I'll warrant, cared to know what life might mean.
To ask that question is a kind of dying.
What matters to a bird a-wing is flying;
What matters to a proper thirst is drinking.
A tree would wither if it got to thinking
Of what the summers and the winters meant!
There was a place to go to, and we went,
High-hearted with a hunger for the new.
The fifty mules and horses felt so too
For all their heavy packs. The brutes are wise
Beyond us, Bob. They can't philosophize
And get the world all tangled in their skulls.
At Utah Lake the mourning of the gulls
Had seemed the last of what was known and dear;
And when we struck the bend of the Sevier
To follow eastward where it cuts the range,
The canyon seemed the doorway to a strange
New world. The ridden critters and the led,
Strung out along the river after Jed,
Pricked ears and listened. Nothing but the whine
Of saddle leather down the toiling line,
Until some cayuse at the canyon's mouth
Neighed; and the empty valley, rising south,
Was full of horses answering the din
Of horses where no horse had ever been
Forever. And the mules brayed, walking faster.
What need of any pasture, greener, vaster,
To pay them for the eager joy of striving?
If living is a matter of arriving,
Why not just start to rotting at the first,

And save the trouble? Thirty died of thirst
And hunger yonder in the desert hells.
Ask God why, when you see Him. If He tells,
You'll hardly be the wiser. Furthermore,
I'll gamble that He won't.

                The valley bore
Southeastward, and there wasn't any game.
Our packs got lighter fast. So when we
      came
To where a small creek entered from the west,
We followed up along it to a crest,
And saw what fed our hunger for the new
But couldn't satisfy it; for it grew
Beyond the feeding. Where a high plateau
Stretched southwardly, a million years or so
Of rain had hewed a great unearthly town
With colored walls and towers that looked down
On winding streets not meant for men to tread.
You half believed an angel race, long dead,
Had built with airy, everlasting stuff
They quarried from the sunrise in the rough
And spent their lives in fashioning, and died
Before the world got old.

                The other side
Of ranges west and south, a dim world ran
Uphill to where eternity began
And time died of monotony at last.
And when that rim of nothing had been
      passed,
Why surely 'twould be California then;
But would we all be long-gray-whiskered men
Before we got there? No one seemed to mind.
God only knew what wonders we might find,
And how He must be weary with His knowing!
No curiosity at all for going
And nothing new to look for anywhere!

Into the clutter of the foothills there
Below, we wound a weary way, and crossed
The valley of a stream we called the Lost—
And lost it was, if ever it had run!
The bare slopes focussed the September sun
Upon the blistering rubble. Round the few
And shallow holes that kept a brackish brew
The fifty critters pawed and fought and screamed,
Blaming each other; and the echoes seemed
To ape the clatter of the hoofs like laughter.

It wasn't any better soon thereafter
Among the tumbled hills gone bald with age
Millenniums ago. The scrubby sage
Was making out to live on memory yet,
But even it had started to forget
What rain was like. Our grub was getting low.
For days we hadn't even seen a crow
To shoot at; but we didn't seem to care,
For we were learning our first lesson there
In what thirst means; and we were walking now.
My roan was pulling like a stubborn cow
Not halter-broke, when, with a shivering slump,
He just sat down awhile upon his rump,
And then keeled over with a tired sigh.
So there was meat we couldn't stop to dry,
For need of water. Little we could eat!
It takes a proper tongue to relish meat,
And not some dead cow's crammed into your mouth!
The balance of the day we hurried south—
A creeping hurry; anyway, as fast
As we could snake the nags along. At last
'Twas night again, and not a blade of grass
Or drop of water. Seemed 'twould never pass.
You dozed, dog-weary, and the dreams you had
Of creeks and springs were just about as bad
As even waking was. A horse would dream—
Of wading, maybe, in a mountain stream—

And neigh himself and all the herd awake;
And there'd be panic neighing, and a break
That ended, in a flounder, with the ropes.
It surely didn't much revive our hopes,
When morning came, to find three others dead.

I thought 'twas kind of funny about Jed
That day. You see, I didn't know him then.
And there was peevish talk among the men
Of how he didn't seem to realize.
There'd be a freshness in his face and eyes
When he came striding from a spell of straying
Off trail somewhere. I know now he'd been praying.
You'd swear he knew a spring along the way,
And kept it for himself! He'd smile and say
We shouldn't doubt, but we should trust and know
There'd soon be water.

                    And, by God, 'twas so—
'Twas so that afternoon!

                    We struck a draw—
The toughest going mortal ever saw—
A dazzling oven, crooked as a snake
And full of boulders. But it seemed to make
Downhill and southward, so we shuffled in.
To think that such a flood had ever been
As rolled those boulders, almost drove you crazy!
I mind that everything was dizzy-hazy
When someone said that Louis Pombert's mare
Was down. What of it? No one seemed to care
Enough to save the saddle.

                    Bye and bye—
Hours later or the batting of an eye
Was all the same, for time just sort of stood
And wobbled like a drunk—a mule sawed wood
Down yonder. Then they all began to saw,

And horses whinnied up along the draw,
If they could manage better than a nicker.
The weakest of them whimpered, stepping quicker,
And when they stumbled, staggered up again
With bloody noses. Presently the men
Were hollering down yonder like a flock
Of addled crows. Another jut of rock,
And there it was—a world of running water!”

“Aw, Arthur, make it just a little hotter!”
The younger pleaded; “just a little drier,
So I can raise a thirst!”

                    “You grieve me, Squire,”
The elder said; “I thought you’d had enough
To be half human! Water’s holy stuff,
Direct from heaven! When the grass gets green,
That’s worship! Bob here gathers what I mean,
Eh Bob? You mind that day; you had the most
Tough water-scrapes with Jed!”

                         “The Holy Ghost,
The dove descending,” Evans mused aloud.

The youngest laughed. “This go-to-meeting crowd
Should rise and let the kiotes lead a hymn!”

“We might be singing with the seraphim,”
Said Evans.

                “Well, there was a church that night,”
Continued Black. “We circled in the light
Of one big fire; and when we had our fill
Of horse meat, which we didn’t have to kill,
Because too much is deadly as the lack,
He got his Bible with the leather back
(That looked a worn-out boot-top, like as not,)
And fuzzy pages bulging with a lot

Of heavy reading. For a little while
He thumbed it, silent. No one cracked a smile
Or said a word, and there were godless cusses,
Whose on'ry fracases and rakehell musses
Had sent them where they were, among the others.
Like pious little boys who mind their mothers,
They sat there waiting, mannerly and prim.
And if they hadn't, there was that in him
To whale the devil out of any man.
I've seen him do it.

             Well, when he began
To read out loud, 'twas not as parsons do.
He said it just like anything that's true—
'The sun is shining,' maybe, or 'the birds
Are singing.' Something got into the words
That made them seem they couldn't be the same
That you remembered. For the Lord became
A gentle shepherd, real as Mr. Jones,
And he had made us rest our weary bones
In that green pasture by the waters there!
Laugh, Squire, and show your raising—I don't care;
I like to see you happy, bless your heart!"

"I didn't mean to spoil your story, Art,"
Explained the other. "Who am I to doubt it?
But what would those dead horses say about it,
Back yonder in the swelter?"

                  "Well, you see,"
Black countered; "that was lack of piety.
I guess they hadn't gone to Sunday schools!"

"You reckon all of your Missouri mules
Were Holy Rollers? Not a one was dead!"
The younger chuckled.

               "Just the same," Black said,
"It wasn't funny and nobody snickered.

It scared me when a happy cayuse nickered,
The place had got so still when he was through.
And then he didn't preach, as parsons do;
He just sat silent, for the Book had said it.
What else was there to do when he had read it,
But let it soak like rain? And if he prayed,
You couldn't hear him do it.

          There we stayed
A couple days to let the critters eat,
And jerk the leavings of the pony meat
Against the chance there'd not be game enough.
For we were down to traps and trading stuff—
Red bolted goods and blankets, fufaraws,
Like beads and looking glasses, for the squaws,
And knives and arrow metal for the men,
So be it we should ever see again
A human face but ours.

          And then we took
Down river—just a wider sort of brook,
But 'Diah named it for the President,
The Adams River. No fine compliment,
We came to think; but not so bad at first.
'Twas still a blessing to be shut of thirst
So long as you remembered how it felt;
But when you saw the packs of jerked horse melt
To nothing, and the red-walled canyon wound,
Until you only rambled round and round
From nowhere, nowhere—not a thing to eat,
But now and then a bite of rabbit meat—
You wondered was there treason in the name!

About to kill a pony when we came
At last to where a little creek broke through
And made a valley. There a garden grew
With tasseled corn and punkin vines between!
You stood and stared, misdoubting you had seen,
But there it flickered, sure as you were born—

The yellow-bellied crawlers and the corn
Late earing in the green!

          We yelled hurrah
For good old garden sass. And then we saw
A little Indian woman running there,
All wibble-wobble and a mess of hair,
Hell-bent for cover—and she needed some,
Not having any more on than your thumb,
But one important patch of rabbit fur!
And, like the devils that she thought we were,
Young hellions cheered her, laughing: 'Go it, Gert!'
And 'Hump it, Maggie!' But the words of dirt
They flung at her stopped quick enough, when Jed
Came riding, looking like a thunder-head
With lightning in it just about to break.
'Respect a woman for your mothers' sake,'
He said, 'or take a licking!'

          Well, he took
Some knives and looking glasses, and the Book
For luck, no doubt, and vanished up the creek
Among the brush. It seemed a weary week
We held the herd till he appeared again,
About a dozen lousy-looking men
And women at his heels, with not a thing
Upon them but an apron and a string
Of rabbit hide. If that was human mud,
'Twas badly baked and furnished with the blood
Of rabbits. 'Diah treated them the same
As folks.

          And while we feasted, others came,
Like cringing cur-dogs that apologize
For being curs, to see with their own eyes
The four-legged spirit-critters and the gods
That rode them; for we made our thunder-rods
Spout cloud and lightning. Anyone would say

We celebrated Independence Day,
If there had been a barrel of lemonade!
For pretty soon nobody was afraid.
The women brought us cakes of pounded seeds
Messed up with cane, and strutted in the beads
They got from us. God-awful homely lasses
And scrawny grandmas peeped at looking glasses
And giggled. Men went running to their wives,
Like tickled boys, to show their shiny knives;
And wee, pot-bellied rascals dared to sneak
Just near enough to give our shirts a tweak
And show their little sisters who was scared!

It kind of looked as if the Lord prepared
A table for us!

         Well, the thought of it
Still fed us—anyway a little bit—
Down river. Anything might happen next,
The way it had, to fit the Bible text
He read that night. And, soon enough, it did!

The canyon narrowed, towering, and hid
The friendly day. A scary twilight fell.
As from the dusky bottom of a well,
We saw the blood-red rim-rock swimming high
Along the jaggéd knife-scar of a sky,
And dim stars mocked the middle afternoon!
We thought at first the place would broaden soon.
The few stars only brightened in the cut,
And, like a heavy snow of kettle-smut,
Night smothered down.

           'Twas long before we slept.
Serenely in the diary he kept,
Jed scribbled by the fire without a word.
Unless a horse complained, you almost heard
Your thinker thinking. All the while the stream

Was like a sick man moaning in a dream
Of dying.

       We were plodding on our way
When first the rim-rock reddened with the day,
But up until the noon 'twas early morning.
It seemed that any minute, without warning,
The worst might happen. Maybe one more bend,
And there we'd come upon the canyon's end,
Some cave without a bottom, yawning black.

There was no hope of 'Diah turning back;
He wouldn't listen to the gloomy talk
Among the men. 'Yea, even though I walk
The valley of the shadow,' said the Book.
His face and eyes would have that freshened look,
When he'd been riding out of sight a spell,
As though he knew some good he wouldn't tell,
Just wanting to surprise us pretty soon.
The whole late evening that was afternoon
We plodded till the few trapped stars were bright.

The weakest of the horses went that night
To fill the pots. It didn't really matter
Which one we ate—unless the leather's fatter
In either of your boot-soles than the other.
The driftwood made a sickly sort of smother;
And while we watched the kettles in despair,
Jed asked old Rogers would he offer prayer;
And Harry would—but offer's not the word.
He took no chances that Jehovah heard,
Or interrupted with an old man's 'Eh?'—
The off ear cupped the hard-of-hearing way—
'Wha's that?' He bellered. 'Twas a fine oration!

Well, when we'd feasted on our transportation
And felt a little better, 'Diah read
Some verses from the Scripture where it said

The whole earth was the Lord's. A sneaking
    doubt
If that was anything to brag about
Grew big enough to dare you to deny it.
Then all at once the canyon got so quiet
The water didn't moan, the soggy wood
Quit wheezing. And the whole round earth was
    good,
The fulness of it—and it made you glad!
No, Squire, 'twas not the bellyful we had
Of leather soup. 'Twas far above the belt.
'Twas like old summers and the way you felt
A barefoot shaver—white clouds going over,
And apple trees and bumblebees and clover,
And warm dust feeling pleasant to your toes,
And wheat fields flowing and the corn in rows,
And stars to twinkle when the day was done,
While people rested, certain of the sun,
All safe and cozy!

            Words are mighty queer!
They try to tell you something, and you hear
Some old familiar rattle in your head
That isn't any nearer what they said
Than mules and mothers; but you think you know!
Then maybe, all at once, *they're simply so—*
And always were! They sprout like seeds and thrive!
If all the words men gargle came alive,
I wonder what would happen! 'Diah's sprouted.

And then he talked. Seemed foolish that we doubted,
So near the Spanish settlements might be.
And soon we ought to make the Siskadee
Old Ashley tried that spring to navigate,
But, getting nearer to St. Peter's gate
Than to the ocean, had to give it up.
And California! That was where the cup
Ran over!

Well, we stumbled down that maze
And counted horses dying. —Also days
Since we had fed in yonder Indian heaven;
And number five was slow, but six and seven
Hung on so long they almost never quit.
The earth was needing axle grease a bit
Before we finished counting nine and ten!
Do you remember, Bob, what happened then,
And what we saw?"

                "The day broke overhead.
The endless canyon ended," Evans said;
And there was desert to the setting sun!"

"I guess we'd better have another one,"
Remarked the Squire, "before we undertake it!
Unless we do, I doubt if we can make it.
We've et an awful lot of harness leather!"

"The skin-rack horses nickered all together,"
The elder mused, as though he didn't hear;
"And up the haunted canyon in the rear
It seemed the dead ones answered. Starving mules
Heehawed, as if to jeer the two-legged fools
Who brought them there. We didn't make a sound;
Just looked across that country, hellward bound,
And filled our eyes with nothing, flabbergasted.
You made up stories while the canyon lasted,
But yonder was the story God had made.
It looked like even Harry hadn't prayed
Quite loud enough!

               Jed didn't seem to care.
Spoke quietly of California there,
And pointed to the white sun blazing down
Beyond that waste! There'd be an Indian town
Along the river we were coming to,

And there we'd rest. He spoke as if he knew,
And made hope certain as geography.
Why, come to think about it, you could see
The corn fields waving by the riverside!

Well, two more horses and a mule had died,
With others on the ragged edge of dying,
Before the Adams finally quit trying
To justify the wearing of the name.
And in the dragging afternoon we came
Upon the Colorado.

       Greasewood throve
Along the valley, and a stunted grove,
That huddled yonder by the river, made
The only promise of a little shade
In all that bowl of glare. Two yapping dogs
Came bristling; and we saw a house of logs
Squat-roofed with 'dobe in among the trees.
A nursing woman, hobbled at the knees
With frightened young ones, peeked at us and ran
Behind the cabin. Then an oldish man,
We took to be a Piute, filled the door.
If anything surprised him any more,
You didn't guess it by the look he had.
Was he amused or just a little sad
Or maybe both? The quiet, puckered way
He looked us over didn't seem to say
A thing for sure, except he didn't scare.
And when we sign-talked at him, asking where
The village was, he waved his hand around
The whole horizon, pointed to the ground,
Then tapped his chest and chuckled pleasantly.
'Twas Crusoe with the desert for a sea,
And he had built an island with his labors
Where there were only well-behaving neighbors—
The sun and moon and stars!

              We feasted there
On garden stuff, and Jed paid more than fair
With trading goods. The mules and horses had
Their fodder, and the little ones were glad
With bells to tinkle, while their mother chose,
With happy little noises in her nose,
The gaudiest of cloth. But all the while
Old Crusoe smiled a pleasant little smile,
Observing with that quiet squint of his,
As though he sort of knew what really is
And always was and shall be evermore,
So that he wasn't bothered looking for
What isn't, wasn't, and will never be."

"Another sort of turnip, seems to me,"
The younger said; "just dumb and half asleep."

"And maybe," Evans added, "rooted deep
In what I call the other side of things,
Where running feet are stilled and eager wings
Are folded, and all seeking is forsaken,
Because there's nothing to be overtaken
In such a peace of being."

               "Well," said Black,
"I've often kind of hankered to go back
And see if I could gather what he knew.
It must have worked on all the others too;
Nobody joked about him. All the way
Down river, when the going, day by day,
Grew harder, with the done-out critters dying,
I thought and thought of how you go on trying
And suffering to find, until you're dead,
When maybe all the while it's in your head
The way it was in his, if you could see.

But when we came to where the Siskadee
Broke out into a valley fat with tillage,

And saw the populous Mojave village
Among the trees, he didn't seem so wise;
For hadn't we arrived at Paradise,
However we had paid in Purgatory?
You're always wanting life to be a story
With some pat end to show what it's about.
Somebody's torn a lot of pages out,
If that's the case! You never quite arrive.

Well, it was mighty good to be alive
Among those gardens yellowing with plenty,
And see our critters, dwindled now to twenty,
Contented in the meadows, making fat.

Could we have read, just one year after that,
The bloody page that would be written, when
With eighteen more, Jed came that way again
From Bear Lake, fought with devils, met as friends,
And fled with eight! I guess the story ends
When anybody turns an empty page—
An ending without end. You'd swear old age
Had found them when they reached our camp beside
The Stanislaus, and told how ten had died
Bare-handed in the treacherous attack.

'Twas lucky, Bob, you didn't try it back
With Jed and Silas Gobel, your old friend
Of desert days. But what a rousing end
Old Silas made before his page went blank!
The eight had crossed, and from the western bank
They saw it happen on the further shore—
The whole tribe swarming inward, with the roar
A cloudburst makes, upon the helpless ten—
Men drowning quickly in a flood of men,
Save where old Silas, hardened at the forge,
And looming like a boulder in a gorge
Bankfull with freshet, labored with a limb
Of mesquite for a hammer at his grim

Last smithing job. If God has set the Right
To prove its mettle in the losing fight
Forever, 'twas another score for God!
Not all the horses Silas ever shod
Outweighed the burden of the spears that bowed
Those blacksmith shoulders; and the milling crowd
Rained arrows till the club no longer whirled
About him. When a howling eddy swirled
And slowly closed at last above his head,
The watchers yonder knew that he was dead
As any coward. Then the running fight—
Few rifles, many bows. And all that night
They fled until the desert blazed with day.

But that was still a good long year away,
And we were happy, being richly fed
With more than garden stuff. For Rumor said,
And 'twas the clearer being vague, somewhere
Far off beyond the jealous desert there
The ripened days of all the wide world went
To make a lazy country of content
Where it was always Spring—a dream of Spain,
Come true forever! Not a wish was vain
In yonder climate kind to all desires!
Hard-bitten youngsters, squatting 'round the fires,
Half tight already with imagined wine,
Discussed it, till you felt the soft sun shine
On drowsy vineyards; heard beneath the stars
The castanets, the strumming of guitars,
The singing senoritas! There it lay,
And only Boston clippers knew the way—
Ten thousand miles down under 'round the Horn!
To think that we, of all our breed, were born
To see it first by land!

           Our luck was good.
You, Squire, would say Jehovah understood
We'd lack for horses, and provided some.

Well, anyway, some Indians had come
Across the desert with a stolen herd
Of Spanish Mission horses! Seemed absurd
Such scurvy rascals hailed from Paradise!
What scenes had filled their slinking, sleepy eyes
That didn't seem to care! Reubasco knew
Their Spanish lingo; and the wonder grew
The bigger for the little that they told.
'Twas late October, and the moon was old,
As we were, when we hit Mojave town.
'Twas young again, as we were, going down
The trail of sunset to the Promised Land,
Our first camp out. We scooped the seeping sand
Along a wash to make a little spring,
And didn't sleep much, for the whinnying
Of horses, waiting for the hole to fill
Again and yet again.

        The blue-black chill
Wore out and whitened to a withering blaze;
And after that we didn't count the days
Or nights of endless plodding, nor the sleeps
That ran to tangled dreams of water seeps
Clawed out in vain. We only counted drinks.
Dry washes running into empty sinks,
Bankfull with starlight, mocked us when we tramped
From sunset to the white of dawn, and camped,
Holed up in sand against the blistering light,
Until the purple chill came. Mind the night
We found the lake, Bob?"

          "I can see it yet,"
The other mused. "The moon about to set;
The ghostly yucca trees around us there,
Transfigured by some ultimate despair
That filled the stillness of the solitude;
The slimy cabbage cactus that I chewed;
The rasping, hollow sound of critters panting;

The sudden clearing, and the low moon slanting—
The low moon slanting on a lake! Dry salt!
A crazy notion 'twas the yuccas' fault
Seemed true, and yet I couldn't make it track!"

"Well, even though it wasn't wet," said Black,
"It made the going easy. Anyway,
    You mind it ended with the break of day
    And how that cool spring sparkled in the sun
    There where the river that forgot to run
    Spread wide to fill the lake that wasn't wet!
'Twas something queer you wouldn't soon forget—
The spooky yucca trees that seemed to know
The end of us and didn't care—the low
Half moon across the salt! But Oh, the night
We saw the full moon glitter on the white
Peaks yonder!"

                "I remember," Evans said.
"The journey's end! And yet, the day when Jed
    Went hunting water for us seems to glow
    The brighter now. With burning sand for snow,
    The blizzard booming down the empty river,
    And 'Diah calmly praying to the Giver
Of all good things, before he left us there
Among the huddled horses! Could a prayer
Make headway yonder where the sun at noon
Ran through the howling smother like a moon
Gone mad with thirst? It seemed a cruel joke.
Yet there was something in the way he spoke
Of finding water—something in his face—"

"As if," Black said; "it might be any place
    For anybody who could look that way!"

"And I believed the balance of the day,"
    The other said. "But when the storm was through
    At sundown, and the still cold moonlight grew

Around us, I forgot enough to doubt him.
The moon denied it knew a thing about him;
The silence said he wasn't coming back."

"It didn't know old 'Diah!" chuckled Black.
"Remember how he made us kneel to thank
The Giver of Good Things before we drank,
There where the river, hiding underground,
Came up as if to have a look around
And made a pool before it hid again?"

"The very horses kneeling with the men,
Eye-deep in joy! The moon near full and sinking,
And morning coming on while we were drinking,"
The other mused. "I like that picture better
Than yours, Art."

        "Well, that water did seem wetter
Somehow," Black said, "than any other brew
This side of where the Squire is going to,
Unless he mends his ways. He won't, alas!
But what about the day we topped the pass
And stopped to stare—with all of that behind us,
And only missing horses to remind us
Of what it cost? The Promised Land at last!
And when we climbed the mountain, saw the vast
Land lazing there with nothing left to seek
Forevermore—the high, thin silver streak
That must have been the ocean—scattered droves
In happy meadows—greenery of groves
And vineyards! Wasn't that a better sight?
And yonder, drowsing in the golden light,
The Mission of the Padres! Journey's end!"

He thought awhile in silence. "No, my friend,"
He said, "you win. The men and horses kneeling
Around the pool, the white of morning stealing—
It's better. Queer the way a man remembers!"

He gazed awhile upon the dreaming embers,
With silent laughter mounting to his eyes.
"And so," he chuckled, "there was Paradise,
And all us lanky, ragamuffin scamps
A-faunching! What does 'Diah do? He camps
To shave his whiskers!"

V

Chin to chest and nodding,
The younger, startled by the elder's prodding,
Jerked back to waking with a hostile glare
That softened to a silly grin. "We're there!
Wake up!" Black shouted.

Leaving with a leap
Some rabbit heaven of his broken sleep,
The dog lit snarling, shook himself to clear
The addled world, sat up and pricked an ear
To point the question of an injured whine.

"Where?" growled the Squire.

"The Land of Corn and Wine!"
Laughed Black; "and dark-eyed senoritas too!
But here you squat, you lazy loafer you,
And snooze!"

"Why, Arthur, I was only thinking
Of what's the use in talking about drinking,"
Explained the other. "Why not have a drink?
You just don't realize how hard I think
When I think hard. To prove I was awake,
I saw you all go swimming in that lake
To scrub yourselves. I'll bet you needed peeling!
And I know all about the fellow stealing
The horses at the come-to-glory meeting!
Well then, we're there! So how about some
        eating
And maybe just a gurgle? Woo! I'm froze!"

He shook himself, dog-fashion, as he 'rose,
And, yawning, vanished creekward. Snapping brush
Upon the treble of the harplike hush
Plucked desultory discord. He returned
Arm-laden; nursed the embers till they burned,
Blue-stemming into blossom round the logs;
Then moved the slashed hump nearer, with the dog's
High, whimpering approval. "There!" said he,
Now pass the moonshine, so as I can see
Your senoritas!"

Edging nearer while
The trio drank, the fourth, with tongueful smile
Of ready gratitude, and both intense
Ears focussed on the simmering succulence,
Leaned hard as though his patience were a chain.
The humblest, prayerful whimpers proving vain,
He snapped the leash, and, with explosive barks,
Made pointed, if not impious, remarks
Upon the doings of Divinity.
Whereat the youngest of the Trinity
Gave heed at last and opened heaven's gate.

The Fork's returning chatter, as they ate,
Made bold against the canyon's phasic moaning—
Time troubling and Eternity intoning
The never and forever that are one.
It grew upon them when the feast was done;
And each sat silent, suddenly alone,
Negotiating, as the dog the bone,
Some all but meatless leaving of the past.

A warwhoop shattering the spell at last,
The lonely little worlds flowed back together.
"I sure do like this California weather,"
The Squire remarked, with hands before the flame.
"I'll need more educating, just the same,
Before I see your senoritas clear.

If yonder's any pleasanter than here,
I wonder why you beggars didn't stay."

"Well, take the donkey and his bait of hay."
Black stroked his whiskers sagely. "Round the mill
He chases fodder that is yonder still
Regardless of how far or fast he goes.
And why? Because a proper donkey knows
If he just chases hard enough, he'll beat it.
And maybe, when he's too done out to eat it,
He'll come to fodder heaven if he's pious!"

"Jed told me once God gave us goals to try us,"
Said Evans; "living was a kind of weaning.
We needed sugar-teats of worldly meaning
For some unworldly purpose of the soul.
It seemed the goal was learning that a goal
Is just the fleeing shadow that you cast,
Until pursuing teaches you at last
What mattered was the light upon your back."

"Just like old 'Diah," meditated Black,
Scarce breaking silence—"just the way he'd be
When there was no one left but him and me
And we'd be camping, maybe on the Snake.
All still, but for the sound the fire would make,
And then you'd notice he was looking through you,
That way he had. You wondered if he knew you.
You wondered if you knew him, even more.
And then he'd tell what he'd been groping for
Down deep inside of him; and while he told,
Like dreaming, something in him very old
And gentle made you happy to be sad.
For suddenly some precious thing you had
Or thought you had or would have, wasn't so;
And yet the very hurt of letting go
Was like a joy—till he turned young again.
Just thirty-eight now, counting nine from then!

You somehow just can't think of him as dead."
"I saw him very old once," Evans said,
"And gentle. Often when I sleep I see
Again, between a white-hot sky and me,
That look of glowing rain—like joy and tears.
I've lived upon it all these lonely years
From dream to dream. And when I see and wake,
It seems awhile that nothing is opaque
Or commonplace, but luminously new
With what it was that I saw coming through
His face that morning."

                  "Must have been the time,"
Said Black, "the whole caboodle tried to climb
The high Sierras for the shorter way
Back yonder to the Lake from San Jose,
The spring of 'twenty-seven. Peak on peak,
And not a pass! A snow-hell of a week,
With horses balking in the drifts to drowse
And stiffen, standing. Camped on Stanislaus
To wait and wonder how could he and you
And Silas ever live to make it through.
And then the desert yonder! Seemed to be
He never wanted much to talk to me
About it."

       "Yes," said Evans, "it was hell;
But there was heaven too. I want to tell
About the lives we lived, the deaths we died
Together. I've been telling it inside
These empty years alone.

                  You mind, no doubt,
'Twas late in May before we started out
With seven horses—one a little mare
Grown wise in leading packers; and a pair
Of rangy mules. 'Twas comical the way
Their long necks turtled under loads of hay

Lashed shell-wise! Seemed to know it, and revolted!
Remember how the camp cheered when they bolted,
Expressing what they thought of diamond hitching—
All bray and flying hay and corkscrew pitching,
Until they had enough of it to follow?

They grazed that night along a flowery hollow
Beside a mountain brook where grass was
    growing
Lush green and tender. Next night it was snowing
Upon our camp between high canyon walls;
And like a momentary hush that falls
Before disaster, long drawn out with fear,
All night it snowed. The sky began to clear
At sunrise, and the dazzling heights ahead
Repeated what that falling silence said,
In cruel splendor.

        Shallowing by noon,
With sloping walls, the canyon promised soon
To reach a pass. The tall pines crowding round
Appeared to know, and watched without a sound
Our sweating labor in the biting glare.
Loud in the knife-edge thinning of the air,
The panting of the horses only made
The muffled stillness deeper. And the grade
Grew steeper with the waning of the day.

The pack mules had no quarrel with the hay
That night.

       We scooped a clearing in the snow,
And, dozing with their muzzles to the glow
Of logs, the mules and horses made a wall
About us. 'Twasn't any time at all
Until the peaks were floating in the dawn;
And when they glittered, we were wading on,
Knee-deep.

The stunted pines were getting scant,
And more and more the critters balked to pant
With straining nostrils, when we made a bend,
And there ahead we saw the canyon's end—
A sheer-walled pocket!

          Nothing else to do
But double back to where a gulch broke through
The southward wall. And 'twas a stubborn climb
Before we scrambled out by camping time
Upon a granite shoulder. In the last
Of day, we stared dumbfounded at a vast
White mountain maze beyond. The west went out,
And blue night came upon us like the doubt
That kept us silent. It was crystal cold.
A single squatting pine, that looked as old
And weathered as the granite, gave us fire.
God only knows what maniac desire
To live and flourish, packed into a cone,
Could bite into that rock and fight alone
For centuries! Gnarled, flattened like a flame
By ancient winds, it fought until we came
To burn it!"

      "Surely does sound queer enough,"
Remarked the elder, "for the sort of stuff
To make religion out of. 'Diah could,
I'll warrant!"

      "When you think of all it stood,"
Said Evans, "seems a crazy waste of trouble
For one warm night! He'd say we're seeing double,
The striving of the Spirit being one.
Well, howsoever, ours had just begun
Next morning; for the shoulder fell abrupt,
A swimmy distance, into valleys cupped
With crowding peaks that glittered blinding white.
We got the outfit down at fall of night

By angling back beneath the granite crest
To where the mountain steepened south and west
Into a canyon winding south and east.
Halfway to noon it seemed that neither beast
Nor man could make it to the canyon bed,
Unless a goat might. Bothered even Jed,
Until we came to where a rubble slide
Broke through the wall-rim. Looked like suicide
To try it; but the only chance was there.

It took some coaxing for the little mare
To lead the way. She pawed and shook her head,
All nervous like a woman—but she led,
Stiff-kneed and mincing, sliding on her tail.
A-slither in the wallow of her trail,
The horses followed; but the mules agreed
That horses were an idiotic breed,
And wouldn't budge without a lot of booting.
Well, finally they started out a-scooting
To get it over—and they did it brown!

Old 'Diah and the mare were half way down
And right side up, when, mortally insulted
And fighting mad, those critters catapulted
Against the rear. The rest of it was snow,
A little blizzard roaring there below
With heads and tails and hoofs and squealing in it!
It got to be a mighty long half minute
Before it ended, and the canyon thundered
Far off and dim.

       We held our breaths and wondered
How Jed was faring in the drift that churned
With scrambled horses."

       "That was where you learned
It's hard to kill a Christian, I'll allow,"
The younger bantered.

"Didn't, anyhow,"
Said Evans. "Saw him crawling out as cool
As ever—maybe more so! Not a mule
Or horse had suffered in the cushioned tumble.
The mules appeared to be a bit more
    humble,
I noticed, when we skidded down the slope
And finished rolling.

    There's a lift of hope
In climbing, even though you want to drop,
Done out. A sort of something at the top,
That isn't there, is going to be good.
But yonder was the top, and there we stood
Spilled out along the bottom of a pit.
No way at all to climb back out of it,
If we'd a mind to. Had to go ahead;
And into what new trap that canyon led,
God knew; and He was keeping deathly still.
We mended cinches broken in the spill,
Re-set the packs, and waded on again.
The going wasn't very bad, and when
The pines had gathered round us, and the blue
Of twilight came, the canyon widened
    through
The cliffside of the valley we had seen
At sunrise.

    If you gather what I mean,
It sent a scary tickle up your spine
To feel that snow-hushed solitude of pine
Grow darker, darker, darker, listening.
And 'twasn't any sort of mortal thing,
That made you almost glad to be afraid.
It came on me that night, while 'Diah prayed,
That maybe 'twas the Everlasting Word—
That silence; maybe something really heard—
Not Sunday-like, but really!

All the same,
We wakened just as there when morning came.
The forest listened on without a sound.
If God had heard, He hadn't got around
To doing anything about it yet!
But all day long you couldn't quite forget
That feeling, even when the snow had deepened.
And when the way grew rockier and steepened
Against the coming mountain, it was night.
There wasn't any blueing of the light;
It grayed and blackened: for the sky began
To cloud near evening. And a moaning ran
Across the forest-roof that dusted snow
Upon us in the quiet far below—
That waiting quiet.

　　　　　Wakened in the black
Of dying fires, we heard the timber crack
And groan above a steady ocean roar,
And spindrift scudded on the forest floor
In gusty whirls.

　　　　　Thank God it wasn't snowing,
With hell a-popping and a high wind blowing,
When finally the long night faded gray.
We couldn't wait. There wasn't any hay;
There wasn't anything a horse could eat,
Except the precious bags of Spanish wheat
They carried—not enough, for all we knew,
To see them to the Salt Lake rendezvous
Across a land no man had ever seen.

We struck an open where we had to lean
Against the howling suck along a draw
That led us upward. Straight ahead we saw,
By snatches in the blur of stinging sight,
The jumble of the mountains, height on height
At hide-and-seek behind the broken flurries.

But we were willing that tomorrow's worries
Should worry us tomorrow; for the hollow
Was drifting bad. The string began to wallow
Breast-deep by middle day, and we were walking,
If that is what you'd call it!

                No use talking,
We couldn't make it—and we couldn't camp.
And so we headed up a rocky ramp
Along the mountain's flank upon our right;
And if we had a stiffer wind to fight,
It swept the footing cleaner.

                Leaning low
And stopping often for the nags to blow,
We climbed. The hollow sagged away from under
And was a canyon flowing snow and thunder
A dizzy drop beneath a granite ledge
We snaked along. The precipice's edge
Was coming nearer. Pausing often, pinned
Between a wall of rock and wall of wind,
We fought to breathe.

              There was a jutting bend
To leftward, where the ledge appeared to end
In nothing. I can see old 'Diah there,
Lean inward, leading. I can see the mare
Step daintily and study with her nose
The doubtful trail; three horses after those,
And looming in the middle of the string
The bulk of Gobel. I was following
The willing mule and tugging at the other,
A balky brute.

           Above the howling smother
I heard old Silas, saw the stumbling critter
He guided, scramble in the pebble-skitter
To get its footing. Then it disappeared,
Hoofs up. The next two horses screamed and reared

Against the mule ahead of me. I guess
'Twas over in the telling time or less;
And there was Silas staring back at me,
Mouth open. There was nothing else to see
But empty ledge, between, and flying snow!

The steady thunder loudened there below
A rumbling moment. Then I heard Jed shout
My name, and saw him yonder, leaning out
Around the mare. He seemed about to fall.
And when he saw me huddled by the wall,
His frosted face went empty of the wild,
Scared look it had. It gentled, and he smiled—
By God, he smiled, and I can see him now!

We made it round the jutting point somehow,
And there the ledge swung rightward, and we saw
The rim-rock of a deep confluent draw
Slope up to where the mountain sagged away
To eastward. We were yonder when the day
Began to muddy; and the black night found us
Well down the ridge, a forest roaring round us,
The snow scooped back to make a cozy wall
About our fire.

       We hardly talked at all
Before we swooned into a heavy sleep.
I wakened when the cold began to creep
About the smouldering logs. The wind was dead.
I listened. Not a whisper overhead.
It seemed that something knew that nothing mattered.
I hurried with the fire until it chattered
About the logs. I didn't want to hear
A meaning in the stillness. 'Twasn't fear
Of storm and cold and hunger or of dying.
'Twas doubt if there was any use in trying:
And maybe if the Everlasting Word
Was silence, and its meaning could be heard,
'Twould be there was no meaning anywhere.

I watched the others sleeping soundly there
And wondered at the peace on 'Diah's face,
The look of nothing being out of place
In his world. Not a doubt what he would say!
And Gobel getting ready for the day
That was to come, with all that might of his
Unloosened; wise the way a good horse is
Without a thought of wisdom! So I slept.

The cold was not so bad when morning crept
Among the pines. The edge of it was round,
Or sort of cotton-muffled, like the sound
Of pot and skillet and the pawing feet
Of horses begging us for more to eat
Than we dared give them now.

                  The sun seemed warm,
By midday, in a sky swept clean with storm;
And yet the ghostly summer that we felt
Upon our backs was not enough to melt
The crusted drifts we broke and sweated in.

A valley forest had begun to thin
Against a granite rise, and we could see,
Ahead and to the right, southeastwardly,
A maze of summits floating in the blue—
The same it seemed that we were coming to
Before we lost the critters. To the left,
Northeastward, where a barren hollow cleft
The rise ahead, there soared a single peak
Above a roll of shoulders.

                'Twas a week
That morning since the critters tasted grass,
And it was time we happened on a pass
Into a greener land. Their lightened packs
Grew heavier—ribs getting to be racks
To hang a skin. The water that they got

Had been the snow we melted in a pot
For days now. It was time to find a way.

We topped the drifted hollow when the day
Had faded out. With only brush to burn,
And scant at that, one kept the fire by turn,
And it was mine to wait the morning in,
That stretched-out moment when the wall is thin
Between two worlds, a brief forevermore
When time sleeps. Even Gobel didn't snore;
The mule and horses seemed to hold their breaths
While some hushed answer, more profound than
     death's,
Made starry splendor out of old despair.
Then suddenly the peaks were all a-stare
To southward, and the morning star was dim
Above the whitening horizon rim
Without a mountain! We had found a pass!

By noon the snow gave out, and there was grass
Along a canyon brook. Before the night
Came on us, we had made it from the height
Of January into blooming May
Among the foothills.

         So we camped a day
Beside a brook. The critters grazed their fill,
And, groaning with pot bellies, greedy still,
Rolled in the lush green, hungry to the hide.
Deer stole upon us, gazing Eden-eyed
And wondering, to make a pleasant feast;
And we gave thanks that night.

           A day northeast
We came upon a little river's mouth
And camped there by a lake. Then, riding south
And east by north, we kept the water's edge,
Where many a wild-fowl paradise of sedge,

All clack and chatter with another Spring's
Old promises, exploded into wings
That dimmed the sun.

           A range of barren breaks
Loomed eastward in the twilight from the lake's
Far border. We could hardly wait to see
What sort of country it was going to be
The other side. Before the morning broke
We wakened when the ducks and geese awoke
To gossip drowsily along the shore;
And wingéd thunders, roar on dimming roar,
Fled in the starlight when I filled the pot.
The venison was fried, the coffee hot
Before the starry dusk began to pale;
And yonder at the summit of the trail
Across the breaks, we faced the level might
Of sunrise.

          Vaguer for the blast of light,
Appalling vastness lay before us there.
No echo answered when the little mare
Neighed nervously. We cupped our eyes to gaze.
Deep in the blear transparency of haze,
Yet strangely near, the saw-tooth silhouette
Of mountains, black with day behind them yet,
Began abruptly to the east and ran
To southward. Far beyond where they began
We made out others, patterned on the high
Horizon in the very stuff of sky,
Where earth and air were getting to be one.

We headed downward straight into the sun;
For yonder, if our reckoning was true,
A crow would fly to find the rendezvous
Beyond the world's end. Little likelihood,
You'd say, that any ever did or could,
To look across that country.

                     All forenoon
It almost seemed we'd pass those mountains soon,
So near they blackened, featureless and flat
Against the dazzling sky. But after that,
They turned to light and shadow, floating there
As little solid as the oily air
They drifted on to keep the pace we made.
'Twas blazing hot, without a wisp of shade
To spell the horses in; and far ahead
As where it seemed the floating mountains fled,
It looked as if they'd had to wait for water.

But when it seemed the slanting day grew hotter,
Before the sudden coming of the cool,
We found a seeping spring that fed a pool
Sun-steeping in a gully, where the land
Of broken ridges gave away to sand
And sage-brush flats. We called it ''Diah's luck.'

And while the critters drank, blue shadow struck
The world, as though you saw the sudden chill.
It slowly climbed the mountains there, until
The tallest blued and deepened into black.
A thin new moon was floating on its back
Above the peaks behind us, gleaming white
With day yet, when already it was night
Upon the desert."

               Evans stirred the fire
And gazed upon it. "Bob," remarked the Squire,
"We'll need a better drink before we start
Across that country. How about it, Art?
Bob's gully stew ain't fit for man or beast!"
They passed the jug around.

                     "'Twas wet, at least,"
Said Evans. "And I doubt, if we had known
What that would mean when yonder moon had grown

And waned and darkened and was new again,
If even 'Diah would have ventured then
With all that lake and paradise of snow
Behind us. Now I'm glad we didn't know,
Because of what I saw when I had learned."

"It sounds like something Arthur's donkey earned,"
The younger chuckled.
                    "But he ground the grain,"
Laughed Black; "he turned the mill!"

                            "The mill of pain,"
Mused Evans, poring on the flame that curled
About the logs. As though a tortured world
Moaned in its sleep, the distant canyon took
The vast night silence from the nearby brook
And filled it.

           "Well, you'd swear that while we slept,"
Continued Evans, "yonder range had crept
Upon us to surprise us when we woke,
So sharply near it loomed when morning broke
Behind it. And before that day was done,
It towered in the slanting of the sun,
A bare black wall behind us to the right.

Jed thought we'd better travel on that night,
For straight ahead as far as we could see
To where the shimmering immensity
Dissolved in air and hazy mountains rose
From nothing, there was nothing short of
      those
That promised water. Was it even there?

We stopped to rest the horses when the air
Was chilling blue again, where they could eat
Their fill of greasewood, for it saved the wheat
And, being green, was wetter than the grain.

The black wall yonder loosened from the plain
And hovered with the growing of the gloom.
'Twas queer the way it seemed a trap of doom
About to close, just pausing to remind us
The water of the world was left behind us
Forever with the disappointed hope
When we had crossed that broken northern slope,
Searching the bone-dry gullies for a hole.
And when the day-old slice of moon, a bowl
Of phantom water, slowing sinking, slipped
Behind the range, it seemed the trap was tripped
In silence.

      We had walked a lot that day
To save the nags, and by the wheezing way
They breathed it wasn't time for riding then.
God only knew when they would drink again,
If ever; while we had a sup or two
Still hoarded in the horns—and that might do
Until we reached the mountains we had seen.

I told myself the country might be green
Beyond the range. How could you ever guess,
I argued with the dragging weariness
That wasn't me, about the lake and snow
Back yonder? But the very mule said no,
And balked by fits.

        —You didn't climb the range;
You sort of floated over with a strange
Convincingness, and there it was. You knew
The pasture that the creek went winding through
To where the big elm, leaning to the pond,
Made cool blue lace; the mumbling mill beyond
The shady quiet; cattle feeding, lazy—
The brindle cow that kicked, and good old Daisy
With speckled face and crumpled water-horn
With nothing in it; weary earing corn

Beyond the fence, nid-nodding; time for bed;
The new moon going down behind the shed
To fill itself back yonder at the lake;
And suddenly you stumbled broad awake
And walking yet. Or were you still asleep?
No, that was 'Diah wading shoulder-deep
In darkness yonder. What a killing stride!
Because the meadow on the other side
Was green, and sparkled dewy in the cool
Of morning!

       —Damn a hammer-headed mule
That wouldn't let you sleep!

         —The tripping sage,
The slipping sand, and every other age
A pause to spell the horses.

        —Getting cold.
You thought of frost. The night was turning old
And looked it. Tired stars that didn't care
At all if we were getting anywhere
Or if there'd ever be another dawn.

Then, all at once, you knew the night was gone,
And wondered vaguely when and where it went.
Somehow it should have been a big event
When finally the costly morning came.
The black range looming near us seemed the same
We left behind us when the moon was setting;
But, like some dream the desert was forgetting,
The other was a blur along the west
To southward, lying low.

       We stopped to rest
And have a bite; but when we spilled the wheat
Upon the blankets, not a nag would eat;
Just nuzzled it and wilted, standing propped

And dead asleep. The way the mule's ears flopped,
His long-drawn look of gloating in his plight,
Abandoned to the curse of being right
In all our quarrels, wakened, half and half,
A catch of fellow feeling and a laugh
Too weak for sound. Between a breath and breath,
It seemed I slept a sleep as deep as death
And long as weary time; for when Jed shook
The unchanged landscape back, it had the look
Of something that had happened lives away.
He spoke of water yonder where the day
Was like a wild beast crouching for the leap
Across the black wall. Wasn't time to sleep
Until the horses drank. And when I said
The rigmarole that grumbled in my head,
How I'd believe in water that I saw,
There came that flint-hard setting of the jaw,
That long-range hawk-gaze penetrating through you,
The way you said, Art,—wondered if he knew you
Or you knew him. And then his eyes went kind.
"That saying, Bob," he said, "is for the blind.
Believing is a better way to see."

It didn't make a bit more sense to me
Than to the mule I jerked and kicked awake.
The horns bone-dry and hell about to break
The black dam yonder, and the going tougher!
The plain wore out; the land was getting rougher—
Low ridges, crookéd, cactus-haunted draws
On fire with day, and no less dry because
You couldn't see a drink that wasn't there.

By noon you almost tried to touch the bare
Black walls and shoulders where a canyon yawned,
Moon-empty. Would they always stare beyond
That glass of distance there? We didn't talk—
Just moved. The very mule forgot to balk.
The ganted horses in a panting doze,

With hoofs too slow to overtake a nose,
Just kept on trying in a feeble way.

Now mind you, Squire, I don't pretend to say
It had a meaning. Who am I to know?
I'm only saying that it happened so,
And you can say no wonder that I wondered—
A bit heat-crazy, maybe.

     But it thundered—
Right in the empty hell of afternoon!
I guess we'd all been sort of in a swoon
And busy with the stagger of the ground,
Or we'd have seen before. 'Twas less like sound
Than white-hot stillness throbbing, or the dull
Blood-mumble in the hollow of your skull,
Until a roar and tumbling rumble shook
The earth; and there was 'Diah shouting, 'Look!
Rain in the mountain, boys!'

     You tried to doubt,
But sure enough a peak was blotted out
With cloud that poured, the way molasses does,
To where the canyon wasn't now, but was,
Moon-empty, just a look or two ago.
It sounded like stampeding buffalo
Where yonder patch of darkness boiled, and blazed
With slashers from the hidden height that raised
A thousand-bellied bawling in the herd.
We just stood gawking at it—not a word
For quite a spell—till Silas looked at Jed
As though a mule had kicked him. 'Well!' he said,
'By God!'

    Now, Squire, I'm willing to confess
That when I heard old 'Diah mutter, 'Yes,
Who else, indeed?' it struck me he'd been praying
And 'twas the answer. Maybe what I'm saying

Sounds loony; but that empty glare of sky
And desert—all the nags about to die—
And then it thundered!—Was I loony, Art?"

"Well," chuckled Black, "not being very smart,
I wouldn't know, because I wonder too.
I mind a black old codger of the Sioux
Who seemed to make it rain. The Squire would say
He had a weather eye, and didn't pray
Until it had a mind to rain without him!
But I don't know.—Yes, 'Diah had about him
A way that made things wonderful and strange."

"Come on now, let's be getting to the range!"
The younger bantered. "Argufying whether
God did it, or the two of them together,
Won't make the water wetter, you'll allow!"

"But there was something in the thought, some how,"
Continued Evans, "like a lift of wings;
As though the stubborn stuff of earthly things
Was thinner than you knew, or only seemed,
And suddenly the agony you dreamed
Evaporated in a waking wonder.

Arousing to the miracle of thunder
The little mare, with pricked ears, whinnied shrill
And set the horses nickering, until
The slow-believing mule awakened too
And, lifting up the only song he knew,
Mourned hopefully.

                    It met us on the run;
Against a broad arroyo's blast of sun
It rushed to meet us in a tumbling flood,
The tousled, rowdy water, full of mud
And sand and laughter. God! but it was good!
And then, as though the mountains understood

And said it for us, where the thunder-smoke
Trailed off along the range, a rainbow broke
And spanned the canyon with a gate of awe;
And you could hear the waters cry hurrah,
Beneath the glory of it far away.

We made the canyon in the slant of day
And fed the nags, but didn't eat a bite—
Just drank. And then—there wasn't any night.
The white sun blazing yonder never set;
You rubbed your eyes, and it was blazing yet—
But it was blazing on the other side
Above the mountain!

          Seemed that you had died,
And found the way back, half a life the younger
And all a-tingle with a happy hunger,
Into a world that, after all, was kind.

I've often wondered what it is you find
Down yonder at the bottom of a sleep—
Not shoaling slumber, but the ocean-deep
And dreamless sort. There's something that you touch,
And what you call it needn't matter much
If you can reach it. Call it only rest,
And there is something else you haven't guessed—
The Everlasting, maybe. You can try
To live without it, but you have to die
Back into it a little now and then.
And maybe praying is a way for men
To reach it when they cannot sleep a wink
For trouble. Surely I was on the brink
Of knowing what I mean a blink or two
That morning there; and what I nearly knew
Gave everything a wonder-haunted look.

When we had eaten, 'Diah thumbed the Book
And read us snatches, letting silence speak

While he went on thumb-hunting others.—
  Seek
And you would find. You only had to knock,
And it would open. Water from the rock.
The hills of help. 'Twas what his silence said
Between the snatches, more than what he read—
As if some wise old-timer really meant
A plenty that he didn't just invent,
But something in the saying wasn't true
Until the words turned inside out for you,
And there it was, less meaning than a thrill
Upon the edge of meaning. In the still
Cool morning shadow of the canyon walls
It lingered; and the little waterfalls
Made singing of it when he prayed awhile,
His still lips saying with a happy smile
Whatever 'twas the reading hadn't told.
And then he shaved his whiskers, two-days old,
Discussing, while he slowly reappeared,
Boy-eager, from behind the mask of beard
And lather, certain stories rumor knew
About the country we were coming to—
About the Buenaventure, for the most.
We know that river was the kind of ghost
That likes to wander where a map is blank;
But there's no other river I can thank
As I can thank that happiest of streams.
It kept me going, singing in my dreams
By day and night out yonder in the waste,
And such bright water I will never taste
This side of Jordan. 'Diah made you feel
At least 'twas so deserving to be real
That we could hardly miss its upper reach.
I mind that even Silas made a speech
About it, catching 'Diah's eagerness.
He must have said a dozen words or less
That morning!

When the sun was overhead
We started up the canyon, and it led,
Box-walled and boulder-cluttered, to a pass
That gashed the granite of the mountain mass,
A sheer and narrow gorge. We made it through
And saw, below, a canyon brimming blue
With swimming haze and shadow from the height;
And, farther on, the crawling edge of night
Upon some vast dead valley of a star
Where only emptiness and silence are
Forever and forever. Seeming steep
From where we stood, the desert, rising deep
Into the distance, faded to a line
Of mountains gleaming in the level shine
Of evening.

Nothing like a river there.
It should have fetched a feeling of despair,
But somehow didn't, and I wondered why.
There wasn't any difference in the sky;
There wasn't any difference in the earth;
But something that had never suffered birth
And couldn't die, lived mighty in the scene
Of desolation; and I think I mean
The very same that trees appear to know.
You've seen the still, enchanted way they grow.
It wasn't in the desert we had crossed;
But now it seemed you never could be lost,
For always you were in it any place;
And by the look that came upon his face,
I knew what 'Diah called it, gazing there.

We scrambled down a gulch that led to where
The purple canyon deepened, and the change
Upon the desert and the distant range
Was like a revelation. Red as blood
Above the lavender, transparent flood
Of twilight, every summit was a rose,

And half the heavens quickened back of those
With ghostly colors. Maybe it was Jed
And how he felt; but 'twas as though it said,
'With this, and only this, to die into,
How can it matter what becomes of you
Or when, or where?'"

                He pored upon the flame
A little while and then, "When daylight came,
We heard the wind across the canyon rim;
And when we reached the mouth and saw the dim
Range yonder streaked against the dirty dawn,
It wasn't easy to go plodding on,
With quiet places and the pools of rain
Behind us there.

             By noon the sagebrush plain
Became a stinging smother in the dun
Sand-scurry and the swelter of the sun,
Moon-dim and hurrying.

                 Our camp was dry
That night. There was no wonder in the sky.
We knew the sun was setting by the weird
And sickly half-light breaking in the bleared
Abruptly chilling air that darkened soon.
The wind gave out and died. The dusty moon
Hung dry above the rain pools far away.
It must have been the first or second day
Thereafter—no, I guess it was the first—
We lost another horse. It wasn't thirst—
We drank at noon. It happened after that.
A spring pool stewing in a sagebrush flat—
We stumbled on it in the stifling blow.
The roan went shoulder-lame and wouldn't go;
Gave up, done out with limping in the sand.
And Silas—well he never was a hand
For talking. Did his thinking dumb and hid it;

But when the time to do it came, he did it,
Stone-cold. I see that vise of hairy paw
Upon the horse's nose; the other draw
The hunting knife; the bubbling gush of
    red
Along a bulging forearm. Nothing said,
Excepting what the wind-pipe tried to say.

Against the strangled moaning of the day
We plodded, silent. Couldn't stop for meat;
And one nag yonder had a bag of wheat
He wouldn't need.

           As I remember now,
About the killing of the roan, somehow,
Or drinking at the puddle in the smother,
The changing of one life into another
Began for me. It may have been that luck
Forgot us there—three days before we
    struck
Another water hole—or was it two?
It must have been the stifling wind that blew
Three days on end. Another range to climb,
And, like a picture of forgotten time,
That emptiness beyond! The days of hope
And of despair begin to telescope
In there, as I remember. Dawns and noons
And sunsets tangle with the icy moons;
And ranges loom and vanish, yet remain
Forever rising from the rim of plain
Asleep with heavy heat. But in the mixed,
Unsteady flow are pictures strangely fixed
And sharp with vivid colors that are fast.
A moment, maybe, when you felt at last
The miracle of water singing through you,
And suddenly it seemed the desert knew you
And was a breast that pitied, and the blind,
Wide stare of heaven softened and was kind.

I mind the stillness, mightier than wind,
That dizzy noon we squatted there and skinned
The sorrel in the blister of the sun,
Because the days of hunger had begun,
And nights of phantom feasting. Couldn't eat
For swollen tongues. The scarlet strips of meat
Draped round us in the cactus patch to dry.
The heat-dim desert empty to the sky,
Blue-fretted with the everlasting range.
It's queer the way the picture doesn't change.
The strips don't blacken, and the sorrel's eyes
In everlasting, terrified surprise
Still look at me. The high sun doesn't set,
But I can see the way the moon looked yet,
Beyond the half that night. The purple air,
The glassy hush, the horses drooping there,
The ghostly cactuses and 'Diah praying;
And I can hear the mule's tongue-muffled braying
Like sorrow breaking into devil laughter.

I know it had to be the day thereafter
We drank—altho' I'm vague about the setting—
For how could I be sitting here forgetting,
By half, a story never to be told?
It must have been the day was getting old
Before we drank. I feel the driving sun
Upon my back. I see my shadow run
And reach ahead, unwearyingly swift,
Because it hadn't any feet to lift
Or any wooden tongue it couldn't swallow.
'Twas hard to follow, cruel hard to follow,
Because it had to keep the drunken road
That led to where the Buenaventure flowed
Bright waters in a heaven of a valley.
It didn't tally—something didn't tally
About the fleeing shadow that you cast,
Until pursuing teaches you at last
That nothing matters but the driving light

Behind you. I can feel the burly might
Of Gobel's arm, the hairy fingers close
About my shoulder—no, the sorrel's nose,
Or maybe it was roan. No matter whether.
Then three of us were dancing on together,
And they were saying that it wasn't far.

There was a drop of water like a star
That glowed back yonder where the sorrel bled
Along the sky-rim. Mountain overhead,
A burning mountain fading into sleep.
Of all the jumbled pictures that I keep,
That seems to be the one that fits the best.

Suns glaring in the east and in the west;
The swift nights turning into ghostly days
With growing moons; the same blue range to raise,
So often set behind us, yet the same.
And in that blurred eternity we came
To where a sharpened moment lingers still
And doesn't blur. There was a rocky hill
Beyond a soda flat. It seemed to float
Upon a bright white water. Creosote
And greasewood grew and gaudy cactus bloomed
All over it. Beyond, the mountains loomed
Not very far away. And when we neared
The gray-green hill, there suddenly appeared
A man and woman, standing to the waist
In brush. Clear-cut against the sky, they faced
The sloping day. A moment they were there
Above us, withered faces, tangled hair
And scrawny bodies blackened by the sun.
But while we gaped, there wasn't anyone
In all the world but us. We climbed to see
If there might be a village. Seemed to me
That we had dreamed those faces. Nothing stirred.
The broken land stared emptily. We heard
Our shortened breath. But, coming down, we found

A hollow rock they'd squatted by to pound
Grasshoppers! Made it easier to eat
The leather leavings of the sorrel meat
There in the haunted silence of a draw
That evening. Might have doubted what we saw
But for the footprints crowding in the sand
Below a spring. They made the lonely land
Seem lonelier and more remote from men.

It gets to be a troubled dream again
Beyond that range. The days of windy smother
And burning stillness overlap each other
And run together wearily the same.
But Oh! the valley where the deer were tame
And many, and the Buenaventure made
So cool a road of silver in the shade
Of leaning elm and rustling cottonwood!
No other meat can ever be so good
As that meat was, so tender and so fat!
Just one more range to cross, and, after that,
The tame deer feeding belly-deep in grass!
One night holds changeless—blown of purple glass
And haunted with a deathly hush of light.
I never saw the full moon burn so bright
Before or since. The cactus looked appalled;
And I can see the way our shadows crawled
Like living things. You sort of floated on,
A dream of torture, with a dream of dawn
And food and water floating on ahead
Forever. Maybe you were lying dead
Back yonder, staring sightless at the sky,
But what you died of couldn't ever die
And had to wander on forever so.
The ghostly desert's mockery of snow,
The cold moon's ghostly mockery of day,
The sound of feet forever on the way
To emptiness, the hollow-sounding breath
Of horses in the stillness that was death

And didn't hear! What was it that you knew—
With this and only this to die into?—
But that was far away before you died,
Past memory beyond the other side
Of mountains, many past remembering.

Now if you say it was a foolish thing
That happened there, I will not blame you, Squire.
There's half of me here sitting by the fire
Will share your laughter if you want to laugh,
Without denying that the other half
May somehow be the wiser, just the same.

Tall, out of purple emptiness it came
Serenely slow, and stopped to look at me.
It should have been a common yucca tree,
And was, except for something it was saying
Without a sound. That yucca tree was praying,
And had to pray forevermore in vain
With wide arms waiting wearily for rain—
A ghost that didn't know that it had died
Of thirst, and went on waiting, crucified
Forever!

    Then from very far away,
There was a voice remembered—*'Though He slay'*—
Why, it was 'Diah reading!

       Say it seemed
I came awake then, have it that I dreamed;
But still it's something that the dream was good;
And in a world so little understood,
There should be room for two to be mistaken.
Well, if I dreamed, the yucca seemed to waken,
And wasn't waiting any more in vain.
The lifted arms were drinking in a rain
Of living glory, like no earthly shower;
And now I saw the yucca was in flower—
Tall beauty pluming in a quiet light!

I don't know how much came to me that night,
And how much later when I mulled it o'er.
I know I wasn't weary any more
Till moondown faded in the morning.

                    Well,
I see it's like a dream you try to tell,
And wonder why it seemed to mean so much;
But if a dream can be a sort of crutch,
I leaned upon it often—till I 'woke
Again; or did I only dream it broke
And left three scarecrows limping in despair?—
No Buenaventure river anywhere,
No haunted yucca drinking in a rain
Of glory, making beauty out of pain
And ugly need!

              But often, broad awake,
It seized me. Once it was a rattlesnake
That brought it back! The very devil's land
It was—all tumbled rock and shale and sand
Where squatty cactus starved and no sage grew.
It was the time the moon was starving too
And came up late and feeble, withering
Because there was a curse on everything
In all the world. There was a whirring sound
That made the land be still—and there he
     wound,
A deadly puddle stewing in the sun,
Head up to end what hunger had begun,
And weariness and thirst. A rage to kill
One foe at least just left me staring still
And wondering. Then suddenly it came!
It was the same, it was the very same
Still beauty saying what I couldn't hear,
So far away it was; with fangs of fear
Or thorns of bitter need to guard some good
Against a strange world neither understood
Nor understanding. Like a flower he grew,

Slow waving in a breeze that never blew
This side of heaven. Then he crawled away,
Still beautiful with what he couldn't say,
And scared because it never could be said.

It happened when the starved old moon was dead
And all our little talk was of the Lake,
There was a ridge ahead. Beyond would break
The sky-wide gleam of it; and there would be
Deer grazing by the rivers of that sea,
A little way beyond the ridge's brow.
The Buenaventure was behind us now;
And maybe if it really had been there,
The buzzards would have banqueted somewhere
This side of hope.

          There was a little spring
In yonder ridge, but not a living thing,
It seemed, had ever found that blessèd pool
Until three men, two horses and a mule
Came staggering—or ever would again.

We saw it from the ridge's summit when
The day began to brighten. Was it land
Or water there beyond the tumbled sand—
That still white sheet of nothing sloping high
Until it was the nothing of the sky
On fire again? One look at 'Diah told
The answer that I knew. It was an old,
Old man I saw a moment in his place,
The look of something broken in his face
That wasn't to be mended any more.
I see that I had never known before
How much I'd leaned upon him like a child,
Until he turned that face on me and smiled—
When nothing but the smile of it was Jed.
'You see, it's just beyond the salt,' he said,
'A little way.' And for a moment there,

Not anything but hearing Silas swear
Beneath his breath was left to fill the lack,
Until I saw that hawk-gaze coming back,
That long-range look of something that he saw
Beyond you; and the setting of the jaw
Was cruel in the face that it denied.
I didn't know how lean and hollow-eyed
It was until the light of it went dim,
That quicksand moment when I pitied him—
The leaner on his pity—even I!
Well, yonder looked as good a place to die
As any other then. But now I know
I went because he wanted me to go;
For more than pity happened in that bleak,
Forsaken moment when I saw him weak
Upon that ridge. I'd just begun to love him,
And something in the breaking manhood of him
Was stronger than his old unbroken might.

By noon the very hush was blinding white;
The world had shrunken to a tiny, round
White island, floating lost in a profound
White dazzle of a sea without a shore.
The more we toiled, the island moved the more,
To keep us toiling in the center still.
I think what drove me wasn't hope or will,
But just the stagger and the baffled stare
Of Silas, striving like a wounded bear
To crush a foe he couldn't overtake;
And 'Diah's haunted eyes upon a lake
He didn't see, those hollow, haunted eyes.

There's something happens when your last wish dies
I wish I could remember—something good;
But just about when it is understood
There isn't anything to tie it to
Of all the tangled wishes that were you;
But surely it is good.

I still can see
The mule, like something in a comedy
Beyond the mere indecency of mirth;
The horse's muzzle to the lifeless earth,
Negotiating where to leave a skin
Too big and heavy for the bones within
To carry long. I see the little mare.
That woman-patience in her eyes of care,
The drooping head, the placing of her feet
Just so—and so—brought back the chimney seat
At home, and me a boy, with Granny sitting
Forever there, her nose among her knitting
For fear the feeble fingers might forget.

It must have been the sun about to set
That conjured there ahead of us the ghost
Of breakers beating silent on a coast
Of silence. That was where the tumbled sand
Began again.

                    We made the broken land
Beyond it, where the cold stars whirled away.
And there was nothing—there was dazzling day
On sandy, cedar-spotted hills that ran
To northward where the higher range began,
Patched black with cedar scrub.

                              I wonder still,
Sometimes, what really happened on a hill,
Unsteady with the burden of the sun
That day; if truly there was anyone
Below us in the draw, and if we dreamed
That Indian woman and the way she screamed
As though we'd come upon her by surprise.
But in the mirror of her face and eyes
I still can see the horrors that she saw;
And surely there were youngsters in the draw,
With frightened faces peeping from the brush.

She offered weed seed messed into a mush,
And tried to tell us it was all she had,
While, plainly starving and as clearly mad,
Three nightmare creatures croaked a single
    word
The louder, hoping if she only heard
She'd give them water. Surely it was true,
For I can see the knowing look that grew
Upon her black face, terror-frozen still,
And how she pointed off across a hill,
Then took another look at us, and ran!
There must have been a tall tale for a man
To hear that night!

        There was another side
To those hot hills, somehow; and by a wide
Sun-swimming flat, with cedar hills beyond,
The dizzy dazzle focussed in a pond
Of water—water—water! It was wet;
But I can see the whimpering critters fret
And slobber over it—the mule, with curled
Lip skyward, making faces at the world
To tell it what he hadn't breath to bray.

We weren't any better off next day,
Remembering that sickly tang of brine;
And if the horse's belly felt like mine,
'Twas little wonder he was satisfied,
At last, with any place to dump a hide,
And did it in the sand without a fuss.

I mind the antelope that stared at us
And vanished, floating. Didn't make you
    think
Of eating—only where they went to drink;
And so you floated after them, and came
Upon it, swooping giddily—the same
Sick pool back there.

I know now we had turned
Northeastward, heading for a peak that burned
Away off yonder. When the twilight grew,
We stood upon a rise and saw a blue
Unending valley running north and south;
And 'Diah, talking of the valley's mouth
To northward and the lake that might be there,
Seemed far away—as far away as where
That snowy summit slowly lost the glow
And kept the secret that it seemed to know
In everlasting silence.

Down that slope,
'Twas gravity that moved us more than hope
Of water short of yonder paling height.
But deeper in the blueing of the light
Upon the still, cool sage-brush solitude,
We stopped to listen. Was it doves that cooed?
Doves in the desert? Water must be near
If there were doves about! But did we hear
Or dream the yearning homesick ache of it?
We stood there wondering what to make of it,
And gaped upon each other's faces. *There!*
Doves in the cool blue hush! The little mare
Heard too and whimpered; but the mule forgot
His burden of a head, and, doves or not,
Slept heavily.

We didn't find the spring,
For all our dragging search—not anything
But sage; and when it grew too dark to seek,
We headed up the valley where the peak
Had vanished with the secret that it knew.

Last year I found it, camped there in the blue
Of twilight when the doves began to moan—
For 'Diah yonder by the Cimarrone
And Silas by the Siskadee, asleep

With all their might unloosened. It was deep
And wide enough to swim us! By the cool
Sweet water, homesick for the very mule,
And thirsting just for thirst with Jed again,
I marvelled, if we hadn't missed it then,
How much I would have missed!

                      The whole night through
We stumbled toward a vanished peak that knew
The reason why the doves kept mourning so—
Beyond the barn lot, dim and far ago
At twilight—just before the crickets wake—
The rusty pulley grieving at the lake,
The well, the lake, the well—the bucket sinking,
Blub—and the greedy gurgle of it drinking—
A dusty bucket in a well gone dry.

And all at once, the peak was gleaming high
Up yonder in a lake the sorrel bled—
The roan—the sorrel. 'Diah there ahead
And Silas in between the mule and mare—
All hunting with a microscopic care
For doves among the sage brush long ago.

But why was 'Diah talking like a crow
And pointing at the peak? Because it swam
And tossed so with the breaking of the dam,
The flood of fire.—

                    I wakened in the shade
And quiet that a stunted cedar made.
I know it was a little cedar now;
But then I wasn't anywhere, somehow,
And it was chilly. Stooping there above,
An old, old man was looking for a dove,
And it was someone that I used to know;
But he had lost the dove so long ago,
I couldn't find the waste of bone and skin

His hunting, sunken eyes were burning in—
I couldn't find it in the sage at all.
But he was leaning from a canyon wall
And smiling, and a storm of doves moaned by;
And very far away I heard him cry
A name I knew—and every one of those
Dim mountains far away became a rose,
And he was blooming—like a yucca tree—
All gentle light. And leaning over me
Was 'Diah."

       Evans brooded for a space,
Until the glow that came upon his face,
And wasn't from the embers, died away.
"I lived upon it waiting there that day,"
He said at length "—that look of joy and tears.
I've lived upon it all these lonely years
From dream to dream. And I have seen it break
Upon the drab world, even when awake,
As though the common hills and valleys knew
In some deep way. And when it seems they do,
I almost know what happens in a seed,
How cactuses can make of bitter need
Such beauty; and there's something in the look
Like hearing 'Diah with the dog-eared Book,
Still reading, on the further side of sound:
'Take off thy shoes. The place is holy ground
Whereon thou standest.'

       Day was nearly done,
And I was troubled for a sinking sun
That couldn't rise again, it grew so weak.
Then there was 'Diah, back from yonder peak,
With water in a kettle!
       Noon was pouring
White-hot on Silas when we found him snoring
Beside the spring, the mule and little mare
Drooped over him.

Another day from there—
Or was it more?—it seems like many more—
A lone butte rising from the valley floor
Was looking northward into empty sky.
I still can see Jed climbing, hear him cry
'The lake! the lake!'

That night the moon was new."

VI

The low intoning of the canyon grew,
Filling the silence of a story told
With something immemorially old,
Beyond all telling; till the Squire arose
And with a boot heel broke the glowing doze
Of gutted logs that startled into flame.
"I still can see the five of you that came
To Bear Lake camp," he said. "If you had died,
No buzzard would have thanked you for the hide
And rags you packed!—We'll need another log."
He melted into darkness; and the dog,
'Roused by the quiet of the brooding pair,
Sat up, limp-eared, and with a surly air
Flopped down again and snuggled into sleep.

The brittle mock of axes, biting deep
Into the crystal distances of night,
Died out. The Squire stooped back into the light,
Cast down his load upon the flame, and said:
"It's queer the way the night seems full of Jed
Out yonder—sort of hiding everywhere,
As though you'd maybe see him standing there
Behind you, if you just turned quick enough—
Taller than men and made of starry stuff
And stillness."

                    While they passed the jug around
The silence deepened with the busy sound
The new wood made. "When he turned up again,"
Said Black at length, "with less than half his men,
Beside the Stanislaus, it seems to me

The graybeard that he wouldn't live to be
Had somehow come to haunt him like a ghost.
I felt it all the way along the coast
To Oregon. And when we camped beside
The Umpqua where it bitters with the tide,
You know what happened. We had gone that day,
Just he and I, to find a solid way
Among the marshes. Two escaped to tell,
Of all our comrades, how the Umpquas fell
Upon the camp—a scrambled tale and queer,
As though they'd had a nightmare; nothing clear
But Rogers towering and the axe he plied
Before he died the way old Silas died
Down yonder on the Colorado shore.

I felt the other 'Diah more and more
Until we met the others up the Snake
About the forks. Sometimes he'd seem to take
A trail I couldn't follow, all alone—
Who knows?—somewhere beyond the Cimarrone
As like as not. Beside a fire together,
Or maybe rubbing knees and saddle leather,
I'd know he'd gone exploring far away.
And then he'd get that long-range look and say
What made me feel 'twas good where he had been,
But 'twas no country I was ever in,
Or likely would be; something wise and old
As light and growing, but, in being told,
As new as morning or the first green grass.
'Twould be like seeing darkly in a glass,
Then face to face, the way he often read it;
And you would feel, the gentle way he said it,
A little shaver listening to his mother.
Between the common 'Diah and the other
There might have been a thousand years or two.
I often wonder if the other knew
That he was getting near to where he is.
Concerned, for all that might and youth of his,

About the vanity of worldly gain!
And making worldly trouble seem like rain
Upon the desert of our mortal stuff!
He used to tell me that he had enough
Of worldly goods to help his folks and others—
So no more beaver!"

    "Had a mess of brothers,"
Observed the Squire. "I hear 'twas on the way
To set them up in trade with Santa Fé
He got his hair raised."

     "Going to retire,"
Mused Black, "—and did."

     "I wonder," yawned the Squire,
With lazy stretching. "Got a horse to bet
He's nowhere or there's blue horizon yet
He's chasing after with that hungry stride!"

"I should have been there with him," Evans sighed;
"I should have followed anywhere he went."
With grave and unintentional assent
The elder nodded, and the canyon's moan
Took up the old regret—*alone, alone,
Alone.* The younger, slumped upon his pack,
Blinked dreamily. "But when he started back
For California with another band—
And Silas—all the torture of that land
Came on me like a nightmare. I was gray
And old inside. And so he went away
Forever, maybe; but a thrilling doubt
Has grown upon me.

    Well, I knocked about
Among the mountains, hunting beaver streams,
Alone—no, not alone, for there were dreams
And memories that grew. And more and more
I knew, whatever I was hunting for,
It wasn't beaver. When the evening blued,

The listening stillness of the solitude
Would come alive with something he had read,
Or just a passing word or two he said,
Too trivial for memory till then.
And all our story would begin again
Self-spinning in the quiet—always new,
And more like longing livingly come true
Than memory. Or maybe on a rise
I'd see that look of breaking in his eyes
Far off; or suddenly a hill or draw
Would sadden with the vision that I saw
Beside the stunted cedar.

                Well, I spent
That winter down at Santa Fé, and went
Back to the mountains trapping in the Spring,
And all that Summer didn't hear a thing
Of 'Diah. I was hunting beaver sign
Along this way, the Fall of 'twenty-nine,
Before I heard about him from a pair
Of trappers—him and all the band somewhere
Up Teton way. But yonder up the Green
Beyond the Sandy, Indians had seen
The white men cross the Pass a moon ago
With many horses.

                Wasn't time for snow,
Not heavy snow, although 'twas getting late
For proper mountain doings. It was fate
That I would never see him any more;
And so an early blizzard shut the door
Behind him, and I couldn't make it through.
I wintered at the Bear Lake rendezvous
With half a dozen men of Hudson Bay,
Who met the band up north and heard them say
He planned to winter at the Powder's mouth,
And calculated to be heading south
Back to the States for good, come early grass.

And winter getting deeper in the Pass,
And deeper! Hardest that I ever saw,
That winter! Didn't even fix to thaw
Till 'way along in March sometime, and then
It caught its breath and started in again
To snow and bluster. Seemed the hand of God
Was in it."

    Jerking backward from a nod,
The elder muttered: "Stayed until July—
Wind River—."

     "Hadn't heart enough to try
To overtake him when at last the snows
Were gone!" said Evans.

     Studying his nose,
The younger brooded owl-like, breathing deep.

"But there was one more rendezvous to keep,"
Continued Evans; "one more rendezvous.
It wasn't till July of 'thirty-two
I heard, and 'twas a year ago that May
It happened! I was down at Santa Fé—
A brawling mess of traders from the Plains
And mountain men and tangled wagon trains
From Independence. Just an idle word
Across the glasses, and it seemed absurd!
So many Smiths! It couldn't have been Jed!
For when I tried to think of him as dead,
It wouldn't fit the picture anyhow.
It isn't fitting better even now,
These lonely years away! But, bit by bit,
The tale grew bigger than the doubt of it,
And ended in the emptiness of air.
Killed southward of the wagon trail,
  somewhere
Along the Cimarrone! And it was told
With half an air of being rather old

To matter in the brawling summertide
Of lusty, living men. But where he died
His brothers, even, didn't rightly know,
Recalling, with already seasoned woe,
How he went hunting water for the train,
And how they watched until the lonely plain
Went empty in the shimmer of the sun—
Forever. But they had his rifle gun
And silver-mounted pistols, dearly bought
From certain hangdog Mexicans who brought
The news to Santa Fé. And, word by word,
I bought their tale through, feeling, as I heard,
'Twas measured for the market or they knew
Too much by plenty.

                    One more rendezvous—
And only silence waiting after all!

The nights were nippy with a tang of Fall
Along the lone road leading to the States—
The season when the dying Summer waits
To listen for the whisper of the snow
A long way off. Three horseback days below
The Arkansaw, and twelve from Santa Fé
I crossed the Cimarrone; another day
Beyond the waterholes, and that was where
He left the wagons.

                    All around me there
Was empty desert, level as a sea,
And like a picture of eternity
Completed for the holding of regret.
But I could almost see the oxen yet
Droop, panting, in the circled wagon train;
The anxious eyes that followed on the plain
A solitary horseman growing dim;
And, riding south, I almost sighted him
Along the last horizon—many moons
Ahead of me.

                    Beyond a strip of dunes
I came upon the Cimarrone once more,
A winding flat no wetter than the shore,
Excepting when you clawed a hole, it filled.
But hunting for the spot where he was killed
Was weary work. There had to be a ledge
Of sandstone jutting from the river's edge
Southwestwardly; and, balanced at the tip,
A bowlder, waiting for a flood, to slip
And tumble in the stream; and just below,
Not any farther than a good knife-throw,
A hiding place behind a point of clay.

But there was sand—and sand.

                        The second day,
When I was sure the Mexicans had sold
The buyer's wish, with twilight getting cold
And blue along a northward bend, I came
Upon it with a start—the very same,
Except the bowlder bedded in the stream!
And like one helpless in an evil dream,
I seemed to see it all. The burning glare,
The pawing horse, and 'Diah clawing there
Beneath the ledge, beyond the reach of sound
To warn him of the faces peering round
The point of clay behind; a sheath-knife thrown,
Bows twanging; 'Diah fighting all alone,
A-bristle with the arrows and the knife—
Alone, alone, and fighting for his life
With twenty yelling devils; left for dead,
The bloody, feathered huddle that was Jed,
Half buried in Comanches, coming to;
The slow red trail, the hard, last trail that grew
Behind him, crawling up the bank to seek
The frightened horse; too dizzy sick and weak
To make it past the sepulcher of shade
The sandstone ledge and balanced bowlder made

Against the swimming dazzle of the sun;
The band returning for the horse and gun
To find him there, still moaning, in his tomb
And roll the bowlder on him.

                          —Only gloom
And silence left!"

                 The voice of sorrow rose
And ceased. Assenting in a semi-doze,
The elder nodded sagely; and the Squire
Breathed deeper. Feeling by the fallen fire
The mystery of sorrow in the cry,
The dog sat up and, muzzle to the sky,
Mourned for the dear one mourning.

The Song

of the Indian Wars

To *Alice*, three years old

When I began the gift I bear
It seemed you weren't anywhere;
But being younger now I know
How even fifty moons ago
The apple bloom began to seek
The proper tinting for a cheek;
The skies, aware of thrilling news,
Displayed the loveliest of blues
For whoso fashions eyes to choose.
And all that prehistoric spring
Experimental grace of wing
And tentatively shapen forms,
From crocuses to thunderstorms
And happy sound and sunny glow
Rehearsed you fifty moons ago.
Why, even I was toiling too
Upon a little gift for you!
And now that we are wise and three,
And I love you and you love me,
We know the whole conspiracy!

THE SOWING OF THE DRAGON

I

At last the four year storm of fratricide
Had ceased at Appomattox, and the tide
Of war-bit myriads, like a turning sea's,
Recoiled upon the deep realities
That yield no foam to any squall of change.

Now many a hearth of home had gotten strange
To eyes that knew sky-painting flares of war.
So much that once repaid the striving for
No longer mattered. Yonder road that ran
At hazard once beyond the ways of Man
By haunted vale and space-enchanted hill,
Had never dreamed of aught but Jones's Mill—
A dull pedestrian! The spring, where erst
The peering plowboy sensed a larger thirst,
Had shoaled from awe, so long the man had drunk
At deeper floods. How yonder field had shrunk
That billowed once mysteriously far
To where the cow-lot nursed the evening star
And neighbored with the drowsing moon and sun!
For O what winds of wrath had boomed and run
Across what vaster fields of moaning grain—
Rich seedings, nurtured by a ghastly rain
To woeful harvest!

                    So the world went small.
But 'mid the wreck of things remembered tall
An epidemic rumor murmured now.
Men leaned upon the handles of the plow

To hear and dream; and through the harrow-smoke
The weird voice muttered and the vision broke
Of distant, princely acres unpossessed.

Again the bugles of the Race blew west
That once the Tigris and Euphrates heard.
In unsuspected deeps of being stirred
The ancient and compelling Aryan urge.
A homing of the homeless, surge on surge,
The valley roads ran wagons, and the hills
Through lane and by-way fed with trickling rills
The man-stream mighty with a mystic thaw.
All summer now the Mississippi saw
What long ago the Hellespont beheld.
The shrewd, prophetic eyes that peered of eld
Across the Danube, visioned naked plains
Beyond the bleak Missouri, clad with grains,
Jewelled with orchard, grove and greening
          garth—
Serene abundance centered in a hearth
To nurture lusty children.

                    On they swirled,
The driving breed, the takers of the world,
The makers and the bringers of the law.
Now up along the bottoms of the Kaw
The drifting reek of wheel and hoof arose.
The kiotes talked about it and the crows
Along the lone Republican; and still
The bison saw it on the Smoky Hill
And Solomon; while yonder on the Platte
Ten thousand wagons scarred the sandy flat
Between the green grass season and the brown.

A name sufficed to make the camp a town,
A whim unmade. In spaces wide as air,
And late as empty, now the virile share
Quickened the virgin meadow-lands of God;

And lo, begotten of the selfsame sod,
The house and harvest!

        So the Cadmian breed,
The wedders of the vision and the deed
Went forth to sow the dragon-seed again.

But there were those—and they were also men—
Who saw the end of sacred things and dear
In all this wild beginning; saw with fear
Ancestral pastures gutted by the plow,
The bison harried ceaselessly, and how
They dwindled moon by moon; with pious dread
Beheld the holy places of their dead
The mock of aliens.

        Sioux, Arapahoe,
Cheyenne, Commanche, Kiowa and Crow
In many a council pondered what befell
The prairie world. Along the Musselshell,
The Tongue, the Niobrara, all they said
Upon the Platte, the Arkansaw, the Red
Was echoed word by peril-laden word.
Along Popo Agie[1] and the Horn they heard
The clank of hammers and the clang of rails
Where hordes of white men conjured iron trails
Now crawling past the Loup Fork and the Blue.
By desert-roaming Cimarron they knew,
And where La Poudre heads the tale was known,
How, snoring up beyond the Yellowstone,
The medicine-canoes breathed flame and steam
And, like weird monsters of an evil dream,
Spewed foes—a multitudinary spawn!

Were all the teeming regions of the dawn
Unpeopled now? What devastating need

1. Pronounced *Po-po-zha*.

Had set so many faces pale with greed
Against the sunset? Not as men who seek
Some meed of kindness, suppliant and meek,
These hungry myriads came. They did but look,
And whatsoever pleased them, that they took.
Their faded eyes were icy, lacking ruth,
And all their tongues were forked to split the truth
That word and deed might take diverging ways.
Bewildered in the dusk of ancient days
The Red Men groped; and howsoever loud
The hopeful hotheads boasted in the crowd,
The wise ones heard prophetic whisperings
Through aching hushes; felt the end of things
Inexorably shaping. What should be
Already was to them. And who can flee
His shadow or his doom? Though cowards stride
The wind-wild thunder-horses, Doom shall ride
The arrows of the lightning, and prevail.
Ere long whole tribes must take the spirit trail
As once they travelled to the bison hunt.
Then let it be with many wounds—in front—
And many scalps, to show their ghostly kin
How well they fought the fight they could not win,
To perish facing what they could not kill.

So down upon the Platte and Smoky Hill
Swept war; and all their valleys were afraid.
The workers where the trails were being laid
To speed the iron horses, now must get
Their daily wage in blood as well as sweat
With gun and shovel. Often staring plains
Beheld at daybreak gutted wagon-trains
Set foursquare to the whirling night-attack,
With neither hoof nor hand to bring them back
To Omaha or Westport. Every week
The rolling coaches bound for Cherry Creek
Were scarred in running battle. Every day
Some ox-rig, creeping California way—

That paradise of every hope fulfilled—
Was plundered and the homesick driver killed,
Forlornly fighting for his little brood.
And often was the prairie solitude
Aware by night of burning ricks and roofs,
Stampeding cattle and the fleeing hoofs
Of wild marauders.

RED CLOUD

II

                    Sullenly a gale
That blustered rainless up the Bozeman Trail
Was bringing June again; but not the dear
Deep-bosomed mother of a hemisphere
That other regions cherish. Flat of breast,
More passionate than loving, up the West
A stern June strode, lean suckler of the lean,
Her rag-and-tatter robe of faded green
Blown dustily about her.

                    Afternoon
Now held the dazzled prairie in a swoon;
And where the Platte and Laramie unite,
The naked heavens slanted blinding light
Across the bare Fort Laramie parade.
The groping shadow-arm the flag-pole swayed
To nightward, served to emphasize the glare;
And 'mid Saharan hollows of the air
One haughty flower budded from the mast
And bloomed and withered as the gale soughed past
To languish in the swelter.

                    Growing loud,
When some objection wakened in the crowd,
Or dwindling to a murmur of assent,
Still on and on the stubborn parley went
Of many treaty makers gathered here.
Big talk there was at Laramie that year
Of 'sixty-six; for lo, a mighty word

The Great White Father spoke, and it was heard
From peep of morning to the sunset fires.
The southwind took it from the talking wires
And gave it to the gusty west that blew
Its meaning down the country of the Sioux
Past Inyan Kara to Missouri's tide.
The eager eastwind took and flung it wide
To where lush valleys gaze at lofty snow
All summer long. And now Arapahoe
The word was; now Dakota; now Cheyenne;
But still one word: 'Let grass be green again
Upon the trails of war and hatred cease,
For many presents and the pipe of peace
Are waiting yonder at the Soldier's Town!'
And there were some who heard it with a frown
And said, remembering the White Man's guile:
"Make yet more arrows when the foemen smile."
And others, wise with many winters, said:
"Life narrows, and the better days are dead.
Make war upon the sunset! Will it stay?"
And some who counselled with a dream would say:
"Great Spirit made all peoples, White and Red,
And pitched one big blue tepee overhead
That men might live as brothers side by side.
Behold! Is not our country very wide,
With room enough for all?" And there were some
Who answered scornfully: "Not so they come;
Their medicine is strong, their hearts are bad;
A little part of what our fathers had
They give us now, tomorrow come and take.
Great Spirit also made the rattlesnake
And over him the big blue tepee set!"

So wrought the Great White Father's word; and yet,
Despite remembered and suspected wrong,
Because the Long Knife's medicine was strong,
There lacked not mighty chieftains who obeyed.
A thousand Ogalalas Man Afraid

And Red Cloud marshalled on the council trail;
A thousand Brulés followed Spotted Tail.
Cheyennes, Arapahoes came riding down
By hundreds; till the little Soldier Town
Was big with tepees.

              Where the white June drowse
Beat slanting through a bower of withered boughs
That cast a fretwork travesty of shade,
Now sat the peace-commissioners and made
Soft words to woo the chieftains of the bands.
'They wanted but a roadway through the lands
Wherein the Rosebud, Tongue and Powder head,
That white men, seeking for the yellow lead
Along the Madison, might pass that way.
There ran the shortest trail by many a day
Of weary travel. This could do no harm;
Nor would there be occasion for alarm
If they should wish to set a fort or two
Up yonder—not against Cheyenne and Sioux,
But rather that the Great White Father's will
Might be a curb upon his people still
And Red Men's rights be guarded by the laws.'

Adroitly phrased, with many a studied pause,
In which the half-breed spokesmen, bit by bit,
Reshaped the alien speech and scattered it,
The purpose of the council swept at last
Across the lounging crowd. And where it passed
The feathered headgear swayed and bent together
With muttering, as when in droughty weather
A little whirlwind sweeps the tasseled corn.
Some bull-lunged Ogalala's howl of scorn
Was hurled against the few assenting "hows"
Among the Brulés. Then the summer drowse
Came back, the vibrant silence of the heat;
For Man Afraid had gotten to his feet,
His face set hard, one straight arm rising slow

Against the Whites, as though he bent a bow
And yonder should the fleshing arrow fly.
So stood he, and the moments creeping by
Were big with expectation. Still and tense,
The council felt the wordless eloquence
Of Man Afraid; and then:

                    "I tell you no!
When Harney talked to us ten snows ago
He gave us all that country. Now you say
The White Chief lied. My heart is bad today,
Because I know too well the forkéd tongue
That makes a promise when the moon is young,
And kills it when the moon is in the dark!"

The Ogalalas roared; and like a spark
That crawls belated when the fuse is damp,
The words woke sequent thunders through the
        camp
Where Cheyennes heard it and Arapahoes.
Then once again the chieftain's voice arose:
"Your talk is sweet today. So ever speak
The white men when they know their hands are
        weak
That itch to steal. But once your soldiers pitch
Their tepees yonder, will the same hands itch
The less for being stronger? Go around.
I do not want you in my hunting ground!
You scare my bison, and my folk must eat.
Far sweeter than your words are, home is sweet
To us, as you; and yonder land is home.
In sheltered valleys elk and bison roam
All winter there, and in the spring are fat.
We gave the road you wanted up the Platte.
Make dust upon it then! But you have said
The shortest way to find the yellow lead
Runs yonder. Any trail is short enough
That leads your greedy people to the stuff

That makes them crazy! It is bad for you.
I, Man Afraid, have spoken. *Hetchetu!*"

How, how, how, how! A howl of fighting men
Swept out across the crowd and back again
To break about the shadow-mottled stand
Where Colonel Maynadier, with lifted hand,
Awaited silence. 'As a soldier should,
He spoke straight words and few. His heart was
     good.
The Great White Father would be very sad
To know the heart of Man Afraid was bad
And how his word was called a crooked word.
It could not be that Man Afraid had heard.
The council had not said that Harney lied.
It wanted but a little road, as wide
As that a wagon makes from wheel to wheel.
The Long Knife chieftains had not come to steal
The Red Men's hunting ground.'

                  The half-breeds cried
The speech abroad; but where it fell, it died.
One heard the flag a-ripple at the mast,
The bicker of the river flowing past,
The melancholy crooning of the gale.

Now 'mid the bodeful silence, Spotted Tail
Arose, and all the people leaned to hear;
For was he not a warrior and a seer
Whose deeds were mighty as his words were wise?
Some droll, shrewd spirit in his narrowed eyes
Seemed peering past the moment and afar
To where predestined things already are;
And humor lurked beneath the sober mien,
But half concealed, as though the doom foreseen
Revealed the old futility of tears.
Remembering the story of his years,
His Brulé warriors loved him standing so.

And some recalled that battle long ago
Far off beside the upper Arkansaw,
When, like the freshet of a sudden thaw,
The Utes came down; and how the Brulés, caught
In ambush, sang the death-song as they fought,
For many were the foes and few were they;
Yet Spotted Tail, a stripling fresh from play,
Had saved them with his daring and his wit.
How often when the dark of dawn was lit
With flaming wagon-tops, his battle-cry
Had made it somehow beautiful to die,
A whirlwind joy! And how the leaping glare
Had shown by fits the snow-fall of despair
Upon the white men's faces! Well they knew
That every brave who followed him was two,
So mighty was the magic of his name.
And none forgot the first time Harney came—
His whetted deaths that chattered in the sheath,
The long blue snake that set the ground beneath
A-smoulder with a many-footed rage.
What bleeding of the Brulés might assuage
That famished fury? Vain were cunning words
To pay the big arrears for harried herds
And desolated homes and settlers slain
And many a looted coach and wagon-train
And all that sweat of terror in the land!
Who now went forth to perish, that his band
Might still go free? Lo, yonder now he stood!
And none forgot his loving hardihood
The day he put the ghost paint on his face
And, dressed for death, went singing to the place
Where Harney's soldiers waited.

                              "Brothers, friends!"
Slow words he spoke. "The longest summer ends,
And nothing stays forever. We are old.
Can anger check the coming of the cold?
When frosts begin men think of meat and wood

And how to make the days of winter good
With what the summer leaves them of its cheer.
Two times I saw the first snow deepen here,
The last snow melt; and twice the grass was brown
When I was living at the Soldier's Town
To save my Brulés. All the while I thought
About this alien people I had fought,
Until a cloud was lifted from my eyes.
I saw how some great spirit makes them wise.
I saw a white Missouri flowing men,
And knew old times could never be again
This side of where the spirit sheds its load.
Then let us give the Powder River road,
For they will take it if we do not give.
Not all can die in battle. Some must live.
I think of those and what is best for those.
Dakotas, I have spoken."

            Cries arose
From where his band of Brulé warriors sat—
The cries that once sent Panic up the Platte,
An eyeless runner panting through the gloom.
For though their chief had seen the creeping doom
Like some black cloud that gnaws the prairie rim,
Yet echoes of their charges under him
Had soared and sung above the words he said.
Now silence, like some music of the dead
That holds a throng of new-born spirits awed,
Possessed the brooding crowd. A lone crow cawed.
A wind fled moaning like a wildered ghost.

So clung that vatic hush upon the host
Until the Bad Face Ogalala band
Saw Red Cloud coming forward on the stand,
Serene with conscious might, a king of men.
Then all the hills were ululant again
As though a horde of foes came charging there;
For here was one who never gave despair

A moral mien, nor schooled a righteous hate
To live at peace with evil. Tall and straight
He stood and scanned the now quiescent crowd;
Then faced the white commissioners and bowed
A gracious bow—the gesture of a knight
Whose courage pays due deference to might
Before the trumpets breathe the battle's breath.
Not now he seemed that fearful lord of death,
Whose swarm of charging warriors, clad in red,
Were like a desolating thunder-head
Against an angry sunset. Many a Sioux
Recalled the time he fought alone and slew
His father's slayers, Bull Bear and his son,
While yet a fameless youth; and many a one
About the fort, remembering Grattán
And all his troopers slaughtered by a man
So bland of look and manner, wondered much.
Soft to the ear as velvet to the touch,
His speech, that lacked but little to be song,
Caressed the fringing hushes of the throng
Where many another's cry would scarce be clear.

"My brothers, when you see this prairie here,
   You see my mother. Forty snows and four
Have blown and melted since the son she bore
First cried at Platte Forks yonder, weak and blind;
And whether winter-stern or summer-kind,
Her ways with me were wise. Her thousand laps
Have shielded me. Her ever-giving paps
Have suckled me and made me tall for war.
What presents shall I trade my mother for?
A string of beads? A scarlet rag or two?"

Already he was going ere they knew
That he had ceased. Among the people fled
A sound as when the frosted oaks are red
And naked thickets shiver in the flaws.
Far out among the lodges keened the squaws,

Shrill with a sorrow women understand,
As though the mother-passion of the land
Had found a human voice to claim the child.

With lifted brows the bland commission smiled,
As clever men who share a secret joke.

At length the Brulé, Swift Bear, rose and spoke,
'Twixt fear and favor poised. He seemed a man
Who, doubting both his ponies, rode the span
And used the quirt with caution. Black Horse then
Harangued the crowd a space, the words, Cheyenne,
Their sense, an echo of the White Man's plea,
Rebounding from a tense expectancy
Of many pleasing gifts.

                            But all the while
These wrestled with the question, mile on mile
The White Man's answer crept along the road—
Two hundred mule-teams, leaning to the load,
And seven hundred soldiers! Middle May
Had seen their dust cloud slowly trail away
From Kearney. Rising ever with the sun
And falling when the evening had begun,
It drifted westward. When the low-swung moon
Was like a cradle for the baby June,
They camped at Julesburg. Yet another week
Across the South Platte's flood to Pumpkin Creek
They fought the stubborn road. Beneath the towers
Of Court House Rock, awash in starry showers,
Their fagged herd grazed. Past Chimney Rock they
        crawled;
Past where the roadway narrows, dizzy walled;
Past Mitchell Post. And now, intent to win
Ere dusk to where the Laramie comes in,
The surly teamsters swore and plied the goad.
The lurching wagons grumbled at the road,

The trace-chains clattered and the spent mules
    brayed,
Protesting as the cracking lashes played
On lathered withers bitten to the red;
And, glinting in the slant glare overhead,
A big dust beckoned to the Soldier's Town.

It happened now that Red Cloud, peering down
The dazzling valley road with narrowed eyes,
Beheld that picture-writing on the skies
And knitted puzzled brows to make it out.
So, weighing this and that, a lonely scout
Might read a trail by moonlight. Loudly still
The glib logicians wrangled, as they will,
The freer for the prime essential lacked—
A due allowance for the Brutal Fact,
That, by the vulgar trick of being so,
Confounds logicians.

        Lapsing in a flow
Of speech and counter-speech, a half hour passed
While Red Cloud stared and pondered. Then at last
Men saw him rise and leave his brooding place,
The flinty look of battle on his face,
A gripping claw of wrath between his brows.
Electric in the sullen summer drowse,
The silence deepened, waiting for his word;
But still he gazed, nor spoke. The people heard
The river lipping at a stony brink,
The rippling flag, then suddenly the clink
Of bridle-bits, the tinkling sound of spurs.
The chieftains and the white commissioners
Pressed forward with a buzzing of surprise.
The people turned.

        Atop a gentle rise
That cut the way from fort to ford in half,
Came Carrington a-canter with his staff,

And yonder, miles behind, the reeking air
Revealed how many others followed there
To do his will.

              Now rising to a shout,
The voice of Red Cloud towered, crushing out
The wonder-hum that ran from band to band:
"These white men here have begged our hunting land.
Their words are crookéd and their tongues are split;
For even while they feign to beg for it,
Their soldiers come to steal it! Let them try,
And prove how good a warrior is a lie,
And learn how Ogalalas meet a thief!
You, Spotted Tail, may be the beggar's chief—
I go to keep my mother-land from harm!"
He tapped his rifle nestled in his arm.
"From now I put my trust in this!" he said
With lowered voice; then pointing overhead,
"Great Spirit, too, will help me!"

                    With a bound
He cleared the bower-railing for the ground,
And shouting "Bring the horses in," he made
His way across the turbulent parade
To where the Ogalala lodges stood.
So, driving down some hollow in a wood,
A great wind shoulders through the tangled ruck
And after it, swirled inward to the suck,
The crested timber roars.

               Then, like a bird
That fills a sudden lull, again was heard
The clink of steel as Carrington rode through
The man-walled lane that cleft the crowd in two;
And, hobbling after, mindless of the awe
That favors might, a toothless, ancient squaw
Lifted a feeble fist at him and screamed.

THE COUNCIL ON THE POWDER

III

Serenely now the ghost of summer dreamed
On Powder River. 'Twas the brooding time,
With nights of starlight glinting on the rime
That cured the curly grass for winter feed,
And days of blue and gold when scarce a reed
Might stir along the runnels, lean with drouth.
Some few belated cranes were going south,
And any hour the blizzard wind might bawl;
But still the tawny fingers of the Fall,
Lay whist upon the maw of Winter.

                             Thrice
The moon had been a melting boat of ice
Among the burning breakers of the west,
Since Red Cloud, bitter-hearted, topped the crest
Above the Fort and took the homeward track,
The Bad Face Ogalalas at his back
And some few Brulés. Silently he rode,
And they who saw him bent as with a load
Of all the tribal sorrow that should be,
Pursued the trail as silently as he—
A fateful silence, boding little good.
Beyond the mouth of Bitter Cottonwood
They travelled; onward through the winding halls
Where Platte is darkened; and the listening walls
Heard naught of laughter—heard the ponies blow,
The rawhide creak upon the bent travaux,
The lodge-poles skid and slidder in the sand.
Nor yet beyond amid the meadowland

Was any joy; nor did the children play,
Despite the countless wooers by the way—
Wild larkspur, tulip, bindweed, prairie pea.
The shadow of a thing that was to be
Fell on them too, though what they could not tell.

Still on, beyond the Horseshoe and La Prele,
They toiled up Sage Creek where the prickly pear
Bloomed gaudily about the camp. And there
The Cheyenne, Black Horse, riding from the south,
Came dashing up with sugar in his mouth
To spew on bitter moods. "Come back," he whined;
"Our good white brothers call you, being kind
And having many gifts to give to those
Who hear them." But the braves unstrung their bows
And beat him from the village, counting *coup,*
While angry squaws reviled the traitor too,
And youngsters dogged him, aping what he said.
Across the barren Cheyenne watershed
Their ponies panted, where the sage brush roots
Bit deep to live. They saw the Pumpkin Buttes
From Dry Fork. Then the Powder led them down
A day past Lodge Pole Creek.

        Here Red Cloud's town,
With water near and grass enough, now stood
Amid a valley strewn with scrubby wood;
And idling in the lazy autumn air
The lodge-smoke rose. The only idler there!
For all day long the braves applied their hate
To scraping dogwood switches smooth and straight
For battle-arrows; and the teeth that bit
The gnarly shaft, put venom into it
Against the day the snarling shaft should bite.
Unceasingly from morning until night
The squaws toiled that their fighting men might eat,
Nor be less brave because of freezing feet.
By hundreds they were stitching rawhide soles

To buckskin uppers. Many drying-poles
Creaked with the recent hunt; and bladders, packed
With suet, fruit and flesh, were being stacked
For hungers whetted by the driving snow.
Fresh robes were tanning in the autumn glow
For warriors camping fireless in the cold.
And noisily the mimic battles rolled
Among the little children, grim in play.

The village had been growing day by day
Since Red Cloud sent a pipe to plead his cause
Among the far-flung Tetons. Hunkpapas,
Unhurried by the fear of any foe,
Were making winter meat along Moreau
The day the summons came to gird their loins.
The Sans Arcs, roving where the Belle Fourche joins
The Big Cheyenne, had smoked the proffered pipe
When grapes were good and plums were getting ripe.
Amid the Niobrara meadowlands
And up the White, the scattered Brulé bands,
That scorned the talk at Laramie, had heard.
Among the Black Hills went the pipe and word
To find the Minneconjoux killing game
Where elk and deer were plentiful and tame
And clear creeks bellowed from the canyon beds.
Still westward where the double Cheyenne heads,
The hunting Ogalalas hearkened too.
So grew the little camp as lakelets do
When coulees grumble to a lowering sky.

Big names, already like a battle cry,
Were common in the town; and there were some
In which terrific thunders yet were dumb
But soon should echo fearsome and abhorred:
Crow King, Big Foot, the younger Hump, and Sword,
Black Leg and Black Shield, Touch-the-Cloud and Gall;
And that one fear would trumpet over all—
Young Crazy Horse; and Spotted Tail, the wise;

Red Cloud and Man Afraid, both battle-cries;
Rain-in-the-Face, yet dumb; and Sitting Bull.

'Twas council time, for now the moon was full;
The time when, ere the stars may claim the dark,
A goblin morning with the owl for lark
Steals in; and ere the flags of day are furled,
Pressed white against the window of the world
A scarred face stares astonished at the sun.
The moonset and the sunrise came as one;
But ere the daybreak lifted by a span
The frosty dusk, the tepee tops began
To burgeon, and a faery sapling grove
Stood tall, to bloom in sudden red and mauve
And gold against the horizontal light.
Still humped, remembering the nipping night,
The dogs prowled, sniffing, round the open flaps
Where women carved raw haunches in their laps
To feed the kettles for the council feast.
Amid the silence of the lifting east
The criers shouted now—old men and sage,
Using the last sad privilege of age
For brief pathetic triumphs over youth.
Neat saws and bits of hortatory truth
They proffered with the orders of the day.
And names that were as scarlet in the gray
Of pending ill they uttered like a song—
The names of those who, being wise or strong,
Should constitute the council. 'Round and 'round,
The focal centers of a spreading sound,
The criers went. The folk began to fuse
In groups that seized the latest bit of news
And sputtered with the tongue of fool and seer.
A roaring hailed some chanted name held dear;
Or in a silence, no less eloquent,
Some other, tainted with suspicion, went
Among the people like a wind that blows
In solitary places.

Day arose
A spear-length high. The chattering became
A bated hum; for, conscious of their fame,
And clad in gorgeous ceremonial dress,
The Fathers of the Council cleft the press
In lanes that awe ran on before to clear;
And expectation closed the flowing rear
Sucked in to where the council bower stood.
Long since the busy squaws had fetched the wood
And lit the council fire, now smouldering.
The great men entered, formed a broken ring
To open eastward, lest the Light should find
No entrance, and the leaders of the blind
See darkly too. With reverential awe
The people, pressed about the bower, saw
The fathers sit, and every tongue was stilled.

Now Red Cloud took the sacred pipe and filled
The bowl with fragrant bark, and plucked a brand
To light it. Now with slowly lifted hand
He held it to the glowing sky, and spoke:
"Grandfather, I have filled a pipe to smoke,
And you shall smoke it first. In you we trust
To show good trails." He held it to the dust.
"Grandmother, I have filled a pipe for you,"
He said, "and you must keep us strong and true,
For you are so." Then offering the stem
To all four winds, he supplicated them
That they should blow good fortune. Then he smoked;
And all the Fathers after him invoked
The Mysteries that baffle Man's desire.

Some women fetched and set beside the fire
The steaming kettles, then with groundward gaze
Withdrew in haste. A man of ancient days,
Who searched a timeless dusk with rheumy stare
And saw the ghosts of things that struggle there
Before men struggle, now remembered Those

With might to help. Six bits of meat he chose,
The best the pots afforded him, and these
He gave in order to the Mysteries,
The Sky, the Earth, the Winds, as was their due.
"Before I eat, I offer this to you,"
He chanted as he gave; "so all men should.
I hope that what I eat may do me good,
And what you eat may help you even so.
I ask you now to make my children grow
To men and women. Keep us healthy still,
And give us many buffalo to kill
And plenty grass for animals to eat."
Some youths came forth to parcel out the meat
In order as the councillors were great
In deeds of worth; and each, before he ate,
Addressed the mystic sources of the good.

The feast now being finished, Red Cloud stood
Still pondering his words with mouth set grim;
But men felt thunder in the hush of him
And knew what lightning struggled to be wise
Behind the hawklike brooding of the eyes,
The chipped flint look about the cheek and jaw.
The humming of a hustling autumn flaw
In aspen thickets swept the waiting crowd.
It seemed his voice would tower harsh and loud.
It crooned.

"My friends, 'twas many snows ago
When first we welcomed white men. Now we know
Their hearts are bad and all their words are lies.
They brought us shining things that pleased the eyes
And weapons that were better than we knew.
And this seemed very good. They brought us too
The spirit water, strong to wash away
The coward's fear, and for a moment stay
The creeping of old age and gnawing sorrow.
My friends, if you would have these things tomorrow,

Forget the way our fathers taught us all.
As though you planned to live till mountains fall,
Seek out all things men need and pile them high.
Be fat yourself and let the hungry die;
Be warm yourself and let the naked freeze.
So shall you see the trail the white man sees.
And when your tepee bulges to the peak,
Look round you for some neighbor who is weak
And take his little too. Dakotas, think!
Shall all the white man's trinkets and his drink,
By which the mind is overcome and drowned,
Be better than our homes and hunting ground,
The guiding wisdom of our old men's words?
Shall we be driven as the white man's herds
From grass to bitter grass? When Harney said
His people, seeking for the yellow lead,
Would like an iron trail across our land,
Our good old chieftains did not understand
What snake would crawl among us. It would pass
Across our country; not a blade of grass
Should wither for that passing, they were told.
And now when scarce the council fire is cold,
Along the Little Piney hear the beat
Of axes and the desecrating feet
Of soldiers! Are we cowards? Shall we stand
Unmoved as trees and see our Mother Land
Plowed up for corn?"

           Increasing as he spoke,
The smothered wrath now mastered him, and 'woke
The sleeping thunder all had waited for.
Out of a thrilling hush he shouted: *"War!"*—
A cry to make an enemy afraid.
The grazing ponies pricked their ears and neighed,
Recalling whirlwind charges; and the town
Roared after like a brush-jam breaking down
With many waters.

When the quiet fell
Another rose with phrases chosen well
To glut the tribal wrath, and took his seat
Amid the crowd's acclaim. Like chunks of meat,
Flung bloody to a pack, raw words were said
By others; and the rabble's fury, fed,
Outgrew the eager feeding. Who would dare
To rise amid the blood-lust raging there
And offer water?

          Spotted Tail stood up;
And since all knew no blood was in the cup
That he would give, dumb scorn rejected him.
He gazed afar, and something seen made dim
The wonted quizzic humor of the eyes.
The mouth, once terrible with battle-cries,
Took on a bitter droop as he began.

"*Hey—hey'-hey!* So laments an aging man
Who totters and can never more be free
As once he was. *Hey—hey'-hey!* So may we
Exclaim today for what the morrow brings.
There is a time, my brothers, for all things,
And we are getting old. Consider, friends,
How everything begins and grows and ends
That other things may have their time and grow.
What tribes of deer and elk and buffalo
Have we ourselves destroyed lest we should die!
About us now you hear the dead leaves sigh;
Since these were green, how few the moons have
     been!
We share in all this trying to begin,
This trying not to die. Consider well
The White Man—what you know and what men
     tell
About his might. His never weary mind
And busy hands do magic for his kind.
Those things he loves we think of little worth;

And yet, behold! he sweeps across the earth,
And what shall stop him? Something that is true
Must help him do the things that he can do,
For lies are not so mighty. Be not stirred
By thoughts of vengeance and the burning word!
Such things are for the young; but let us give
Good counsel for the time we have to live,
And seek the better way, as old men should."

He ended; yet a little while he stood
Abashed and lonely, seeing how his words
Had left as little trace as do the birds
Upon the wide insouciance of air.
He sat at length; and round him crouching there
The hostile silence closed, as waters close
Above the drowned.

       Then Sitting Bull arose;
And through the stirring crowd a murmur 'woke
As of a river yielding to the stroke
Of some deft swimmer. No heroic height
Proclaimed him peer among the men of might,
Nor was his bearing such as makes men serve.
Bull-torsed, squat-necked, with legs that kept a
    curve
To fit the many ponies he had backed,
He scarcely pleased the eyes. But what he lacked
Of visible authority to mould
Men's lives, was compensated manifold
By something penetrating in his gaze
That searched the rabble, seeming to appraise
The common weakness that should make him
    strong.
One certainty about him held the throng—
His hatred of the white men. Otherwise,
Conjecture, interweaving truth and lies,
Wrought various opinions of the man.
A mountebank—so one opinion ran—

A battle-shirking intimate of squaws,
A trivial contriver of applause,
A user of the sacred for the base.
Yet there was something other in his face
Than vanity and craft. And there were those
Who saw him in that battle with the Crows
The day he did a thing no coward could.
There ran a slough amid a clump of wood
From whence, at little intervals, there broke
A roaring and a spurt of rifle-smoke
That left another wound among the Sioux.
Now Sitting Bull rode down upon the slough
To see what might be seen there. What he saw
Was such as might have gladdened any squaw—
A wounded warrior with an empty gun!
'Twas then that deed of Sitting Bull was done,
And many saw it plainly from the hill.
Would any coward shun an easy kill
And lose a scalp? Yet many saw him throw
His loaded rifle over to the Crow,
Retreat a space, then wheel to charge anew.
With but a riding quirt he counted *coup*
And carried back a bullet in his thigh.
Let those who jeered the story for a lie
Behold him limping yet! And others said
He had the gift of talking with the dead
And used their clearer seeing to foretell
Dark things aright; that he could weave a spell
To make a foeman feeble if he would.

Such things the people pondered while he stood
And searched them with a quiet, broad-browed stare.
Then suddenly some magic happened there.
Can men grow taller in a breathing span?
He spoke; and even scorners of the man
Were conscious of a swift, disarming thrill,
The impact of a dominating will
That overcame them.

"Brothers, you have seen
The way the spring sun makes the prairie green
And wakes new life in animal and seed,
Preparing plenty for the biggest need,
Remembering the little hungers too.
The same mysterious quickening makes new
Men's hearts, for by that power we also live.
And so, till now, we thought it good to give
All life its share of what that power sends
To man and beast alike. But hear me, friends!
We face a greedy people, weak and small
When first our fathers met them, now grown tall
And overbearing. Tireless in toil,
These madmen think it good to till the soil,
And love for endless getting marks them fools.
Behold, they bind their poor with many rules
And let their rich go free! They even steal
The poor man's little for the rich man's weal!
Their feeble have a god their strong may flout!
They cut the land in pieces, fencing out
Their neighbors from the mother of all men!
When she is sick, they make her bear again
With medicines they give her with the seed!
All this is sacrilegious! Yet they heed
No word, and like a river in the spring
They flood the country, sweeping everything
Before them! 'Twas not many snows ago
They said that we might hunt our buffalo
In this our land forever. Now they come
To break that promise. Shall we cower, dumb?
Or shall we say: 'First kill us—here we stand!'"

He paused; then stooping to the mother-land,
He scraped a bit of dust and tossed it high.
Against the hollow everlasting sky
All watched it drifting, sifting back again
In utter silence. "So it is with men,"
Said Sitting Bull, his voice now low and tense;

"What better time, my friends, for going hence
Than when we have so many foes to kill?"

He ceased. As though they heard him speaking still,
The people listened; for he had a way
That seemed to mean much more than he could say
And over all the village cast a spell.
At length some warrior uttered in a yell
The common hate. 'Twas like the lean blue flash
That stabs a sultry hush before the crash
Of heaven-rending thunder and the loud
Assault of winds. Then fury took the crowd
And set it howling with the lust to slay.

The councillors were heard no more that day;
And from the moony hill tops all night long
The wolves gave answer to the battle-song,
And saw their valley hunting-grounds aflare
With roaring fires, and frenzied shadows there
That leaped and sang as wolves do, yet were men.

FORT PHIL KEARNEY

IV

Long since the column, pushing north again
With Carrington, had left the little post
On Laramie; unwitting how the ghost
Of many a trooper, lusty yet and gay,
Disconsolately drifting back that way,
Should fill unseen the gaps of shattered ranks.

Scarce moved to know what shadows dogged their flanks,
Till all the winds that blew were talking spies
And draws had ears and every hill-top, eyes,
And silence, tongues, the seven hundred went.
How brazenly their insolent intent
Was flaunted! Even wolves might understand
These men were going forth to wed the land
And spawn their breed therein. Behold their squaws!
Could such defend the Great White Father's laws?
So weak they were their warriors hewed the wood,
Nor did they tend the pots, as women should,
Nor fill them.

   Powder River caught the word
Of how they swam their long-horned cattle herd
At Bridger's Ferry. Big Horn and the Tongue
Beheld through nearer eyes the long line flung
Up Sage Creek valley; heard through distant ears
The cracking lashes of the muleteers
The day the sandy trail grew steep and bleak.
The Rosebud saw them crossing Lightning Creek,
Whence, southward, cone outsoaring dizzy cone,

Until the last gleamed splendidly alone
They viewed the peak of Laramie. When, high
Between the head of North Fork and the Dry
They lifted Cloud Peak scintillant with snows,
The Cheyenne hunters and Arapahoes,
Far-flung as where the Wind becomes the Horn,
Discussed their progress. Spirits of the morn,
That watched them break the nightly camp and leave,
Outwinged the crane to gossip with the eve
In distant camps. Beyond the Lodge Pole's mouth
Relentless Red Cloud, poring on the south,
Could see them where the upper Powder ran
Past Reno Post, and counted to a man
The soldiers left there. Tattlings of the noon
Were bruited by the glimmer of the moon
In lands remote; till, pushing northward yet
Past Crazy Woman's Fork and Lake DeSmedt,
They reached the Big and Little Piney Creeks.

Some such a land the famished hunter seeks
In fever-dreams of coolness. All day long
The snow-born waters hummed a little song
To virgin meadows, till the sun went under;
Then tardy freshets in a swoon of thunder,
That deepened with the dark, went rushing by,
As 'twere the Night herself sang lullaby
Till morning. Cottonwoods and evergreens
Made music out of what the silence means
In timeless solitudes. And over all,
White towers dizzy on a floating wall
Of stainless white, the Big Horn Mountains rose.
Absoraka, the Country of the Crows,
A land men well might fight for!

                              Here they camped,
Rejoicing, man and beast. The work-mule champed
The forage of the elk, and rolled to sate
His lust for greenness. Like a voice of fate,

Foretelling ruthless years, his blatant bray
With horns of woe and trumpets of dismay
Crowded the hills. The milk cow and the steer
In pastures of the bison and the deer
Lowed softly. And the trail-worn troopers went
About their duties, whistling, well content
To share this earthly paradise of game.

But scarcely were the tents up, when there came—
Was it a sign? One moment it was noon,
A golden peace hypnotic with the tune
Of bugs among the grasses; and the next,
The spacious splendor of the world was vexed
With twilight that estranged familiar things.
A moaning sound, as of enormous wings
Flung wide to bear some swooping bat of death,
Awakened. Hills and valleys held their breath
To hear that sound. A nervous troop-horse neighed
Shrill in the calm. Instinctively afraid,
The cattle bellowed and forgot to graze;
And raucous mules deplored the idle day's
Untimely end. Then presently there fell
What seemed a burlesque blizzard out of hell—
A snow of locusts—tawny flakes at strife,
That, driven by a gust of rabid life,
Smothered the windless noon! The lush grass bent,
Devoured in bending. Wagon-top and tent
Sagged with the drift of brown corrosive snow.
Innumerable hungers shrilled below;
A humming fog of hungers hid the sky,
Until a cool breath, falling from the high
White ramparts, came to cleanse the stricken world.
Then suddenly the loud rack lifted, swirled
To eastward; and the golden light returned.

Now day by day the prairie people learned
What wonders happened where the Pineys flowed;
How many wagons rutted out a road

To where the pines stood tallest to be slain;
What medicine the White Man's hand and brain
Had conjured; how they harnessed up a fog
That sent a round knife screaming through a log
From end to end; how many adzes hewed;
And how the desecrated solitude
Beheld upon a level creek-side knoll
The rise of fitted bole on shaven bole,
Until a great fort brazened out the sun.
And while that builded insolence was done,
Far prairies saw the boasting banner flung
Above it, like a hissing adder's tongue,
To menace every ancientry of good.

Long since and oft the workers in the wood
Had felt the presence of a foe concealed.
The drone of mowers in the haying-field
Was silenced often by the rifle's crack,
The arrow's whirr; and often, forging back
With lash and oath along the logging road,
The scared mule-whacker fought behind his load,
His team a kicking tangle. Oft by night
Some hill top wagged a sudden beard of light,
Immediately shorn; and dark hills saw
To glimmer sentient. Hours of drowsy awe
Near dawn had heard the raided cattle bawl,
Afraid of alien herdsmen; bugles call
To horse; the roaring sally; fleeing cries.
And oft by day upon a distant rise
Some naked rider loomed against the glare
With hand at brow to shade a searching stare,
Then like a dream dissolved in empty sky.

So men and fate had labored through July
To make a story. August browned the plain;
And ever Fort Phil Kearney grew amain
With sweat of toil and blood of petty fights.
September brought the tingling silver nights

And men worked faster, thinking of the snows.
Aye, more than storm they dreaded. Friendly Crows
Had told wild tales. Had they not ridden through
The Powder River gathering of Sioux?
And lo, at one far end the day was young;
Noon saw the other! Up along the Tongue
Big villages were dancing! Everywhere
The buzzing wasp of war was in the air.

October smouldered goldenly, and gray
November sulked and threatened. Day by day,
While yet the greater evils held aloof,
The soldiers wrought on wall, stockade and roof
Against the coming wrath of God and Man.
And often where the lonely home-trail ran
They gazed with longing eyes; nor did they see
The dust cloud of the prayed-for cavalry
And ammunition train long overdue.
By now they saw their forces cut in two,
First Reno Post upon the Powder, then
Fort Smith upon the Big Horn needing men;
And here the center of the brewing storm
Would rage.

        Official suavities kept warm
The wire to Laramie—assurance bland
Of peace now reigning in the prairie land;
Attest the treaty signed! So said the mail;
But those who brought it up the Bozeman Trail
Two hundred miles, could tell of running fights,
Of playing tag with Terror in the nights
To hide by day. If peace was anywhere,
It favored most the growing graveyard there
Across the Piney under Pilot Hill.

December opened ominously still,
And scarce the noon could dull the eager fang
That now the long night whetted. Shod hoofs rang

On frozen sod. The tenuated whine
And sudden shriek of buzz-saws biting pine
Were heard far off unnaturally loud.
The six-mule log-teams labored in a cloud;
The drivers beat their breasts with aching hands.
As yet the snow held off; but prowling bands
Grew bolder. Weary night-guards on the walls
Were startled broad awake by wolf-like calls
From spots of gloom uncomfortably near;
And out across the crystal hemisphere
Weird yammerings arose and died away
To dreadful silence. Every sunny day
The looking-glasses glimmered all about.
So, clinging to the darker side of doubt,
Men took their boots to bed, nor slumbered
     soon.

It happened on the sixth December noon
That from a hill commanding many a mile
The lookout, gazing off to Piney Isle,
Beheld the log-train crawling up a draw
Still half way out. With naked eye he saw
A lazy serpent reeking in the glare
Of wintry sunlight. Nothing else was there
But empty country under empty skies.
Then suddenly it seemed a blur of flies
Arose from each adjacent gulch and break
And, swarming inward, swirled about the snake
That strove to coil amid the stinging mass.
One moment through the ill-adjusted glass
Vague shadows flitted; then the whirling specks
Were ponies with their riders at their necks,
Swung low. The lurching wagons spurted smoke;
The teams were plunging.

              Frantic signals woke
The bugles at the fort, the brawl of men
Obeying "boots and saddles."

Once again
The sentry lifts his glass. 'Tis like a dream.
So very near the silent figures seem
A hand might almost touch them. Here they come
Hell-bent for blood—distorted mouths made dumb
With distance! One can see the muffled shout,
The twang of bow-thongs! Leaping fog blots out
The agitated picture—flattens, spreads.
Dull rumblings wake and perish. Tossing heads
Emerge, and ramrods prickle in the rack.
A wheel-mule, sprouting feathers at his back,
Rears like a clumsy bird essaying flight
And falls to vicious kicking. Left and right
Deflected hundreds wheel about and swing
To charge anew—tempestuous galloping
On cotton! Empty ponies bolt away
To turn and stare high-headed on the fray
With muted snorting at the deeds men do.
But listen how at last a sound breaks through
The deathly silence of the scene! Hurrah
For forty troopers roaring down the draw
With Fetterman! A cloud of beaten dust
Sent skurrying before a thunder-gust,
They round the hogback yonder. With a rush
They pierce the limpid curtain of the hush,
Quiescing in the picture. Hurry, men!
The rabid dogs are rushing in again!
Look! Hurry! No, they break midway! They see
The squadron dashing up. They turn, they flee
Before that pack of terriers—like rats!
Yell, yell, you lucky loggers—wave your hats
And thank the Captain that you've kept your hair!
Look how they scatter to the northward there,
Dissolving into nothing! Ply the spurs,
You fire-eaters! Catch that pack of curs
This side the Peno, or they'll disappear!
Look out! They're swooping in upon your rear!
Wherever did they come from? Look! Good God!

The breaks ahead belch ponies, and the sod
On every side sprouts warriors!

                   Holy Spoons!
The raw recruits have funked it! Turn, you loons,
You cowards! Can't you see the Captain's game
To face them with a handful? Shame! O shame!
They'll rub him out—turn back—that's not the way
We did it to the Johnnies many a day
In Dixie! Every mother's baby rides
As though it mattered if they saved their hides!
Their empty faces gulp the miles ahead.
Ride on and live to wish that you were dead
Back yonder where the huddled muskets spit
Against a sea!

               Now—now you're in for it!
Here comes the Colonel galloping like sin
Around the hill! Hurrah—they're falling in—
Good boys! It's little wonder that you ran.
I'm not ashamed to say to any man
I might have run.

                Ah, what a pretty sight!
Go on, go on and show 'em that you're white!
They're breaking now—you've got 'em on the run—
They're scattering! Hurrah!

                  The fight was done;
No victory to boast about, indeed—
Just labor. Sweat today, tomorrow, bleed—
An incidental difference. And when
The jaded troopers trotted home again
There wasn't any cheering. Six of those
Clung dizzily to bloody saddle-bows;
And Bingham was the seventh and was dead;
And Bowers, with less hair upon his head

Than arrows in his vitals, prayed to die.
He did that night.

                  Now thirteen days went by
With neither snow nor foe; and all the while
The log-trains kept the road to Piney Isle.
Soon all the needed timber would be hauled,
The work be done. Then, snugly roofed and walled,
What need for men to fear? Some came to deem
The former mood of dread a foolish dream,
Grew mellow, thinking of the holidays
With time for laughter and a merry blaze
On every hearth and nothing much to do.
As for the bruited power of the Sioux,
Who doubted it was overdrawn a mite?
At any rate, they wouldn't stand and fight
Unless the odds were heavy on their side.
It seemed the Colonel hadn't any pride—
Too cautious. Look at Fetterman and Brown,
Who said they'd ride the whole Sioux nation down
With eighty men; and maybe could, by jing!
Both scrappers—not afraid of anything—
A pair of eagles hungering for wrens!

And what about a flock of butchered hens
In Peno valley not so long ago
But for the Colonel? Bowers ought to know;
Go ask him! Thus the less heroic jeered.
These Redskins didn't run because they feared;
'Twas strategy; they didn't fight our way.

Again it happened on the nineteenth day
The lookout saw the logging-train in grief;
And Captain Powell, leading the relief,
Returned without a single scratch to show.
The twentieth brought neither snow nor foe.
The morrow came—a peaceful, scarlet morn.
It seemed the homesick sun in Capricorn

Had found new courage for the homeward track
And, yearning out across the zodiac
To Cancer, brightened with the conjured scene
Of grateful hills and valleys flowing green,
Sweet incense rising from the rain-soaked sward,
And color-shouts of welcome to the Lord
And Savior.

   Ninety took the logging-road
That morning, happy that the final load
Would trundle back that day, and all be well.
But hardly two miles out the foemen fell
Upon them, swarming three to one. And so
Once more the hill-top lookout signalled woe
And made the fort a wasp-nest buzzing ire.

The rip and drawl of running musket fire,
The muffled, rhythmic uproar of the Sioux
Made plain to all that what there was to do
Out yonder gave but little time to waste.
A band of horse and infantry soon faced
The Colonel's quarters, waiting for the word.
Above the distant tumult many heard
His charge to Powell, leader of the band;
And twice 'twas said that all might understand
The need for caution: "Drive away the foe
And free the wagon-train; but do not go
Past Lodge Trail Ridge."

    A moment's silence fell;
And many in the after-time would dwell
Upon that moment, little heeded then—
The ghostly horses and the ghostly men,
The white-faced wives, the gaping children's eyes
Grown big with wonder and a dread surmise
To see their fathers waiting giant-tall;
That mumbling voice of doom beyond the wall;
The ghastly golden pleasance of the air;

And Fetterman, a spectre, striding there
Before the Colonel, while the portals yawn.
As vivid as a picture lightning-drawn
Upon the night, that memory would flash,
More vivid for the swooping backward crash
Of gloom. 'Twas but the hinges of the gates
That shrieked that moment, while the eager Fates
Told off the waiting band and gloated: *Done!*
He asked for eighty—give him eighty-one!
Then Fetterman, unwitting how the rim
Of endless outer silence pressed on him
And all his comrades, spoke: "With deference due
To Captain Powell, Colonel, and to you,
I claim command as senior captain here."

So ever is the gipsy Danger dear
To Courage; so the lusty woo and wed
Their dooms, to father in a narrow bed
A song against the prosing after-years.

And now the restive horses prick their ears
And nicker to the bugle. Fours about,
They rear and wheel to line. The hillsides shout
Back to the party. Forward! Now it swings
High-hearted through the gate of common things
To where bright hazard, like a stormy moon,
Still gleams round Hector, Roland, Sigurd, Fionn;
And all the lost, horizon-hungry prows,
Eternal in contemporary nows,
Heave seaward yet.

       The Colonel mounts the wall,
And once again is heard his warning call:
"Relieve the wagon-train, but do not go
Past Lodge Trail Ridge." And Fetterman, below,
Turns back a shining face on him, and smiles
Across the gap that neither years nor miles
May compass now.

A little farther still
They watched him skirt a westward-lying hill
That hid him from the train, to disappear.
"He'll swing about and strike them in the rear,"
The watchers said, "and have the logging crew
For anvil."

Now a solitary Sioux
Was galloping in circles on a height
That looked on both the squadron and the fight—
The prairie sign for "many bison seen."
A lucky case-shot swept the summit clean
And presently the distant firing ceased;
Nor was there sound or sight of man or beast
Outside for age-long minutes after that.

At length a logger, spurring up the flat,
Arrived with words of doubtful cheer to say.
The Indians had vanished Peno way;
The train was moving on to Piney Isle.
He had no news of Fetterman.

RUBBED OUT

V

                    Meanwhile
Where ran the Bozeman Road along the bleak
North slope of Lodge Trail Ridge to Peno
    Creek,
Big hopes were burning. Silence waited there.
The brown land, even as the high blue air,
Seemed empty. Yet the troubled crows that flew
Keen-eyed above the sunning valley knew
What made the windless slough-grass ripple so,
And how a multitude of eyes below
Were peering southward to the road-scarred rise
Where every covert was alive with eyes
That scanned the bare horizon to the south.

The white of dawn had seen the Peno's mouth
A-swarm with men—Cheyennes, Arapahoes,
Dakotas. When the pale-faced sun arose—
A spectre fleeing from a bath of blood—
It saw them like a thunder-fathered flood
Surge upward through the sounding sloughs and
    draws—
Afoot and mounted, veterans and squaws,
Youths new to war, the lowly and the great—
A thousand-footed, single-hearted hate
Flung forward. Now their chanted battle-songs
Dismayed the hills. Now silent with their wrongs
They strode, the sullen hum of hoofs and feet,
Through valleys where aforetime life was sweet,
More terrible than songs or battle cries.

The sun had traversed half the morning skies
When, entering the open flat, they poured
To where the roadway crossed the Peno ford
Below the Ridge. Above them wheeled and pried
The puzzled crows, to learn what thing had died,
What carcass, haply hidden from the ken
Of birds, had lured so large a flock of men
Thus chattering with lust. There, brooding doom,
They paused and made the brown December bloom
With mockeries of August—demon flowers
And lethal, thirsting for the sanguine showers
That soon should soak the unbegetting fields—
The trailing bonnets and the pictured shields,
The lances nodding in the warwind's breath,
And faces brave with paint to outstare Death
In some swift hush of battle!

                              Briefly so
They parleyed. Then the spears began to flow
On either side the Ridge—a double stream
Of horsemen, winking out as in a dream
High up among the breaks that flanked the
        trail.
Amid the tall dry grasses of the vale
The footmen disappeared; and all the place
Was still and empty as a dead man's face
That sees unmoved the wheeling birds of prey.

The anxious moments crawled. Then far away
Across the hills a muffled tumult grew,
As of a blanket being ripped in two
And many people shouting underground.
The valley grasses rippled to the sound
As though it were a gusty wind that passed.

Far off a bugle's singing braved the vast
And perished in a wail.

The tall grass stirred.
The rumor of the distant fight was heard
A little longer. Suddenly it stopped;
And silence, like a sky-wide blanket, dropped
Upon the landscape empty as the moon.

The sun, now scarce a lance-length from the noon,
Seemed waiting for whatever might occur.
Across the far Northwest a purplish blur
Had gathered and was crawling up the sky.

Now presently a nearer bugle cry
Defied the hush—a scarlet flower of sound
That sowed the sterile silences around
With futile seed of music.

             Once again
The sound of firing and the cries of men
Arose; but now 'twas just beyond the place
Where, climbing to the azure rim of space,
The roadway topped the Ridge and disappeared.
The tongueless coverts listened, thousand-eared,
And heard hoof-thunders rumbling over there.

Then suddenly the high blue strip of air
Was belching warriors in a wind of cries.
In breakneck rout they tumbled from the skies,
Wheeled round to fling more arrows at a foe,
And fled to where the breast-deep grass below
Swayed wildly.

              Now a crow-black stallion 'rose,
And looming huge against the blue noon doze,
Raced back and forth across the Ridge's rim,
While, shooting from beneath the neck of him,
The Cheyenne Big Nose held the roaring rear;
Nor did the snarling musket-balls come near,
So mighty was his medicine, they say.

Now presently the high blue wall of day
Spewed cavalry along the Ridge; and then
A marvel for the tongues and ears of men
Amazed the hidden watchers of the height.
For like a thunder-stridden wind of night
That rages through a touselled poplar grove,
The rider of the stallion charged, and drove
Straight through the middle of the mounted crowd.
Men saw his bonnet tossing in a cloud
Of manes and tails; and sabre lightnings played
About it. Then, emerging undismayed,
He charged back through and galloped down the hill
With bullets that were impotent to kill
Spat-pinging all around.

      The firing ceased.
The fugitives were half a mile at least
Beyond the Peno ford. There, circling wide
With bows and lances brandished, they defied
The foe to come and fight with them. By now
The infantry had crossed the Ridge's brow.
It joined the troop a little way below;
Then all together, cautiously and slow,
Came down the hated road. And silence lay
On summit, slope and valley, deep as day
And doomful, as they came. The flat could hear
The murmur of the straining saddle-gear,
The shuffling feet, the clinking of the bits;
And when a nervous troop-horse neighed by fits,
The ponies, lurking in the broken lands
That flanked the Ridge, kept silence for the hands
That gripped their nostrils.

      Now the eighty-one
Were half way down the hill. The nooning sun
Slipped fearfully behind a flying veil,
And from the gray northwest a raw-cold gale
Came booming up. The fugitive decoys,

Off yonder in the flat, like playing boys
Divided now and waged a mimic fight.
Immediately half way up the height
Among the breaks appeared a warrior's torse.
A thousand hidden eyes knew Little Horse,
The Cheyenne chieftain; saw him wave a spear
Left-handed; pass it round him in the rear
To seize it with the right.

                 The whole flat swarmed
With footmen. Mounted warriors thunder-stormed
By hundreds from the breaks above; and one
Came dashing down the ridge-road at a run
And plunged among the soldiery to die
Beneath the frantic sabres. With a cry
That set the horses wild, the swarm closed in.

The cavalry, as hoping yet to win
The summit of the Ridge, wheeled round and hewed
A slow way upward through the solitude
Of lances, howling in the arrow-storm.
The rest, already circled by the swarm,
Took cover in a patch of tumbled rock
Where, huddled like a blizzard-beaten flock,
They faced the swirling death they could not stem.
A little while before it smothered them
The dwindling few toiled mightily, men say,
With gun-butts swinging in the dim mêlée
Of battle-clubs and lances; then were still.

The wave broke over, surging up the hill;
For yonder yet the battle smoked and roared
Where, midway 'twixt the summit and the ford,
The little band of troopers held the height—
Green manhood withering in a locust flight
Of arrows! Aye, a gloaming of despair
The shuttling arrows wove above them there,
So many were the bows. Cheyenne and Sioux

Went down beneath the shafts their brothers drew;
Arapahoes struck down Arapahoes
Unwittingly. And many a red gout froze
Along the slopes, so keen had grown the gale.

A little while those makers of a tale
Gave battle like a badger in a hole;
Nor could the ponies charge the narrow knoll,
For either slope was steep and gully-scrawled.
Still up and up the cautious bowmen crawled,
And still the troopers overawed the field.

Then presently, men say, a white chief reeled;
Rolled from his saddle; like a man gone daft
Got up and doddered, tugging at a shaft
That sprouted from his belly. Then a yell
Of many bowmen mocked him as he fell,
His writhing body feathered like a goose.

The troops began to turn their horses loose,
Retreating up the ridge, a hopeless crowd.
A lull of battle thinned the arrow-cloud
Above them; for the mounted warriors knew
The soldiers doomed whatever they might do,
And fell to rounding up the runaways.
Meanwhile the broken troopers in a daze
Of desperation scrambled up the slope.
Strewn boulders yonder woke a lying hope,
And there they waited, living, in their grave.

The horse-chase ended. Once again the wave
Began to mount the steep on either side,
While warriors hailed their fellows and replied:
Be ready!—We are ready, brothers!

                                            Then
The hillsides bellowed with a surf of men
Flung crowding on the boulders. 'Twas the end.

Some trooper's wolfhound, mourning for his
    friend,
Loped fortward, pausing now and then to cry
His urgent question to the hostile sky
That spat a stinging frost. And someone said:
"Let yonder dog bear tidings of the dead
To make the white men tremble over there."
"No, teach them that we do not even spare
Their dogs!" another said. An arrow sang
Shrill to the mark. The wolfhound yelped and
    sprang,
Snapped at the feather, wilted, and was still.

And so they perished on that barren hill
Beside the Peno. And the Winter strode
Numb-footed down that bloody stretch of road
At twilight, when a squadron came to read
The corpse-writ rune of battle, deed by deed,
Between the Ridge's summit and the ford.

The blizzard broke at dusk. All night it roared
Round Fort Phil Kearney mourning for the slain.

THE WAGON BOXES

VI

Besieging January made the plain
One vast white camp to reinforce the foe
That watched the fort. Mad cavalries of snow
Assaulted; stubborn infantries of cold
Sat round the walls and waited. Wolves grew
     bold
To peer by night across the high stockade
Where, builded for the Winter's escalade,
The hard drifts leaned. And often in the deep
Of night men started from a troubled sleep
To think the guards were fighting on the wall
And, roaring over like a waterfall,
The wild hordes pouring in upon the lost.
But 'twas the timber popping in the frost,
The mourning wolves. Nor did the dawn
     bring cheer.
Becandled like a corpse upon a bier
The lifeless sun, from gloom to early gloom,
Stole past,—a white procession to a tomb
Illumining the general despair.

Meanwhile Omniscience in a swivel chair,
Unmenaced half a continent away,
Amid more pressing matters of the day
Had edited the saga of the dead.
Compare the treaty where it plainly said
There was no war! All duly signed and sealed!
Undoubtedly the evidence revealed
The need of an official reprimand.

Wherefore stern orders ticked across the land
From Washington to Laramie. Perhaps
No blizzard swept the neat official maps
To nip a tracing finger. Howsoe'er,
Four companies of horse and foot must bear
To Fort Phil Kearney tidings of its shame.
Through ten score miles of frozen hell they came—
Frost-bitten, wolfish—with the iron word
Of Carrington dishonored and transferred
To Reno Post. The morning that he went,
The sun was like a sick man in a tent,
Crouched shivering between two feeble fires.
Far off men heard his griding wagon tires
Shriek fife-like in the unofficial snow,
His floundering three-span mule-teams blaring
    woe
Across the blue-cold waste; and he was gone.

Without a thaw the bitter spell wore on
To raging February. Days on days
Men could not see beyond the whirling haze
That made the fort's the world's wall fronting
    sheer
On chaos. When at times the sky would clear
And like a frozen bubble were the nights,
Pale rainbows jigged across the polar heights
And leafy rustlings mocked the solitude.
Men sickened with the stale and salty food,
For squadrons hunt at best with ill success;
And quiet days revealed the wilderness
Alert with fires, so doggedly the foe
Guarded the deer and elk and buffalo
That roamed the foothills where the grass was
    good.
A battle often bought a load of wood;
And arrows swept the opening water-gate
From where the wily bowmen lurked in wait
Along the brush-clad Piney.

                              March went past
A lion, crouched or raging, to the last;
And it was April—in the almanac.
No maiden with the southwind at her back
Ran crocus-footed up the Bozeman Road.
A loveless vixen swept her drear abode
With brooms of whimsic wrath, and scolded shrill.
Men pined to think of how the whippoorwill
Broidered the moony silences at home.
There now a mist-like green began to roam
The naked forest hillward from the draws;
The dogwood's bloom was vying with the haw's;
The redbud made a bonfire of its boughs.
And there, perchance, one lying in a drowse
At midnight heard the friendly thunder crash,
The violet-begetting downpour lash
The flaring panes; and possibly one heard
The sudden rapture of a mocking bird
Defy the lightning in a pitch-black lull.

Here dull days wore the teeth of Winter dull.
Drifts withered slowly. Of an afternoon
The gulches grumbled hoarsely, ceasing soon
When sunset faded out. The pasque flower broke
The softened sod, and in a furry cloak
And airy bonnet brazened out the chill.
The long grave yonder under Pilot Hill,
Where eighty lay, was like a wound unwrapped.
The cottonwoods, awaking sluggish-sapped,
Prepared for spring with wavering belief.
May stole along the Piney like a thief.

And yet, another sun made summer now
In wild hearts given glebe-like to the plow
Of triumph. So miraculously fed
With slaughter, richly seeded with the dead,
The many-fielded harvest throve as one.

And Red Cloud was the summer and the sun.

In many a camp, in three great tribal tongues,
That magic name was thunder in the lungs
Of warriors. Swift, apocalyptic light,
It smote the zenith of the Red Man's night
With dazzling vision. Forts dissolved in smoke,
The hated roadway lifted, drifted, broke
And was a dust; the white men were a tale;
The green, clean prairie bellowed, hill and vale,
With fatted bison; and the good old days
Came rushing back in one resistless blaze
Of morning!

         It was good to be a youth
That season when all dreaming was the truth
And miracle familiar! Waning May
Could hear the young men singing on the way
To Red Cloud. Pious sons and rakehell scamps,
Unbroken colts, the scandals of their camps,
And big-eyed dreamers never tried by strife,
One-hearted with the same wild surge of life,
Sang merrily of dying as they came.
Aloof amid his solitude of fame,
The battle-brooding chieftain heard, to dream
Of great hordes raging like a flooded stream
From Powder River to the Greasy Grass,
That never after might a wagon pass
Along that hated highway of deceit.

The meadows of Absoraka grew sweet
With nursing June. War-ponies, winter-thin,
Nuzzled the dugs of ancient might therein
Against the day of victory. July
Poured virile ardor from a ruthless sky
To make stern forage—that the hardened herds
Might speed as arrows, wheel and veer as birds,
Have smashing force and never lack for breath,

Be fit for bearing heroes to their death
In that great day now drawing near.

                           Meanwhile
Once more the solitude of Piney Isle
Was startled with a brawl of mules and men.
The Long Knives' wagons clattered there again;
The axes bit and rang, saws whined and gnawed;
And mountain valleys wakened to applaud
The mighty in their downfall, meanly slain.

Now close to Piney Isle there lay a plain
Some three long bow-shots wide. Good grazing land
It was, and empty as a beggar's hand.
Low foothills squatted round with bended knees,
And standing mountains waited back of these
To witness what the hunkered hills might view.
They saw a broad arena roofed with blue
That first of August. Where the mid-plain raised
A little knoll, the yellow swelter blazed
On fourteen wagon-beds set oval-wise—
A small corral to hold the camp supplies,
Flour, salt, beans, ammunition, grain in sacks.
Therein, forestalling sudden night attacks,
The mules were tethered when the gloaming starred
The laggard evening. Soldiers, sent to guard
The logging crew, had pitched their tents around.
And all of this was like a feeble sound
Lost in the golden fanfare of the day.
Across the Piney Fork, a mile away,
Unseen among the pines, the work-camp stood;
And trundling thence with loads of winter wood,
Stript wagon-trucks creaked fortward.

                           Twilight awe
Among the pines now silenced axe and saw.
With jingling traces, eager for their grain,
Across the creek and up the gloaming plain

The work mules came, hee-hawing at the glow
Of fires among the tents. The day burned low
To moonless dusk. The squat hills seemed to lift,
Expectant. Peaks on shadow-seas adrift,
Went voyaging where lonely wraiths of cloud
Haunted the starry hushes. Bugs grew loud
Among the grasses; cynic owls laughed shrill;
Men slept. But all night long the wolves were still,
Aware of watchers in the outer dark.
And now and then a sentry's dog would bark,
Rush snarling where it seemed that nothing
    stirred.
But those who listened for a war-cry, heard
The skirling bugs, the jeering owls, the deep
Discordant snoring of the men asleep
Upon their guns, mules blowing in the hay.

At last the blanching summits saw the day.
A drowsy drummer spread the news of morn.
The mules began to nicker for their corn
And wrangle with a laying back of ears.
Among them went the surly muleteers,
Dispensing feed and sulphurous remarks.
The harness rattled, and the meadow larks
Set dawn to melody. A sergeant cried
The names of heroes. Common men replied,
Sing-songing down the line. The squat hills heard
To seize and gossip with the running word—
Here! Here! Here! Coffee steaming in the pot,
Wood-smoke and slabs of bacon, sizzling hot,
Were very good to smell. The cook cried "chuck!"
And when the yellow flood of sunrise struck
The little prairie camp, it fell on men
Who ate as though they might not eat again.
Some wouldn't, for the day of wrath arose.
And yet, but for a cruising flock of crows,
The basking world seemed empty.

                                        Now the sun
Was two hours high. The axes had begun
Across the Piney yonder. Drowsy draws
Snored with the lagging echoes of the saws.
The day swooned windless, indolently meek.
It happened that the pickets by the creek
Were shaken from a doze by rhythmic cries
And drumming hoofs. Against the western skies,
Already well within a half a mile,
Came seven Indians riding single file,
Their wiry ponies flattened to the quirt.
A sentry's Springfield roared, and hills, alert
With echoes, fired a ghostly enfillade.
The ball fell short, bit dust and ricocheted.
The foremost pony, smitten in the breast,
Went down amid the rearing of the rest
And floundered to a dusty somersault.
Unhurt, the tumbled brave emerged to vault
Behind a comrade; and the seven veered
To southward, circling round the spot they feared
Where three far-stinging human hornets stood.
Now one of these went running to the wood
To see what made the logging camp so still.
Short breath sufficed to tell the tale of ill
He brought—the whole crew making off in
        stealth
And going to the mountains for their health,
The mules stampeded!

                        Things were looking blue.
With shaking knees, uncertain what to do,
The pickets waited. Whisperings of death
Woke round them, and they felt the gusty breath
Of shafts that plunked and quivered in the sod.
As though men sprouted where the ponies trod,
The circling band now jeered them, ten to one.
They scanned the main camp swinking in the sun.
No signal to return! But all the men

Were rushing round there, staring now and then
To where the foothills, northward, broke the flat.

A pointing sentry shouted: "Look at that!
Good God! There must be thousands over there!"
Massed black against the dazzle of the air,
They made the hilltops crawlingly alive—
The viscid boiling over of a hive
That feels the pale green burning of the spring.
Slow-moving, with a phasic murmuring
As of a giant swarm gone honey-wild,
They took the slope; and still the black rear piled
The wriggling ridges. What could bar the way?
Dwarfed in the panorama of the day,
The camp was but a speck upon the plain.
And three remembered eighty lying slain
Beside a ford, and how the Winter strode
Numb-footed down a bloody stretch of road
Across strange faces lately known and dear.

"I guess we'd better hustle out of here,"
The sergeant said. To left, to right, in front,
Like starving kiotes singing to the hunt,
Yet overcautious for a close attack,
Scores pressed the fighting trio, falling back
Across the Piney campward. One would pause
To hold the rear against the arrow-flaws,
The pelting terror, while the two ran past;
Then once again the first would be the last,
The second, first. And still the shuttling hoofs
Wove closelier with gaudy warps and woofs
The net of death; for still from brush and break
The Piney, like a pregnant water snake,
Spewed venomous broods.

                          So fleeing up the slope
The pickets battled for the bitter hope
Of dying with their friends. And there was one

Who left the wagon boxes at a run
And, dashing past the now exhausted three,
Knelt down to rest his rifle on his knee
And coolly started perforating hides.
Bare ponies, dragging warriors at their sides
And kicking at the unfamiliar weight,
Approved his aim. The weaving net of hate
Went loose, swung wide to southward.

        So at last
They reached the camp where, silent and aghast,
The men stood round and stared with haunted eyes.
'Tis said a man sees much before he dies.
Were these not dying? O the eighty-one
Bestrewn down Lodge Trail Ridge to Peno Run
That blizzard evening! Here were thirty-two!
And no one broached what everybody knew—
The tale there'd be and maybe none to tell
But glutted crows and kiotes. Such a spell
As fastens on a sick room gripped the crowd—
When tick by tick the doctor's watch is loud,
With hours between. And like the sound of leaves
Through which a night-wind ominously grieves,
The murmur of that moving mass of men
To northward rose and fell and rose again,
More drowsing music than a waking noise.

And Captain Powell spoke: "Get ready, boys;
Take places; see their eyes, then shoot to kill."

Some crouched behind the boxes, staring still
Like men enchanted. Others, seeming fain
To feel more keenly all that might remain
Of ebbing life, paced nervously about.
One fortified the better side of doubt
With yokes of oxen. That was Tommy Doyle.
(Alas, the total profit of his toil
Would be a hot slug crunching through his skull!)

And Littman yonder, grunting in the lull,
Arranged a keg of salt to fight behind;
While Condon, having other things in mind
Than dying, wrestled with a barrel of beans.
And others planned escape by grimmer means.
Old Robertson, with nothing in his face,
Unlaced a boot and noosed the leather lace
To reach between a trigger and a toe.
He did not tell, and no one asked to know
The meaning of it. Everybody knew.
John Grady and McQuarie did it too,
And Haggirty and Gibson did the same,
And many others. When the finish came,
At least there'd be no torturing for them.

Now as a hail-cloud, fraying at the hem,
Hurls ragged feelers to the windless void,
The nearing mass broke vanward and deployed
To left and right—a dizzy, flying blear,
Reek of a hell-pot boiling in the rear.
And now, as when the menaced world goes strange
And cyclone sling-shots, feeling out the range,
Spatter the waiting land agape with drouth,
The few first arrows fell. Once more the south
Was humming with a wind of mounted men
That wove the broken net of death again
Along the creek and up the campward rise.

Then suddenly, with wolfish battle-cries
And death-songs like the onset of a gale
And arrows pelting like a burst of hail,
The living tempest broke. There was no plain;
Just head-gear bobbing in a toss of mane,
And horses, horses, horses plunging under.
Paunch-deep in dust and thousand-footed thunder,
That vertigo of terror swarmed and swirled
About the one still spot in all the world—
The hushed cyclonic heart. Then that was loud!

The boxes bellowed, and a spurting cloud
Made twilight where the flimsy fortress stood;
And flying splinters from the smitten wood
And criss-cross arrows pricked the drifting haze.
Not now, as in the recent musket days,
The foe might brave two volleys for a rush
Upon the soldiers, helpless in a hush
Of loading. Lo, like rifles in a dream
The breech-fed Springfields poured a steady
     stream
That withered men and horses roaring in!
And gut-shot ponies screamed above the din;
And many a wounded warrior, under-trod
But silent, wallowed on the bloody sod—
Man piled on man and horses on the men!

They broke and scattered. Would they come again?
Abruptly so the muted hail-storm leaves
Astonished silence, when the dripping eaves
Count seconds for the havoc yet to come
Weird in the hush, a melancholy hum,
From where the watching women of the Sioux
Thronged black along the circling summits, grew
And fell and grew—the mourning for the dead.

One whispered hoarsely from a wagon-bed,
"Is anybody hit?" But none replied.
Awe-struck at what they did and hollow-eyed,
All watched and waited for the end of things.

Then even as the fleeing hail-cloud swings
Before some freakish veering of the gale,
Returning down its desolated trail
With doubled wrath, the howling horsemen came.
Right down upon the ring of spurting flame
The quirted ponies thundered; reared, afraid
Of that bad medicine the white men made,
And, screaming, bolted off with flattened ears.

So close the bolder pressed, that clubs and spears
Were hurled against the ring.

                    Again they broke,
To come again. Now flashing through the smoke,
Like lightning to the battle's thunder-shocks,
Ignited arrows, streaming to the nocks,
Fell hissing where the fighting soldiers lay;
And flame went leaping through the scattered hay
To set the dry mule-litter smouldering.

Half suffocated, coughing with the sting
Of acrid air, like scythemen in a field
The soldiers mowed. And gaudy man-flower reeled
To wriggling swaths. And still the mad Sioux fought
To break this magic that the white men wrought—
Heroic flesh at grapple with a god.

Then noon was glaring on the bloody sod;
And broken clouds of horsemen down the plain
Went scudding; hundreds, heavy with the slain
And wounded, lagging in the panic rout.

Again the ridges murmured round about
Where wailed the wives and mothers of the Sioux.
Some soldier whispered, asking for a chew,
As though he feared dread sleepers might arise.
Young Tommy Doyle with blood upon his eyes
Gaped noonward and his fighting jaw sagged loose.
Hank Haggirty would never need a noose
To reach between a trigger and a toe.
Jenness would never hear a bugle blow
Again, so well he slept. Around the ring
Men passed the grisly gossip, whispering—
As though doomed flesh were putting on the ghost.

A sound grew up as of a moving host.
It seemed to issue from a deep ravine

To westward. There no enemy was seen.
A freak gust, gotten of a sultry hush,
May mumble thus among the distant brush
Some moments ere a dampened finger cools.
But still the smudgy litter of the mules
Plumed straight against the dazzle of the day.
Upon a hilltop half a mile away
To eastward, Red Cloud presently appeared
Among his chieftains, gazing where the weird
Susurrus swelled and deepened in the west;
And to and from him dashed along the crest
Fleet heralds of some new-begotten hope.

Once more the Piney spread along the slope
A dizzy ruck of charging horse. They broke
Before those stingers in a nest of smoke,
Fled back across the creek, and waited there.
For what?

              The voice of it was everywhere—
A bruit of waters fretting at a weir.
The woman-peopled summits hushed to hear
That marching sound.

                    Then suddenly a roar,
As from the bursting open of a door,
Swept out across the plain; and hundreds, pressed
By hundreds crowding yonder from the west,
Afoot and naked, issued like a wedge,
With Red Cloud's nephew for the splitting edge,
A tribe's hot heart behind him for a maul.

Slow, ponderously slow, the V-shaped wall
Bore down upon the camp. The whirlwind pace
Of horsemen seemed less terrible to face
Than such a leisure. Brave men held their breath
Before that garish masquerade of Death
Aflaunt with scarlets, yellows, blues and greens.

Then Condon there behind his barrel of beans,
Foreseeing doom, afraid to be afraid,
Sprang up and waved his rifle and essayed
Homeric speech according to his lights.
"Come on!" he yelled, "ye dairty blatherskites,
Ye blitherin' ijuts! We kin lick yez all,
Ye low-down naygurs!" Shafts began to fall
About him raging. Scattered muskets roared
Along the fraying fringes of the horde.
"Get down there, Jim!" men shouted. "Down!" But
     Jim
Told Death, the blackguard, what he thought of him
For once and all.

          Again the Springfields crashed;
And where the heavy bullets raked and smashed
The solid front and bored the jostling mass,
Men withered down like flame-struck prairie grass;
But still the raging hundreds forged ahead
Pell mell across their wounded and their dead,
Like tumblebugs. The splitting edge went blunt.
A momentary eddy at the front
Sucked down the stricken chief. The heavy rear,
With rage more mighty than the vanward fear,
Thrust forward. Twenty paces more, and then—
'Twould be like drowning in a flood of men.
Already through the rifts one saw their eyes,
Teeth flashing in the yawn of battle-cries,
The sweat-sleek muscles straining at the bows.

Forgotten were the nooses for the toes.
Tomorrows died and yesterdays were naught.
Sleep-walkers in a foggy nowhere fought
With shadows. So forever from the first,
Forever so until this dream should burst
Its thin-blown bubble of a world. And then,
The shadows were a howling mass of men
Hurled, heavy with their losses, down the plain

Before that thunder-spew of death and pain
That followed till the last had disappeared.
The hush appalled; and when the smoke had
    cleared,
Men eyed each other with a sense of shock
At being still alive.

                    'Twas one o'clock!

One spoke of water. Impishly the word
Went round the oval, mocking those who heard.
The riddled barrel had bled from every stave;
And what the sun-stewed coffee-kettles gave
Seemed scarcely wet.
                        Off yonder on the hill
Among his chieftains Red Cloud waited still—
A tomcat lusting for a nest of mice.
How often could these twenty-nine suffice
To check his thousands? Someone raised a sight
And cursed, and fell to potting at the height;
Then others. Red Cloud faded into air.

What fatal mischief was he brewing there?
What ailed the Fort? It seemed beyond belief
That Wessels yonder wouldn't send relief!
The hush bred morbid fancies. Battle-cries
Were better than this buzzing of the flies
About Jenness and Haggirty and Doyle.
Wounds ached and smarted. Shaken films of oil
Troubled the yellow dazzle of the grass.
The bended heavens were a burning glass
Malevolently focussed. Minutes crawled.
Men gnawed their hearts in silence where they
    sprawled,
Each in the puddle of his own blue shade.

But hear! Was that a howitzer that bayed?
Look! Yonder from behind the eastward steep

Excited warriors, like a flock of sheep
That hear the wolves, throng down the creekward
    slope
And flee along the Piney!

                Slow to hope,
Men searched each other's faces, silent still.

A case-shot, bursting yonder on the hill,
Sent dogging echoes up the foe-choked draws.
And far hills heard the leather-lunged hurrahs
And answered, when the long blue skirmish line
Swept down the hill to join the twenty-nine
Knee-deep in standing arrows.

VII

Summer turned.
Where blackbirds chattered and the scrub oaks
burned
In meadows of the Milk and Musselshell,
The fatted bison sniffed the winter-smell
Beneath the whetted stars, and drifted south.
Across the Yellowstone, lean-ribbed with drouth,
The living rivers bellowed, morn to morn.
The Powder and the Rosebud and the Horn
Flowed backward freshets, roaring to their heads.
Now up across the Cheyenne watersheds
The manless cattle wrangled day and night.
Along the Niobrara and the White
Uncounted thirsts were slaked. The peace
that broods
Aloof among the sandhill solitudes
Fled from the bawling bulls and lowing cows.
Along the triple Loup they paused to browse
And left the lush sloughs bare. Along the Platte
The troubled myriads pawed the sandy flat
And snorted at the evil men had done.
For there, from morning sun to evening sun,
A strange trail cleft the ancient bison world,
And many-footed monsters whirred and whirled
Upon it; many-eyed they blinked, and screamed;
Tempestuous with speed, the long mane streamed
Behind them; and the breath of them was loud—
A rainless cloud with lightning in the cloud
And alien thunder.

Thus the driving breed,
The bold earth-takers, toiled to make the deed
Audacious as the dream. One season saw
The steel trail crawl away from Omaha
As far as ox-rigs waddled in a day—
An inchworm bound for San Francisco Bay!
The next beheld a brawling, sweating host
Of men and mules build on to Kearney Post
While spring greens mellowed into winter browns,
And prairie dogs were giving up their towns
To roaring cities. Where the Platte divides,
The metal serpent sped, with league-long strides,
Between two winters. North Platte City sprang
From sage brush where the prairie sirens sang
Of magic bargains in the marts of lust;
A younger Julesburg sprouted from the dust
To howl a season at the panting trains;
Cheyenne, begotten of the ravished plains,
All-hailed the planet as the steel clanged by.
And now in frosty vacancies of sky
The rail-head waited spring on Sherman Hill,
And, brooding further prodigies of will,
Blinked off at China.

So the man-stream flowed
Full flood beyond the Powder River road—
A cow path, hardly worth the fighting for.
Then let grass grow upon the trails of war,
Bad hearts be good and all suspicion cease!
Beside the Laramie the pipe of peace
Awaited; let the chieftains come and smoke!

'Twas summer when the Great White Father spoke.
A thousand miles of dying summer heard;
And nights were frosty when the crane-winged word
Found Red Cloud on the Powder loath to yield.
The crop from that rich seeding of the field
Along the Piney flourished greenly still.

The wail of many women on a hill
Was louder than the word. And once again
He saw that blizzard of his fighting men
Avail as snow against the August heat.
"Go tell them I am making winter meat;
No time for talk," he said; and that was all.

The Northwind snuffed the torches of the fall,
And drearily the frozen moons dragged past.
Then when the pasque-flower dared to bloom
      at last
And resurrected waters hailed the geese,
It happened that the flying word of peace
Came north again. The music that it made
Was sweet to Spotted Tail, and Man Afraid
Gave ear, bewitched. One Horn and Little Chief
Believed; and Two Bears ventured on belief,
And others who were powers in the land.
For here was something plain to understand:
As long as grass should grow and water flow,
Between Missouri River and the snow
That never melts upon the Big Horn heights,
The country would be closed to all the Whites.
So ran the song that lured the mighty south.
It left a bitter taste in Red Cloud's mouth,
No music in his ears. "Go back and say
That they can take their soldier-towns away
From Piney Fork and Crazy Woman's Creek
And Greasy Grass. Then maybe I will speak.
Great Spirit gave me all this country here.
They have no land to give."

                The hills went sere
Along the Powder; and the summer grew.
June knew not what the white men meant to do;
Nor did July. The end of August came.
Bullberries quickened into jets of flame
Where smoky bushes smouldered by the creeks.

Grapes purpled and the plums got rosy cheeks.
The nights were like a watching mother, yet
A chill as of incipient regret
Foretold the winter when the twilight fell.
'Twas then a story wonderful to tell
Went forth at last. In every wind it blew
Till all the far-flung bison hunters knew;
And Red Cloud's name and glory filled the tale.
The soldier-towns along the hated trail
Were smoke, and all the wagons and the men
Were dust blown south! Old times had come again.
Unscared, the fatted elk and deer would roam
Their pastures now, the bison know their home
And flourish there forever unafraid.
So when the victor's winter-meat was made
And all his lodges ready for the cold,
He listened to the word, now twelve moons old,
Rode south and made his sign and had his will.

Meanwhile the road along the Smoky Hill
Was troubled. Hunters, drifting with the herd
The fall before, had scattered wide the word
Of Red Cloud's victory. "Look north," they said;
The white men made a road there. It is red
With their own blood, and now they whine for peace!"
The brave tale travelled southward with the geese,
Nor dwindled on the way, nor lacked applause.
Comanches, South Cheyennes and Kiowas,
Apaches and the South Arapahoes
Were glad to hear. Satanta, Roman Nose,
Black Kettle, Little Raven heard—and thought.
Around their winter fires the warriors fought
Those far-famed battles of the North again.
Their hearts grew strong. "We, too," they said,
    "are men;
And what men did up yonder, we can do.
Make red the road along the Smoky too,
And grass shall cover it!"

So when the spring
Was fetlock-deep, wild news ran shuddering
Through Kansas: women captured, homes ablaze,
Men slaughtered in the country north of Hays
And Harker! Terror stalking Denver way!
Trains burned along the road to Santa Fe,
The drivers scalped and given to the flames!
All summer Panic babbled demon names.
No gloom but harbored Roman Nose, the Bat.
Satanta, like an omnipresent cat,
Moused every heart. Out yonder, over there,
Black Kettle, Turkey Leg were everywhere.
And Little Raven was the night owl's croon,
The watch-dog's bark. The setting of the moon
Was Little Rock; the dew before the dawn
A sweat of horror!

All that summer, drawn
By vague reports and captive women's wails,
The cavalry pursued dissolving trails—
And found the hotwind. Loath to risk a fight,
Fleas in the day and tigers in the night,
The wild bands struck and fled to strike anew
And drop the curtain of the empty blue
Behind them, passing like the wrath of God.

The failing year had lit the goldenrod
Against the tingling nights, now well begun;
The sunflowers strove to hoard the paling sun
For winter cheer; and leagues of prairie glowed
With summer's dying flare, when fifty rode
From Wallace northward, trailing Roman Nose,
The mad Cheyenne. A motley band were those—
Scouts, hunters, captains, colonels, brigadiers;
Wild lads who found adventure in arrears,
And men of beard whom Danger's lure made young—
The drift and wreckage of the great war, flung
Along the brawling border. Two and two,

The victor and the vanquished, gray and blue,
Rode out across the Kansas plains together,
Hearts singing to the croon of saddle leather
And jingling spurs. The buffalo, at graze
Like dairy cattle, hardly deigned to raise
Their shaggy heads and watch the horsemen pass.
Like bursting case-shot, clumps of blue-joint grass
Exploded round them, hurtling grouse and quail
And plover. Wild hens drummed along the trail
At twilight; and the antelope and deer,
Moved more by curiosity than fear,
Went trotting off to pause and gaze their fill.
Past Short Nose and the Beaver, jogging still,
They followed hot upon a trail that shrank
At every tangent draw. Their horses drank
The autumn-lean Republican and crossed;
And there at last the dwindled trail was lost
Where sandhills smoked against a windy sky.

Perplexed and grumbling, disinclined to try
The upper reaches of the stream, they pressed
Behind Forsyth, their leader, pricking west
With Beecher there beside him in the van.
They might have disobeyed a lesser man;
For what availed another wild goose chase,
Foredoomed to end some God-forsaken place
With twilight dying on the prairie rim?
But Fame had blown a trumpet over him;
And men recalled that Shenandoah ride
With Sheridan, the stemming of the tide
Of rabble armies wrecked at Cedar Creek,
When thirty thousand hearts, no longer weak,
Were made one victor's heart.

                              And so the band
Pushed westward up the lonely river land
Four saddle days from Wallace. Then at last
They came to where another band had passed

With shoeless ponies, following the sun.
Some miles the new trail ran as lean creeks run
In droughty weather; then began to grow.
Here other hoofs had swelled it, there, travaux;
And more and more the circumjacent plains
Had fed the trail, as when torrential rains
Make prodigal the gullies and the sloughs,
And prairie streams, late shrunken to an ooze,
Appal stout swimmers. Scarcity of game
(But yesterday both plentiful and tame)
And recent pony-droppings told a tale
Of close pursuit. All day they kept the trail
And slept upon it in their boots that night
And saddled when the first gray wash of light
Was on the hill tops. Past the North Fork's mouth
It led, and, crossing over to the south,
Struck up the valley of the Rickaree—
So broad by now that twenty, knee to knee,
Might ride thereon, nor would a single calk
Bite living sod.

          Proceeding at a walk,
The troopers followed, awed by what they dared.
It seemed the low hills stood aloof, nor cared,
Disowning them; that all the gullies mocked
The jingling gear of Folly where it walked
The road to Folly's end. The low day changed
To evening. Did the prairie stare estranged,
The knowing sun make haste to be away?
They saw the fingers of the failing day
Grow longer, groping for the homeward trail.
They saw the sun put on a bloody veil
And disappear. A flock of crows hurrahed.

Dismounting in the eerie valley, awed
With purple twilight and the evening star,
They camped beside the stream. A gravel bar
Here split the shank-deep Rickaree in two

And made a little island. Tall grass grew
Among its scattered alders, and there stood
A solitary sapling cottonwood
Within the lower angle of the sand.

No jesting cheered the saddle-weary band
That night; no fires were kindled to invoke
Tales grim with cannon flare and battle smoke
Remembered, and the glint of slant steel rolled
Up roaring steeps. They ate short rations cold
And thought about tomorrow and were dumb.

A hint of morning had begun to come;
So faint as yet that half the stars at least
Discredited the gossip of the east.
The grazing horses, blowing at the frost,
Were shadows, and the ghostly sentries tossed
Their arms about them, drowsy in the chill.

Was something moving yonder on the hill
To westward? It was there—it wasn't there.
Perhaps some wolfish reveller, aware
Of dawn, was making home. 'Twas there again!
And now the bubble world of snoring men
Was shattered, and a dizzy wind, that hurled
Among the swooning ruins of the world
Disintegrating dreams, became a shout:
"Turn out! Turn out! The Indians! Turn out!"
Hearts pounding with the momentary funk
Of cold blood spurred to frenzy, reeling drunk
With sleep, men stumbled up and saw the hill
Where shadows of a dream were blowing still—
No—mounted men were howling down the slopes!
The horses, straining at their picket ropes,
Reared snorting. Barking carbines flashed and
    gloomed,
Smearing the giddy picture. War drums boomed
And shaken rawhide crackled through the din.

A horse that trailed a bounding picket pin
Made off in terror. Others broke and fled.
Then suddenly the silence of the dead
Had fallen, and the slope in front was bare
And morning had become a startled stare
Across the empty prairie, white with frost.

Five horses and a pair of pack mules lost!
That left five donkeys for the packs. Men poked
Sly banter at the mountless ones, invoked
The "infantry" to back them, while they threw
The saddles on and, boot to belly, drew
Groan-fetching cinches tight.

                   A scarlet streak
Was growing in the east. Amid the reek
Of cowchip fires that sizzled with the damp
The smell of coffee spread about the camp
A mood of peace. But 'twas a lying mood;
For suddenly the morning solitude
Was solitude no longer. "Look!" one cried.
The resurrection dawn, as prophesied,
Lacked nothing but the trump to be fulfilled!
They wriggled from the valley grass! They spilled
Across the sky rim! North and south and west
Increasing hundreds, men and ponies, pressed
Against the few.

                 'Twas certain death to flee.
The way left open down the Rickaree
To where the valley narrowed to a gap
Was plainly but the baiting of a trap.
Who rode that way would not be riding far.
"Keep cool now, men! Cross over to the bar!"
The colonel shouted. Down they went pell-mell,
Churning the creek. A heaven-filling yell
Assailed them. Was it triumph? Was it rage?
Some few wild minutes lengthened to an age

While fumbling fingers stripped the horses' backs
And tied the horses. Crouched behind the packs
And saddles now, they fell with clawing hands
To digging out and heaping up the sands
Around their bodies. Shots began to fall—
The first few spatters of a thunder squall—
And still the Colonel strolled about the field,
Encouraging the men. A pack mule squealed
And floundered. "Down!" men shouted. "Take it
    cool,"
The Colonel answered; "we can eat a mule
When this day's work is over. Wait the word,
Then see that every cartridge wings a bird.
Don't shoot too fast."

                The dizzy prairie spun
With painted ponies, weaving on the run
A many colored noose. So dances Death,
Bedizened like a harlot, when the breath
Of Autumn flutes among the shedding boughs
And scarlets caper and the golds carouse
And bronzes trip it and the late green leaps.
And then, as when the howling winter heaps
The strippings of the hickory and oak
And hurls them in a haze of blizzard smoke
Along an open draw, the warriors formed
To eastward down the Rickaree, and stormed
Against the isle, their solid front astride
The shallow water.

          "Wait!" the Colonel cried;
"Keep cool now!"—Would he never say the word?
They heard the falling horses shriek; they heard
The smack of smitten flesh, the whispering rush
Of arrows, bullets whipping through the brush
And flicked sand *phutting;* saw the rolling eyes
Of war-mad ponies, crooked battle cries
Lost in the uproar, faces in a blast

Of color, color, and the whirlwind last
Of all dear things forever.

                    "Now!"
                         The fear,
The fleet, sick dream of friendly things and dear
Dissolved in thunder; and between two breaths
Men sensed the sudden splendor that is Death's,
The wild clairvoyant wonder. Shadows screamed
Before the kicking Spencers, split and streamed
About the island in a flame-rent shroud.
And momently, with hoofs that beat the cloud,
Winged with the mad momentum of the charge,
A war horse loomed unnaturally large
Above the burning ring of rifles there,
Lit, sprawling, in the midst and took the air
And vanished. And the storming hoofs roared by.
And suddenly the sun, a handbreadth high,
Was peering through the clinging battle-blur.

Along the stream, wherever bushes were
Or clumps of blue-joint, lurking rifles played
Upon the isle—a point-blank enfilade,
Horse-slaughtering and terrible to stand;
And southward there along the rising land
And northward where the valley was a plain,
The horsemen galloped, and a pelting rain
Of arrows fell.

                Now someone, lying near
Forsyth, was yelling in his neighbor's ear
"They've finished Sandy!" For a giant whip,
It seemed, laid hot along the Colonel's hip
A lash of torture, and his face went gray
And pinched. And voices boomed above the fray,
"Is Sandy dead?" So, rising on a knee
That anyone who feared for him might see,
He shouted: "Never mind—it's nothing bad!"

And noting how the wild face of a lad
Yearned up at him—the youngest face of all,
With cheeks like Rambeau apples in the fall,
Eyes old as terror—"Son, you're doing well!"
He cried and smiled; and that one lived to tell
The glory of it in the after days.

Now presently the Colonel strove to raise
The tortured hip to ease it, when a stroke
As of a dull ax bit a shin that broke
Beneath his weight. Dragged backward in a pit,
He sat awhile against the wall of it
And strove to check the whirling of the land.
Then, noticing how some of the command
Pumped lead too fast and threw their shells away,
He set about to crawl to where they lay
And tell them. Something whisked away his hat,
And for a green-sick minute after that
The sky rained stars. Then vast ear-hollows rang
With brazen noises, and a sullen pang
Was like a fire that smouldered in his skull.
He gazed about him groggily. A lull
Had fallen on the battle, and he saw
How pairs of horsemen galloped down the draw,
Recovering the wounded and the dead.
The snipers on the river banks had fled
To safer berths; but mounted hundreds still
Swarmed yonder on the flat and on the hill,
And long range arrows fell among the men.

The island had become a slaughter pen.
Of all the mules and horses, one alone
Still stood. He wobbled with a gurgling moan,
Legs wide, his drooping muzzle dripping blood;
And some still wallowed in a scarlet mud
And strove to rise, with threshing feet aloft.
But most lay still, as when the spring is soft
And work-teams share the idleness of cows

On Sunday, and a glutted horse may drowse,
Loose-necked, forgetting how the plowshare drags.
Bill Wilson yonder lay like bundled rags,
And so did Chalmers. Farley over there,
With one arm limp, was taking special care
To make the other do; it did, no doubt.
And Morton yonder with an eye shot out
Was firing slowly, but his gun barrel shook.
And Mooers, the surgeon, with a sightless look
Of mingled expectation and surprise,
Had got a bullet just above the eyes;
But Death was busy and neglected him.

Now all the while, beneath the low hill rim
To southward, where a sunning slope arose
To look upon the slaughter, Roman Nose
Was sitting, naked of his battle-gear.
In vain his chestnut stallion, tethered near,
Had sniffed the battle, whinnying to go
Where horses cried to horses there below,
And men to men. By now a puzzled word
Ran round the field, and baffled warriors heard,
And out of bloody mouths the dying spat
The question: "Where is Roman Nose, the Bat?
While other men are dying, where is he?"
So certain of the mighty rode to see,
And found him yonder sitting in the sun.
They squatted round him silently. And one
Got courage for a voice at length, and said:
"Your people there are dying, and the dead
Are many." But the Harrier of Men
Kept silence. And the bold one, speaking then
To those about him, said: "You see today
The one whom all the warriors would obey,
Whatever he might wish. His heart is faint.
He has not even found the strength to paint
His face, you see!" The Flame of Many Roofs

Still smouldered there. The Midnight Wind of
    Hoofs
Kept mute. "Our brothers, the Arapahoes,"
Another said, "will tell of Roman Nose;
Their squaws will scorn him; and the Sioux
    will say
'He was not like the men we were that day
When all the soldiers died by Peno ford!'"

They saw him wince, as though the words had
    gored
His vitals. Then he spoke. His voice was low.
"My medicine is broken. Long ago
One made a bonnet for a mighty man,
My father's father; and the good gift ran
From sire to son, and we were men of might.
For he who wore the bonnet in a fight
Could look on Death, and Death would fear him
    much,
So long as he should let no metal touch
The food he ate. But I have been a fool.
A woman lifted with an iron tool
The bread I ate this morning. What you say
Is good to hear."

He cast his robe away,
Got up and took the bonnet from its case
And donned it; put the death-paint on his face
And mounted, saying "Now I go to die!"
Thereat he lifted up a bull-lunged cry
That clamored far among the hills around;
And dying men took courage at the sound
And muttered "He is coming."

Now it fell
That those upon the island heard a yell
And looked about to see from whence it grew.

They saw a war-horse hurtled from the blue,
A big-boned chestnut, clean and long of limb,
That did not dwarf the warrior striding him,
So big the man was. Naked as the day
The neighbors sought his mother's lodge to say
'This child shall be a trouble to his foes'
(Save for a gorgeous bonnet), Roman Nose
Came singing on the run. And as he came
Mad hundreds hailed him, booming like a flame
That rages over slough grass, pony tall.
They formed behind him in a solid wall
And halted at a lifting of his hand.
The troopers heard him bellow some command.
They saw him wheel and wave his rifle high;
And distant hills were peopled with the cry
He flung at Death, that mighty men of old,
Long dead, might hear the coming of the bold
And know the land still nursed the ancient breed.
Then, followed by a thundering stampede,
He charged the island where the rifles brawled.
And some who galloped nearest him recalled
In after days, what some may choose to doubt,
How suddenly the hubbuboo went out
In silence, and a wild white brilliance broke
About him, and the cloud of battle smoke
Was thronged with faces not of living men.
Then terribly the battle roared again.
And those who tell it saw him reel and sag
Against the stallion, like an empty bag,
Then slip beneath the mill of pony hoofs.

So Roman Nose, the Flame of Many Roofs,
Flared out. And round the island swept the foe—
Wrath-howling breakers with an undertow
Of pain that wailed and murmuring dismay.

Now Beecher, with the limp he got that day
At Gettysburg, rose feebly from his place,

Unearthly moon-dawn breaking on his face,
And staggered over to the Colonel's pit.
Half crawling and half falling into it,
"I think I have a fatal wound," he said;
And from his mouth the hard words bubbled red
In witness of the sort of hurt he had.
"No, Beecher, no! It cannot be so bad!"
The other begged, though certain of the end;
For even then the features of the friend
Were getting queer. "Yes, Sandy, yes—goodnight,"
The stricken muttered. Whereupon the fight
No longer roared for him; but one who grieved
And fought thereby could hear the rent chest heaved
With struggling breath that couldn't leave the man.
And by and by the whirling host began
To scatter, most withdrawing out of range.
Astonished at the suddenness of change
From dawn to noon, the troopers saw the sun.

To eastward yonder women had begun
To glean the fallen, wailing as they piled
The broken loves of mother, maid and child
On pony-drags; remembering their wont
Of heaping thus the harvest of the hunt
To fill the kettles these had sat around.

Forsyth now strove to view the battleground,
But could not for the tortured hip and limb;
And so they passed a blanket under him
And four men heaved the corners; then he saw.
"Well, Grover, have they other cards to draw,
Or have they played the pack?" he asked a scout.
And that one took a plug of chewing out
And gnawed awhile, then spat and said: "Dunno;
I've fit with Injuns thirty year or so
And never see the like of this till now.
We made a lot of good ones anyhow,
Whatever else—."

Just then it came to pass
Some rifles, hidden yonder in the grass,
Took up the sentence with a snarling rip
That made men duck. One let his corner slip.
The Colonel tumbled, and the splintered shin
Went crooked, and the bone broke through
          the skin;
But what he said his angel didn't write.

'Twas plain the foe had wearied of the fight,
Though scores of wary warriors kept the field
And circled, watching for a head revealed
Above the slaughtered horses. Afternoon
Waned slowly, and a wind began to croon—
Like memory. The sapling cottonwood
Responded with a voice of widowhood.
The melancholy heavens wove a pall.
Night hid the valley. Rain began to fall.

How good is rain when from a sunlit scarp
Of heaven falls a silver titan's harp
For winds to play on, and the new green swirls
Beneath the dancing feet of April girls,
And thunder-claps applaud the meadow lark!
How dear to be remembered—rainy dark
When Youth and Wonder snuggle safe abed
And hear creation bustling overhead
With fitful hushes when the eave *drip-drops*
And everything about the whole house stops
To hear what now the buds and grass may think!

Night swept the island with a brush of ink.
They heard the endless drizzle sigh and pass
And whisper to the bushes and the grass,
Sh—sh—for men were dying in the rain;
And there was that low singing that is pain,
And curses muttered lest a stout heart break.

As one who lies with fever half awake
And sets the vague real shepherding a drove
Of errant dreams, the broken Colonel strove
For order in the nightmare. Willing hands
With knife and plate fell digging in the sands
And throwing out a deep surrounding trench.
Graves, yawning briefly in the inky drench,
Were satisfied with something no one saw.
Carved horse meat passed around for wolfing raw
And much was cached to save it from the sun.

Now when the work about the camp was done
And all the wounds had got rude handed care,
The Colonel called the men about him there
And spoke of Wallace eighty miles away.
Who started yonder might not see the day;
Yet two must dare that peril with the tale
Of urgent need; and if the two should fail,
God help the rest!

         It seemed that everyone
Who had an arm left fit to raise a gun
And legs for swinging leather begged to go.
But all agreed with old Pierre Trudeau,
The grizzled trapper, when he ''lowed he knowed
The prairie like a farmer did a road,
And many was the Injun he had fooled.'
And Stillwell's youth and daring overruled
The others. Big he was and fleet of limb
And for his laughing pluck men honored him,
Despite that weedy age when boys begin
To get a little conscious of the chin
And jokers dub them "Whiskers" for the lack.
These two were swallowed in the soppy black
And wearily the sodden night dragged by.

At last the chill rain ceased. A dirty sky
Leaked morning. Culver, Farley, Day and Smith

Had found a comrade to adventure with
And come upon the country that is kind.
But Mooers was slow in making up his mind
To venture, though with any breath he might.
Stark to the drab indecency of light,
The tumbled heaps, that once were horses, lay
With naked ribs and haunches lopped away—
Good friends at need with all their fleetness gone.
Like wolves that smell a feast the foe came on,
A skulking pack. They met a gust of lead
That flung them with their wounded and their
      dead
Back to the spying summits of the hills,
Content to let the enemy that kills
Without a wound complete the task begun.

Dawn cleared the sky, and all day long the sun
Shone hotly through a lens of amethyst—
Like some incorrigible optimist
Who overworks the sympathetic rôle.
All day the troopers sweltered in the bowl
Of soppy sand, and wondered if the two
Were dead by now; or had they gotten through?
And if they hadn't—What about the meat?
Another day or two of steaming heat
Would fix it for the buzzards and the crows;
And there'd be choicer banqueting for those
If no one came.
      So when a western hill
Burned red and blackened, and the stars came chill,
Two others started crawling down the flat
For Wallace; and for long hours after that
Men listened, listened, listened for a cry,
But heard no sound. And just before the sky
Began to pale, the two stole back unhurt.
The dark was full of shadow men, alert
To block the way wherever one might go.
Alas, what chance for Stillwell and Trudeau?

That day the dozen wounded bore their plight
Less cheerfully than when the rainy night
Had held so great a promise. All day long,
As one who hums a half forgotten song
By poignant bits, the dying surgeon moaned;
But when the west was getting sober-toned,
He choked a little and forgot the tune.
And men were silent, wondering how soon
They'd be like that.

          Now when the tipping Wain,
Above the Star, poured slumber on the plain,
Jack Donovan and Pliley disappeared
Down river where the starry haze made weird
The narrow gulch. They seemed as good as dead;
And all next day the parting words they said,
"We won't be coming back," were taken wrong.
The fourth sun since the battle lingered long.
Putrescent horseflesh now befouled the air.
Some tried to think they liked the prickly pear.
Some tightened up their belts a hole or so.
And certain of the wounded babbled low
Of places other than the noisome pits,
Because the fever sped their straying wits
Like homing bumblebees that know the hive.
That day the Colonel found his leg alive
With life that wasn't his.

          The fifth sun crept;
The evening dawdled; morning overslept.
It seemed the dark would never go away;
The kiotes filled it with a roundelay
Of toothsome horses smelling to the sky.

But somehow morning happened by and by.
All day the Colonel scanned the prairie rims
And found it hard to keep away the whims
That dogged him; often, wide awake, he dreamed.

The more he thought of it, the more it seemed
That all should die of hunger wasn't fair;
And so he called the sound men round him there
And spoke of Wallace and the chance they stood
To make their way to safety, if they would.
As for himself and other cripples—well,
They'd take a chance, and if the worst befell,
Were soldiers.

       There was silence for a space
While each man slyly sought his neighbor's face
To see what better thing a hope might kill.
Then there was one who growled: "The hell we will!
We've fought together and we'll die so too!"
One might have thought relief had come in view
To hear the shout that rose.

          The slow sun sank.
The empty prairie gloomed. The horses stank.
The kiotes sang. The starry dark was cold.

That night the prowling wolves grew over bold
And one was cooking when the sun came up.
It gave the sick a little broth to sup;
And for the rest, they joked and made it do.
And all day long the cruising buzzards flew
Above the island, eager to descend;
While, raucously prophetic of the end,
The crows wheeled round it hungrily to pry;
And mounted warriors loomed against the sky
To peer and vanish. Darkness fell at last;
But when the daylight came and when it passed
The Colonel scarcely knew, for things got mixed;
The moment was forever, strangely fixed,
And never in a moment. Still he kept
One certain purpose, even when he slept,
To cheer the men by seeming undismayed.
But when the eighth dawn came, he grew afraid

Of his own weakness. Stubbornly he sat,
His tortured face half hidden by his hat,
And feigned to read a novel one had found
Among the baggage. But the print went round
And wouldn't talk however it was turned.

At last the morning of the ninth day burned.
Again he strove to regiment the herds
Of dancing letters into marching words,
When suddenly the whole command went mad.
They yelled; they danced the way the letters had;
They tossed their hats.

     Then presently he knew
'Twas cavalry that made the hillside blue—
The cavalry from Wallace!

Autumn's goad

VIII Had thronged the weed-grown Powder River
Road
With bison following the shrinking green.
Again the Platte and Smoky Hill had seen
The myriads nosing at the dusty hem
Of Summer's robe; and, drifting after them,
The wild marauders vanished. Winter came;
And lo! the homesteads echoed with a name
That was a ballad sung, a saga told;
For, once men heard it, somehow it was old
With Time's rich hoarding and the bardic lyres.
By night the settlers hugged their cowchip fires
And talked of Custer, while the children heard
The way the wild wind dramatized the word
With men and horses roaring to the fight
And valiant bugles crying down the night,
Far-blown from Cedar Creek or Fisher's Hill.
And in their sleep they saw him riding still,
A part of all things wonderful and past,
His bright hair streaming in the battle blast
Above a surf of sabres! Roofs of shale
And soddy walls seemed safer for the tale,
The prairie kinder for that name of awe.
For now the Battle of the Washita
Was fought at every hearthstone in the land.
'Twas song to talk of Custer and his band:
The blizzard dawn, the march from Camp
Supply,

Blind daring with the compass for an eye
To pierce the writhing haze; the icy fords,
The freezing sleeps; the finding of the hordes
That deemed the bitter weather and the snows
Their safety—Kiowas, Arapahoes,
Cheyennes, Comanches—miles of river flat
One village; Custer crouching like a cat
Among the drifts; the numbing lapse of night;
The brass band blaring in the first wan light,
The cheers, the neighing, and the wild swoop
    down
To widow-making in a panic town
Of widow-makers! O 'twas song to say
How Old Black Kettle paid his life that day
For bloody dawns of terror! Lyric words
Dwelt long upon his slaughtered pony herds,
His lodges burning for the roofs that blazed
That dreadful year! Rejoicing Kansas raised
Her eyes beyond the days of her defeat
And saw her hills made mighty with the wheat,
The tasselled corn ranks marching on the plain;
The wonder-working of the sun and rain
And faith and labor; plenty out of dearth;
Man's mystic marriage with the virgin Earth,
A hard-won bride.

        And April came anew;
But there were those—and they were human too—
For whom the memory of other springs
Sought vainly in the growing dusk of things
The ancient joy. Along the Smoky Hill
The might they could no longer hope to kill
Brawled west again, where maniacs of toil
Were chaining down the violated soil,
And plows went wiving in the bison range,
An alien-childed mother growing strange
With younger loves. May deepened in the sloughs
When down the prairie swept the wonder news

Of what had happened at the Great Salt Lake,
And how, at last, the crawling iron snake
Along the Platte had lengthened to the sea.
So shadows of a thing that was to be
Grew darker in the land.

               Four years went by,
And still the solemn music of a lie
Kept peace in all the country of the Sioux.
Unharried yonder, still the bison knew
The meadows of Absoraka and throve;
But now no more the Hoary Herdsman drove
His countless cattle past the great Platte road.
Still honoring the treaty, water flowed,
And grass grew, faithful to the plighted word.
Then yonder on the Yellowstone was heard
The clank of sabers; and the Red Men saw
How Yellow Hair, the Wolf of Washita,
Went spying with his pack along the stream,
While others, bitten with a crazy dream,
Were driving stakes and peeping up the flat.
Just so it was that summer on the Platte
Before the evil came. And devil boats
Came up with stinking thunder in their throats
To scare the elk and make the bison shy.
So there was fighting yonder where the lie
Was singing flat; though nothing came of it.

And once again the stunted oaks were lit,
And down across the prairie howled the cold;
And spring came back, exactly as of old,
To resurrect the waters and the grass.
The summer deepened peacefully—alas,
The last of happy summers, cherished long
As Sorrow hoards the wreckage of a song
Whose wounding lilt is dearer for the wound.
The children laughed; contented mothers crooned
About their lodges. Nothing was afraid.

The warriors talked of hunting, in the shade,
Or romped with crowing babies on their backs.
The meat was plenty on the drying racks;
The luscious valleys made the ponies glad;
And travellers knew nothing that was bad
To tell of any village they had known.
No white men yonder on the Yellowstone,
Nor any sign of trouble anywhere!

Then once again the name of Yellow Hair
Was heard with dread; for Summer, turning brown,
Beheld him lead a thousand horsemen down
To pierce the Hills where Inyan Kara towers,
Brawl southward through that paradise of flowers
And deer and singing streams to Frenchman Creek;
Beheld him even climbing Harney Peak
To spy the land, as who should say him no!
Had grasses failed? Had water ceased to flow?
Were pledges wind?

                    Now scarce the sloughs were sere
When Custer, crying in the wide world's ear
What every need and greed could understand,
Made all men see the Black Hills wonderland
Where Fortune waited, ready with a bow.
What fertile valleys pining for the plow!
What lofty forests given to the birds,
What luscious cattle pastures to the herds
Of elk and deer! What flower-enchanted parks,
Now lonely with the quails and meadowlarks,
Awaited men beneath the shielding peaks!
And in the creeks—in all the crystal creeks—
The blesséd creeks—O wonder to behold!—
Free gold—the god of rabbles—holy gold—
And gold in plenty from the grass roots down!

The Black Hills Country! Heard in every town,
That incantation of a wizard horn

Wrought madness. Farmers caught it in the corn
To shuck no more. No glory of the sward
Outdazzled yonder epiphanic Lord—
The only revelation that was sure!
And through the cities went the singing lure,
Where drearily the human welter squirms
Like worms that lick the slime of other worms
That all may flourish. Squalor saw the gleam,
And paupers mounted in a splendid dream
The backs of luckless men, for now the weak
Inherited the earth! The fat, the sleek
Envisaged that apocalypse, and saw
Obesity to put the cringe of awe
In knees of leanness!

        Sell the family cow!
Go pawn the homestead! Life was knocking now!
There might not ever be another knock.
Bring forth the hoarding of the hidden sock,
Poor coppers from the dear dead eyes of Joy!
Go seek the god that weighs the soul by troy;
Be saved, and let the devil take the rest!
The West—the golden West—the siren West—
Behold the rainbow's end among her peaks!
For in the creeks—in all the crystal creeks—
The blesséd creeks—!

        So wrought the rueful dream.
Chinooks of hope fed full the human stream,
Brief thawings of perennial despair.
And steadily the man-flood deepened there
With every moon along the Sioux frontier,
Where still the treaty held—a rotten wier
Already trickling with a leak of men.
And some of those came drifting back again,
Transfigured palmers from the Holy Lands,
With true salvation gleaming in their hands
Now cleansed of labor. Thus the wonder grew.

And there were flinty hearts among the Sioux
That fall and winter. Childish, heathen folk,
Their god was but a spirit to invoke
Among the hushes of a lonely hill;
An awfulness when winter nights were still;
A mystery, a yearning to be felt
When birds returned and snow began to melt
And miracles were doing in the grass.
Negotiable Divinity, alas,
They had not yet the saving grace to know!

Nor did the hard hearts soften with the snow,
When from the high gray wilderness of rain
Johannine voices of the goose and crane
Foretold the Coming to a world enthralled;
For still along the teeming border brawled
The ever growing menace.

                Summer bloomed;
But many, with the prescience of the doomed,
Could feel the shaping of the end of things
In all that gladness. How the robin sings
The sweeter in the ghastly calm that aches
With beauty lost, before the cyclone breaks!
And helpless watchers feel it as a pang,
Because of all the times the robin sang
Scarce noted in the melody of then.
About the lodges gray and toothless men
Bemoaned the larger time when life was good.
Hey-hey, what warriors then, what hardihood!
What terror of the Sioux among their foes!
What giants, gone, alas, these many snows—
And they who knew so near their taking off!
Now beggars at the Great White Father's trough
Forgot the bow and waited to be swilled.
The woman-hearted god the White Man killed
Bewitched the people more with every moon.
The buffalo would join the fathers soon.

The world was withered like a man grown old.
A few more grasses, and the Sioux would hold
A little paper, dirtied with a lie,
For all that used to be. 'Twas time to die.
Hey-hey, the braver days when life was new!

But there were strong hearts yet among the Sioux
Despite the mumbling of the withered gums.
That summer young men chanted to the drums
Of mighty deeds; and many went that fall
Where Crazy Horse and Sitting Bull and Gall
Were shepherding their people on the Tongue
And Powder yet, as when the world was young,
Contemptuous of alien ways and gods.

Now when the candles of the goldenrods
Were guttering about the summer's bier,
And unforgetting days were hushed to hear
Some rumor of a lone belated bird,
It came to pass the Great White Father's word
Assembled many on the White to meet
The Long Knife chieftains. Bitter words and sweet
Grew rankly there; and stubbornly the wills
Of children met the hagglers for the Hills,
The lust for gold begetting lust for gold.
The young moon grew and withered and was old,
And still the latest word was like the first.

Then talking ended and the man-dam burst
To loose the living flood upon the West.
All winter long it deepened, and the crest
Came booming with the February thaw.
The torrent setting in through Omaha
Ground many a grist of greed, and loud Cheyenne
Became a tail-race running mules and men
Hell-bent for Eldorado. Yankton vied
With Sidney in the combing of the tide
For costly wreckage. Giddily it swirled

Where Custer City shouted to the world
And Deadwood was a howl, and Nigger Hill
A cry from Pisgah. Unabated still,
Innumerable distant freshets flowed.
The bison trail became a rutted road
And prairie schooners cruised the rolling Spring.
In labor with a monstrous farrowing,
The river packets grunted; and the plains
Were startled at the spawning of the trains
Along the Platte.

        So, bitten by the imp
Of much-for-nought, the gambler and the pimp,
The hero and the coward and the fool,
The pious reader of the golden rule
By decimals, the dandy and the gawk,
The human eagle and the wingless hawk
Alert for prey, the graybeard and the lad,
The murderer, the errant Galahad,
Mistaken in the color of the gleam—
All dreamers of the old pathetic dream—
Pursued what no pursuing overtakes.

THE VILLAGE OF CRAZY HORSE

IX

Meanwhile among the Powder River breaks,
Where cottonwoods and plums and stunted oaks
Made snug his village of a hundred smokes,
Young Crazy Horse was waiting for the spring.
Well found his people were in everything
That makes a winter good. But more than food
And shelter from the hostile solitude
Sustained them yonder when the sun fled far
And rustling ghost-lights capered round the Star
And moons were icy and the blue snow whined;
Or when for days the world went blizzard blind
And devils of the North came howling down.
For something holy moved about the town
With Crazy Horse.

        No chieftainship had run,
Long cherished in the blood of sire and son,
To clothe him with the might he wielded then.
The Ogalalas boasted taller men
But few of fairer body. One might look
And think of water running in a brook
Or maybe of a slender hickory tree;
And something in his face might make one see
A flinty shaft-head very keen to go,
Because a hero's hand is on the bow,
His eye upon the mark. But nothing seen
About his goodly making or his mien
Explained the man; and other men were bold.
Unnumbered were the stories that were told

(And still the legend glorified the truth)
About his war-fond, pony-taming youth
When Hump the Elder was a man to fear;
And where one went, the other would be near,
For there was love between the man and lad.
And it was good to tell what fights they had
With roving bands of Utes or Snakes or Crows.
And now that Hump was gone these many snows,
His prowess lingered. So the legend ran.
But neither Hump nor any other man
Could give the gift that was a riddle still.
What lonely vigils on a starry hill,
What fasting in the time when boyhood dies
Had put the distant seeing in his eyes,
The power in his silence? What had taught
That getting is a game that profits naught
And giving is a high heroic deed?
His plenty never neighbored with a need
Among his band. A good tough horse to ride,
The gear of war, and some great dream inside
Were Crazy Horse's wealth. It seemed the dim
And larger past had wandered back in him
To shield his people in the days of wrong.
His thirty years were like a brave old song
That men remember and the women croon
To make their babies brave.

                Now when the moon
Had wearied of December and was gone,
And bitterly the blizzard time came on,
The Great White Father had a word to say.
The frost-bit runners rode a weary way
To bring the word, and this is what it said:
"All bands, before another moon is dead,
Must gather at the agencies or share
The fate of hostiles." Grandly unaware
Of aught but its own majesty and awe,
The big word blustered. Yet the people saw

The snow-sift snaking in the grasses, heard
The Northwind bellow louder than the word
To make them shudder with the winter fear.
"You see that there are many children here,"
Said Crazy Horse. "Our herd is getting lean.
We can not go until the grass is green.
It is a very foolish thing you say."
And so the surly runners rode away
And Crazy Horse's people stayed at home.

And often were the days a howling gloam
Between two howling darks; nor could one tell
When morning broke and when the long night
      fell;
For 'twas a winter such as old men cite
To overawe and set the youngsters right
With proper veneration for the old.
The ponies huddled humpbacked in the cold
And, dog-like, gnawed the bark of cottonwood.
But where the cuddled rawhide lodges stood
Men laughed and yarned and let the blizzard roar,
Unwitting how the tale the runners bore
Prepared the day of sorrow.

                  March boomed in,
And still the people revelled in their sin
Nor thought of woe already on the way.
Then, when the night was longer than the day
By just about an old man's wink and nod,
As sudden as the storied wrath of God,
And scarce more human, retribution came.

The moony wind that night was like a flame
To sear whatever naked flesh it kissed.
The dry snow powder coiled and struck and hissed
Among the lodges. Haloes mocked the moon.
The boldest tale was given over soon
For kinder evenings; and the dogs were still

Before the prowling foe no pack might kill,
The subtle fang that feared not any fang.
But ever nearer, nearer, shod hoofs rang
To southward, unsuspected in the town.
Three cavalry battalions, flowing down
The rugged canyon bed of Otter Creek
With Reynolds, clattered out across the bleak
High prairie, eerie in the fitful light,
Where ghostly squadrons howled along the night,
Their stinging sabers gleaming in the wind.
All night they sought the village that had sinned
Yet slept the sleep of virtue, unafraid.
The Bear swung round; the stars began to fade;
The low moon stared. Then, floating in the puffs
Of wind-whipped snow, the Powder River bluffs
Gloomed yonder, and the scouts came back to tell
Of many sleeping lodges.

           Now it fell
That when the bluffs were paling with the glow
Of dawn, and still the tepee tops below
Stood smokeless in the stupor of a dream,
A Sioux boy, strolling down the frozen stream
To find his ponies, wondered at the sound
Of many hoofs upon the frozen ground,
The swishing of the brush. He paused to think.
The herd, no doubt, was coming for a drink;
He'd have to chop a hole. And while he stood,
The spell of dawn upon him, from the wood—
How queer!—they issued marching four by four
As though enchanted, breasts and muzzles hoar
With frozen breath! Were all the ponies dead,
And these their taller spirits?

               —Then he fled,
The frightened trees and bushes flowing dim,
The blanching bluff tops flinging back at him
His many-echoed yell. A frowsy squaw

Thrust up a lodge flap, blinked about her—saw
What ailed her boy, and fell to screaming shrill.
The startled wolf-dogs, eager for a kill,
Rushed yelping from the lodges. Snapping sharp,
As 'twere a short string parting in a harp,
A frosty rifle sounded. Tepees spilled
A half clad rabble, and the valley filled
With uproar, spurting into jets of pain;
For now there swept a gust of killing rain
From where the plunging horses in a cloud
Of powder smoke bore down upon the crowd
To set it scrambling wildly for the breaks.
The waddling grandmas lost their precious aches
In terror for the young they dragged and drove;
Hysteric mothers staggered as they strove
To pack the creepers and the toddlers too;
And grandpas, not forgetting they were Sioux,
Made shift to do a little with the bows,
While stubbornly the young men after those
Retreated fighting through the lead-swept town
And up the sounding steeps.

                There, looking down
Along the track of terror splotched with red
And dotted with the wounded and the dead,
They saw the blue-coats rage among their roofs,
Their homes flung down and given to the hoofs
Of desecrating wrath. And while they gazed
In helpless grief and fury, torches blazed
And tepees kindled. Casks of powder, stored
Against a doubtful future, belched and roared.
The hurtled lodge poles showered in the gloom,
And rawhide tops, like glutted bats of doom,
Sailed tumbling in the dusk of that despair.

Not long the routed warriors cowered there
Among the rocks and gullies of the steep.
The weakness of a panic-broken sleep

Wore off. Their babies whimpered in the frost.
Their herd was captured. Everything seemed lost
But life alone. It made them strong to die.
The death-song, stabbed with many a battle cry,
Blew down the flat—a blizzard of a sound—
And all the rocks and draws and brush around
Spat smoke and arrows in a closing ring.
There fell a sudden end of plundering.
Abruptly as they came the raiders fled,
And certain of their wounded, men have said,
Were left to learn what hells are made of wrath.

Now, gleaning in that strewn tornado path
Their dead and dying, came the mourning folk
To find a heap for home, a stinking smoke
For plenty. Senseless to the whirling snow,
About the bitter honey of their woe
They swarmed and moaned. What evil had
    they done?
Dear eyes, forever empty of the sun,
Stared up at them. These little faces, old
With pain, and pinched with more than winter
    cold—
Why should they never seek the breast again?
A keening such as wakes the wolf in men
Outwailed the wind. Yet many a thrifty wife,
Long used to serve the urgencies of life
That make death seem a laggard's impudence,
Descended in a rage of commonsense
Upon the wreck, collecting what would do
To fend the cold.

        Now while the village grew,
A miracle of patches, jerry-built,
The young men, hot upon the trail of guilt
With Crazy Horse, found many a huddled stray
Forlorn along the thousand-footed way
The stolen herd had gone. And all day long

Their fury warmed them and their hearts were
    strong
To meet with any death a man might die;
For still they heard the wounded children cry,
The mourning of the women for the dead.
Nor did they deem that any hero led
The raiders. Surely nothing but the greed
Of terror could devour at such a speed
That pony-laming wallow, drift on drift.

The blue dusk mingled with the driven sift,
And still it seemed the trail of headlong flight
Was making for the wilderness of night
And safety. Then, a little way below
The mouth of Lodge Pole Creek, a dancing glow
Went up the bluff. Some few crept close to see,
And what they saw was listless misery
That crouched and shivered in a smudge of sage.
How well they cooled their baby-killing rage,
Those tentless men without a bite to eat!
And many, rubbing snow upon their feet,
Made faces that were better to behold
Than how their shaking horses took the cold
With tight-tailed rumps against the bitter flaw.
Beyond the camp and scattered up the draw
The hungry ponies pawed the frozen ground,
And there was no one anywhere around
To guard them. White-man medicine was weak.

Now all the young men, hearing, burned to wreak
Their hate upon the foe. A wiser will
Restrained them. "Wait a better time to kill,"
Said Crazy Horse. "Our lives are few to give
And theirs are many. Can our people live
Without the herd? We must not die today.
The time will come when I will lead the way
Where many die."

Like hungry wolves that prowl
The melancholy marches of the owl
Where cows and calves are grazing unafraid,
The pony stalkers went. A stallion neighed,
Ears pricked to question what the dusk might bring;
Then all the others fell to whinnying
And yonder in the camp the soldiers heard.
Some rose to point where many shadows, blurred
With driven snow and twilight, topped a rise
And vanished in the smother. Jeering cries
Came struggling back and perished in the bruit
Of charging wind. No bugles of pursuit
Aroused the camp. Night howled along the slough.

THE SUN DANCE

X

Now wheresoever thawing breezes blew
And green began to prickle in the brown,
There went the tale of Crazy Horse's town
To swell a mood already growing there.
For something more than Spring was in the air,
And, mightier than any maiden's eyes,
The Lilith-lure of Perilous Emprise
Was setting all the young men's blood astir.
How fair the more than woman face of her
Whose smile has gulfed how many a daring prow!
What cities burn for jewels on her brow;
Upon her lips what vintages are red!
Her lovers are the tallest of the dead
Forever. When the streams of Troas rolled
So many heroes seaward, she was old;
Yet she is young forever to the young.

'Twas now the murmur of the man-flood, flung
Upon the Hills, grew ominously loud.
The whole white world seemed lifted in a cloud
To sweep the prairie with a monstrous rain.
Slay one, and there were fifty to be slain!
Give fifty to the flame for torturing,
Then count the marching multitude of Spring
Green blade by blade!

              Still wilder rumors grew;
They told of soldiers massed against the Sioux
And waiting till the grass was good, to fall

On Crazy Horse and Sitting Bull and Gall
That all the country might be safe for theft,
And nothing of a warrior race be left
But whining beggars in a feeding pen.
Alas, the rights of men—of other men—
That centenary season of the Free!
No doubt the situation wanted tea
To make it clear! But long before the green
Had topped the hills, the agencies grew lean
Of youth and courage. Did a watch dog bark
Midway between the owl and meadowlark?—
Then other lads with bow and shield and lance
Were making for the Region of Romance
Where Sitting Bull's weird medicine was strong
And Crazy Horse's name was like a song
A happy warrior sings before he dies,
And Gall's a wind of many battle cries
That flings a thousand ponies on the doomed.

So where the Powder and the Rosebud boomed,
Men met as water of the melting snows.
The North Cheyennes and North Arapahoes,
Become one people in a common cause
With Brulés, Minneconjoux, Hunkpapas,
Sans Arcs and Ogalalas, came to throng
The valleys; and the villages were long
With camp on camp. Nor was there any bluff,
In all the country, that was tall enough
To number half the ponies at a look.
Here young June came with many tales of Crook,
The Gray Fox, marching up the Bozeman Road.
How long a dust above his horsemen flowed!
How long a dust his walking soldiers made!
What screaming thunder when the pack-mules
      brayed
And all the six-mule wagon teams replied!
The popping of the whips on sweaty hide,
How like a battle when the foe is bold!

And from the North still other tales were told
By those who heard the steamboats wheeze and
     groan
With stuffs of war along the Yellowstone
To feed the camps already waiting there.
Awaiting what? The might of Yellow Hair
Now coming from the Heart's mouth! Rumor
     guessed
How many Snakes were riding from the West
To join the Whites against their ancient foes;
How many Rees, how many of the Crows
Remembered to be jealous of the Sioux.
Look north, look south—the cloud of trouble grew.
Look east, look west—the whole horizon frowned.
But it was better to be ringed around
With enemies, to battle and to fail,
Than be a beggar chief like Spotted Tail,
However fattened by a hated hand.

Now when the full moon flooded all the land
Before the laughter of the owls began,
They turned to One who, mightier than Man,
Could help them most—the Spirit in the sun;
For whatsoever wonder-work is done
Upon the needy earth, he does it all.
For him the whole world sickens in the fall
When streams cease singing and the skies go gray
And trees and bushes weep their leaves away
In hopeless hushes empty of the bird,
And all day long and all night long are heard
The high geese wailing after their desire.
But, even so, his saving gift of fire
Is given unto miserable men
Until they see him face to face again
And all his magic happen, none knows how.
It was the time when he is strongest now;
And so a holy man whose heart was good
Went forth to find the sacred cottonwood

Belovéd of the Spirit. Straight and high,
A thing of worship yearning for the sky,
It flourished, sunning in a lonely draw;
And there none heard the holy man nor saw
What rites were done, save only one who knows
From whence the new moon comes and whither
    goes
The old, and what the stars do all day long.
Thereafter came the people with a song,
The men, the boys, the mothers and the maids,
All posy-crowns and blossom-woven braids,
As though a blooming meadow came to see.
And fruitful women danced about the tree
To make the Spirit glad; for, having known
The laughter of the children of their own,
Some goodness of the earth, the giving one,
Was in them and was pleasing to the Sun,
The prairie-loving nourisher of seed.

A warrior who had done the bravest deed
Yet dared that year by any of the Sioux
Now struck the trunk as one who counts a *coup*
Upon a dreaded foe; and prairie gifts
He gave among the poor, for nothing lifts
The heart like giving. Let the coward save—
Big hoard and little heart; but still the brave
Have more with nothing! Singing virgins came
Whose eyes had never learned to droop with shame,
Nor was there any present, man or youth,
Could say them aught of ill and say the truth,
For sweet as water in a snow-born brook
Where many birches come and lean to look
Along a mountain gorge, their spirits were.
And each one took the ax they gave to her
And smote the tree with many a lusty stroke;
And with a groan the sleeper in it 'woke
And far hills heard the falling shout of him.
Still rang the axes, cleaving twig and limb

Along the tapered beauty of the bole,
Till, naked to the light, the sacred pole
Lay waiting for the bearers.

                They who bore
Were chieftains, and their fathers were before,
And all of them had fasted, as they should;
Yet none dared touch the consecrated wood
With naked fingers, out of pious fear.
And once for every season of the year
They paused along the way, remembering
With thanks alike the autumn and the spring,
The winter and the summer.

                 Then it fell
That many warriors, lifting up a yell
That set their ponies plunging, thundered down
Across the center of the circled town
Where presently the holy tree should stand;
For whosoever first of all the band
Could strike the sacred spot with bow or spear
Might gallop deep among the dead that year
Yet be of those whom busy Death forgot.
And sweaty battle raged about the spot
Where screaming ponies, rearing to the thrust
Of screaming ponies, clashed amid the dust,
And riders wrestled in the hoof-made gloam.

So, having safely brought the sun-tree home,
The people feasted as for victory.

And on the second day they dressed the tree
And planted it with sacred songs and vows,
And round it reared a wall of woven boughs
That opened to the mystic source of day.
And with the next dawn mothers came to lay
Their babies down before the holy one,
Each coveting a hero for a son

Or sturdy daughters fit to nurse the bold.
Then when the fourth dawn came the war drums
    rolled;
And from their lodges, lean and rendered pure
With meatless days, those vowing to endure
The death-in-torture to be born again,
Came naked there before the holy men
Who painted them with consecrated paint.
And if a knee seemed loosened, it was faint
With fast and weary vigil, not with dread;
For lo! the multitudinary dead
Pressed round to see if heroes such as they
Still walked the earth despite the smaller day
When 'twas not half so easy to be brave.
Now, prone beneath the pole, as in a grave,
Without a wince each vower took the blade
In chest or back, and through the wound it made
Endured the passing of the rawhide thong,
Swung from the pole's top; raised a battle song
To daunt his anguish; staggered to his feet
And, leaning, capered to the war drum's beat
A dizzy rigadoon with Agony.

So all day long the spirit-haunted tree
Bore bloody fruitage, groaning to the strain,
For with the dropping of the ripe-in-pain,
Upon the stem the green-in-courage grew.
And seldom had there fallen on the Sioux
So great a wind of ghostly might as then.
Boys tripped it, bleeding, with the tortured men.
The mothers, daughters, sisters, sweethearts, wives
Of those who suffered, gashed their flesh with knives
To share a little of the loved one's pang;
And all day long the sunning valley rang
With songs of courage; and the mother sod
Received the red libation; and the god
Gave power to his people.

THE SEVENTH MARCHES

XI

Far away,
One foggy morning in the midst of May,
Fort Lincoln had beheld the marshalling
Of Terry's forces; heard the bugle sing,
The blaring of the band, the brave hurrah
Of Custer's men recalling Washita
And confident of yet another soon.
How gallantly in column of platoon
(So many doomed and given to the ghost)
Before the weeping women of the post
They sat their dancing horses on parade!
What made the silence suddenly afraid
When, with a brazen crash, the band went whist
And, dimmer in the clinging river mist,
The line swung westward? Did the Ree squaws know,
Through some wise terror of the ancient foe,
To what unearthly land their warriors led
The squadrons? Better suited to the dead
Than to the quick, their chanting of farewell
Grew eerie in the shadow, rose and fell—
The long-drawn yammer of a lonely dog.
But when at length the sun broke through the fog,
What reassurance in the wide blue air,
The solid hills, and Custer riding there
With all the famous Seventh at his heel!
And back of those the glint of flowing steel
Above the dusty infantry; the sun's
Young glimmer on the trundled Gatling guns;
And then the mounted Rees; and after that

The loaded pack mules straggling up the flat
And wagons crowding wagons for a mile!

What premonition of the afterwhile
Could darken eyes that saw such glory pass
When, lilting in a muffled blare of brass
Off yonder near the sundering prairie rim,
The Girl I Left Behind Me floated dim
As from the unrecoverable years?
And was it nothing but a freak of tears,
The vision that the grieving women saw?
For suddenly a shimmering veil of awe
Caught up the van. One could have counted ten
While Custer and the half of Custer's men
Were riding up a shining steep of sky
As though to join the dead that do not die
But haunt some storied heaven of the bold.
And then it seemed a smoke of battle rolled
Across the picture, leaving empty air
Above the line that slowly shortened there
And dropped below the prairie and was gone.

Now day by day the column straggled on
While moody May was dribbling out in rain
To make a wagon-wallow of the plain
Between the Muddy and the upper Heart
Where lifeless hills, as by demonic art,
Were hewn to forms of wonderment and fear,
Excited echoes flocked about to hear,
And any sound brought riotous applause,
So long among the scarps and tangled draws
Had clung that silence and the spell of it.
Some fiend-deserted city of the Pit
The region seemed, with crumbling domes and
        spires;
For still it smoked with reminiscent fires,
And in the midst, as 'twere the stream of woe,
A dark flood ran.

June blustered in with snow,
And all the seasons happened in a week.
Beyond the Beaver and O'Fallon creek
They toiled. Amid the wilderness of breaks
The drainage of the lower Powder makes,
They found a way and brought the wagons through;
Nor had they sight or sign of any Sioux
In all that land. Here Reno headed south
With packs and half the troopers for the mouth
Of Mispah, thence to scout the country west
About the Tongue; while Terry and the rest
Pushed onward to the Yellowstone to bide
With Gibbon's men the news of Reno's ride.

Mid June drew on. Slow days of waiting bred
Unhappy rumors. Everybody said
What no one, closely questioned, seemed to know.
Enormous numerations of the foe,
By tentative narration made exact
And tagged with all the circumstance of fact,
Discredited the neat official tale.
'Twas well when dawn came burning down the vale
And river fogs were lifting like a smoke
And bugles, singing reveille, awoke
A thousand-throated clamor in the herd.
But when the hush was like a warning word
And taps had yielded darkness to the owl,
A horse's whinny or a kiote's howl
Made true the wildest rumors of the noon.

So passed the fateful seventeenth of June
When none might guess how much the gossip
        lacked
To match the unimaginative fact
Of what the upper Rosebud saw that day:
How Crook, with Reno forty miles away,
Had met the hordes of Crazy Horse and Gall,
And all the draws belched cavalries, and all

The ridges bellowed and the river fen
Went dizzy with the press of mounted men—
A slant cyclonic tangle; how the dark
Came not a whit too early, and the lark
Beheld the Gray Fox slinking back amazed
To Goose Creek; what a dust the victors raised
When through the Chetish Hills by many a pass
They crowded down upon the Greasy Grass
To swell the hostile thousands waiting there.

Alas, how wide they made for Yellow Hair
That highway leading to the shining Past!

Now came the end of waiting, for at last
The scouting squadrons, jogging from the south,
Had joined their comrades at the Rosebud's mouth
With doubtful news. That evening by the fires,
According to their dreads or their desires,
The men discussed the story that was told
About a trail, not over three weeks old,
That led across the country from the Tongue,
Struck up the Rosebud forty miles and swung
Again to westward over the divide.
Some said, "We'll find blue sky the other side,
Then back to Lincoln soon!" But more agreed
'Twould not be so with Custer in the lead.
"He'll eat his horses when the hardtack's gone
Till every man's afoot!" And thereupon
Scarred veterans remembered other days
With Custer—thirsty marches in the blaze
Of Texas suns, with stringy mule to chew;
And times when splinters of the North Pole blew
Across the lofty Colorado plains;
And muddy going in the sullen rains
Of Kansas springs, when verily you felt
Your backbone rub the buckle of your belt
Because there weren't any mules to spare.
Aye, there were tales to make the rookies stare

Of Custer's daring and of Custer's luck.
And some recalled that night before they struck
Black Kettle's village. Whew! And what a night!
A foot of snow, and not a pipe alight,
And not a fire! You didn't dare to doze,
But kept your fingers on your horse's nose
For fear he'd nicker and the chance be lost.
And all night long there, starry in the frost,
You'd see the steaming Colonel striding by.
And when the first light broke along the sky,
Yet not enough to make a saber shine,
You should have seen him gallop down the line
With hair astream! It warmed your blood to see
The way he clapped his hat beneath his knee
And yelled "Come on!" 'Go ask him if we came!'

And so they conjured with a magic name;
But, wakeful in the darkness after taps,
How many saddened, conscious of the lapse
Of man-denying time!

     The last owl ceased.
A pewee sensed the changing of the east
And fluted shyly, doubtful of the news.
A wolf, returning from an all-night cruise
Among the rabbits, topped a staring rim
And vanished. Now the cooks were stirring dim,
Waist-deep in woodsmoke crawling through the damp.
The shadow lifted from the snoring camp.
The bugle sang. The horses cried ha! ha!
The mule herd raised a woeful fanfara
To swell the music, singing out of tune.
Up came the sun.

     The Seventh marched at noon,
Six hundred strong. By fours and troop by troop,
With packs between, they passed the Colonel's group
By Terry's tent; the Rickarees and Crows

Astride their shaggy paints and calicoes;
The regimental banner and the grays;
And after them the sorrels and the bays,
The whites, the browns, the piebalds and the blacks.
One flesh they seemed with those upon their backs,
Whose weathered faces, like and fit for bronze,
Some gleam of unforgotten battle-dawns
Made bright and hard. The music of their going,
How good to hear!—though mournful beyond knowing;
The low-toned chanting of the Crows and Rees,
The guidons whipping in a stiff south breeze
Prophetical of thunder-brewing weather,
The chiming spurs and bits and crooning leather,
The shoe calks clinking on the scattered stone,
And, fusing all, the rolling undertone
Of hoofs by hundreds rhythmically blent—
The diapason of an instrument
Strung taut for battle music.

                        So they passed.
And Custer, waking from a dream at last
With still some glory of it in his eyes,
Shook hands around and said his last goodbyes
And swung a leg across his dancing bay
That champed the snaffle, keen to be away
Where all the others were. Then Gibbon spoke,
Jocosely, but with something in the joke
Of its own pleasantry incredulous:
"Now don't be greedy, Custer! Wait for us!"
And Custer laughed and gave the bay his head.
"I won't!" he cried. Perplexed at what he said,
They watched the glad bay smoking up the draw
And heard the lusty welcoming hurrah
That swept along the column. When it died,
The melancholy pack mules prophesied
And ghost-mules answered.

XII

Now it came to pass,
That late June morning on the Greasy Grass,
Two men went fishing, warriors of the Sioux;
And, lonesome in the silence of the two,
A youngster pictured battles on the sand.
Once more beneath the valor of his hand
The execrated troopers, blotted out,
Became a dust. Then, troubled with a doubt,
He ventured: "Uncle, will they find us here—
The soldiers?" 'Twas a buzzing in the ear
Of Red Hawk where he brooded on his cast.
"The wind is coming up," he said at last;
"The sky grows dusty." "Then the fish won't bite,"
Said Running Wolf. "There may be rain tonight"
Said Red Hawk, falling silent. Bravely then
The youngster wrought himself a world of men
Where nothing waited on a wind of whim,
But everything, obedient to him,
Fell justly. All the white men in the world
Were huddled there, and round about them swirled
More warriors than a grownup might surmise.
The pony-thunder and the battle-cries,
The whine of arrows eager for their marks
Drowned out the music of the meadowlarks,
The rising gale that teased the cottonwoods
To set them grumbling in their whitened hoods,
The chatter of a little waterfall.
These pebbles—see!—were Crazy Horse and
    Gall;

Here Crow King raged, and Black Moon battled
    there!
This yellow pebble—look!—was Yellow Hair;
This drab one with a little splotch of red,
The Gray Fox, Crook! Ho ho! And both were dead;
And white men fell about them every place—
The leafage of the autumn of a race—
Till all were down. And when their doom was sealed,
The little victor danced across the field
Amid the soundless singing of a throng.
The brief joy died, for there was something wrong
About this battle. Mournfully came back
That other picture of a dawn attack—
The giant horses rearing in the fogs
Of their own breath; the yelping of the dogs;
The screaming rabble swarming up the rise;
The tangled terror in his mother's eyes;
The flaming lodges and the bloody snow.
Provokingly oblivious of woe,
The two still eyed the waters and were dumb.

"But will they find us, Uncle? Will they come?"

Now Red Hawk grunted, heaving at his line,
And, wrought of flying spray and morning-shine,
A spiral rainbow flashed along the brook.
"*Hey hey!*" said Red Hawk, staring at his hook,
"He got my bait! Run yonder to the bluff
And catch some hoppers, Hohay. Get enough
And you shall see how fish are caught today!"

Half-heartedly the youngster stole away
Across a brawling riffle, climbed the steep
And gazed across the panoramic sweep
Of rolling prairie, tawny in the drouth,
To where the Big Horns loomed along the south,
No more than ghosts of mountains in the dust.
Up here the hot wind, booming gust on gust,

Made any nook a pleasant place to dream.
You could not see the fishers by the stream;
And you were grown so tall that, looking down
Across the trees, you saw most all the town
Strung far along the valley. First you saw
The Cheyennes yonder opposite the draw
That yawned upon the ford—a goodly sight!
So many and so mighty in a fight
And always faithful brothers to the Sioux!
Trees hid the Brulé village, but you knew
'Twas half a bow-shot long from end to end.
Then Ogalalas filled a river bend,
And next the Minneconjoux did the same.
A little farther south the Sans Arc came,
And they were neighbors to the Hunkpapas.—
The blackened smoke-vents, flapping in the flaws,
Were like a startled crow flock taking wing.—
Some Ogalalas played at toss-the-ring
And many idlers crowded round to see.—
The grazing ponies wandered lazily
Along the flat and up the rolling west.

Now, guiltily remembering his quest,
He trotted farther up the naked hill,
Dropped down a gully where the wind was still—
And came upon a hopping army there!
They swarmed, they raged—but Hohay didn't care;
For suddenly it seemed the recent climb
Had been a scramble up the height of time
And Hohay's name was terror in the ears
Of evil peoples. Seizing weeds for spears,
He charged the soldiers with a dreadful shout.
The snapping of their rifles all about
Might daunt a lesser hero. Never mind;
His medicine made all their bullets blind,
And 'twas a merry slaughter. Then at last
The shining glory of the vision passed,
And hoppers were but hoppers as before,

And he, a very little boy once more,
Stood dwarfed and lonely on a windy rise.
The sun was nearly up the dusty skies.
'Twas white with heat and had a funny stare—
All face! The wind had blown away its hair.
It looked afraid; as though the sun should fear!

Now, squinting downward through the flying blear,
He scanned the town. And suddenly the old
Remembered dawn of terror struck him cold.
Like startled ants that leave a stricken mound
In silence that is felt as panic sound
By one who sees, the squaws and children poured
Along the valley northward past the ford;
And men were chasing ponies every place,
While many others ran, as in a race,
To southward.

       Hohay, taking to his heels,
Made homeward like a cottontail that feels
A kiote pant and whimper at his tail.
He reached the bluff rim, scrambled to the vale
And crossed the stream. The fishermen were gone.
A hubbub in the village led him on
Pell-mell among the snatching underwood,
Till, checked as by a wall of sound, he stood
Apant and dripping in the howling town.

A bent old man there hobbled up and down
Upon a staff and sang a cackling song
Of how his heart was young again and strong;
But no one heeded. Women ran with guns
And bows and war clubs, screaming for their sons
And husbands. Men were mounting in a whirl
Of manes and tails to vanish in a swirl
Of scattered sand; and ever louder blew
The singing wind of warriors riding through
To battle. Hohay watched them, mouth agape,

Until he felt a hand upon his nape
That shoved him north, and someone shouted
 "Run!"
He scampered.

    Meanwhile, nearer to the sun,
A rifle shot beyond the village end,
Came Reno's troopers pouring round a bend,
Their carbines ready at their saddle bows.
A bugle yammered and a big dust rose
And horses nickered as the fours swung wide
In battle order; and the captains cried,
And with a running thunder of hurrahs
The long line stormed upon the Hunkpapas
Strung thin across the open flat. They fled
Like feeble ghosts of men already dead
Beneath the iron feet that followed there;
For now they deemed the far-famed Yellow Hair,
The Wolf of Washita, with all his pack
Potential in the dust cloud at his back,
Bore down upon them.

    Flame along a slough
Before a howling wind, the terror grew
As momently increased the flying mass,
For all the others running up were grass
Before that flame; till men became aware
Of how another voice was booming there,
Outsoaring Panic's, smashing through the brawl
Of hoofs and wind and rifles.

    It was Gall.
A night wind blowing when the stars are dim,
His big black gelding panted under him;
And scarce he seemed a man of mortal race,
His naked body and his massive face
Serene as hewn from time-forgotten rock,
Despite the horse's rearing to the shock

Of surging men. Boy-hearted warriors took
New courage from the father in his look
And listened in a sudden lull of sound.
"The foe is there!" he shouted. "Turn around!
Die here today!" And everywhere he rode
A suck of men grew after him and flowed
To foeward.

         Now it seemed the routed fear
Had joined the halted troops. They ceased to cheer.
Dismounting with their right upon the trees
Along the river, and the Rickarees
Upon their left, they flung a blazing dam
Across the valley. Like a river jam
The eager rabble deepened on the front,
For other hundreds, howling to the hunt,
Were dashing up with ponies. Then they say
A sound was heard as when a jam gives way
Before a heaped up freshet of the Spring,
And ponies in a torrent smote the wing
Where, mounted yet, the little Ree band stood.

Now those, remembering where life was good,
Regretting that they ever chose to roam
So far from kindly faces, started home
Without farewells; and round the crumpled flank
The Sioux came thronging, bending back the rank
Upon the pivot of the farther troop,
Till, crowded in a brushy river loup,
The soldiers fought bewildered and forlorn.
Behind them from across the Little Horn
The long range rifles on the bluff rim spat
A hornet swarm among them; and the flat
Before them swam with ponies on the run—
A vertigo of shadows; for the sun
Went moony in the dust and disappeared.
Inverted faces of a nightmare leered
Beneath the necks of ponies hurtling past;

And every surge of horsemen seemed the last,
So well their daring fed upon their rage.

It might have been a moment or an age
The troopers gripped that slipping edge of life,
When some along the left saw Bloody Knife,
By Reno, straighten from his fighting squat.
And heard him scream, and saw the wound he got
Spew brains between the fingers clutching there.
Then like a drowning man with hands in air
He sank. And some who fought nearby have said
The Major's face, all spattered with the red
Of that snuffed life, went chalky, and his shout
Scarce reached the nearer troopers round about:
"Back to the bluffs!" But when a few arose
To do his will, they say he raged at those:
"Get down! Get down!" Then once again he cried:
"Get to the bluffs!"—And was the first to ride.

Now some along the right, who had not heard,
But saw the mounting, passed a shouted word
That groped, a whisper, through the roaring smoke:
"We're going to charge!" And where it fell, it broke
The ragged line. Men scrambled to the rear
Where now the plunging horses shrieked with fear
And fought their holding "fours"—nor all in vain,
For whole quadrigæ, fastened bit to rein,
Ramped down that stormy twilight of the Sioux.
The nearest empty saddle seat would do
For any lucky finder. Rout or charge—
What matter? All along the river marge
The man storm raged, and all the darkened vale
Was tumult. To retreat was to assail,
Assault was flight. The craven and the bold
Seemed one that moment where the loud dust
      rolled,
Death-strewing, up along the Little Horn.

About the loup a mockery of morn
Broke in upon the gloaming of the noon,
And horseless troopers, starting from the swoon
Of battle, saw, and knew themselves alone
And heard the wounded wailing and the moan
Of dying men around them. Even these,
Forlorn among the bullet-bitten trees,
Were scarce less lucky than the fleeing ranks
With crowding furies snapping at their flanks,
Death in the rear and frantic hope ahead.
'Twas like a bison hunt, the Sioux have said,
When few bulls battle and the fat cows run
Less fleet than slaughter. Hidden from the sun,
How many a boy, struck motherless, belied
The whiskered cheek; what heroism died,
Fronting the wild white glory!

                           Funk or fight,
Lost in the noon's anomaly of night,
The troopers struggled, groping for a ford.
But more and more the pressure of the horde
Bore leftward, till the steep-banked river spread
Before them, and the bluffs that loomed ahead
Were like the domes of heaven to the damned.
A shrinking moment, and the flood was jammed
With men and horses thrashing belly deep;
And down upon them, jostled to the leap,
The rear cascaded. Many-noted pain
Sang medley in the roaring rifle rain
That swept the jetting water, gust on gust.
And many a Sioux, gone wild with slaughter lust,
Plunged after. Madmen grappled in the flood,
And tumbling in the current, streaked with blood,
Drank deep together and were satisfied.

Now scrambling out upon the further side,
The hunted troopers blundered at a steep
More suited to the flight of mountain sheep

Than horses; for a narrow pony trail,
That clambered up a gully from the vale,
Immediately clogged with brutes and men.
Spent horses skittered back to strive again,
Red-flanked and broken-hearted. Many bore
Their riders where no horse had gone before,
Nor ever shall go. Bullets raked the slope,
And from the valley to the heights of hope
The air was dirty with the arrow-snow.
The heights of hope? Alas, that stair of woe,
Strewn with the bleeding offal of the rout,
Led only to an eminence of doubt,
A more appalling vision of their plight;
For in the rear and on the left and right
The nearer bluffs were filling with the Sioux,
And still along the flat beneath them blew
The dust of thousands yelping for the kill.

They say that good men broke upon the hill
And wept as children weep. And there were some
Who stared about them empty eyed and dumb,
As though it didn't matter. Others hurled
Profane irrelevancies at the world
Or raved about the jamming of their guns.
And yet there lacked not level-headed ones,
Unruffled shepherds of the flock, who strove
For order in the milling of the drove
With words to soothe or cheer, or sting with scorn.

Now up the valley of the Little Horn
Wild news came crying from the lower town
Of other soldiers yonder riding down
Upon the guardless village from the east;
And every tongue that sped the news increased
The meaning of it. Victory forsook
Big hearts that withered. Lo, the Gray Fox, Crook,
Returning for revenge—and not alone!
How many camps along the Yellowstone

Were emptied on the valley there below?
The whipped were but a sprinkle of the foe,
And now the torrent was about to burst!
With everything to know, they knew the worst,
And saw the clearer in that no one saw.
Then broke a flying area of awe
Across the rabble like a patch of sun
Upon the troubled corn when gray clouds run
And in the midst a glowing rift is blown.
Pressed back before the plunging white-faced roan
Of Crazy Horse, men brightened. How they knew
That lean, swift fighting-spirit of the Sioux,
The wizard eyes, the haggard face and thin,
Transfigured by a burning from within
Despite the sweat-streaked paint and battle grime!
Old men would ponder in the wane of time
That lifting vision and alluring cry:
"There never was a better day to die!
Come on, Dakotas! Cowards to the rear!"

Some hundreds yonder held the net of fear
Round Reno's hill; but in the cloud that spread
Along the valley where the fleet roan led
Were thousands.

          Now the feeble and the young,
The mothers and the maidens, terror-flung
Beyond the lower village to the west,
Had seen the soldiers loom along a crest
Beyond the town, and, heading down a swale
By fours, with guidons streaming in the gale,
Approach the ford. 'Twas Custer with the grays,
A sorrel troop and thrice as many bays—
Two hundred and a handful at the most;
But 'twas the bannered onset of a host
To those who saw and fled. Nor could they know
The numbers and the valiance of the foe
Down river where the bulls of war were loud;

For even then that thunder and the cloud
Came northward. Were they beaten? Had they won?
What devastation, darkening the sun,
Was tearing down the valley? On it roared
And darkled; deepened at the lower ford
And veered cyclonic up the yawning draw
To eastward. Now the breathless people saw
The dusty ponies darting from the van
And swarming up the left. The guns began,
A running splutter. Yonder to the south
The big dust boiling at a coulee's mouth
Was pouring ponies up around the right.
Grown dimmer in the falling battle-night,
The stormy guidons of the troopers tossed,
Retreating upward, lessened and were lost
Amid a whirling cloud that topped the hill.
And steadily the valley spouted still
The double stream of warriors.

                      Then a shout
Enringed the battle, and the scene went out
In rumbling dust—as though a mine were lit
Beneath the summit and the belch of it
Gloomed bellowing. A windy gloaming spread
Across the ridges flicked with errant lead
And wayward arrows groping for a mark.
And horses, hurtled from the central dark,
With empty saddles charged upon the day.

Meanwhile on Reno's hill four miles away
Men heartened to a rousing cheer had seen
The bays and blacks and sorrels of Benteen,
Hoof-heavy with their unavailing quest
Among the valleys to the south and west,
Toil upward. Unmolested by the foe,
The pack mules, trumpeting "We told you so,"
Trudged in a little later. By the cheers
It might have been reunion after years;

And was in truth; for there were graying locks,
That night, to mock the pedantry of clocks,
Untroubled by the ages life can pack
Between the ticks.

        The fire had fallen slack
Upon the watching summits round about
And in a maze of wonderment and doubt
Men scanned the north that darkled as with war.
'What was it that the Major waited for?
He'd best be doing something pretty quick
Or there'd be Custer with a pointed stick
To look for him!' So growled a bolder few.
But many thought of little else to do
Than just to dodge the leaden wasp that kills
Sent over by the snipers on the hills
In fitful swarms.

        Now like a bellowed word
The miles made inarticulate, they heard
A sound of volley-firing. *There! and there!*
Hoarse with a yet incredible despair
That incoherent cry of kin to kin
Grew big above the distant battle din—
The sequent breakers of a moaning sea.
And twice the murmuring veil of mystery
Was rent and mended. Then the tearing drawl
Was heard no more where Fury, striding tall,
Made one in dust the heavens and the earth.
'He's pitching into them for all he's worth,'
Some ventured;—'was there nothing else to do
But hug that hill?'

        Then suddenly there grew
A voice of wrath, and many lying near,
Who heard it, looked—and it was Captain Wier
By Reno yonder; and the place went still:
"Then, Major, if you won't, by God I will,

And there'll be more to say if we get back!"
They saw him fling a leg across his black
And take the northward steep with face set grim;
And all the black horse troop rode after him
Across the gulch to vanish on a rise.

Two miles away from where the smudgy skies
Of afternoon anticipated night,
They halted on a space-commanding height
And, squinting through the dusty air ahead,
Were puzzled. For the silence of the dead
Had fallen yonder—only now and then
A few shots crackled. Groups of mounted men—
Not troopers—by the rifting dust revealed,
Were scattered motionless about the field,
As wearily contented with a work
Well done at last.

        Then suddenly the murk
Began to boil and murmur, like a storm
Before the wind comes. Ponies in a swarm
Were spreading out across the ridgy land
Against the blacks.

        By now the whole command
Was coming up, and not a whit too soon;
For once again the sun became a moon
Amid the dust of thousands bearing down.

Now farther back upon a bleak bluff crown
The troop of Godfrey waited for the fight,
Not doubting that their comrades held the right,
When orders, riding with an urgent heel,
Arrived with more of prudence to reveal
Than pluck: *Withdraw at once!* A startled stare
Made plain how all the flanking hills were bare
And not a sign of Reno in the rear!
Just then the fleeing troops of French and Wier

Came roaring down across a ridge in front
And, close upon their heels, the howling hunt
Made dimmer yet the summit of the slope.
And Godfrey, seeing very little hope
If all should flee those thousands, overjoyed
With some great *coup,* dismounted and deployed
To fight on foot, and sent the horses back.
And so he dared the brunt of the attack,
Retreating slowly like a wounded bear
With yelping dogs before him everywhere
Regardful of the eager might at bay.
And so the whole command got back that day
Of big despairs; and men remember still.

Then all the ridges circling Reno's hill
Were crowded. In among the flattened men,
Now desperately fighting one to ten,
Hell hornets snarled and feathered furies crooned
A death song; and the sun was like a wound
Wherewith the day bled dizzy. Yet from all
The muddled nightmare of it, men recall
Deeds brighter for the years: how Captain French,
Like any stodgy tailor on his bench,
Sat cross-legged at the giddy edge of life
Serenely picking with a pocket knife
The shell-jammed guns and loading them anew;
How, seemingly enamoured of the view,
Deliberate, Johnsonian of mien,
His briar drawing freely, strolled Benteen
Along his fighting line; how Wallace, Wier
And Godfrey yonder, fearing only fear,
Walked round among the troopers, cheering them.
And some remember Happy Jack of M,
The way his gusty laughter served to melt
The frost of terror, though the joy he felt
Seemed less to mark a hero than a fool.
And once, they say, an ammunition mule
Broke loose and bolted, braying, as he went,

Defiance and a traitorous intent
To quit the Whites forever. Then they tell
How Sergeant Hanley with an Irish yell
Took horse and followed, jealous for the pack;
And all the line roared after him, "Come back!
Come back, you fool!" But Hanley went ahead.
At times you hardly saw him for the lead
That whipped the dust up. Blindly resolute,
The traitor with the Irish in pursuit
Struck up along a hostile ridge that burned
And smoked and bellowed. Presently he turned
And panted home, an image of remorse;
And Hanley, leaping from his winded horse,
Lay down and went to work among the rest.

The wounded day bled ashen in the west;
The firing dwindled in the dusk and ceased;
The frightened stars came peeking from the east
To see what anguish moaned. The wind went down—
A lull of death. But yonder in the town
All night the war drums flouted that despair
Upon the hill, and dancers in the glare
Of fires that lowered filled the painted dark
With demon exultation, till the lark
Of doom should warble. Heavy-lidded eyes
Saw often in the sage along a rise
The loom of troops. If any shouted "Look!"
And pointed, all the others cheered for Crook
Or Terry coming; and the bugles cried
To mocking echoes. When the sick hope died,
They fell to sullen labor, scraping up
The arid earth with plate and drinking cup
Against the dreaded breaking of the day.
And here and there among the toilers lay
The winners of an endless right to shirk;
While many panted at a harder work,
The wage whereof is nothing left to buy.

It seemed that all were men about to die,
Forlornly busy there among the dead—
Each man his sexton. Petulant with dread,
They talked of Custer, grumbling at a name
Already shaping on the lips of Fame
To be a deathless bugle-singing soon.
For no one guessed what now the tardy moon
Was poring over with a face of fright
Out yonder: naked bodies gleaming white
The whole way to the summit of the steep
Where Silence, brooding on a tumbled heap
Of men and horses, listened for a sound. . . .
A wounded troop horse sniffed the bloody ground
And ghosts of horses nickered when he neighed.

Now scarcely had the prairie owls, afraid
Of morning, ceased, or waiting hushes heard
A timid, unauthoritative bird
Complain how late the meadowlarks awoke,
When suddenly the dreaded fury broke
About the sleepless troopers, digging still.
It raked the shallow trenches on the hill;
It beat upon the little hollow where
The mules and horses, tethered in a square
About the wounded, roared and plunged amain,
Tight-tailed against no pasture-loving rain;
And many fell and floundered. What of night
From such a morning? For the hostile light
Increased the fury, and the battle grew.

That day it seemed the very sun was Sioux.
The heat, the frenzy and the powder gas
Wreaked torture. Men were chewing roots of grass
For comfort ere the day had well begun.
Bare to the grim mid-malice of the sun,
The wounded raved for water. Far below,
Cool with the melting of the mountain snow,

The river gleamed; and, queasy with the smell
Of bodies bloating in a stew of hell,
Men croaked about it. Better to be killed
Half way to yonder joy than perish grilled
Between that grid of earth and burning air!

So nineteen troopers volunteered to dare
A grisly race. The twentieth who ran,
Invisible and fleeter than a man,
With hoofs of peril flicked the dusty sod
Where pluckily the sprinting water squad
Made streamward. Giddy with a wound he got,
A trooper tumbled, and his cooking pot
Pursued the others with a bounding roll.
A second runner crumpled near the goal.
And when the sprawling winners drank, they say
The bullets whipped the water into spray
About their heads; for yonder in the brush
The Sioux kept watch, but dared not make a rush
Because of marksmen stationed on the bluff.
And when the greedy drinkers had enough,
With brimming kettles and the filled canteens
They toiled along the tortuous ravines
And panted up a height that wasn't Fame's.
Men still recall the water; but the names
Enrich that silence where the millions go.

The shadows had begun to overflow
Their stagnant puddles on the nightward side,
When presently the roar of battle died
On all the circling summits there. Perplexed
With what the wily foe might purpose next,
The troopers lay and waited. Still the swoon
Of silence held the stifling afternoon,
Save for a low monotony of pain,
The keening of the gnats about the slain
That festered. Nothing happened. Shadows crept
A little farther nightward. Many slept,

Dead to the sergeant's monitory shake;
And some, for very weariness awake,
Got up and dared to stretch a leg at last,
When from the summits broke a rifle blast
That banished sleep and drove the strollers in.

Abruptly as it started, ceased the din
And all the hills seemed empty as before.

And, breath by breath, the weary waiting wore
The hours out. Every minute, loath to pass,
Forewarned the next of some assault in mass
Preparing in the hush. A careless head
Above a horse's carcass drew the lead
Of lurking marksmen. What would be the end?
The prayed-for dark itself might prove no friend
For all its pity.

        Now the early slant
Of evening made the thirsty horses pant
And raise a running whimper of despair,
When, seemingly ignited by the glare,
The very prairie smouldered. Spire by spire,
Until the whole fat valley was afire,
Smoke towered in the windless air and grew
Where late the league long village of the Sioux
Lay hidden from the watchers on the hill;
And like the shadow of a monster ill
Untimely gloaming fell across the height.
Yet nothing but the failing of the light
Upon the distant summits came to pass.
The muffled murmur of the burning grass
Was all the reeking valley had of sound;
And when the troopers dared to walk around,
No spluttering of rifles drove them back.

The shadows in the draws were getting black
When someone lifted up a joyous cry

That set the whole band staring where the sky,
To southward of the smoke, remembered day.
And there they saw, already miles away—
A pictographic scrawl upon the glow—
The tangled slant and clutter of travaux
By crowding hundreds; ponies that pursued,
A crawling, milling, tossing multitude,
A somber river brawling out of banks;
And glooms of horsemen flowing on the flanks—
The whole Sioux village fleeing with the light
To where the Big Horn Mountains glimmered
     white
And low along the south!

              The horses neighed
To swell the happy noise their masters made.
The pack mules sang the only song they knew.
And summits, late familiar with the Sioux,
Proclaimed a new allegiance, cheer on cheer.
For who could doubt that news of Terry near
Had driven off the foe?

THE TWILIGHT

A moon wore by,

XIII

And in the rainless waning of July
Ten thousand hearts were troubled where the creeks,
Young from the ancient winter of the peaks,
Romped in the mountain meadows green as May.
The very children lost the heart to play,
Awed by the shadow of an unseen thing,
As covies, when the shadow of a wing
Forebodes a pounce of terror from the skies.
They saw it in the bravest father's eyes—
That shadow—in the gentlest mother's face;
Unwitting how there fell upon a race
The twilight of irreparable wrong.
The drums had fallen silent with the song,
And valiant tales, late eager to be told,
Were one with all things glorious and old
And dear and gone forever from the Sioux.

For now the hunted prairie people knew
How powerful the Gray Fox camp had grown
On Goose Creek; how along the Yellowstone
The mounted soldiers and the walking ones—
A multitude—had got them wagon guns,
Of which the voice was thunder and the stroke,
Far off, a second thunder and a smoke
That bit and tore. A little while, and then
Those open jaws, toothed terribly with men,
Would move together, closing to the bite.
What hope was left in anything but flight?

And whither? O the world was narrow now!
South, east, the rat-like nibbling of the plow
Had left them but a little way to go.
The mountains of the never melting snow
Walled up the west. Beyond the northern haze,
There lay a land of unfamiliar ways,
Dark tongues and alien eyes.

           As waters keep
Their wonted channels, yearning for the deep,
The homeless rabble took the ancient road.
From bluff to bluff the Rosebud valley flowed
Their miles of ponies; and the pine-clad heights
Were sky-devouring torches in the nights
Behind them, and a rolling gloom by day;
And prairies, kindled all along the way,
Bloomed balefully and blackened. Noon was dark,
Night starless, and the fleeing meadowlark
Forgot the morning. Where the Bluestone runs
Their dust bore east; and seldom did the suns
Behold them going for the seed they strewed
To crop the rearward prairie solitude
With black starvation even for the crow.
Creeks, stricken as with fever, ceased to flow
And languished in a steaming ashen mire.
But more than grass was given to the fire—
O memories no spring could render young!
And so it was that, marching down the Tongue,
The Gray Fox, seeking for the hostile bands,
Saw nothing but the desolated lands
Black to the sky; and when a dreary week
Had brought him to the mouth of Bluestone Creek,
Lo, Terry with another empty tale!

Broad as a road to ruin ran the trail
Of driven pony herds, a livid scar
Upon a vast cadaver, winding far
To eastward as the tallest hill might look.

And thither pressed the horse and foot of Crook,
Their pack mules, lighter for a greater speed,
With scant provisions for a fortnight's need
Upon their saddles.

              Burning August waned
About the toiling regiments. It rained—
A sodden, chill monotony of rains—
As though the elements had cursed the plains,
And now that flame had stricken, water struck.
The scarecrow horses struggled with the suck
Of gumbo flats and heartbreak hills of clay;
And many a bone-bag fell beside the way
Too weak to rise, for still the draws were few
That were not blackened. Crows and buzzards knew
How little eager claws and whetted beaks
Availed them where so many hollow cheeks
Had bulged about a brief and cookless feast.

Still wearily the main trail lengthened east
By hungry days and fireless bivouacs;
And more and more diverging pony tracks,
To north and south, and tangent lodge pole trails
Revealed the hunted scattering as quails
Before a dreaded hunter. Eastward still
They staggered, nourished by a doggéd will,
Past where a little river apes in mud
And name the genius of a titan flood
That drinks it. Crumbling pinnacles of awe
Looked down upon them; domes of wonder saw
The draggled column slowly making head
Against the muck; the drooping horses, led,
Well loaded with their saddles; empty packs,
Become a cruel burden on the backs
Of plodding mules with noses to the ground.
Along the deeps of Davis Creek they wound,
To where the Camel's Hump and Rosebud Butte
Behold the Heart's head.

Here the long pursuit,
It seemed, had come to nothing after all.
The multitude of Crazy Horse and Gall
Had vanished in that God-forsaken place
And matched their fagged pursuers for a race
With something grimmer than a human foe.
Four marches east across the dim plateau
Fort Lincoln lured them. Twice as many days
Beyond the dripping low September haze,
Due south across the yet uncharted lands,
Lay Deadwood, unprotected from the bands
Of prowling hostiles. 'Twas enough for Crook.
Half-heartedly the ragged column took
The way of duty.

And the foe appeared!
Where, like a god-built stadium, the tiered
Age-carven Slim Buttes watch the Rabbit's Lip
Go groping for the ocean, in the drip
And ooze of sodden skies the battle raged;
And presences, millennially aged
In primal silence, shouted at the sight.
Until the rifles gashed the front of night
With sanguinary wounds, they fought it out;
And darkness was the end of it, and doubt
And drizzle. Unrejoicing victors knew
What enemy, more mighty than the Sioux,
Would follow with no lagging human feet;
And early morning saw them in retreat
Before that foe. Above their buried slain
A thousand horses trampled in the rain
That none might know the consecrated ground
To violate it.

Up and up they wound
Among the foggy summits, till the van
Was checked with awe. Inimical to Man,
Below them spread a featureless immense,

More credibly a dream of impotence
Than any earthly country to be crossed—
A gloomy flat, illimitably lost
In gauzes of the downpour.

                Thither strove
The gaunt battalions. And the chill rain drove
Unceasingly. Through league on league of mire
Men straggled into camps without a fire
To wolf their slaughtered horses in the red;
And all the wallow of the way they fled
Was strewn with crowbaits dying in the bogs.
About them in the forest of the fogs
Lurked Crazy Horse, a cougar mad for blood;
And scarce the rearguard-battles in the mud
Aroused the sullen plodders to the fore.
The Deer's Ears loomed and vanished in the pour;
The Haystack Buttes stole off along the right;
And men grew old between a night and night
Before their feeble toil availed to raise
The Black Hills, set against the evil days
About a paradise of food and rest.

Now Crazy Horse's people, turning west,
Retraced the trail of ruin, sick for home.
Where myriads of the bison used to roam
And fatten in the golden autumn drowse,
A few rejected bulls and barren cows
Grew yet a little leaner. Every place
The good old earth, with ashes on her face,
Was like a childless mother in despair;
Though still she kept with jealous, loving care
Some little hoard of all her youth had known
Against the dear returning of her own;
But where the starving herd of ponies passed,
The little shielded hollows, lately grassed,
Were stricken barren even as with fire.
And so they reached the place of their desire,

The deep-carved valley where the Powder flows.
Here surely there was peace.

                But when the snows
Came booming where the huddled village stood
And ponies, lean with gnawing cottonwood,
Were slain to fill the kettles, Dull Knife came,
The great Cheyenne. The same—O not the same
As he who fought beside the Greasy Grass
And slew his fill of enemies! Alas,
The beggar in his eyes! And very old
He seemed, for hunger and the pinch of cold
Were on him; and the rabble at his back—
Despairing hundreds—lacked not any lack
That flesh may know and live. The feeble wail
Of babies put an edge upon the tale
That Dull Knife told.

             "There was a fight" he said.
"I set my winter village at the head
Of Willow Creek. The mountains there are tall.
A canyon stood about me for a wall;
And it was good to hear my people sing,
For there was none that wanted anything
That makes men happy. We were all asleep.
The cold was sharp; the snow was very deep.
What enemy could find us? We awoke.
A thunder and a shouting and a smoke
Were there among us, and a swarm of foes—
Pawnees, Shoshones and Arapahoes,
And soldiers, many soldiers. It was night
About us, and we fought them in the light
Of burning lodges till the town was lost
And all our plenty. Bitter was the frost
And most of us were naked from the bed.
Now many of our little ones are dead
Of cold and hunger. Shall the others die?"

There was a light in Crazy Horse's eye
Like moony ice. The other spoke again.
"As brothers have Dakota and Cheyenne
Made war together. Help us. You have seen
We can not live until the grass is green,
My brother!"

        Then the other face grew stone;
The hard lips moved: "A man must feed his own,"
Said Crazy Horse, and turned upon his heel.
But now the flint of him had found the steel
In Dull Knife, and the flare was bad to see.
"Tashunka Witko, dare to look at me
That you may not forget me. We shall meet.
The soldiers yonder have enough to eat,
And I will come, no beggar, with the grass!"

And silently the people saw him pass
Along the valley where the snow lay blue,
The plodding, silent, ragamuffin crew
Behind him. So the evil days began.

Now Crazy Horse, they say, was like a man
Who, having seen a ghost, must look and look
And brood upon the empty way it took
To nowhere; and he scarcely ate at all;
And there was that about him like a wall
To shut men out. He seemed no longer young.

Bleak January found them on the Tongue
In search of better forage for the herd—
A failing quest. And hither came the word
Of many walking soldiers coming down
With wagon guns upon the starving town
That might not flee; for whither could they go
With ponies pawing feebly in the snow
To grow the leaner? Mighty in despair,

They waited on a lofty summit there
Above the valley.

                Raw gray dawn revealed
A scaly serpent crawling up a field
Of white beneath them. Leisurely it neared,
Resolving into men of frosty beard
With sloping rifles swinging to the beat
And melancholy fifing of their feet
Upon the frost; and shrill the wagon tires
Sang rearward. Now the soldiers lighted fires
And had their breakfast hot, as who should say:
"What hurry? It is early in the day
And there is time for what we came to do."
With wistful eyes the rabble of the Sioux
Beheld the eating; knew that they defied
In vain their own misgivings when they cried:
"Eat plenty! You will never eat again!"
It was not so; for those were devil men
Who needed nothing and were hard to kill.

The wagon-guns barked sharply at the hill
To bite the summit, always shooting twice;
And scrambling upward through the snow and ice
Came doggedly, without a sign of fear,
The infantry of Miles. They didn't cheer,
They didn't hurry, and they didn't stop,
For all the rifles roaring at the top,
Until the gun-butt met the battle-ax.
Still fighting with their children at their backs
The Sioux gave slowly. Wind came on to blow,
A hurrying northwester, blind with snow,
And in the wild white dusk of it they fled.

But when they reached the Little Powder's head,
So much of all their little had been lost,
So well had wrought their hunger and the frost,
One might have thought 'twas Dull Knife coming there.

The country had a cold, disowning stare;
The burned-off valleys could not feed their own.

The moon was like a frozen bubble, blown
Along the rim of February nights,
When Spotted Tail, the lover of the Whites,
Came there with mighty words. His cheeks were full,
His belly round. He spoke of Sitting Bull
And Gall defeated, driven far away
Across the line; of Red Cloud getting gray
Before his time—a cougar in a cage,
Self-eaten by a silent, toothless rage
That only made the watching sentry smile.
And still the story saddened. All the while
The scattered Sioux were coming in to save
Their children with the food the soldiers gave
And laying down their guns and making peace.
He told how Dull Knife's fury did not cease
But grew upon the soldier food he ate;
And how his people fattened, nursing hate
For Crazy Horse. And many more than these
But waited for the grass—the Loup Pawnees,
The Utes, the Winnebagoes and the Crows,
Shoshones, Bannocks and Arapahoes,
With very many more Dakotas too!

"Now what could Crazy Horse's people do
Against them all?" said Spotted Tail, the Wise.
And with the ancient puzzle in his eyes
That only death may riddle; gazing long
Now first upon the fat one in the wrong
And now upon the starving in the right,
The other found an answer: "I could fight!
And I could fight till all of us were dead.
But now I have no powder left," he said;
"I can not fight. Tell Gray Fox what you saw;
That I am only waiting for a thaw
To bring my people in."

THE DEATH OF CRAZY HORSE

And now 'twas done.

XIV

Spring found the waiting fort at Robinson
A half-moon ere the Little Powder knew;
And, doubting still what Crazy Horse might do
When tempted by the herald geese a-wing
To join the green rebellion of the spring,
The whole frontier was troubled. April came,
And once again his undefeated name
Rode every wind. Ingeniously the West
Wrought verities from what the East had guessed
Of what the North knew. Eagerly deceived,
The waiting South progressively believed
The wilder story. April wore away;
Fleet couriers, arriving day by day
With but the farthing mintage of the fact,
Bought credit slowly in that no one lacked
The easy gold of marvelous surmise.
For, gazing northward where the secret skies
Were moody with a coming long deferred,
Whoever spoke of Crazy Horse, still heard
Ten thousand hoofs.

But yonder, with the crow

And kiote to applaud his pomp of woe,
The last great Sioux rode down to his defeat.
And now his people huddled in the sleet
Where Dog Creek and the Little Powder met.
With faces ever sharper for the whet
Of hunger, silent in the driving rains,

They straggled out across the blackened plains
Where Inyan Kara, mystically old,
Drew back a cloudy curtain to behold,
Serene with Time's indifference to men.
And now they tarried on the North Cheyenne
To graze their feeble ponies, for the news
Of April there had wakened in the sloughs
A glimmering of pity long denied.
Nor would their trail across the bare divide
Grow dimmer with the summer, for the bleach
Of dwindled herds—so hard it was to reach
The South Cheyenne. O sad it was to hear
How all the pent-up music of the year
Surged northward there the way it used to do!
In vain the catbird scolded at the Sioux;
The timid pewee queried them in vain;
Nor might they harken to the whooping crane
Nor heed the high geese calling them to come.
Unwelcome waifs of winter, drab and dumb,
Where ecstacy of sap and thrill of wing
Made shift to flaunt some color or to sing
The birth of joy, they toiled a weary way.
And giddy April sobered into May
Before they topped the summit looking down
Upon the valley of the soldier's town
At Robinson.

       Then eerily began
Among the lean-jowled warriors in the van
The chant of peace, a supplicating wail
That spread along the clutter of the trail
Until the last bent straggler sang alone;
And camp dogs, hunger-bitten to the bone,
Accused the heavens with a doleful sound;
But, silent still, with noses to the ground,
The laden ponies toiled to cheat the crows,
And famine, like a wag, had made of those
A grisly jest.

So Crazy Horse came in
With twice a thousand beggars.

                                    And the din
Died out, though here and there a dog still howled,
For now the mighty one, whom Fate had fouled,
Dismounted, faced the silent double row
Of soldiers haughty with the glint and glow
Of steel and brass. A little while he stood
As though bewildered in a haunted wood
Of men and rifles all astare with eyes.
They saw a giant shrunken to the size
Of any sergeant. Now he met the glare
Of Dull Knife and his warriors waiting there
With fingers itching at the trigger-guard.
How many comrade faces, strangely hard,
Were turned upon him! Ruefully he smiled,
The doubtful supplication of a child
Caught guilty; loosed the bonnet from his head
And cast it down. "I come for peace," he said;
"Now let my people eat." And that was all.

The summer ripened. Presages of fall
Now wanted nothing but the goose's flight.
The goldenrods had made their torches bright
Against the ghostly imminence of frost.
And one, long brooding on a birthright lost,
Remembered and remembered. O the time
When all the prairie world was white with rime
Of mornings, and the lodge smoke towered straight
To meet the sunlight, coming over late
For happy hunting! O the days, the days
When winds kept silence in the far blue haze
To hear the deep-grassed valleys running full
With fatling cows, and thunders of the bull
Across the hills! Nights given to the feast
When big round moons came smiling up the east
To listen to the drums, the dancing feet,

The voices of the women, high and sweet
Above the men's!

        And Crazy Horse was sad.
There wasn't any food the white man had
Could find his gnawing hunger and assuage.
Some saw a blood-mad panther in a cage,
And some the sulking of a foolish pride,
For there were those who watched him narrow-eyed
The whole day long and listened for a word,
To shuttle in the warp of what they heard
A woof of darker meaning.

              Then one day
A flying tale of battles far away
And deeds to make men wonder stirred the land:
How Nez Perce Joseph led his little band,
With Howard's eager squadrons in pursuit,
Across the mountains of the Bitter Root
To Big Hole Basin and the day-long fight;
And how his women, fleeing in the night,
Brought off the ponies and the children too.
O many a heart beat fast among the Sioux
To hear the way he fled and fought and fled
Past Bannack, down across the Beaverhead
To Henry's Lake, relentlessly pursued;
Now swallowed by the dreadful solitude
Where still the Mighty Spirit shapes the dream
With primal fires and prodigies of steam,
As when the fallow night was newly sown;
Now reappearing down the Yellowstone,
Undaunted yet and ever making less
That thousand miles of alien wilderness
Between a people's freedom and their need!

O there was virtue in the tale to feed
The withered heart and make it big again!
Not yet, not yet the ancient breed of men

Had vanished from the aging earth! They say
There came a change on Crazy Horse the day
The Ogalala village buzzed the news.
So much to win and only life to lose;
The bison making southward with the fall,
And Joseph fighting up the way to Gall
And Sitting Bull!

                  Who knows the dream he had?
Much talk there was of how his heart was bad
And any day some meditated deed
Might start an irresistible stampede
Among the Sioux—a human prairie-fire!
So back and forth along the talking wire
Fear chattered. Yonder, far away as morn,
The mighty heard—and heard the Little Horn
Still roaring with the wind of Custer's doom.
And there were troopers moving in the gloom
Of midnight to the chaining of the beast;
But when the white light broke along the east,
There wasn't any Ogalala town
And Crazy Horse had vanished!

                  Up and down
The dusty autumn panic horsemen spurred
Till all the border shuddered at the word
Of how that terror threatened every trail.

They found him in the camp of Spotted Tail,
A lonely figure with a face of care.
"I am afraid of what might happen there"
He said. "So many listen what I say
And look and look. I will not run away.
I want my people here. You have my guns."

But half a world away the mighty ones
Had spoken words like bullets in the dark
That wreak the rage of blindness on a mark
They can not know.

     Then spoke the one who led
The soldiers: "Not a hair upon your head
Shall suffer any harm if you will go
To Robinson for just a day or so
And have a parley with the soldier chief."
He spoke believing and he won belief,
So Crazy Horse went riding down the west;
And neither he nor any trooper guessed
What doom now made a rutted wagon road
The highway to a happier abode
Where all the dead are splendidly alive
And summer lingers and the bison thrive
Forever.

    If the better hope be true,
There was a gate of glory yawning through
The sunset when the little cavalcade
Approached the fort.

      The populous parade,
The straining hush that somehow wasn't peace,
The bristling troops, the Indian police
Drawn up as for a battle! What was wrong?
What made them hustle Crazy Horse along
Among the gleaming bayonets and eyes?
There swept a look of quizzical surprise
Across his face. He struggled with the guard.
Their grips were steel; their eyes were cold
  and hard—
Like bayonets.

     There was a door flung wide.
The soldier chief would talk with him inside
And all be well at last!

      The stifling, dim
Interior poured terror over him.
He blinked about—and saw the iron bars.

O nevermore to neighbor with the stars
Or know the simple goodness of the sun!
Did some swift vision of a doom begun
Reveal the monstrous purpose of a lie—
The desert island and the alien sky,
The long and lonely ebbing of a life?
The glimmer of a whipped-out butcher knife
Dismayed the shrinking squad, and once again
Men saw a face that many better men
Had died to see! Brown arms that once were kind,
A comrade's arms, whipped round him from behind,
Went crimson with a gash and dropped aside.
"Don't touch me! I am Crazy Horse!" he cried,
And, leaping doorward, charged upon the world
To meet the end. A frightened soldier hurled
His weight behind a jabbing belly-thrust,
And Crazy Horse plunged headlong in the dust,
A writhing heap. The momentary din
Of struggle ceased. The people, closing in,
Went ominously silent for a space,
And one could hear men breathing round the place
Where lay the mighty. Now he strove to rise,
The wide blind stare of anguish in his eyes,
And someone shouted *Kill that devil quick!*

A throaty murmur and a running click
Of gun-locks woke among the crowding Sioux,
And many a soldier whitened. Well they knew
What pent-up hate the moment might release
To drop upon the bungled farce of peace
A bloody curtain.

        One began to talk;
His tongue was drunken and his face was chalk;
But when a halfbreed shouted what he spoke
The crowd believed, so few had seen the stroke,
Nor was there any bleeding of the wound.
It seemed the chief had fallen sick and swooned;

Perhaps a little rest would make him strong!
And silently they watched him borne along,
A sagging bundle, dear and mighty yet,
Though from the sharp face, beaded with the sweat
Of agony, already peered the ghost.

They laid him in an office of the post,
And soldiers, forming in a hollow square,
Held back the people. Silence deepened there.
A little while it seemed the man was dead,
He lay so still. The west no longer bled;
Among the crowd the dusk began to creep.
Then suddenly, as startled out of sleep
By some old dream-remembered night alarm,
He strove to shout, half rose upon an arm
And glared about him in the lamp-lit place.

The flare across the ashes of his face
Went out. He spoke; and, leaning where he lay,
Men strained to gather what he strove to say,
So hard the panting labor of his words.
"I had my village and my pony herds
On Powder where the land was all my own.
I only wanted to be let alone.
I did not want to fight. The Gray Fox sent
His soldiers. We were poorer when they went;
Our babies died, for many lodges burned
And it was cold. We hoped again and turned
Our faces westward. It was just the same
Out yonder on the Rosebud. Gray Fox came.
The dust his soldiers made was high and long.
I fought him and I whipped him. Was it wrong
To drive him back? That country was my own.
I only wanted to be let alone.
I did not want to see my people die.
They say I murdered Long Hair and they lie.
His soldiers came to kill us and they died."

He choked and shivered, staring hungry-eyed
As though to make the most of little light.
Then like a child that feels the clutching night
And cries the wilder, deeming it in vain,
He raised a voice made lyrical with pain
And terror of a thing about to be.
"I want to see you, Father! Come to me!
I want to see you, Mother!" O'er and o'er
His cry assailed the darkness at the door;
And from the gloom beyond the hollow square
Of soldiers, quavered voices of despair:
"We can not come! They will not let us come!"

But when at length the lyric voice was dumb
And Crazy Horse was nothing but a name,
There was a little withered woman came
Behind a bent old man. Their eyes were dim.
They sat beside the boy and fondled him,
Remembering the little names he knew
Before the great dream took him and he grew
To be so mighty. And the woman pressed
A hand that men had feared against her breast
And swayed and sang a little sleepy song.
Out yonder in the village all night long
There was a sound of mourning in the dark.
And when the morning heard the meadowlark,
The last great Sioux rode silently away.
Before the pony-drag on which he lay
An old man tottered. Bowed above the bier,
A little wrinkled woman kept the rear
With not a sound and nothing in her eyes.

Who knows the crumbling summit where he lies
Alone among the badlands? Kiotes prowl
About it, and the voices of the owl
Assume the day-long sorrow of the crows,
These many grasses and these many snows.

The Song

of the Messiah

To *Mona* "—His woman was a mother to the Word."

"And it shall come to pass in the last days, saith God, I will pour out of my Spirit upon all flesh; and your sons and your daughters shall prophesy, and your young men shall see visions, and your old men shall dream dreams."—Acts 2–17.

"Is it not, indeed, the core of man's mystery, that in his greatest follies his last wisdom lies enfurled?"—Fülop-Miller.

THE VOICE IN THE WILDERNESS

The Earth was dying slowly, being old.
A grandam, crouched against an inner cold
Above the scraped-up ashes of the dear,
She babbled still the story of the year
By hopeless moons; but all her bloom was
     snow.
Mere stresses in a monody of woe,
Her winters stung the moment, and her springs
Were only garrulous rememberings
Of joy that made them sadder than the fall.
And mournful was the summer, most of all,
With fruitfulness remembered—bounteous
     sap
For happy giving, toddlers in her lap
And nuzzlers at her breast, and more to be,
And lovers eager still, so dear was she,
So needed and so beautiful to woo!

Ten years had grown the sorrow of the Sioux,
Blood-sown of one ingloriously slain,[1]
Whose dusty heart no sorcery of rain
Would sprout with pity, flowering for his own;
Nor could the blizzard's unresolving moan
Remind him of his people unconsoled.
Old as the earth, the hearts of men were old
That year of 'eighty-seven in the spring.

1. Crazy Horse.

O once it was a very holy thing,
Some late March night, to waken to the moan
Of little waters, when the South, outblown,
Had left the soft dark clear of other sound;
When you could feel things waking underground
And all the world turned spirit, and you heard
Still thunders of the everlasting Word
Straining the hush.—Alas, to lie awake
Remembering, when time is like the ache
Of silence wedded, barren, to a wraith!

True to an empty ritual of faith,
The geese came chanting as they used to do
When there was wonder yet; when, blue on blue,
The world was wider than a day in June,
And twice the northbound bison lost the moon
Trailing the summer up the Sioux domain.
What myriads now would hear the whooping
     crane
And join the green migration?

                Vision, sound,
Song from the green and color from the ground,
Scent in the wind and shimmer on the wing,
A cruel beauty, haunting everything,
Disguised the empty promise. In the sloughs
The plum brush, crediting the robin's news,
Made honey of it, and the bumblebee
Hummed with the old divine credulity
The music of the universal hoax.
Among the public cottonwoods and oaks
The shrill jays coupled and the catbird screamed,
Delirious with the dream the old Earth dreamed
Of ancient nuptials, ecstasies that were.
For once again the warm Rain over her
Folded the lover's blanket; nights were whist
To hear her low moan running in the mist,
Her secret whispers in the holy dark.

And every morning the deluded lark
Sang hallelujah to a widowed world.

May sickened into June. The short-grass curled.
Of evenings thunder mumbled 'round the sky;
But clouds were phantoms and the dawns were
      dry,
And it were better nothing had been born.
Sick-hearted in the squalor of the corn,
Old hunters brooded, dreaming back again
The days when earth still bore the meat of men—
Bull-thunders in a sky-wide storm of cows!—
Till bow-grips tightened on the hated plows
And spear-hands knuckled for an empty thrust.
The corn-stalks drooping in the bitter dust,
Despairing mothers widowed in the silk,
With swaddled babies dead for want of milk,
Moaned to the wind the universal dearth.

There was no longer magic in the earth;
No mystery was vital in the air;
No spirit in the silence anywhere
Made doubly sure a wonder that was sure.
To live was now no more than to endure
The purposeless indignity of breath,
Sick for the brave companion that was Death,
Now grown a coward preying on the weak.
However might the hungry-hearted seek
Upon a starry hill, however high,
A knowing Presence, everywhere the sky
Was like a tepee where the man lies stark
And women wail and babble in the dark
Of what the dawn can never bring to light.

The big Cheyenne lay dying, and the White;
And all the little creeks forgot their goals.
Crows feasted by the dusty water-holes.
Gaunt grew the Niobrara, ribbed with sand.

A wasting fever fed upon the Grand
And with the famishing Moreau it crawled.
All day and every day the hotwind bawled.
The still nights panted in a fever-swoon.
Dead leaves were falling in the harvest moon
And it was autumn long before the frost.
Back came the wild geese wailing for the lost—
Not there, not there! Back came the mourning crane.
A sunset darkened with a loveless rain;
The Northwest wakened and a blind dawn howled.

The winter deepened. Evil spirits prowled
And whimpered in the jungles of the cold,
Wolves of the ancient darkness that were old
Before the Morning took the Land to wife
And all the souls came loving into life
Save these alone, the haters of the warm.
Men heard them screaming by upon the storm;
And when the sharp nights glittered and were still
And any sound was big enough to fill
The world with clamor, they were gnawing fear.

The strangely wounded bodies of the dear
Grew alien. Scarce the father knew the child
So stricken, and the mother, so defiled,
By her own fire became a dreaded thing.
Wide roamed the evil spirits, ravening,
Till every village fed the Faceless Guest
With little hungers that forgot the breast
And agèd wants too long denied to care.

In vain against the formless wolves of air
The holy men wrought magic. Songs that ran
Beyond the hoarded memories of man,
With might beyond the grip of words, they sang;
But still the hidden claw and secret fang
Were mightier, and would not go away.
Grotesqueries of terror shaped in clay

To simulate the foe, and named with names
Of dreadful sound, were given to the flames;
But it was hope that perished. Empty air
Was peopled for the haunted fever-stare;
And when some final horror loosed the jaw,
What shape could image what the dying saw
That none might ever see and live to tell?

By night when sleep made thin the hollow shell
Between what is forever and what seems,
Came voices, awful in a hush of dreams,
Upon the old; and in that dreams are wise
When hearing is but silence and the eyes
Are dark with sun and moon, the weird news
      spread.
"There is no hope for us," the old men said,
"For we have sold our Mother to the lust
Of strangers, and her breast is bitter dust,
Her thousand laps are empty! She was kind
Before the white men's seeing made us blind
And greedy for the shadows they pursue.
The fed-on-shadows shall be shadows too;
Their trails shall end in darkness. We have sinned;
And all our story is a midnight wind
That moans a little longer and is still.
There was a time when every gazing hill
Was holy with the wonder that it saw,
And every valley was a place of awe,
And what the grass knew never could be told.
It was the living Spirit that we sold—
And what can help us?"

          Still the evil grew.
It fell upon the cattle, gaunt and few,
That pawed the crusted winter to the bone.
The weirdly wounded flesh of them was blown
To putrid bubbles. Diabolic fire
Burned out the vain last animal desire

In caving paunches, and their muzzles bled.
They staggered, staring. And the wolves were fed.

So Hunger throve. And many of the lean,
Who, having eyes for seeing, had not seen,
And, having ears for hearing, had not heard,
Fed hope a little with the wrathful word
And clamored 'round the agencies. "Our Lands,"
They said, "we sold to you for empty hands
And empty bellies and a white man's lie!
Where is the food we bought? Our children die!
The clothing? For our people shiver. Look!
The money for the ponies that you took
Ten snows ago? The Great White Father's friends
Have stolen half the little that he sends.
The starving of our babies makes them fat.
We want to tell the Great White Father that.
We cannot live on promises and lies."

But there were weighty matters for the wise
In Washington, and bellies that were round;
And gold made music yonder, and the sound
Of mourning was a whisper.

                So the young,
In whom wild blood was like a torrent flung
Upon a rock, grew sullen, brooding war.
What was it that the Sioux were waiting for?
To die like cattle starving in a pen?
Was it not better men should run as men
To meet the worst?

                And wrinkled warriors sighed,
Remembering the way their brothers died
Of old to make the living rich in tales.
"Go up the hills," they said, "and search the vales,
And count our battle-ponies by their breaths—
Ten thousand smokes! The grass they eat is death's,

And spirits hear the whisper of their feet.
Dream back for fighting men their bison meat;
Unlive these many winters of our sin
That makes us weak: then let the war begin,
And we will follow mighty men and tall.
Where are they?"

      And the young men thought of Gall,
The wild man-reaper of the Little Horn,
Grown tame at last, a sweater in the corn,
A talker for the white man and his way.
They thought of Red Cloud, doddering and gray,
And of the troubled twilight of his eyes,
Turned groundward now; of Spotted Tail, the wise,
Become a story seven winters old;
And, better to be sung than to be told,
The glory that was Crazy Horse. Alas!
Somewhere the heart and hand of him were grass
Upon a lonely hill!

      The winter died.
Once more, as though a wish too long denied,
Became creative in a fond belief,
The old Earth cast her ragged weeds of grief,
And listened for the well-belovèd's words,
Until her hushes filled with singing birds
And many-rivered music. Only men
Were paupers in the faith to dream again,
Rebuilding heaven with the stuff of woe.

But when the northern slopes forgot the snow
And song betrayed the secret of the nest
Too dear to keep, begotten of the West
A timid rumor wandered—vaguely heard,
As troubled sleepers hear the early bird
And lose it in the unbelieving night.
'Twas all of wrong grown weaker than the right,
Of fatness for the lowly and the lean,

And whirlwinds of the spirit sweeping clean
The prairie for the coming of the dead.
And many strove to say what someone said
That someone said, who had it from the Crows,
To whom Cheyennes or else Arapahoes
Had brought it from the Snakes. And one by one
Strange tongues had brought it from the setting sun
Across the starving lands where men endure
To live upon the locust and are poor
And rabbit-hearted. And a valley lay
Among the mountains where the end of day
Clings long, because those mountains are the last
Before the prairie that is never grassed
Rolls on forever in dissolving hills.
And in that valley where the last light spills
From peaks of vision, so the rumor ran,
There lived a man—or was he but a man?—
Who once had died, and verily had trod
The Spirit Land, and from the lips of God
He knew how all this marvel was to be.

'Twas very far away.

A naked tree
Awakened by the fingers of the Spring,
But lacking the believing sap to sing,
Has nothing but the winter moan to give.

The vague tale made it harder still to live
Where men must dream the right and bear the wrong.
And so another summer, like a song,
Sad with an unforgettable refrain—
Green promises forgotten by the Rain—
Droned to the dying cadence of the leaves.
And winter came.

But as the wood believes
At last the evangelic winds of March,

When eagerly the bare apostate larch
Avows the faith of cedars in the sun,
And cottonwoods confess the Living One,
And scrub-oaks, feeling tall against the blue,
Grow priestly with the vision; so the Sioux
Thought better of the iterated tale.
For every westwind knew about the vale
Beneath the shining summits far away;
And southwinds hearkened what they had to say,
And northwinds listened, ceasing to deride.
The man had died, and yet he had not died,
And he had talked with God, and all the dead
Were coming with the whirlwind at their head,
And there would be new earth and heaven!

                                        So
It happened, when the grass began to grow
That spring of 'eighty-nine, the dream took root
In hearts long fallow. And the fateful fruit
Greened in the corn-denying summer heat;
And dry moons mellowed it and made it sweet
Before the plum took color, or the smoke
That was the gray-green rabbit-berry broke
Along the gullies into ruddy sparks.
It seemed no secret to the meadow larks.
In clamorous and agitated flights
The crows proclaimed it. In the stifling nights,
When latent wonder made the four winds still,
The breathless watching of a starry hill
Revealed some comprehension not for speech.
And wheresoever men might gather, each
Would have some new astonishment to share.

But when the smell of frost was in the air
Of mornings, though the noons were summer yet,
The oft-shared wonder only served to whet
The hunger for a wonder real as cold
And empty bellies.

So the wise and old
Held council. "Let us see him with our eyes
And hear him with our ears—this man who dies
And talks to God—that we may know the way;
For all our words are shadows, and the day
Is yonder, if the day be anywhere.
And who would go?"

Good Thunder, Kicking Bear,
Short Bull, Flat Iron would, and Yellow Breast.
So once again the man-compelling West,
Sad mother of dissolving worlds, lured on.
And when the awed adventurers were gone,
Behind them fell the curtain of the snow.

And now the moon was like an elkhorn bow
Drawn to the shaft-head, wanting but a mark;
And now a shield against the doubting dark;
And now it withered, and was lost again:
And as the moon, the phasic hope of men
Measured the winter, slow with many a lack.
For less and less the jaded news came back
From regions nearer to the setting sun—
Re-echoings of wonders said and done—
That faith might flourish briefly in the green:
And sorrow filled the silences between
With troubled voices. What if, far away,
As sunset proves but ordinary day,
The dream-pursuers only sped their dreams?

But when along the cataleptic streams
Spasmodic shudders ran; and in the lee
Of browning slopes the furred anemone,
Already awed by what might happen next,
Stood waiting; and the silences were vexed,
Between crank winds, with moaning in the sloughs—
Though still the grasses slumbered—came the news
Of those five seekers homing. Like a fire

Before a banked-up southwind of desire
Unleashed at last, it swept the tawny land.
The smoke of it was all along the Grand
When first the valley of Moreau took light
From where it bloomed in tumult on the White,
Seeding the fallows of the Big Cheyenne.
The living Christ had come to earth again!
And those who saw Him face to face, and heard,
Were bringing back the wonder of the Word
Whereby the earth and heavens would be new!

And suddenly the prairie took the hue
Of faith again. The rivers understood;
And every budding, gaunt-limbed cottonwood
Experienced the Cleansing of the Blood.
The tall clouds bent above the lowly mud.
A holy passion whitened into flame
Among the plum-brush.

                        Then the seekers came
With awe upon their faces.

THE COMING OF THE WORD

II

          Was it fright,
Some prescience of the whirlwind of the light
About to break, that gripped the white men's
      hearts
At Pine Ridge? How the foolish dreamer starts
And strives to hold his futile world of sleep,
When lo, it is the morning, deep on deep,
That takes the world! Could agency police
Arrest the Word? And would the Wonder cease
To be the Wonder even in a jail?
Too deep for laughter, humor sped the tale
Of four returning seers behind the bars!
Was not their story written in the stars
When first the gleaming bubble of the air
Was blown amid the darkness?

              Silent there
The knowers waited, patient as the stone
That has the creeping æons for its own
And cares not how the little moment drips.
The prison key had only locked the lips
Against a word already on the wing.
Two days endured the white men's questioning
Before those faces that were like the sky
When clouds have vanished and the nightwinds
      die
And daybreak is a marvel to the hills.
And when that silence conquered jaded wills,
The four emerged with nothing less to say.

Now Kicking Bear, sojourning on the way
To learn among the north Arapahoes
What slant of vision might illumine those,
Came burning with a story for the Sioux.
Already was the Wonder coming true
Along Wind River where the people trod
The dances taught them by the Son of God,
And there were signs and portents of the end!
The eyes that Death had emptied of the friend
Were being filled again, but not with tears.
The sudden sleep that falls among the spears
And arrows, when the dizzy sun goes black
And all the hoofs are hushed, was giving back
The healed young bodies of the sons and sires.
Dead mothers came to mend the family fires
Long fed by lonely hands; and young they were,
Each fairer for the garment folding her—
The richly beaded years!

                And now there ran
Among the Ogalalas, man by man,
A secret whisper. And it came to pass
When early stars had found a looking glass
In White Clay Creek, and others came to stare,
The owls were startled in a valley there,
And all the kiotes hushed to hear the rills
Of people trickle inward from the hills
And merge into a murmur by the stream.

Now where the chattering campfire dimmed the
      gleam
Of stars, to build with momentary light
A wall of blindness, inward from the night
A shadow moved, took substance from the flare,
And half a man and half a ghost stood there
Searching the breathing darkness round about.
A sudden hush acclaimed him like a shout;

For in his flame-lit face, as though they heard,
Men saw the singing splendor of the Word,
Before he strove to darken into words
What only thunderstorms and mating birds
Might utter in the heyday of the sap,
When Earth with all her children in her lap
Has made her story credible again.

The hush grew big with miracle; and then
Good Thunder spoke. "My relatives," he said,
"Believe and cry no more! The dear, the dead
Are coming with a spring forever green!
Already they are marching! We have seen;
These eyes have seen the Savior! He has come!
His feet are on the prairie!"

                              Stricken dumb,
With breathless, open mouth and startled eyes,
He seemed to hear in lingering surprise
The trailing thunder and the meadow lark
Of what was uttered. From the outer dark,
As though it were the unbelieving world
That fretted yet awhile, a hoot-owl hurled
Its jeering laughter through the knowing hush.

The Word came back upon him with the rush
Of spring delayed, of rain and river-thaw
And universal burgeoning. "We saw!
With little hearts our journey was begun,
For maybe we were men who chased the sun
To find the land where always there is light;
They race with their own weakness, and the night
Outcreeps their running. So the way stretched long,
But still the right was weaker than the wrong;
Earth starved her children still; the same sky stared;
The people prayed and suffered; nothing cared
That there was woe wherever there were men.
And often when the day went out again,

Homesick beneath the old familiar star,
The same fear mocked us. Who by going far
Shall find the good? And who by going fast
Shall overtake it?

     But we came at last
Upon the holy valley. It was bare;
And if the summer ever had been there,
Now nothing but the gray old sagebrush knew.
Around it, higher than the eagles flew,
The shining mountains stood, and every peak
Was listening to hear the stillness speak
With tongues of thunder; but our steps were loud.

And then we saw—we saw!

      There was a crowd
That spoke strange tongues. With every wind that
  blows,
From lands where almost no one ever goes,
From countries, maybe, near to where earth ends,
Queer peoples came and mingled and were friends
With us and with our neighbors; for the wings
That bore the holy news were like the Spring's,
And nowhere had men questioned what it meant
In any tongue; but everywhere it went,
Dry hearts were greening. Is there any land
So far and strange it cannot understand
The drumming thunder and the singing rain?

And then he came—he came!

      We saw him plain;
For suddenly, across a little draw
Upon the higher bank beyond, we saw
A Piute man; and that, at first, was all.
His hair was to the ears, and he was tall,
And maybe he was thirty winters old.

His face was broad. He wore against the cold
A coat and hat and boots that white men wear.
It could have been a white man standing there,
But for his face. He carried in his hand
An eagle's wing. We could not understand,
For only with our eyes we saw him yet.
Who travels far shall see the same sun set;
Upon the longest trail the home stars rise;
And while we saw him only with our eyes
The Holy One was nothing but a man.

He smiled upon us kindly and began
To speak strange words, and they were dark like smoke;
But while I stood and wondered what he spoke,
There came a meaning like a spirit flame;
And then I saw the man was not the same.
He burned until his body was all light;
And if he were a brown man or a white,
I did not think at all. I only knew
How all that we had heard was coming true;
But all I knew no tongue can ever say.
Then like a shadow fell the common day,
And with my eyes I saw him as before,
A Piute man; but there was something more
That made me cry, though like a rustling tree
My body was, and like a bird in me
My heart was glad.

                    Awhile his words ran loud
And buzzed in many tongues among the crowd
Till all had heard them and the tongues were stilled.
Then I was feeling how his low voice filled
The world again; and it was like a light
That made me see how everything was right,
And nothing ever died or could be old.

So, bit by bit, we heard the story told
In many broken words. You too shall hear;

But feeble is the tongue and dull the ear,
And it is with the heart that you shall know.

Now all this came to pass three snows ago,
About the time when plums were getting good,
And he had gone to make his winter wood
Among the mountains. He was feeling strong.
His woman and his children went along,
And all of them were happy there together.
The air was sharp, but it was sunny weather;
The winds were still.

         Now while the children sang
And laughed and chattered, and the axe strokes rang
Against the mountain, he could feel a change
Come over him, till everything was strange.
He listened for the noise the children made;
But all the air was empty and afraid
Of something coming. Then he tried to call
His woman; but he made no sound at all.
And while he wondered, with his axe held high,
The hollow stillness of the earth and sky
Broke down in thunder, and the mountains bowed
And flowed together, whirling like a cloud
A big wind strikes. Then everything was black.

But right away, it seemed, the world came back,
So queer and bright he knew that he had died.
The light of things was coming from inside
And cast no shade! It was like dreaming deep
And waking on the other side of sleep
To know that he had never waked before.
Still in a way that would have been a roar
In this world, all at once the pines became
The rushing up of something like white flame
That spread and hovered at the top, and then
Drooped back with many limbs and fell again
In burning showers, wonderful to see;

For all the seasons of an earthly tree
Were shortened to the blinking of an eye.
He saw the spirit forests flashing by
In generations up the mountainside;
They came and went, but nothing ever died
Nor could be old. The shapes that went and came
Were ways in which the something like a flame
Lived young forever; and the flame, he knew,
Was Wakantanka;[1] for the mountains too
Were holy with it, and the soft earth glowed,
Till it was only light that lived and flowed
To make the shapes of animal and man,
The rooted and the winged. Where one began
The other did not end, for they were one,
All coming from and going to a sun,
That drew him now. And as he rose to go,
He saw his other body there below
Burn swiftly with the holy flame and pass
Into a happy greening that was grass
Along some hill remembered from a dream.
Then he was flowing with a mighty stream
Of living light that did not make him small,
Though he was lost in it. He lived in all
The stream at once, for everything that is
Became one glowing body that was his,
And there was nothing in it near or far.
He was alive, alive in every star,
And he could feel the rivers and the rills,
The grass roots nursing on a thousand hills.

Then, all at once, some meadow of the air
Was sweet with faces blooming everywhere
About him. There were many that he knew,
But all were dear. Dim shadow-bodies grew
Beneath them, swaying with a mournful sound

1. The Great Spirit.

And feeling for remembered shadow ground
To root in—hills of fog and valleys dim
With autumn rain, that he could feel in him
Like all the tears that men have ever shed.

But when he would have wept, behold there spread
New earth beneath; and from the glow thereof
The shadow-forms took flesh, and all above
Was living blue; and eyes have never seen
The green with which that breathing land was green,
The day that made the sunlight of our days
Like moonlight when the bitten moon delays
And shadows are afraid. It did not fall
From heaven, blinding; but it glowed from all
The living things together. Every blade
Of grass was holy with the light it made,
And trees breathed day and blooms were little suns.
And through that land the Ever-Living Ones
Were marching now, a host of many hosts,
So brightly living, we it is are ghosts
Who haunt these shadows feeding on tomorrows.
Like robes of starlight, their forgotten sorrows
Clung beautiful about the newly dead;
And eyes, late darkened with the tears they shed,
Were wide with sudden morning. It was spring
Forever, and all birds began to sing
Above them, marching in a cloud that glowed
With every color. All the bison lowed
Along the holy pastures, unafraid;
And horses, never to be numbered, neighed
Like thunders laughing. Down the blooming plains,
A river-thaw of tossing tails and manes,
They pranced and reared rejoicing in their might
And swiftness. In the streams of living light
The fishes leaped and glittered, marching too;
For everything that lived looked up and knew
What Spirit yonder, even in that day,
Was blooming like a sunrise.

                                    And the way
Was shortened all at once, and here was there,
And all the living ones from everywhere
Were hushed with wonder. For behold! there grew
A tree whose leafage filled the living blue
With sacred singing; and so tall it 'rose,
A thousand grasses and a thousand snows
Could never raise it; but all trees together,
When warm rains come and it is growing weather
And every root and every seed believes,
Might dream of having such a world of leaves
So high in such a happiness of air.

And now, behold! a man was standing there
Beneath the tree, his body painted red,
A single eagle feather on his head,
His arms held wide. More beautiful he seemed
Than any earthly maiden ever dreamed,
In all the soft spring nights that ever were,
Might be the one of all to look on her.
He had a father's face, but when he smiled,
To see was like the waking of a child
Who feels the mother's goodness bending low.
A wound upon his side began to glow
With many colors. Memories of earth,
They seemed to be—of dying and of birth,
Of sickness and of hunger and of cold,
Of being young awhile and growing old
In sorrow. Now he wept, and in the rain
Of his bright tears the holy flower of pain
Bloomed mightily and beautiful to see
Beyond all earthly blooming, and the tree
Was filled with moaning. All the living things,
With roots and leaves, with fins or legs or wings,
Were bowed, beholding; and a sudden change
Came over them, for all that had been strange
Between them vanished. Nothing was alone,
But each one knew the other and was known,

And saw the same; for it had come to pass
The wolf and deer, the bison and the grass,
The birds and trees, the fishes in the streams,
And horse and man had lost their little dreams
And wakened all together.

           Softly crooned
The Tree, for now the colors of the wound
Became a still white happiness that spread
And filled the world of branches overhead
With blossom and the murmuring of birds.
One life of light the peoples and the herds
Lived with the winged, the rooted and the
        finned.

The man was gone; but like a sacred wind
At daybreak, when the star is low and clear
And all the waking world is hushed to hear,
His spirit moved. The whisper of his word
Was thunder in the silences that heard,
And whirlwind in the quiet: "They shall see
At last, and live beneath the Blooming Tree
Forever!"

        Then so great a sunrise broke
Upon the man who died, that he awoke;
But it was when he wakened that he died.

He was no longer on the mountainside,
But home again and lying on his bed.
He looked about him, and the mourners fled,
Filling the door with chatterings and cries;
And, with a frightened stranger in her eyes,
His woman hugged their weeping little ones
And huddled in a corner.

          Dead four suns,
He 'rose and walked before her; but his face

Now shone with such a kindness, and the place
Was filled with light so beautiful, she knew
It was a holy vision shining through,
And wept with joy. And so, before she heard,
His woman was a mother to the Word,
The first of all believers to believe.

"My people, O my people, do not grieve,
For soon shall break the ever-living Dawn."

Good Thunder ceased, and presently was gone,
A spectre fading in the ember light.
The breathing silence of the peopled night
Still felt the low voice flowing like a song,
The round face saddened with a people's wrong
And soft with pity; till a sudden flare
Revealed the whetted face of Kicking Bear,
The hungry gaze, the body taut and lean.

In wildernesses never to be green,
It seemed, his eager spirit dwelt apart,
Wild honey of the solitary heart,
The locust of the lonely soul, for food.
Now crying from an inner solitude
His voice arose and cut across the night:

"These eyes have seen the whirlwind of the Light!
These eyes have seen the marching of the dead!
These eyes have seen the Savior at their head,
And there shall be new earth and heaven soon!
I tell you, in the fullness of the Moon
Of Tender Grass Appearing[1] it shall be
That with the sprouting of the Holy Tree
The earth will shake and thunder. Hills will flow
As water, for a spirit wind will blow,

1. April, 1891.

And all that is not real, but only seems,
And all who have not faith, shall be as dreams
Before that whirlwind waking in the spring.
Like chickens hovered by the mother's wing
The faithful shall be safe beneath the Tree,
And they shall lift their eyes and they shall see
The new earth and the ever-living Day.

My brother spoke, but there is more to say;
O there is more than any tongue can speak!
We did not find the one we went to seek,
A prophet, but a man like other men.
I tell you He is Jesus come again!
I saw the marks upon Him! It is so!
Have not the Black Robes[1] told how long ago
One came to save the people? It is He!
Did not Wasichus[2] nail Him to a tree?
Did they not torture Him until he died?
I saw the spear-wound bleeding in His side!
His lifted palms—I saw them white with scars!"

Unto the awful stillness of the stars
He gave the uttered marvel for a space,
Its latent thunder in his litten face,
The lightning of it in his burning stare.
"I saw!" he cried, "and many others there
Have said they saw it too, although the rest
Saw nothing. It was when He faced the West
And lifted up His hands to pray and said:
'Now I will show you the returning dead
And Him who leads them.' For a little while
His eyes were closed, and with a gentle smile
He moved His lips in silence. It was still,
And things turned strange; but nothing came until
His eyes were opened and He said: 'Behold!'

1. Catholic priests.
2. White men.

I looked; and yonder mighty waters rolled,
Dark waters that were filled with mournful sound
And crowded with the faces of the drowned
And drowning. And I knew the cries of birth
And death and all the sorrows of the earth
Were mingled yonder where a black wind swept
The desert of the waters; and I wept
For all of them I saw but could not save.
And suddenly beyond the farthest wave
A cloud appeared, a whirling, fearful cloud.
Its front was lightning and its rear was loud
With marching thunder. Rising very fast,
It grew, until it stood above the vast
Black flood, now whitened with the hands of prayer,
Beyond all counting, that were lifted there
For mercy. Then it seemed that all sound died,
And silences were voices that replied
To silences, so quiet was the world.
And in that sudden peace the cloud that whirled,
A dark and flaming fury in the van
Of endless cloud, was shapen to a man
With moons upon His robe of starry light.
The feet of Him were rooted in the night;
But upward, still and beautiful and far,
His face was daybreak, and the morning star
Was low upon his brow.

                    A moment so
I saw, and almost knew what none may know
And linger in these shadows here to tell.
But as I gazed, a wind of burning fell
Upon that peace; and roaring from its deep,
The sunrise took the heavens at a leap,
And like a mighty wound the sky rained blood,
And from the sudden scarlet of the flood,
All white the souls of thousands who believed
Arose; but whom the eyes and ears deceived,
I saw them sinking.

Then a singing cry
Of multitudes of voices filled the sky.
Four times I heard it singing—hey-a-hey!
And, looking up, I saw that it was day
Forever. Light no eye has ever seen
Was in the green, the spirit of all green,
That was the earth; the spirit of all blue
That was the sky. And in the midst there grew,
Most beautiful of all, the Blooming Tree.
And through that land, as far as I could see,
The dead were coming with their hands held high,
And it was they who sent the singing cry
To cheer us in this darkness of the sun.
But when I looked upon the Holy One
Who led the host, it all began to fade.

Then I was staring at the one who prayed,
And knew that it was He! That starry calm
Was on His face. In either lifted palm
A white scar gleamed; and there upon His side
The wound Wasichus gave Him when He died
Was like a scarlet flower.

I saw; and then
I saw a man who seemed like other men
And heard him saying: 'It is yet too soon.
Believe; and in the Grass-Appearing Moon
The change will come.'

My people, it is so!
The Holy One who came so long ago
Is even now upon the earth once more,
Preparing for the end. He came before
To help them, but they tortured Him and slew.
Themselves, they tell it! Are their hearts made new
These many, many grasses since He died?
I saw the wound still fresh upon His side
As when they made it! What shall fill the blind

But everlasting darkness? He was kind
As rain and grass the other time He came.
But I have seen the whirlwind and the flame;
And I have seen the greedy, faithless race
Before the waking fury of His face
Become a dream forgotten in the day;
And I have seen the old earth pass away
And all the faithful happy in the new.
He came to them; but now He comes to you!
He comes to you! And shall He be denied?
Woe to the deaf!"

        Upon a shrill note died
The upward straining voice, as though it failed
Midmost the peak of vision it assailed
Beyond the flight of words. And when he went,
A murmuring of wonder and assent
Was like a nightwind freshening, and blew
Among the darkened people; till they knew
That Yellow Breast stood waiting by the fire.

No lure of unassuagable desire
Had led him far and made his spirit lean.
Earth's tolerance was gentle in his mien;
The light of common day was in his eyes,
That seemed to look with half amused surprise
Upon a riddling world, and left it so.
There, generously bulking in the glow,
The radiating quiet of him spread,
And was a hush.

        "My relatives," he said,
"You know me well, and many present knew
The boy I was, the common way I grew
To be a common man. It is the truth
There came to me no vision in my youth
That I might have the power to behold
The hidden things; and neither am I old

Enough in years to make me very wise.
The good and evil seeing of my eyes
I have believed; and what my ears have heard,
If it might be a straight or crookèd word,
I have considered, often being wrong.
And such a man it was you sent along
With these my brothers here, to see and say
If truly yonder at the end of day
A tale of many wonders might be so.

A man who trails an elk or buffalo
May camp with hunger or may sit to eat;
There will be meat or there will not be meat;
He shall be full or empty at the last.
But who shall trail a story? Not so fast
The blizzard flies; and like the whirling snows,
The shapes of it keep changing as it goes.
The bison is no bison, but a deer,
Or else a wolf; and it is never here,
But always it is yonder. Over there
It is an elk that changes into air.
The hunger and the hunted are the same;
And whosoever feeds upon that game,
He shall be very lean.

        And so I said
About this tale of the returning dead
And new earth coming: 'It is far away;
And big; and getting bigger every day.
So are the people's hunger and their sorrow.
The empty belly and the fat tomorrow
Have made a story.'

        But I did not speak.
I went along to see. My heart was weak;
And often as I went I wept alone
To think how big the hunger would have grown
When we came back with nothing.

                                    We are here
And you have heard already. If the ear
Alone had told me half of what I know,
I must have wondered if I heard it so,
Or how good men turned foolish on the way.
But I myself have seen; and I will say
No more than I have seen. I must believe
For what I saw; and if my eyes deceive,
How can I know that I know anything?
The coming of the grasses in the spring—
Is it not strange so wonderful a tale
Is really true? Did mornings ever fail,
Or sleeping Earth forget the time to grow?
How do the generations come and go?
They are, and are not. I am half afraid
To think of what strange wonders all is made!
And shall I doubt another if I see?

No vision in the heavens came to me.
I saw the mountains yonder gleaming tall,
And clouds that burned with evening. That was all.
But while the Holy One was praying there,
I felt a strangeness growing in the air
As when, a boy, I wakened in the night,
And there was something! Faces queerly bright
Were there about me, lifted to the skies;
And I could see some wonder filled their eyes,
Though mine were dark and many others too.

I might believe that everything is true
The Holy One has said and you have heard.
There was a living power in His word
I never felt before; for when He spoke,
It seemed that something lifted like a smoke
And common things were wonderful and new.
But still I could not tell you it is true,
Had I not seen.

This happened on the way
When we were coming home and stopped to pray
Among the Blue Clouds[1] yonder, and to rest.
Of all our neighbors farthest to the west,
They were the first to hear, and first to learn
The dance He said would make the dead return
And new earth blossom. They were dancing then;
And many died and came to life again
Refreshed and very happy; for they said
That they had seen their dear ones who were dead
And visited with them. I longed to see;
I danced, I prayed. But nothing came to me
Until the evening of the seventh day.
They made a feast before we came away,
And it was at the lodge of Sitting Bull,[2]
The holy man. The moon was rising full.
A melting wind had died in pleasant weather,
And we were twenty sitting there together
Around the fire. Two places in the ring
Were empty. Sitting Bull began to sing
A sacred song. Four times he sang, and then
He made a prayer that he might see again
His father and his mother, and that we
Who sat to eat with him might also see
The dearest of our dead.

                      A queerness came
On everything. I could not hear the flame
That chattered in the wood a while before.
A little whisper would have been a roar,
It was so still. Then suddenly it seemed—
And if I dreamed, the twenty of us dreamed
The same dream all together—something grew
Like moon-fog where the places for the two
Had been left empty. Growing from the ground,

1. Arapahoes.
2. Sitting Bull, the Arapahoe.

It shaped itself and thickened, while a sound
Of voices far away came singing through;
And there were faces, many that I knew,
About the fog—a cloud of shining faces.

And then I saw there were no empty places!
A woman and a man were sitting there,
With wrinkled cheeks, at first, and snowy hair,
And with a weary question in their eyes.

But all at once—and there was no surprise
Till afterward—I saw that they were young,
And seemed to know the robes of light that clung
About them were the winters they had known
Together here, all beautifully sewn
With colored sorrows. I could smell the breath
Of green things on the other side of death—
It seemed a kind of singing. Bison herds
Sang with them, weaving voices with the birds,
The horses and the women and the men—
One happy tribe rejoicing. And again
Still as a place of death, the world grew still;
And all around, the night began to fill
With people, people. Eagerly they pressed
About us, happy-faced; and with the rest
My father came, as much alive as I!

Twelve snows ago, it was, I saw him die
That blizzard day we fought beside the Tongue[1]
While with the starving horses and the young
The starving women fled. It was a dim
And fearful battle, and I clung to him,
For something of the boy was in me yet.
We had no powder left. With clubs we met
And struck at shapes that loomed and danced away

1. The fight with Miles on Tongue River, January, 1877.

And roared and blazed about us in the gray
Half-night of snow. I heard my father scream
Beside me there; and often in a dream
I've heard him since, to waken in a chill
Of terror; for the boy was in me still,
Though I was tall. Face downward in the snow
I saw him flounder like a buffalo,
Lung-shot. I stooped to help. He tried to shout
Some word; but only black blood bubbled out.
Then I went killing crazy. Shadows fell
Or fled about me; and I cannot tell
How long it was till nothing but the storm
Was whirling 'round me, and I knew the warm
Wet weight I staggered under."

                        Yellow Breast
Fell brooding, while that battle in the West
Woke in the women memories of woe
That wailed across the dark.

                        "Twelve snows ago,"
He said at length, "I watched my father's face
Bleed empty, and a stranger in his place
Come staring. And I wept and prayed to die.
But now he came, as much alive as I—
O more alive than I have ever been!
His body glowing by a light within,
He came to me and smiled. Upon my head
He laid his hand. 'Believe, my son!' he said;
'Believe, my son!'

                   And whether late or soon,
I do not know; but all at once the moon
Was shining as before. The fire was low,
And twenty sitting in the ember glow
Were staring at each other in dismay;
For all had seen what verily I say
I saw. And I believe it."

Yellow Breast

Was gone, and voices of the dark confessed,

Sweeping the gamut in their reach for awe,

The bright faith shared, until the people saw

The face of Short Bull eager in the gleam.

It was no dreamer's wistful with the dream.

Surely, he dwelt familiarly at ease

Amidst a world where divers certainties

Took root to flower and flourish in a green

Congeniality. The ready mien,

The bustling manner and the bright, shrewd eyes,

Too certain of their seeing to be wise,

Proclaimed the man.

        "My relatives!" he cried;

And, waiting while the distant echo died,

His face went grave with what he meant to say.

"This thing must be set going right away,

And I will tell you all that you must do.

What you have heard is true; but more is true,

And you shall hear and know it for the truth.

I did not doubt this story. From my youth

There had been voices. I was very young

When first the Spirit taught me in the tongue

Of birds. And often in some quiet place

The dead have spoken to me, face to face,

And dreams have shown me things that were to be.

I say this story was not strange to me,

Because I dreamed it just before it came

By living tongues. The Savior is the same

I saw in sleep. I knew it would be so.

His very words I knew. Hear now and know

What wonders He can make.

        One day we sat

To hear Him teach. He wore a broad black hat,

A common hat that any man could wear;

But what He did with it before us there

Not any man could do. He held it, thus,
Before Him, with the hollow turned to us,
And closed His eyes and prayed a little while
In whispers. Then He smiled a happy smile
And passed His eagle feather 'round the brim
And said, 'Behold !'

                I looked into a dim
Deep hollow that was growing; and it grew
Until it was so deep and wide, I knew
That nothing was beyond it, or could be.
And as I wondered at it, I could see
The stars were coming out. They came and came
Until their shining made a soft white flame
That left no empty places in the night.
Then I could see that it was getting light
With dawn that seemed to come from everywhere,
As much like singing and as much like prayer
As seeing. Then the very world was day;
And when I think of it I cannot say
If I was in it, for it seemed inside,
Like being very glad. But it was wide
As I could feel, and there it did not cease.
It went forever in the blue, blue peace
That was the sky; and in the midst there glowed
A green, green world where singing rivers flowed
And leaped and glittered with rejoicing fish;
And deer and elk and bison had their wish
On blooming hills; and happy valleys fed
The singing tribes of men; for none was dead
That ever lived.

              All this I saw, and then
I saw the hollow of the hat again
And it was empty. Truly, some who sat
With us that day saw nothing but a hat,
Because they did not have this gift of mine.

Black Kiote saw, and so did Porcupine,
Almost the same as I; and others too.

There is no end to all that He can do,
This Son of Wakantanka. Beasts and birds,
They say, come close and talk to Him in words,
The same as other people. Trees and grass,
They say, get greener when they feel Him pass,
The way they freshen in a sudden shower.

There is one other story of His Power
That I will tell. Before we came away,
The Savior told us, 'If you stop and pray
When you are very weary, I shall know,
And something good will happen.' It was so.
There was a prairie, dead with thirst, and wide
Beyond a hundred looks. On every side
We stared, and there was nothing anywhere;
And we were weary. So we made the prayer
And slept, believing something would befall.
When we awoke we weren't there at all,
But far upon our journey! This is true.

There is a sacred dance He sent to you
And it will make you see the world of light
And all your dear ones yonder. Every night
The people all shall dance with sacred song,
The little children also. All night long
The fourth night, they shall dance until the day;
Then they shall bathe and all go home to pray
Until the time for dancing comes again!
The Savior, He has said it! Woe to men
Who hear not! I have spoken. Hetchetu!"

He ceased, and as he went the people knew
The eager, whetted voice of Kicking Bear
That from the starry wilderness of air
Shrilled in the hush: "Believe! Be not afraid!

Believe! Believe! And safe within its shade
The Holy Tree will fold you on that day
When all the ancient stars shall blow away
Like autumn leaves, and solid hills shall flow
Like water! Woe to men who hear not! Woe
To faithless men, the blind who will not see!
The Savior, He has said it! Even He,
The Savior said it!"

On a distant hill
The wild voice faltered briefly; and the still
Expectant hollow of the night seemed dense
With dwellers in a breathless imminence
Of whirlwind wonder straining to begin.
A breath might break the world-wall, bubble-thin,
Between this starry seeming and the Light.

The brush-fed embers filled the startled night
With sudden darkness. Presently there came
A shadow moving inward to the flame;
And it was Red Cloud standing in the glow.
Deep voices and the women's tremolo
Acclaimed him still a mighty man and wise,
Despite the wintered hair; the rheumy eyes;
The groundward gaze, incuriously dim;
The once compelling upward thrust of him,
In shrinking shoulder-droop and sagging girth
Now yielding slowly to the woman Earth
The man that was—half woman at the last.
But when at length he raised his face and cast
That unexpecting gaze about him there,
The dignity of stoical despair
Revealed the hero yet.

His voice was low,
Less seeming to be sent than made to grow,
By some indwelling power of the word,
Among the crowd:

"My people, you have heard;
And it is good. The winter and the spring,
The blooming summer and the withering,
The generations and the day and night
Are only moving shadows; but the Light
Is Wakantanka. When our young feet pass
Across the holy mystery of grass,
Our eyes are darkened for the ways we go;
And that is good. We see, and it is so;
We hear, and know it; touch, and it is true.
For to be young is to believe and do,
As rooted things must blossom and be green.
But when the eyes grow weary, having seen,
And flesh begins remembering the ground.
There is a silence wiser than all sound,
There is a seeing clearer than the sun;
And nothing we have tried to do, or done,
Is what the Spirit meant.

The Earth is old;
Her veins are thin, her heart is getting cold;
Her children mumble at her empty paps;
The bison, crowding in her thousand laps,
Have turned to spirit. And the time is near.

This word is good that we have come to hear.
This word is very good."

With gray head bowed,
He stood awhile in silence, and the crowd
Was still as he.
At length he stole away,
A shadow unto shadows.

THE DANCE

III

Every day
No Water's Camp was growing near the mouth
Of White Clay Creek, lean-flowing in the drouth.
What matter if the doomed, unfriendly sky,
The loveless grudging Earth, so soon to die,
Ignored the supplication of the lean?
Rains of the spirit, wonders in the green,
Bloom of the heart and thunders of the Truth,
Waking the deathless meadow lark of youth,
Were yonder. So the village grew. And most
Who came there felt the leading of the ghost;
But if the clever in their own regard,
Amused contenders that the hills were hard
And could not flow, came mockingly to see,
They saw indeed.

They saw the Holy Tree,
A sapling cottonwood with branches lopped,
Set in the center of a ring, and topped
With withered leaves. Around it and around,
Weaving a maze of dust and mournful sound,
The women and the children and the men
Joined hands and shuffled, ever and again
Rounding a weird monotony of song,
Winged with the wail of immemorial wrong,
And burdened with the ancient hope at prayer.
And now and then one turned a knowing stare
Upon the empty dazzle of the skies,
Muttering names, and then, as one who dies,

Slumped to the dust and shivered and was still.
And more and more were seized upon, until
The ring was small of those who could not see;
And weeping there beneath the withered tree,
They sang and prayed.

                          But when the sleepers woke
To stagger from the dust, the words they spoke,
As in a dream, were beautiful and strange.
And many a scoffer felt a still swift change
Come over things late darkened with the light
Of common day; as in a moony night
The rapt sleepwalker lives and is aware,
Past telling, in the landscape everywhere
About him till no alien thing can be,
And every blade of grass and weed and tree,
Seed-loving soil and unbegetting stone,
Glow with the patient secret they have known
These troubled whiles, and even men shall know.
One moment, shrewdly smiling at a show,
The clever ones could see a common pole,
The antic grandmas, little children, droll
With grownup airs, the clowning men who wept,
And dust. But suddenly, as though they slept
And dreamed till then, to wake at last and see,
Swift saps of meaning quickened to a tree
The rootless bole, the earth-forgotten thing
With starveling leafage; and the birds would
      sing
Forever in that shielding holiness.
A joy that only weeping can express
This side of dying, swept them like a rain
Illumining with lightning that is pain
The life-begetting darkness that is sorrow.

So there would be more dancers on the morrow
To swell the camp.

The Moon When Ponies Shed[1]
Had aged and died; and, risen from the dead,
The Moon of Fatness,[2] only in the name,
Haunted the desert heavens and became
A mockery of plenty at the full,
Remembering the thunders of the bull,
The lowing of the countless fatted cows,
Where now it saw the ghostly myriads browse
Along a thousand valleys, still and sere.
But mightily the spirit of the year,
At flood, poured out upon the needy ones
The Light that has the dazzle of the sun's
For shadow, till the very blind could see.

And then it was beneath the withered tree
Young Black Elk stood and sent a voice and wept;
And little had he danced until he slept
The sleep of vision; for a power lay
Upon him from a child, and men could say
Strange things about his seeing that were true,
And of the dying made to live anew
By virtue of the power. When he fell
The sun was high. When he awoke to tell
The silent crowd that pressed about the place
Of what he saw, with awe upon its face
The full moon rose and faltered, listening.

It was, he said, like riding in a swing,
Afraid of falling; for the swing rose high;
And faster, deeper into empty sky
It mounted, till the clutching hands let go,
And, like an arrow leaping from a bow,
He clove the empty spaces, swift and prone.
Alone he seemed, and terribly alone,
For there was nothing anywhere to heed

1. May.
2. June.

The helpless, headlong terror of the speed,
Until a single eagle feather blew
Before him in that emptiness and grew
Into a spotted eagle, leading on
With screaming cries.

        The terror now was gone.
He seemed to float; but looking far below,
He saw strange lands and rivers come and go
In silence yonder. Far ahead appeared
A mighty mountain. Once again he feared,
For it was clothed in smoke and fanged with flame
And voiced with many thunders. On it came
And passed beneath. Then stretching everywhere
Below him, vivid in the glowing air,
A young earth blossomed with eternal spring;
And in the midst thereof a sacred ring
Of peoples throve in brotherly content;
And he could see the good Red Road that went
Across it, south to north; the hard Black Road
From east to west, where bearers of the load
Of earthly troubles wander blind and lost.
But in the center where the two roads crossed,
The roads men call the evil and the good,
The place was holy with the Tree that stood
Earth-rooted yonder. Nourished by the four
Great Powers that are one, he saw it soar
And be the blooming life of all that lives,
The Holy Spirit that the good grass gives
To animals, and animals to men,
And they give back unto the grass again;
But nothing dies.

        On every drying rack,
The meat was plenty. Hunters coming back
Sang on the hills, the laden ponies too.

Now he descended where the great Tree grew
And there a man was standing in the shade;

A man all perfect, and the light He made
Was like a rainbow 'round Him, spreading wide
Until the living things on every side,
Above Him and below, took fire and burned
One holy flame.

       "Then suddenly He turned
Full face upon me and I tried to see,"
Young Black Elk said, "what people His might be;
But there was cloud, and in the cloud appeared
So many stranger faces that I feared,
Until His face came smiling like a dawn.
And then between two blinks the man was gone;
But 'round the Tree there, standing in a ring,
Twelve women and twelve men began to sing:
'Behold! the people's future shall be such!'
I saw their garments and I wondered much
What these might mean, for they were strangely
     wrought.
And even as I thought, they heard my thought
And sang reply: 'The people clad as we
Shall fear no evil thing; for they shall see
As you have seen it. Hundreds shall be flame.'

Then I was blinded with a glow that came
Upon them, and they vanished in bright air
And wordless singing.

         Standing lonely there,
I thought about my father who is dead
And longed to find him. But a great Voice said,
'Go back and tell; for there is yet more wrong
And sorrow!'

       Then a swift wind came along
And lifted me; and once again I knew
The fearful empty speed. Face down I flew
And saw a rushing river full of foam,
And crowds of people trying to get home

Across it; but they could not; and I wept
To hear their wailing. Still the great wind kept
Beneath me. And you see that I am here."

Young Black Elk ceased; and, thinking of the dear
Good days of plenty now become a tale,
A woman, old and withered, raised a wail
Of bitter mourning: "It was even so
The way the young man saw it. Long ago
I can remember it was just the same,
The time before the bad Wasichus came,
That greedy people! All good things are dead,
And now I want to die." Her sorrow spread
Among the women like a song of pain,
As when the ponies, heavy with the slain,
Return from battle and the widows crowd
About them, and the mothers.

                When the shroud
Of moony silence fell upon their woe,
Young Black Elk spoke again: "What shall be so
Forever, I have seen. I did not sleep;
I only woke and saw it. Do not weep;
For it is only being blind that hurts.
Tomorrow you shall make these holy shirts
For us to wear the way I saw them worn.
Clothed in the Holy Spirit, none shall mourn
Or come to harm along the fearful road."

So on the morrow happy women sewed
In all the tepees, singing as they made
Of odds and ends and empty sacks of trade,
The rags and tatters of their earthly need,
Unearthly raiment, richly wrought indeed
For all the love they stitched in every hem.
And good old men of power painted them
With sacred meaning: blue upon the breast,
A moon of promise leading to the west,

The end of days; and, blue upon the back,
A morning star to glimmer on the black
And fearful road; the neck and fringes red,
The hue of life. An eagle feather sped
On either arm the homing of the soul.
And mighty with the meaning of the whole,
The work was finished.

                Death became afraid
Before the dancing people so arrayed
In vision of the deathless. Hundreds burned
With holiness.

             But when the cherries turned
From red to black, while Summer slowly died
And in her waiting hushes prophesied
The locust, and the lark forgot his song,
There fell the shadow of the coming wrong
And yet more sorrow that were left to bear.

The Agent came to see; and he was there
With all his world about him. It was sure
And solid, being builded to endure
With granite guess and rumor of the eyes,
Convincingly cemented with surmise
Against all winds of fancy and of fraud.
The height of it was high; the breadth was broad;
The length was long; and, whether bought or sold,
The worths thereof were weighable in gold,
His one concession to the mysteries.
As common as the growing of its trees,
And natural as having wakened there
Quite obviously living and aware,
His world was known.

                So clearly they were mad,
These dancing heathen, ludicrously clad
For superstitious doings in a day

Of Christian light and progress! Who could say
What devilment they hatched against the whites,
What lonely roofs would flare across the nights
To mark a path of murder!

                It must cease.

Surrounded by the Indian police,
Who sat their mounts importantly, half proud
And half abashed to wear before the crowd
Of relatives the master's coat of blue,
He spoke: "This thing is foolish that you do,
And you must stop it!" Still as though a trance
Had fallen on the interrupted dance,
The people listened while a half-breed hurled
The feeble thunder of a dying world
Among them: "It is bad and you must stop!
Go home and work! This will not raise a crop
To feed you!"

            Yet awhile the silence held,
The tension snapping with a voice that yelled
Some word of fury; and a hubbub broke.

As when across the dust and battle-smoke
The warrior hails the warrior—"Hokahey!
Have courage, brother! Let us die today!"—
The young men clamored, running for their guns.
And swarming back about the hated ones,
They faltered, waiting for the first to kill.
Then momently again the place went still,
But for the clicking locks. And someone cried:
"Your people tortured Jesus till He died!
You killed our bison and you stole our land!
Go back or we will kill you where you stand!
This dance is our religion! Go and bring
Your soldiers, if you will. Not anything

Can hurt us now. And if they want to die,
Go bring them to us!"

Followed by the cry,
As by a stinging whip, the Agent went.

That night one mourned: "It was not what you
meant!"
Alone upon a hill he prayed and wept;
"Not so you taught me when my body slept.
Great Spirit, give them eyes, for they are lost!"

THE SOLDIERS

IV

When plums were mellowing with early frost
And summer was a ghost, with noons that made
The ponies droop in any thinning shade;
With nights that in a hush of tingling air
Still listened for the geese; to Kicking Bear
There came an eager word from Sitting Bull
Up yonder on the Grand: "The winds are full
Of stories. Are they echoes of a lie?
If truly, as we hear, your dancers die
And visit with the dead and then return
Alive and well, my people want to learn.
Come up and teach them."

                   Singing of the day
That was to be, the prophet rode away;
But not alone if what some say be true,
That when he loomed against the shining blue
Upon the final hilltop, strangely large,
The sky was filled with horsemen at the charge
That whirled about him going. Then the sky
And hill were empty.

                   Dreaming days crept by,
And nights were glinting bubbles on the strain,
Blown vast with silence. Then at last the crane
Came crying high; a roaring norther sped
The startled geese, and panic voices fled
Above the sunless and the starless land.
Now came the news of dancing on the Grand

With many tales of wonder-working there;
And of the ghostly might of Kicking Bear
A story lived on every tongue and grew.
It told how, riding northward, rumor flew
Before him, till the Agent heard and feared
At Standing Rock. So when the prophet neared
The home of Sitting Bull, a jingling band
Of Metal Breasts[1] made dust across the land
And trotted up to seize him.

Unafraid

He waited. Then it seemed that something made
A solid wall about him, thin as light;
For suddenly the horses reared in fright
And shied away before him, shivering.
There came a queerness over everything
That made the horses and the riders seem
As though they gazed on terror in a dream,
And could not stir. "My brothers, foolish ones,"
He said, "what have you put into your guns
To kill the Spirit? I am Kicking Bear,
But I am not alone. Behold! the air
Is crowded with my warriors! Look and see!"

He raised an eagle feather. Silently
A little while he prayed; and as he prayed
The horses lifted up their heads and neighed,
Beholding; with a catching of the breath,
Wide-mouthed upon the Other Side of Death
The riders gazed with startled happy eyes,
Like sleepers who have wakened in surprise
To some great joy. A moment so, and then
The horses drooped, the faces of the men
Were empty; for the darkness that is birth,
The sleep that men call waking on the earth

1. Indian police, so named for their metal badges.

Came back upon them. Hardly could they keep
Their saddles for the heaviness like sleep
That fell upon them as they rode away.

Thus mighty was the living Word, they say;
And mightily it flourished on the Grand.

Again a waiting stillness seized the land;
For now the snowless wind blew out and died.
Perhaps the geese had falsely prophesied
And men would never see another snow.
The listening hills and valleys seemed to know,
In that untimely warmth and straining peace,
One bird, believing, almost might release
Immortal springtime. Whisperless with awe,
What vision was it every bare tree saw?
What made the humblest weed-stalk seem aware?
The stillness of the starlight was a prayer,
The dawn a preparation, for the bird.

But in that lull of miracle deferred
Before the Moon of Falling Leaves[1] was dark,
Who listened for the deathless meadow lark
Heard tidings of the trouble yet to be.
The singing people heard on Wounded Knee,
And terror silenced them. On Cut Meat Creek
The dancing Brulès heard, and hearts grew weak,
Lost in the swift return of common day.
The vision fled from hundreds on the Clay,
And eyes of little light went blind again.
For everywhere the feet of marching men
Were rumored. Yonder from the iron road
To south, to west, to northward, load on load,
The soldiers and the horses spawned and spread!
Where were the whirlwind armies of the Dead?

1. November.

The skies were deaf. Far-journeying, the suns
Knew nothing of the Ever-Living Ones,
The shining, good, green Country of the Young.
Fear called the changing tune of many a tongue
Late lyric with the crowd: "We told you so!
Now let us see you make the hard hills flow,
And tell your Christ to hurry! He is late!"
Youths, burning for the rendezvous with Fate,
Were loud for battle. "Let us fight and die!"
They clamored. "Better men than you and I
Have died before us! Crazy Horse is dead!
And will it not be good to go," they said,
"Wherever he went? Living, we are poor!
How rich the dead must be! Let hills endure,
And cowards live forever if they can!"

Remembering, the ancient sorrow ran
Among the women wailing.

                "Even so,"
The old men mourned, "we youngsters long ago
Would die to make a tale. The world is old;
Now all good stories have been lived and told,
And who shall hear them in a few more snows?"

But still the voices of the faithful rose,
Scarce heeded: "We have seen what we have seen!
Not when the world is singing in the green
The Savior comes; but when the leaf is sere
And nothing sings. Already He is near!
The Happy Ones are crowding all the air,
Beholding us! Be strong of heart to bear
This one more sorrow that must come to pass.
The Black Road ends!"

              But withered hearts were grass,
Rich fallow for the seeding of the spark,

And, raging through the horror-painted dark
Of its begetting, panic was a flame.

To Red Leaf's camp the fleeing terrors came
On Wounded Knee, to pause and huddle there,
Fused in a hush of communal despair—
An empty ear for any voice to fill.
And thither, from some lonely vision-hill,
The vessel of an evangelic voice,
Came Short Bull, crying: "Hear me and rejoice!"

A mockery of echoes fled and failed
Among the bluffs. Some little hunger wailed,
Until a crooning mother hushed again
The ancient question only dreams of men
Have ever answered—with how many whys!

The sudden center of a thousand eyes
Made quick with hope or lusterless with care
Or quizzically narrowed, silent there
He filled the silence. For the people saw
A face it seemed some other-worldly awe
Had touched with glory. What ecstatic death
Of self in vision yielded him the breath
Of universal living for a while,
That so upon this trouble he could smile,
With such a look upon this darkness beam?
Or had the weed of self in some vain dream
Grown mightily, till everything was small
Save him, and in the glory of it all
He towered now?

                    Again the shrill voice went
Among the people: "Wakantanka sent
A vision to me on the hill last night
When I was praying. Stillness and a light
Became the world; but what they said to me
Would shake these hills down, if a word could be

To say it. I will tell you what I may.
These troublesome Wasichus, what are they
To run from? Hardly to be called a race,
The color of their death in every face,
Their strength is like a shadow's. Very soon
They shall be nothing. Until now, the Moon
Of Tender Grass Appearing, it was said,
Would see the whirlwind coming of the Dead,
And hear the sprouting-thunder of the Tree.
But by a power the Spirit gave to me,
Because of trouble these Wasichus make
I will not wait until the grasses wake,
Nor shall there fall a single flake of snow,
Before I tell the Tree to sprout and grow;
The Dead to come; these solid hills to run
Like angry water; stars and moon and sun
To be as withered leaves and blow away.
And everything shall hear me and obey,
For Wakantanka said it. I have seen
Among the badlands where the earth is lean
And hardly can the cactus live for need,
The place where even now the holy seed
Lies thirsting in the dust till it shall know
My word of power. Yonder we must go
To sing and pray until the time is right
For me to speak. If soldiers come to fight,
Is not the very power in their guns
The same that lives in grasses and that runs
In winds and rivers and the blood of man,
And birds fly with it? Since the world began,
Of one great Spirit everything is made
And lives and moves. So do not be afraid.
Their guns will not go off. And when I speak,
The hearts of all their horses shall be weak,
Their knees become as water under them.
Then, beautiful with thunder, shall the stem
Burst from the shattered earth, and soar and
     spread

All green and singing, singing! It is said!
The Spirit said it. Hear it and rejoice!"
Astonished silence swallowed up the voice,
And for a timeless moment no one stirred,
While yet the many, fused by what they heard,
Were like a sleeper. Murmuring eddies broke
Among them, spreading as the one awoke
Into the many, mingled and were loud,
With scorn and wonder clashing in the crowd,
Belief and doubt.—'If only all believed!—
If only fools so easily deceived
Were wiser!—If the deaf would only hear!—
Could big talk fill the belly through the ear?
'Twere better to surrender and to eat!—
To fatten on Wasichu lies for meat!
There never was a better day to die!—
Lo, even now the crowding of the sky!
Behold! Believe! It could not now be long!—
The soldiers! They were coming! They were strong,
Not shadows; and the babies would be killed!
The badlands! To the badlands!' Women shrilled
Above the wrangling babble and the shout
Of faith unshaken: 'There the Tree would sprout,
The shielding Tree! They could not murder souls!'

The din died in a clattering of poles,
The sound of stricken lodges coming down,
Where, petulantly buzzing 'round the town,
The women now, as one, were bent on flight
From danger. Children crying in the night
Were those to her, the woman who survives
All man's believings; whom he never wives
For all his wooing, being newly born
Forever in her passion, half a scorn,
But all a shielding fury at the test.

As with a single will the rabble pressed
To northward down the valley of the stream.

For now the driving fear, the leading dream,
The burning of the wild hearts of the young
For deeds and dyings worthy to be sung,
Became one impulse in the straggling ranks.
Far flung, the young men raged along the flanks
And rear; and lonely places were aghast
By night with flaring ranch roofs, where they passed,
Those harriers of cattle and of men,
For whom now briefly had returned again
The very eld of story and of song.
And steadily the rag-and-tatter throng
Grew with the sullen stragglers driven in
To share whatever fate the rest might win,
Whatever hope might feed upon despair.

Beyond the White they fled, along the bare
Unearthly valleys, awed by some intense
Divinity of knowing reticence
About them in the lunar peaks and crags,
Where wearily the questing echo lags
Behind some haunting secret that eludes
To fill the hushes of their solitudes
With sleeping thunder. Yonder, wheeling slow,
Aloofly patient, did the buzzard know
The secret? Were the jeering crows aware?

So great a void, and yet a little prayer
Could fill it and a little question drain!
The trail led steeply to a living plain
Aloft amid the life-forgetting waste,
A lonely island staring stony-faced
Upon the slow encroachment of a sea
Whereof the fluid is eternity,
And time the passing tempest, and the roar
Devouring silence. Still there, as of yore
When Earth was young beneath the primal blue,
Spring keeps with her the ancient rendezvous,
And little needs that run and root and nest

Know in the giving sweetness of her breast
The pity that is water. Grass was good
In plenty there, and stunted growths of wood
Clung to the gulches.

        There they camped to wait
The coming of the good or evil fate
That might befall them. Verily it seemed
To many that their woes were only dreamed,
And this the verge of waking to a deep
Serenity beyond the pain of sleep
Forevermore. But many, scanning far
That desolation of a manless star,
Saw, picture-written in the stuff of sense,
The affirmation of their impotence
And slow despair.

        Through breathless nights of frost
The old moon shrank, delaying, and was lost;
And wonder-weather made the brief days weird.
At last the Moon of Popping Trees[1] appeared,
A ghost above the sunset, leading on
Where all days perish in a deathless dawn,
And still no snow had fallen in the land.
Then Kicking Bear came riding from the Grand,
With words of power: 'Let the people hear
And have strong hearts! The time was very near
When Sitting Bull would come; and then, behold!
The whirlwind of the miracle foretold
Would sweep the world!'

1. December.

SITTING BULL

V

                    Daylong the holy dance
Beside the Grand had murmured in a trance
Of timeless weather. Now, the stars were sharp,
And, tense with frost, the night was like a harp
For any little sound. The young moon sank.
Among the trees along the river bank
The tepees gloomed. Across the open flat
To northward, where a group of cabins sat
Beneath the hills, a window with a lamp
Revealed the one place waking in the camp,
The home of Sitting Bull.

                       The room was dim
With smoke, for there were nine who sat with him
And passed the pipe, in silence for the most,
As though some felt eleventh were a ghost
That moved among them. Tales of long ago
Had failed the mark, as from a sodden bow
Unfleshed the bravest arrows falter spent;
And stories that were made for merriment
Had fallen short of laughter.

                     Now at last
They only sat and listened to the vast
Night silence, heavy with a feel of doom.
The old wife, dreaming in the corner gloom,
Turned with a moaning like a broken song;
And, questioning a universe made wrong,
Far off by fits arose a kiote's cry

That left a deepened silence for reply—
The all-embracing answer.

       Catch-the-Bear
Got up, the startled creaking of his chair,
The shuffle of his feet upon the floor
Loud in the stillness. Striding to the door,
He flung it wide and filled it, listening.
The sharp air entered like a preying thing,
The living body of the hush that prowled
The hollow world. A camp dog woke and howled
Misgiving, and the kennelled hills replied.
The panic clamor trailed away and died;
And there was nothing moving anywhere.

He closed the door, returning to his chair,
And brooded with a troubled face. "My friend,"
He said at length, "I fear how this may end.
I am afraid to see the break of day.
It might be better to be far away,
If they should come. You said that you would go.
What keeps you waiting here?"

         "I do not know,"
Said Sitting Bull, and gazed upon the wall
With eyes that saw not anything at all
But lonely distance that is not of space.
Without the wonted shrewdness in his face,
The lurking wit, it seemed a stranger's stare
He turned upon his friend. "I hardly care,"
He said; "I may be only getting old;
Or maybe what a meadow lark foretold
Is near me; yet I do not feel afraid.

It happened that my circus horse had strayed
One day last summer. So I went to see
A little valley where he likes to be;
But it was empty, even of the crows,

Except for something any still place knows
But sound can never tell it. That was there.
It filled the valley and it filled the air;
It crowded all about me, very still.
I stood there looking at a little hill
That came alive with something that it knew,
And looked at me surprised. The stillness grew.
Then suddenly there came a human cry
From yonder: 'Sitting Bull, your time is nigh!
Your own will kill you!'

              It was loud and clear;
So loud I wondered that I did not hear
An echo. Yet I thought, 'Perhaps a man
Is hiding over there'; and so I ran
To see who said it, maybe out of fun,
Or maybe spite. There wasn't anyone.
But while I wondered had there been a sound
Or had I dreamed, there fluttered from the ground
A meadow lark, and with it rose again
The same cry uttered with the tongue of men,
'Your own will kill you!' Then above my head
Four times it circled rapidly, and fled.

How long I stood there thinking on the hill
I do not know; but, by and by, a shrill
Long neigh aroused me. Looking 'round, I saw
My old gray horse come trotting from a draw
And down the valley. Then the common day
Came back about me."

              Gazing far away,
He brooded. When he spoke again he seemed
As one but half awake. "Last night I dreamed
Of mighty waters, flowing swift and deep
And dark; and on that river of my sleep
I floated in a very frail canoe.
The more I longed to stop, the greater grew

The speed, more terrible for lack of sound.
I thought of help, and when I looked around,
Behold, there floated past on either side
A happy land that flourished in a wide
Blue morning; yet I did not see the sun.
Old camps I had forgotten, one by one,
Came there abreast of me and hurried by.
And someone who was happy, yet was I,
Played 'round his mother's tepee. She was young,
And nothing ever could be said or sung
To tell about the goodness of the place,
And how it was that something in her face
Could make a day so big and blue and clear.
They did not look at me; they could not hear
The cry I sent, though all the stream ahead
Was filled with mocking voices.

                                    Faster sped
The river. Nothing ended or began;
And yet I saw the boy become a man,
And all about him in the whirling change
Were faces falling in and growing strange
Beneath a sudden wintering of hair;
And they were gone, and other faces there
Were round and happy in the Spring they cast,
An eye-blink long; for now the stream was fast
As wind in anger. All the days and nights
That I have lived, the hunts, the feasts, the fights,
Were there again, and being there, were gone,
So swift they were. And still my life came on.
But now the sky was not so blue and wide;
The land was not so green. On either side,
The fury of the wind of days had done
What made me weep. I could not see the sun;
But surely now it sickened to a moon,
And in the ghost of day it made were strewn
The bones of all the buffalo that were.
The Earth, our mother, had the face of her

Who sees her children's children bury theirs,
And, weary of remembering her cares,
Begins the long forgetting.

               There was night
Before me, and a fog of dying light
Behind me, and that ghost of day around;
And under me, too deep for any sound,
The mystery of water and the speed.
Then even sorrow left me in my need,
And fear, the last of friends to flee away.
I drifted into waking, and the day
Was young about me.

           It may happen so.
But still I feel the swift, dark water flow;
I feel it carry me, and do not care."

He scanned that distance with an empty stare
That slowly filled and, brimming with a smile,
Ran over into chuckles for awhile;
And then he said: "What matter? It was good!
Why mourn the young flame laughing in the wood
With tears upon the ashes? I could laugh
All night remembering, forgetting half
The happy times before the world was old.
Do you remember, friends—?"

             And now he told
The story of the fool who, feeling wise,
Would catch a bear, and how that enterprise
Too greatly prospered. Taking either part
With highly circumstantial mimic art
And droll sobriety, as one at ease
With Truth, the chiefest of her devotees,
He built the old tale toweringly tall;
And when at last it toppled to its fall,
And ended with the strangest of all rides,

The men with streaming eyes and aching sides
Defied the vast night silence with a roar
Of laughter, till the woman on the floor
Sat up and scolded. Ever and again
The mirth, subdued, broke out among the ten,
As seeing how the panic people ran
The day the stridden bear brought back the man,
Precariously clinging by its hair,
And shouting wildly: "I have caught a bear!
Behold!"

      But when the final chuckle died,
As though that prowler in the hush outside
Came creeping in, they sat there listening,
Wide-mouthed, alert. There wasn't anything.
They heard their hearts.

            "Yes, truly it was good,"
Said Sitting Bull at length; "but if I could,
I would not live it over from the first.
The goodness of the water is in thirst,
And I have drunk. That day I broke the pipe,
Two moons ago, this heart of mine was ripe
For death already. Shall the ripe grow green?
Beyond a winter's telling I have seen
Enough to make a liar choose the true,
Of wonders these Wasichus dream and do
In crowded lands beyond the rising sun.[1]
I look and see the evil they have done.
My eyes are weary. What is looking worth?

Have I not seen the only mother, Earth,
Full-breasted with the mercy of her Springs,
Rejoicing in her multitude of wings
And clinging roots and legs that leaped and ran?

---

1. He had travelled in Europe with a circus.

And whether winged or rooted, beast or man,
We all of us were little ones at nurse.
And I have seen her stricken with a curse
Of fools, who build their lodges up so high
They lose their mother, and the father sky
Is hidden in the darkness that they build;
And with their trader's babble they have killed
The ancient voices that could make them wise.
Their mightiest in trickery and lies
Are chiefs among them. It shall come to pass
When these at last have stolen all the grass
And all the wood, the water and the meat,
And there is more to burn and drink and eat
Than all could use in many moons of feast,
The starving people shall become a beast,
Denied the very grasses of the chief.
But dreaming each to be the bigger thief
They toil and swarm, not knowing how their
      sweat
Shall turn to blood upon them. Who forget
Their mother, are forgotten at the last.
Already I have seen it in the past
Of spirit vision. It is even so.
These eyes need not to see it.

             Long ago
It happened I was all alone one day
Among the mountains, where the still ones say
In silence what can make men wise to hear.
And while I listened only with the ear,
The pines were giants weeping all around.
Then suddenly there wasn't any sound,
And I could feel that I was not alone.
There was an eagle sitting on a stone
Far up, and all the air was like a crowd
That waits and listens. Then a voice was loud:
'Behold ! Hereafter he shall rule the land !'

I thought and thought; I could not understand.
But I have lived to see it; for behold
The image of the eagle on the gold
These mad Wasichus worship and obey!

The worshippers shall come to be the prey!

You bid me go; but which way lives the Good?
I know my friend would tell me, if he could,
Where greens that land, the weary trail to go,
How many sleeps, and where the grasses grow
The deepest, and the waterholes are sweet.
Then would I ride my horses off their feet
To find that country! But the Spirit keeps
The secret yet awhile.

        How many sleeps?
One sleep, the last and deepest of them all!
I will not ride, my friends."

        Beyond the wall
He gazed again, brows lifted, eyes a-shine,
While louder grew the breathing of the nine
Who watched him. What unutterable day,
Death-deep in night, a heavy sleep away,
Had found the lonely summit of his hope?

They saw the shadow of his waking grope
Across his face.

        He turned to them and said:
"They who have seen this vision of the dead
Have seen what they have seen; and it is good.
But foolish hearts that have not understood,
They make a story out of it that lies.
The blind ones! They would have it with their eyes!
The deaf ones! They would hear it!

Even so,
Almost my heart persuaded me to go.
So big it was with hate and ripe to die,
That it would set men fighting for a lie—
And what to fight with, starving as they are?"

He 'rose. "I wonder if the daybreak star
Is up," he said; "the night is getting old."

Out in the starry glitter of the cold
They followed him and, muffled in their breaths,
Stood shivering, and gazed.

The hush was death's
The East was blind. Knee-deep along the flat,
A fog came crawling. Nothing moved but that.

"My friends," he said at length, "it might be best
To go to bed and get a little rest
Before the morning. It is well with me."

They gripped his hand in silence. Silently,
Like spirits wading in no earthly bog,
They went, and vanished in the deeper fog
Along the river.

Still he waited there,
His ghostly breath ascending like a prayer,
The peace of starlight falling for reply
Upon his face uplifted to the sky,
And 'round his body, like a wraith of doom,
The ground-fog rising.

Presently the gloom,
Where stood the rail corral, gave forth a neigh
That screamed across the night and died away
Into a coaxing nicker. With a start,
The cold, quick clutching of a panic heart,

He turned. There, etched upon a patch of stars,
The old horse thrust his head across the bars,
Ears pricked to question what the master meant.
A warming glow about his heart, he went
And stroked the steaming muzzle that was pressed
With happy little sounds against his breast,
And begging whimpers. Thus remembering,
Again he saw the dazzle of the ring
And heard the heaped-up thunders of applause,
The roaring like a wind that swept in flaws
The hills of men.

        How far it was away!

He threw the old gray horse a feed of hay,
And slapped his neck; then, hunching to the cold,
Went off to bed.

        The slumber of the old
Fell heavy on the night. The stars burned dim.
The East wore thinner.

        Something startled him.
A moment, 'risen from a dreamless deep,
He floated on the surface of his sleep
And knew the fog had found an open door.
It seemed to make a sound along the floor
Of stealthy feet that whispered!

        "Who is there?"
He said. A blue spurt sputtered to a flare
Of yellow. Was the lark's word coming true?
With badges glinting on their coats of blue
And rifles in their hands, the room was full
Of cold-eyed kinsmen!

        "Hurry, Sitting Bull!"
Said one; "Get up and dress!"

The match flare died.
From over yonder by the riverside
A long cry 'rose. The dogs began to bark.
And in the moment's nightmare of the dark
Where startled voices clashed, the woman
    screamed.
A new flare sputtered, and the lamplight gleamed
Upon a witch's face and fury there,
Eyes burning through the tangle of her hair,
Mad with the wrath of terror for the dear.
"Begone!" she raged. "What are you doing here?
You dogs! You jealous woman-hearted men,
I know you! Go, and let us sleep again!
You, Bullhead there! What have we done to you?
Red Tomahawk, for shame! for shame! I knew
Your father, and a man! He lies at rest
And does not see that metal on your breast,
That coward's coat! I do not want to see!
Begone, Dakotas that you ought to be!
Fat dogs you are, that bad Wasichus keep
To sneak and scare old people in their sleep,
And maybe kill them! Ee-yah! Get you hence!"

Stone to the torrent of her impotence,
They crowded 'round the man upon the bed
And strove to dress him. "Hurry up!" they said,
"The White Hair[1] wants you!"

           Placid in their clutch,
He answered: "Friends, you honor me too much!
Am I a warrior going forth to die
That you should dress me? Yet no child am I
That cannot dress himself. Be patient, friends!
If somewhere hereabouts the long trail ends,
I would not reach it naked. Let me dress!"

---

1. McLaughlin, Agent at Standing Rock Reservation.

He stood now, jostled in the eager press
Of men who clamored, angrily afraid,
"Be quick! Be quick!" For all the doubtful aid
Of tangled hands that fumbled, tugged and tore,
And shoved him on, he reached the open door
Not garmentless.

The sounding world seemed black.
But when the vision of the dark came back,
The star-concealing mist, a chill blind gray
With some diluting seepage of the day,
Was full of moving shapes. And there were yells,
The jingling merriment of little bells
About the necks of ponies milling 'round,
And more hoofs rumbling on the frozen ground
Out yonder.

Forth into the dying night,
With Bullhead on his left, and on the right
Red Tomahawk, they crowded him along,
While from the doorway followed, like a song
Of rage that rises on a wing of woe,
The old wife's wailing: "Whither do you go?
There is a name that you have carried far,
My man! Have you forgotten who you are
That cowards come and drag you out of bed?
It would be well if Sitting Bull were dead
And lying in his blood! It would be well!
But now what story will be good to tell
In other winters?"

Desperate alarm
Tightened the fingers clutching either arm;
And in his leaping heart that meadow lark
Sang wildly.

Now against the fading dark
There loomed a bulk he knew for Catch-the-Bear,

And yonder was the old horse waiting there
Already saddled. For a ghost to ride?

He struggled in a net of arms, and cried:
"Hopo-o-o-o Hiyupo! Cola,[1] come ahead!
Come on, I will not go!"

      The great voice fled
Among the people, leaving in its path
An inward surging and a roar of wrath.
Then from the bulk of Catch-the-Bear there broke
The crash and ruddy bloom of powder smoke,
And Bullhead tumbled to a backward sprawl;
But in the very eyeblink of the fall,
His rifle muzzle flared against the back
Of Sitting Bull. A moment hanging slack
Amid a sag of arms, the limp form fell.
A swift hush ended in a howling hell
Of madmen swarming to a bloody work,
And horses screaming in the flame-smeared murk
That hid the slow dawn's apathetic stare.

Now while men fought and died about him there,
The circus horse remembered. Once again
That rainless storm upon the hills of men,
The barking of the guns about the ring,
The plunging of the horses, and the sting
Of powder smoke! He knew it well! He knew
The time had come to do what he could do
The way the master wished it.

      With the proud
Old arching of the neck, he kneeled and bowed;
Then, having waited overlong in vain
To feel the lifting hand upon the rein,

1. Friend.

He 'rose and, squatting on his haunches, sat
With ears alert; for always after that
It thundered.

        Lo now, even as of old
The hills applauded and their thunders rolled
Across the ring! But now they crashed and blazed
About him strangely. Haughtily he raised
A hoof, saluting, as a horse should do,
Though fearfully the storm of voices blew—
Hoarse-throated panic shrilling into yells
Of terror at the bursting of the shells
From where broad daylight lay upon the hill
Alive with soldiers.

        There he waited still
When all his people, save the weary ones
Who slumbered in the silence of the guns,
Had run away, and strangers crowded 'round.
Impatiently he pawed the bloody ground
And nickered for the master.

        People say
It happened in the badlands far away
That certain of the faithful 'rose to see
The morning star. In tense expectancy
They huddled, watching, on a weird frontier
Of sleep and waking wonder, hushed to hear
What meaning labored in the breathless vast
Of silence. Would that morning be the last
Of earthly mornings? Would the old sun rise?
Or did they feel the day that never dies
Preparing 'round them?

        Like the leaden ache
Of some old sorrow, dawn began to break
Beneath the failing star. And then—*he came!*

Gigantic in a mist of moony flame,
He fled across the farther summits there,
That desolation of an old despair
Illumined all about him as he went.
And then, collapsing, like a runner spent,
Upon the world-rim yonder, he was gone.

'Roused in the shiver of the common dawn,
The buzzing village marvelled. 'Lo! the dead
Were drawing near!' "A warning!" others said;
"Some very evil thing will happen soon!"

THE WAY

VI

Now in the bleak fulfillment of the moon
The ragged hundreds of Sitanka's band,
With many who had fought upon the Grand,
Were fleeing southward from the big Cheyenne.
Behind them were the haunts of faithless men,
The feeble-hearted and the worldly wise,
And all the little deaths of compromise
That are the barren living of the blind.
What if the world they strove to leave behind
Still clung a heavy burden on the old,
And starving children shivered in the cold,
And plodding mothers, with the bitter-sweet
Remainder of their aching hearts to eat,
Mourned for the wailing hungers at the breast?
A little farther on there would be rest
Forevermore, there would be warmth and food.

But now the northwind found their solitude
And, like the wolfish spirit of the world
They fled from, all day long it howled and swirled
About their going, loath to let them go,
Too bitter for the pity of the snow
That soothes and covers and is peace at last.

Nightlong about their tepees raved the blast.
The moonset and the morning came as one.
Cold as the sinking moon, a triple sun
Arose to mock them. Day was like a chain
Of little linked eternities of pain

They lengthened step by step. And all day long
With feeble voices tortured into song
They raised again the ancient litany
With freezing tears for answer: "Pity me!
Have pity on me, Father! All is lost!"

Hunched to the driving needles of the frost,
With tucked-in tails and ready for the crow,
The ponies, now one flesh at last in woe
With man, the master, swelled the feeble wail.
They heard the wolves of chaos in the gale,
And nothing heeded, but the pain that cried,
The cry of pain.

       The frail flesh, crucified,
Forgot the Spirit. Truth was in the storm,
And everlasting. Only to be warm,
Only to eat a little and to rest,
Only to reach that Haven of the Blest
Amid the badlands! Were not Kicking Bear
And all his faithful people waiting there
With fire and shelter, food and friendly eyes?
The sick hope built an Earthly Paradise,
A stronghold set against the hounding fear
Of iron-footed furies in the rear,
For surely there the soldiers could not come.

Once more night howled the moon down. Drifting dumb
Before the wind on fire with flying rime,
The aching center of a ring of Time
That was the vast horizon glittering,
All day they searched the south. No living thing
Moved yonder. What had happened to the band
Of young men riding to the Promised Land
For succor? Was it days or years ago?

Hope conjured ponies toiling in a row
Across the prairie rim with heavy packs,

And hunger matched the plenty on their backs
With their delay. But, empty with despair,
The frost-bleared eyes beheld the empty air,
The empty earth.

            An irony of flame,
The blown-out day flared whitely when they came
At last to where the prairie, dropping sheer,
With slowly yielding battlements of fear
Confronts the badlands. Long forgotten rain
Had carved a stairway to the lower plain,
And there beside a clump of stunted plum
They pitched their tepees.

             Purple dusk went numb
With icy silence as the great wind froze
Above the wall and ceased. And the moon 'rose
With nibbled rim, already growing old,
To flood with visibility of cold
The aching stillness. Moaning hungers slept.

But they who woke with dumb despair or wept
Beside the tepee fires they kept alight,
Heard in the moon's mid-climbing of the night
The sound of hoofs approaching and a shout
That set the ponies neighing. Tumbling out,
The village swarmed about the little band,
Their skin-rack horses staggering to a stand
With frosted muzzles drooping to the ground.
There were no packs.

           Men searched without a sound
Those moonlit faces, ghostly to the eyes
That looking on no Earthly Paradise
Had left so hollow and no longer young.
"We saw," one said, dismounting, with a tongue
That stumbled as the feet that sought the warm,
"We saw their ashes blowing in the storm.

They have surrendered. They were starving too.
We saw their ashes."

        Shrill the mourning grew
Among the women for the hope that failed,
And in the tepees children woke and wailed
In terror at the mystery of woe.

But now a brush-heap crackled to a glow
Midmost the village, and a leaping flame
Darkened the moonlight. There Sitanka came
And lifted up a broken voice and cried:
"Be still and hear!"

        The sound of mourning died,
And in a catch of hope the people turned,
Searching the father face of him that yearned
Upon them like a mother's; but his tears
Could not unman it. Bowed with more than years,
His body swayed with feebleness and shook
As with a chill, and ashen in his look
Devouring fever smouldered. When he spoke,
It seemed the slow words strangled with a smoke
Of inner fire beneath the clutching hand
Upon his chest.

        "Be strong to understand,
My children. Keep the faith a little yet.
The Earth forgets us; shall we then forget
The Spirit and that nothing else is true?
The Savior's wound grows beautiful in you!
Lift up your hearts made holy with the spear!
This is the way. The time is very near,
For now we have so little left to lose.
But for this failing flesh that we must use
A little longer, butcher ponies. Eat,
And thank the Spirit not alone for meat.

Choose not between the evil and the good.
Give thanks for everything!"

                  Awhile he stood
With hands upraised. The whispering fire was loud,
So deep the silence of the gazing crowd,
For surely he grew taller by a span
And some deep well of glory over-ran
The tortured face.

              "Great Spirit, give us eyes,"
He prayed, "to see how sorrow can be wise,
And pain a sacred teaching that is kind,
Until the blind shall look upon the blind
And see one face; until their wounds shall ache
One holy wound, and all the many wake
One Being, older than all pain and prayer."

A little longer he stood weeping there,
That morning in his look. Then, old and bent
With suffering, he tottered as he went.
But still the people listened for a space,
As though the meaning of that litten face
Groped in the silence for the ears of men.
Then cold and hunger, mightier again
Than spirit, came upon them with a rush
And not to be denied.

              They gathered brush
And kindled morning, lyric with the lark
Of pain and terror in the outer dark
Where ponies screamed and strangled to the knife.

Alone amid some borderland of life,
Sitanka, in a drowse of fever, dreamed—
Or did he wake? For suddenly it seemed
The stars were icy sweat; the heavens swooned
With anguish of a universal wound
That bled a ghastly gloaming on the night;

And, thronging in that agony of light,
The faces, faces of the living things
That strive with fins or roots or legs or wings,
Were all alike. "It was the Savior cried!"
He gasped. But one there patient at his side
Crooned to her man and stroked his fevered head.
"It was the ponies. Go to sleep," she said.
"But there was one," he muttered, "only one."

Until the low moon faded for the sun,
Gray specters of a prairie *aeons* dead,
Haunting the silence with a word unsaid,
The butte tops glimmered with the festal light,
And heard against the reticence of night
The flesh-fed spirit dare again to sing
Of day, wherein no more the famishing
Would feed upon the famished, pain on pain.

The still dawn came relenting. Not in vain
Now seemd the night's renewal of the hope.
The bright air stung, but every sunward slope
That joined their singing as the people passed
Recalled the ancient yearning to be grassed,
Dreaming of April and the world made new.
Serenely the immense, believing Blue
Awaited, cleansed of cloud and void of wings,
The resurrection of the myriad Springs,
The miracle of thunder-soaring boughs.

Above Sitanka, in a burning drowse
Upon his pony-drag, men leaned to hear;
For in the broken babble of the seer
Were tidings of the Ever-Living Dead,
And mightily their meaning grew and spread
Among the band.

       Before the whet of night
They camped and killed more ponies by the White
And kindled fires and feasted. Sleep came soon.

A crimson dawn burned out the bitten moon.
The Sun came walking with a face benign.
Now up the valley of the Porcupine
They labored, eager with a growing sense
Of some omnipotent Benevolence
Mysteriously busy in the warm
Still air. The naked hills forgot the storm.
The beggared plum-brush, rooted in the lees
Of winter, listened for the bumblebees
And almost heard them.

                    Growing with the sun,
A southwind met the people on the run
And clamored 'round them like a happy throng.

The flanking bluffs gave back their flights of song,
Applauding with the boom of ghostly drums,
Wind-beaten: "Lo! Behold! The Whirlwind comes,
And they shall know each other as they are!—
Upon my forehead shines the daybreak star.
I show it to my children. They shall know!—
A nation marching with the buffalo,
Our dear ones come! The tender grass is stirred!
The tree grows taller, greening for the bird!
A sacred wind is walking with the day!"

Now while they paused to rest beside the way,
Sitanka, rousing from a stupor, cried
A bitter cry. And surely, then, he died:
For when the people crowded 'round him there,
Bleak with the frozen horror of a stare
An alien face appalled them.

                    And the wail
Of women shrilled above the moaning gale,
Lamenting for the well-belovèd one;
And men, with nothing to be said or done,
Stood waiting, waiting, unashamed to weep.

The nightward shadow lengthened from a
    steep
Above them, and the chill of evening ran
Along the wind. The women now began
To make the dear one ready for the grass.

And then it was the wonder came to pass!
He drew a moaning breath. A tremor shook
His limbs. The empty winter of his look
Began to fill. There broke upon his face
From some immeasurably distant place
A growing light. Awhile he lay, a spent
Wayfarer, studying in wonderment
That cloud of frightened faces 'round about,
As though the very miracle of doubt
Amazed him. "Children, children, I have seen!"
He panted; and the shining of his mien
Made morning in the overhanging cloud
Of huddled faces. "Did I cry aloud?
And did you fear for me, and did you weep?
It was a dream that came to me in sleep.
It seemed that we were camped about a hill
With many soldiers; and the place was still
And full of fear. Then from the hillside broke
A whirling storm of powder flame and smoke,
And all the valley in its roaring path
Screamed back for pity to the hill of wrath
That flashed and thundered in the bloody rain.
Then all the voices were a spear of pain,
A great white spear that burned into my side,
And with a voice that filled the world I cried,
'Have pity on us all, for we are blind!'

There came a speaking stillness, very kind.
The whole land listened, and began to green.
Upon the flat and up a long ravine
The heaped and scattered dead began to 'rise,
And faces, glad and shining with surprise,

Were turned on shining faces, brown and white;
And laughing children, with their wounds of light,
Went running to the soldier-men to play,
For those were uncles who had been away
And now were happy to be back again;
And twice I looked to see that they were men,
So very beautiful they were and dear.
And when I thought the Savior must be near
And looked to see Him walking, white and tall,
Across the prairie, there was light; and all
The grasses in the world began to sing,
And every queer and creeping little thing,
That loves the grass, was singing, having shed
Its load of strangeness; and the singing said:
'Behold, behold, behold them! It is He!'

Then such a rain of knowing fell on me,
I bloomed all over.

        It is getting dim;
But still I see we feared and hated Him,
My children. In this blindness of the sun
Are many shadows, but the Light is one;
And even if the soldiers come to kill
The Spirit says that we must love them still,
For they are brothers. Pray to understand.
Not ours alone shall be the Spirit Land.
In every heart shall bloom the Shielding Tree,
And none shall see the Savior till he see
The stranger's face and know it for his own.
This is the secret that the grass has known
Forever, and the Springs have tried to say."

The voice became like singing far away,
And ceased. The people listened yet awhile,
For still it lingered in the loving smile
That faded slowly into quiet sleep.

They heard the wailing wind upon the steep,
Remembering the loneliness of grief.
And eyes of wonder, searching for belief,
Beheld a shining that was not the sun's
In eyes that saw, despite the darkened ones
Of those who tapped their foreheads, being shrewd.

A holy stillness filled the solitude
That night; and tenderly the stars bent low
To share with men the faith that grasses know
And trees are patient with it. All the bare
Hushed hilltops listened and became aware
How nothing in the whole world was afraid.
And when the moon came, withered and delayed,
Like some old woman wedded to the crutch,
She seemed as one who, having mothered much,
Must mother yet wherever there is sorrow.

There woke yet more believers on the morrow
That lacked but bloom and verdure to be May.
And so they made a new song on the way.
Of joy they made it. "Father, I have seen
The stranger's face! Behold, my heart is green!
The stranger's face made beautiful to see!"

Amid the silence like a spirit tree,
Wide-branching, many rooted, soared the tune.

WOUNDED KNEE

Now in the waning of the afternoon
They neared the place where, topping the divide,
A lonely butte[1] can see on every side
Where creeks begin and where they wander to.
And lo! the guidons and the crawling blue
Of cavalry approaching down a hill!

The people halted, staring, and were still
With wonder. Was the vision growing real?
They heard the leather singing with the steel.
The long hoof-murmur deepened. Summits rang
With happy echoes when a bugle sang.
The sleek-necked horses knew their kin and neighed
A joyous greeting. Up the cavalcade
The trailing welcome clamored to the end;
And, rousing to the music of the friend,
The feeble ponies nickered back to those.

Then mightily the people's song arose,
And all the valley was a holy place
To hear it: "Father, I have seen his face,
The stranger's face made beautiful! Behold,
My sprouting heart is green!" Around them rolled
The steel-shod thunder, closing in the rear.
"The stranger's face made beautiful and dear,"
They sang with lifted hands, "I see! I see!"

1. Porcupine Butte.

Along a flat beside the Wounded Knee
They camped at sundown, lacking neither wood
Nor water; and the tattered tepees stood
Within the circled tents beneath a low
And sloping hill where, glooming in a row,
The wagon-guns[1] kept watch upon the town.

A gentle spirit with the night came down,
And like a father was the Soldier Chief.
Strong-hearted, of the plenty of his beef,
The plenty of his bread, he gave to eat;
And plenty was the sugar to make sweet
His many-kettled coffee, good to smell.
And much he did to make the children well
Of coughing, and to give the mothers rest;
And for the burning in Sitanka's breast
His holy man made medicine that night.

One people in a blooming ring of light
They feasted; and within the blooming ring
A song was born: "For every living thing
We send a voice! Lean closer, One Who Gives!
A praying voice for everything that lives!
Lean close to hear!"

                              Sleep came without a care.
Above them, with a face of old despair,
The late moon brooded, watching for the sun.

Almost it seemed the miracle was done
That morning of a weather-breeding day.
The spell of bright tranquility that lay
Upon the land wrought eerily with sound,
And strangely clear the voices were around
The crackling fires, yet dreamily remote.

1. Cannon.

Straight-stemmed, the many smokes arose to float
Dissolving umbels in the hollow blue,
Where, measuring some endless now it knew,
A patient, solitary buzzard wheeled.
Northwestward where the Black Hills lay concealed
Behind the bluest ridge, a faint cloud 'rose,
As though the peaks and flowing slopes of those
Were stretching up to see what might betide.

And now Sitanka, when a bugle cried,
Awakened to the prison of his bed.
A nearer neighbor to the shining dead
Than to the darkly living ones, he lay
And heard, as in a dream and far away,
A deep hoof-rumble running in the land
And briefly singing voices of command,
Clipped upward with an edge to be obeyed.
Again the bugle cried and, ceasing, laid
A sudden stillness over all the camp.

A troop-horse pawed no longer, ceased to champ
The bit and shake the bridle. Awful grew
That stillness of the vision coming true,
That crystal moment of eternity
Complete without a shadow. He could see,
As though his tepee were illumined air,
The whole enchanted picture breathing there
About him: all his ragged band between
The horsemen, southward, skirting the ravine,
And footmen, northward, ranged beneath the hill;
The soldiers on the summit, tall and still
Beside those war-dogs crouched on eager paws
With thunder straining in their iron maws
The leash of peace; the children unafraid,
With thirsting eyes and mouths agape to aid
In drinking all that splendor, gleaming brass
On serried blue!

He listened for the grass.

Scarce real in seeming as the hush it broke,
A voice arose. The Soldier Chieftain spoke.
Remotely clear, the sound itself was kind,
And, trailing it a little way behind,
A voice made meaning that was gentle too.
The speaking ceased. Among the tepees grew
A busy murmur like the buzz and boom
Of bumblebees at work on cherry bloom
In hollows hushed and happy in the sun.

Now surely was the miracle begun,
And all the little strangers without name,
No longer strange, made ready to proclaim
The secret all the Springs have tried to say;
And grasses, greening for the deathless day,
Took breath before the world-renewing song!

And then, as though the dying world of wrong
Cried out before the end, Sitanka heard
The high haranguing voice of Yellow Bird
Above the lulling murmur: "Foolish ones
And blind! Why are you giving up your guns
To these Wasichus, who are hardly men
And shall be shadows? Are you cowards, then,
With hearts of water? Are you fools to heed
A sick man's dreaming? Stab them, and they bleed
No blood of brothers! Look at them and see
The takers of the good that used to be,
The killers of the Savior! Do not fear,
The Nations of the Dead are crowding here
To help us! Shall we shame them? *Do as I!*"

Beneath that final spear-thrust of a cry
The very silence seemed to bleed and ache.
Now!—now!—if but a single seed should wake
And know its Mother, or a grass-root stir,

The sap of pity in the breast of her
Must flood the world with Spring forevermore!

A gun-shot ripped the hush. The panic roar
Outfled the clamor of the hills and died.

And then—as though the whole world, crucified
Upon the heaped Golgotha of its years,
For all its lonely silences of tears,
Its countless hates and hurts and terrors, found
A last composite voice—a hell of sound
Assailed the brooding heavens. Once again
The wild wind-roaring of the rage of men,
The blent staccato thunders of the dream,
The long-drawn, unresolving nightmare scream
Of women and of children over all!
Now—now at last—the peace of love would fall,
And in a sudden stillness, very kind
The blind would look astonished on the blind
To lose their little dreams of fear and wrath!

A plunging fury hurtled from its path
Sitanka's tepee. In a gasp of time
He saw—like some infernal pantomime
A freeze of horror rendered motionless
Forever—horses rearing in a press
Of faces tortured into soundless yells,
Amid the gloaming of the Hotchkiss shells
That blossomed in a horizontal flaw
Of bloody rain that fell not.

                            Then he saw
One face above him and a gun-butt raised;
A soldier's face with haggard eyes that blazed,
A wry wound of a mouth agape to shout,
And nothing but the silence coming out—
An agony of silence. For a span,
Unmeasured as the tragedy of man,

Brief as the weapon's poising and the stroke,
It burned upon him; and a white light broke
About it, even as a cry came through
That stabbed the world with pity. And he knew
The shining face, unutterably dear!
All tenderness, it hovered, bending near,
Half man, half woman, beautiful with scars
And eyes of sorrow, very old—like stars
That seek the dawn. He strove to rise in vain,
To cry "My brother!"

              And the shattered brain

Went out.

         Around the writhing body still,
Beneath the flaming thunders of the hill,
That fury heaped the dying and the dead.
And where the women and the children fled
Along the gully winding to the sky
The roaring followed, till the long, thin cry
Above it ceased.

           The bugles blared retreat.
Triumphant in the blindness of defeat,
The iron-footed squadrons marched away.

And darkness fell upon the face of day.

The mounting blizzard broke. All night it swept
The bloody field of victory that kept
The secret of the Everlasting Word.

Appendix: Prefaces

The Song of Hugh Glass, 1915

The following narrative is based upon an episode taken from that much neglected portion of our history, the era of the American Fur Trade. My interest in that period may be said to have begun at the age of six when, clinging to the forefinger of my father, I discovered the Missouri River from a bluff top at Kansas City. It was flood time, and the impression I received was deep and lasting. Even now I cannot think of that stream without a thrill of awe and something of the reverence one feels for mighty things. It was for me what the sea must have been to the Greek boys of antiquity. And as those ancient boys must have been eager to hear of perils nobly encountered on the deep and in the lands adjacent, so was I eager to learn of the heroes who had travelled my river as an imperial road. Nor was I disappointed in what I learned of them; for they seemed to me in every way equal to the heroes of old. I came to think of them with a sense of personal ownership, for any one of many of them might have been my grandfather—and so a little of their purple fell on me. As I grew older and came to possess more of my inheritance, I began to see that what had enthralled me was, in fact, of the stuff of sagas, a genuine epic cycle in the rough. Furthermore, I realized that this raw material had been undergoing a process of digestion in my consciousness, corresponding in a way to the process of infinite repetition and fond elaboration which, as certain scholars tell us, foreran the heroic narratives of old time. ❖ I decided that some day I would begin to tell these hero tales in verse; and in 1908, as a preparation for what I had in mind, I descended the Missouri in an open boat, and also ascended the Yellowstone for a considerable distance. On the upper river the country was practically unchanged; and for one familiar with what had taken place there, it was no difficult feat of the imagination to revive the details of that time—the men, the trails, the boats, the trading posts where veritable satraps once ruled under the sway of the American Fur Company. ❖ The Hugh Glass episode is to be found in Chittenden's "History of the American Fur Trade" where it is quoted from its three printed sources: the *Missouri Intelligencer,* Sage's "Scenes in the Rocky Mountains," and Cooke's "Scenes in the United States Army." The present narrative begins after that military fiasco known as the Leavenworth Campaign against the Aricaras, which took place at the mouth of the Grand River in what is now South Dakota.

J.G.N.

The Song of Three Friends, 1919

The following narrative, though complete in itself, is designed to be the first piece in a cycle of poems dealing with the fur trade period of the Trans-Missouri region. "The Song of Hugh Glass," which was published in the fall of 1915, is the second in the series. ❖ The four decades during which the fur trade flourished west of the Missouri River may be regarded as a typical heroic period, differing in no essential from the many other great heroic periods that have made glorious the story of the Aryan migration. Jane Harrison says that heroic characters do not arise from any peculiarity of race or even of geographical surroundings; but that, given certain social conditions, they may and do appear anywhere and at any time. The heroic spirit, as seen in heroic poetry, we are told, is the outcome of a society cut loose from its roots, of a time of migrations, of the shifting of populations. Such conditions are to be found during the time of the Spanish conquests of Central and South America; and they are to be found also in those wonderful years of our own West, when wandering bands of trappers were exploring the rivers and the mountains and the plains and the deserts from the British possessions to Mexico, and from the Missouri to the Pacific. ❖ As a result of our individualistic tendencies, our numerous jostling nationalities, and our materialistic temper, we Americans are prone to regard the Past as being separated from us as by an insurmountable wall. We lack the sense of racial continuity. For us it is almost as though the world began yesterday morning; and too much of our contemporary literature is based upon that view. The affairs of antiquity seem to the generality of us to be as remote as the dimmest star, and as little related to our activities. But what we call the slow lapse of ages is really only the blinking of an eye. Sometimes this sense of the close unity of all time and all human experience has come upon me so strongly that I have felt, for an intense moment, how just a little hurry on my part might get me there in time to hear Æschylus training a Chorus, or to see the wizard chisel still busy with the Parthenon frieze, or to hear Socrates telling his dreams to his judges. It is in some such mood that I approach that body of precious saga-stuff which I have called the Western American Epos; and I see it, not as a thing in itself, but rather as one phase of the whole race life from the beginning; indeed, the final link in that long chain of heroic periods stretching from the region of the Euphrates eastward into India and westward to our own Pacific Coast. ❖ Like causes produce like effects; and as we follow the Aryan migration, we find that, over and over again, heroic periods occur; and out of each period have grown epic and saga, celebrating the deeds of the heroes. In India we find the Mahabharata and Ramayana; in Persia, the Shah

Nameh; among the Greeks, the Homeric poems; in
Rome, the Ænid; in Germany, the Niebelungenlied; in
France, the Chanson de Roland; in the Scandinavian
countries, the sagas and the Eddaic poems; in the British
Isles, the Arthurian and Cuchulain cycles. The Race
crosses the Atlantic, and the last lap of the long westward
journey is begun. Still another typical heroic period de-
velops; and where shall we find its epic? Certainly not in
Hiawatha, which is not concerned with our race, and but
little with the real American Indian, for that matter. Cer-
tainly not in Evangeline, which is typical neither in mat-
ter nor manner. Nor is it likely ever to be written on a
theme concerned with the original Colonies, for the rea-
son that in the Colonies society was never cut loose from
its roots. The true American Epos was developed be-
tween the Missouri River and the Pacific Ocean in ap-
proximately the first four decades of the 19th century.
When the settlers began to cross the Missouri, the end of
the epic period was in sight. ❖ As has been the case with
all similar periods, a great body of legend, concerned
with heroic deeds, grew up about those men who ex-
plored that vast wilderness in search of furs. These sto-
ries, which formerly circulated throughout the West as
oral tradition, are now, in the main, known only to spe-
cialists in Western history; for they are to be found chiefly
in contemporary journals and books of travel long since
out of print and difficult to obtain. Any one who has
taken the trouble to explore that spacious and compara-
tively little known field of American history will be likely
to believe with me that the heroes of that time were the
direct descendants, in the epic line, of all the heroes of the
race that have been celebrated in song and saga. ❖ It
would seem that we are now entering upon a period in
which such a work as I propose might logically be writ-
ten, if we are to accept the theory of George Edward
Woodberry. He tells us that those literary works which
embody representative epochs appear upon what he
terms "watersheds of history"; that is to say, at those

times when an old order is passing away, when men look forward hopefully or fearfully to new things, and backward a little wistfully to things that have been. That is the state of the modern world. We are experiencing the wane of individualism; we are beginning to think in terms of the group; and already reactionary voices are being raised in defence of the good old days when a man could do as it pleased him to do. And if we seek for that moment in our national life when individualism was most pronounced, we shall find it in the romantic period with which I am concerned; for in that time society did not exist in the Trans-Missouri country, and there was no law but the whim of the daring and strong. ❖ Obviously, in attempting to embody such a period in a literary work, it is necessary to concentrate upon one representative portion of it. Fortunately, this can be done without sacrifice and without resorting to fictitious means. The story of the two expeditions that ascended the Missouri River under the leadership of Ashley and Henry of St. Louis in the years 1822 and 1823, conprehends every phase of the life of the epoch and covers the entire Trans-Missouri region from the British boundaries to Santa Fé, and from St. Louis to the Spanish Settlements of California. Furthermore, of all the bands of trappers and traders that entered the wilderness during those years, none experienced so many extraordinary adventures as did the Ashley-Henry men. The story of their exploits and wanderings constitutes what I would call the Ashley-Henry Saga; and it is upon this that I am basing my cycle. ❖ The first printed version of the present story is to be found in the files of a short-lived periodical known as *The Western Souvenir,* copied by the *Western Monthly Review* for July, 1829. *The Missouri Intelligencer* for September 4, 1829, and Howe's "Historical Collections of the Great West" contain practically the same version of the tale. A matter-of-fact reference to the episode is made on page 298 of the Letter Book of the Superintendent of Indian Affairs, now among the manuscripts of the Kansas Historical Society at Topeka. ❖ I wish to express a sense of obligation to Mr. Doane Robinson, Secretary of the State Historical Society of South Dakota, for placing his wide knowledge of Western history at my disposal.

John G. Neihardt, Bancroft, Nebraska, 1918

The Song of the Indian Wars, 1925

The Song of the Indian Wars is a part of the Epic Cycle of the West upon which I have been working for eleven years. However, as the reader will note, it is complete in itself, as are the two other parts of the Cycle already published, The Song of Three Friends and The Song of Hugh Glass. ❖ My purpose in writing this cycle is to preserve the great race-mood of courage that was developed west of the Missouri River in the 19th century. The period with which I am dealing is beyond question the great American epic period, beginning in 1822 and ending in 1890. The dates are neither approximate nor arbitrary. In 1822 the first Ashley-Henry band ascended the Missouri and, after Lewis and Clark, the most important explorers of the West were Ashley-Henry men. As to the exploits of those men and the epic nature of the period, the interested reader is referred to the prefatory matter of the The Song of Three Friends and The Song of Hugh Glass in the Modern Readers' Series; also to my volume entitled The Splendid Wayfaring. The Year 1890 marked the end of Indian resistance on the Plains. ❖ In working out my plan for the cycle I have yet to deal with the period of exploration and the period of migration. ❖ The Song of the Indian Wars deals with the last great fight for the bison pastures of the Plains between the westering white men and the prairie tribes—the struggle for the right of way between the Missouri River and the Pacific Ocean. Since the period was one of crucial importance in the process of our national development, I have felt the obligation to be accurate. I have neither fictionized my material nor sentimentalized my characters. It seems unnecessary to list all the printed sources upon which I have drawn during the years I have devoted to the subject. The list would be long, and I doubt if any work of considerable significance bearing on the period has escaped me, whether a government report, a formal history or a personal narrative. But one can not safely trust the printed sources alone, and I have made it a duty to consult many veterans who were themselves a part of what I have to tell. Among these I am especially indebted to the following: ❖ Brigadier-General Anson Mills of Washington, D. C., who served with conspicuous gallantry under Crook both in the Rosebud fight and in the Battle of Slim Buttes; Brigadier-General Edward S. Godfrey of Cookston, N.J., who distinguished himself in the Reno battle on the Little Big Horn; Brigadier-General Walter S. Schuyler of San Francisco, who served under Crook and rendered brilliant service under Mackenzie in the winter battle with the Cheyennes on Willow Creek; Brigadier-General Charles King of Milwaukee, the famous soldier-novelist, who was one of Crook's lieutenants in the campaign of 1876; Major Henry R. Lemly of Washington, D.C., who was Crook's Acting Assistant Adjutant General during the famous "horse-meat march" in pursuit of the Indians after the Custer fight, and who witnessed the death of Crazy Horse; Colonel Homer W. Wheeler of Los Angeles, rich in experience as a plainsman and as an Indian fighter; the late Captain Grant P. Marsh of Bismarck, N.D., who was in command of the steamer Far West during the campaign of 1876 and transported the wounded of Reno's command from the mouth of the Little Big Horn to Fort Abraham Lincoln; Captain James H. Cook of Agate, Nebraska, famous plainsman and army scout, intimate friend of the great Chief Red Cloud and of most other Sioux Leaders; Mrs. George A. Forsyth of Wilkes-

Barre, Penn., wife of the late Brigadier-General George
A. Forsyth, the hero of Beecher's Island: Captain How-
ard Morton of Palo Alto, California, who fought with
Forsyth on the Rickaree Fork of the Republican and
who still carries the bullet that tore out one of his eyes in
that wonderful little battle; Mr. William C. Slaper of
Los Angeles, who served as a private under Reno in the
Battle of the Little Big Horn; Sergeant Max Littman of
St. Louis and Sergeant Samuel Gibson of Omaha, both
of whom were in the Wagon Box fight; Mr. Wallace of
Okarche, Okla., who was one of Custer's scouts in the
winter campaign ending with the Battle of the Washita;
Mr. John Hunton, still living at old Fort Laramie where
he was post trader in the 'sixties; Red Hawk, an Oglala
Sioux, who knew and fought with Crazy Horse; my
"brother-friend," Curly, one of Custer's Crow scouts,
who told me only the truth, however lustily he may have
drawn the long bow for the amazement of over credu-
lous journalists. ❖ Indirectly I have gotten much valu-
able material out of the Indian consciousness through
those who were intimately acquainted with the Sioux,
Cheyenne and Arapahoe during the period of the last
wars. Also much valuable reminiscence of white men,
other than those named, has been made accessible to me
by Mr. E. A. Brininstool of Los Angeles, whose exten-
sive collection of source material bearing on the Indian
Wars has cost him many years of effort and is equalled
by few private collections of the sort in the country. Dr.
Grace R. Hebard of the University of Wyoming,
coauthor with Mr. Brininstool of the Bozeman Trail,
work of the highest authority on the Red Cloud Wars,
gave me generous and timely aid by placing important
original documents in my hands before the publication
of the volume named. Dr. Doane Robinson of Pierre,
Secretary of the State Historical Society of South Dakota
and a high authority on the whole history of the Plains,
has further increased my debt to him, a debt of long
standing. ❖ For some of the Indian speeches I am in-

debted to the works of Dr. Charles A. Eastman, who, himself a Sioux, was intimately acquainted with many of the great leaders of his people. ❖ My years of intimate association with the Omaha Tribe, a Siouan people, at a time when the old generation was still numerous, may have given me some insight into Indian psychology. ❖ As to the country in which my story moves, I have reason to know it well. My acquaintance with it began thirty-seven years ago when I lived with my pioneering grandparents in Kansas on the upper Solomon. Signs of the vanished buffalo were still there, and I have sat by cow-chip fires. Also, I have taken the trouble to study at first hand the topography of the various localities and stretches of country that I have undertaken to describe. ❖ Since my interest in the period treated is not of recent origin, it is impossible to give credit to all who, in one way or another, have helped me; but the foregoing will serve to indicate the means employed by way of getting at the truth and into the mood of the time. ❖ Wherever I have found various versions of particular incidents I have been careful to adopt that one which seemed best supported by the evidence. Perhaps the greatest variation of testimony is to be found in the matter of Custer's last battle. I may say that I am quite familiar with the controversy; nor should those who may resent my account as that of a Custer partisan accuse me of having never seen the report of the Reno investigation. I spent a wonderful day and night with it and I found it a rich mine for the psychologist. ❖ In the interval between a four and a half year task just finished and another soon to be assumed, I may be allowed the satisfaction of noting the steadily increasing success of The Song of Three Friends and The Song of Hugh Glass, both with the general public and in the public schools and colleges. Already the progress made would seem to justify me in devoting my twenty best years to the Cycle.

John G. Neihardt, Branson, Mo., September, 1924

The Song of the Messiah, 1935

"The Song of the Messiah", which will stand as the final narrative poem in my Cycle of the West, is, like the others of the series, complete in itself; but its appeal should be greater to those who are familiar with "The Song of the Indian Wars", since it deals with the last phase of Indian resistance on the Prairies. The action takes place in western South Dakota, chiefly in the country south of the Black Hills.

John G. Neihardt

Appendix: Variora

The Song of the Indian Wars published in the 1971 Bison Book edition of *Twilight of the Sioux* introduced several line changes made at the author's request. Until 1971, the lines had been consistent since the first publication of *The Song of the Indian Wars* in 1925. The Fiftieth Anniversary Edition of *A Cycle of the West* retains the original versions. ❖ The 1971 changes are in lines in section VIII, "The Yellow God," section XI, "The Seventh Marches," and section XII, "High Noon on the Little Horn":

"The Yellow God" (stanza 3, line 12)
Cycle version, p.356:
How Yellow Hair, the Wolf of Washita

1971 version, p.105:
How Long Hair, still the Wolf of Washita

"The Yellow God" (stanza 5, lines 1–3 and 6)
Cycle version, p.357:
Then once again the name of Yellow Hair
Was heard with dread; for Summer, turning brown
Beheld him lead a thousand horsemen down
. . . .
And deer and singing streams to Frenchman Creek;

1971 version, pp.106–7:
Then once again the Wolf with yellow hair
Was on the prowl; for Summer turning brown,
Beheld him lead his men and wagons down
. . . .
And singing streams and pines to French's Creek

"The Seventh Marches" (stanza 6, lines 14–16 and stanza 7)
Cycle version, p.379:
When through the Chetish Hills by many a pass
They crowded down upon the Greasy Grass
To swell the hostile thousands waiting there.

Alas, how wide they made for Yellow Hair
That highway leading to the shining Past!

1971 version, p.131:
Among the Chetish Hills that saw them pass
Triumphant down upon the Greasy Grass
To swell a league-long village. What a road
Their myriad ponies made to that abode.
Where lives the Tallest of the Shining Past!

"High Noon on the Little Horn" (stanza 9, lines 12–16)
Cycle version, p.386:
Beneath the iron feet that followed there;
For now they deemed the far-famed Yellow Hair,
The Wolf of Washita, with all his pack
Potential in the dust cloud at his back
Bore down upon them.

1971 version, p.141:
Beneath those hoofs; for now it seemed they saw
The yellow-headed Wolf of Washita
Already on their heels, with all his pack
Potential in the dust cloud at his back,
A howling fury!

Also in *The Song of the Indian Wars*, the author used
two spellings of *tepee*, sometimes spelling it "tepee" and
sometimes "teepee." Because there is a clear preference
for "tepee," the text has been emended to this spelling
throughout.

Nebraska

This 1991 edition marks the fiftieth year of the University of
Nebraska Press. The text was set in Linotype Galliard by Rose
Kleman at the Press, and printed by Edwards Brothers, Inc.
The paper stock is Finch Opaque White 60 lb. text weight, an
acid-free sheet. The book's designer was Richard Eckersley.